Auer+Weber+Architekten   Arbeiten   1980–2003   Works

Auer+Weber+Architekten

Arbeiten   1980–2003   Works

Andrea Kiock
Herausgeberin / Editor

Birkhäuser – Publishers for Architecture
Basel · Boston · Berlin

Inhalt / Contents

7   **Vorwort der Herausgeberin**
    Editor's preface

8   **Die Schönheit des Gewöhnlichen – und die des Ungewöhnlichen**
    The beauty of the ordinary – and of the unusual
    Einführung von / Introduction by Gert Kähler

25 **Bauten und Projekte 1980 – 2003**
    Buildings and Projects

26 Kurgastzentrum / Spa Center Bad Salzuflen
32 Altenwohn- und Pflegeheim
    Retirement and Nursing Home St. Marien Lemgo
38 Robert-Bosch-Haus / Robert Bosch House Stuttgart
40 Landratsamt / District Office Starnberg
50 Weltausstellung EXPO '92 Sevilla Pavillon der BRD
    EXPO '92, Seville, German Pavilion
56 Stadtportalhäuser / City Portal Buildings Frankfurt am Main
58 Subzentrum Flughafen München / Subcenter at Munich Airport
66 Eiserne Brücke über die Donau / Iron Bridge over the Danube
    Regensburg
70 Verwaltungsgebäude der Stadtwerke / Administration Building
    Reutlingen
74 Helen-Keller-Realschule / Secondary School München-Johanneskirchen
80 Ortszentrum / Town Center Germering
    Stadthalle und Bibliothek / Civic Hall and Library
88 Großvolière in der „Wilhelma" / Large Aviary Stuttgart
94 Theater Hof
102 Ruhrfestspielhaus Recklinghausen
    Umbau und Anbau / Conversion and extension
110 Wohnen am Innenhafen / Living by the Inner Harbor Duisburg
114 Zeppelin Carré Stuttgart
122 Casino und Mensa der Offiziersschule des Heeres
    Army Officers' Mess at the Training College Dresden
128 U-Bahn-Station / Underground Station Westfriedhof München
132 Amazonienhaus in der „Wilhelma" / Amazonian House Stuttgart

136 adidas "World of Sports" Herzogenaurach
140 Hochhauskomplex / High-rise MAX Frankfurt am Main
142 Multifunktionales Sport- und Veranstaltungszentrum
    Sports and Events Center Stuttgart
146 Kurmittelhaus / Spa Center Bad Brambach
152 Überdachung / Roofing Niedersachsenstadion Hannover
156 Hochhausensemble „Münchner Tor" / Twin Towers München
160 Kronen Carré Stuttgart
168 PRISMA-Haus / PRISMA Building Frankfurt am Main
174 Altes Rathaus / Old Town Hall Pforzheim
180 BMW Erlebnis- und Auslieferungszentrum
    BMW Event and Delivery Center München
186 Büropark / Office Park Fasanenhof Stuttgart
190 Neues Fußballstadion / New Soccer Stadium München
196 Hotel der ESO am Cerro Paranal / ESO Hotel Chile
206 Thuringia Versicherung / Insurance Building München
208 Städtebaulicher Masterplan für die Olympiabewerbung
    Master Plan for the Olympic Submission Stuttgart 2012
214 Deutsche Botschaft / German Embassy Mexico City
216 Hochhaus / High-rise Süddeutscher Verlag München
220 Schlossberg Böblingen
222 Zentrum / Center SolarCity Linz
226 Zentraler Omnibusbahnhof / Central Bus Station München
230 Science Park III Ulm
234 Anting New Town Shanghai China
240 Universitätsbibliothek / Library of the University of Magdeburg
246 Max-Planck-Institut für Biophysik / Max-Planck Institute of Biophysics
    Frankfurt am Main

253 **Fragen und Antworten** Andrea Kiock im Gespräch mit Fritz Auer
    Questions and Answers Andrea Kiock in conversation with Fritz Auer

260 **Menschenwerk** Carlo Weber
    A Human Feat Carlo Weber

265 **Anhang**
    Appendix

Vorwort

Vor fünfundzwanzig Jahren traf ich Fritz Auer zum ersten Mal und es begann eine neugierige und wunderbare Freundschaft. Wenig später lernte ich auch Carlo Weber kennen.

Im Juni 2002 saßen wir auf einer Dachterrasse in München und verfielen der Magie von Zahlen und Zeit. Wir stellten fest, dass es in all den Jahren zwar einzelne Veröffentlichungen zu Bauten und Wettbewerben des Büros Auer+Weber gegeben hatte, aber keinen Überblick über die gesamte Entwicklung seit dessen Gründung im Jahr 1980.

Die Freundschaft zu den Architekten und die Begeisterung für ihre Arbeiten waren es, die mich bewogen, Herausgeberin dieses Werkberichts zu werden. Er soll anschaulich gegenwärtiges Bauen in seiner ganzen Vielgestaltigkeit zeigen und damit Architekturfachleute und -liebhaber gleichermaßen ansprechen.

Das nun vorliegende Buch zeigt nicht nur gewonnene und gebaute Projekte, sondern auch nicht gebaute Entwürfe. So wie das Jahr durch Jahreszeiten strukturiert wird, so strukturieren die unterschiedlichen Wettbewerbe die Arbeit des Büros. Durch die Auswahl der Abbildungen und der eigens für das Buch angefertigten Zeichnungen will diese Werkmonografie die Entwicklung des Büros Auer+Weber über die Jahre deutlich machen.

Die Lebendigkeit des Büros wirkt weiter. Die nächste Generation steht bereit.

München, im September 2003

Andrea Kiock

Preface

I met Fritz Auer for the first time twenty-five years ago, and it was the beginning of this wonderful friendship. Shortly thereafter, I made the acquaintance of Carlo Weber.

In June 2002, we were sitting on a rooftop patio in Munich and succumbed to the wizardry of numbers and time. We realized that over the years there had been the occasional publication relating to the competitions and projects in which the Auer+Weber office had been involved, but there was no single monograph that provided an overall view of the development of the company as a whole since it was first founded in 1980.

It was my friendship with the architects and my enthusiasm for their work that prompted me to become the editor of this compilation of their achievements. This book provides visual insight into a wide range of contemporary building, and will appeal to architectural experts and enthusiasts alike.

This book contains not only designs that were subsequently built, but also those that were never realized. Just as a year is structured by the different seasons, various competitions provide a structure for the work of the architectural office. A selection of illustrations and new drawings were produced specifically for this book, and they visually demonstrate the evolution of the Auer+Weber office over the years.

The energy of the office is still a force to be reckoned with. The next generation is raring to go.

Munich, September 2003

Andrea Kiock

Gert Kähler
**Die Schönheit des Gewöhnlichen
– und die des Ungewöhnlichen**
Zur Architektur von Auer+Weber

Gert Kähler
**The Beauty of the Ordinary
and of the Unusual**
The architecture of Auer+Weber

Fritz Auer und Carlo Weber, 1961

Vorweg

Siebzig Jahre alt ist der eine, Fritz Auer, gerade geworden; der andere, Carlo Weber, wird es im nächsten Jahr. Im Jahr darauf feiert ihr gemeinsames Architekturbüro seine 25-jährige Existenz. Das klingt nach Jubiläum, nach Rückblick, besonders, wenn das erste „richtige" Buch über ihr berufliches Lebenswerk erst jetzt erscheint.

Wenn man die beiden kennt, dann vergehen Gedanken zu Abschied und Rückzug aufs Altenteil. Sie scheinen zu neugierig auf die Zukunft zu sein, zu neugierig darauf, was diese an Aufgaben bringt – und zu neugierig darauf, wie sie diese bewältigen können. Man hat das Gefühl, sie haben noch einen „Vorrat an kreativem Potential" in sich, der abgearbeitet werden muss.

Und dennoch – da das Leben (nach Tucholsky) geschmacklos genug ist, einfach weiter zu gehen, und die natürlichen Abläufe nur begrenzt umgangen werden können, bekommt dieses Buch zwangsläufig den Charakter einer Bilanz, oder sagen wir: einer Zwischenbilanz nach fast 25 Jahren gemeinsamer Arbeit. Und damit stellen sich fast von allein Fragen wie die, woher der Antrieb kam zur gemeinsamen Arbeit, welche Ziele man verfolgte, welche Seitenwege man bisweilen einschlug, nach den Motivationen neben dem bloßen Broterwerb. Denn Architekten sind Überzeugungstäter.

Die Antworten sind freilich bis zu einem gewissen Grade spekulativ, nicht nur, weil sie von außen gegeben werden, sondern auch, weil die eigenen Überlegungen, die der beiden Partner, nur eine Annäherung sein können an unbewusste Vorgänge. – „Du glaubst zu schieben, und du wirst geschoben" heißt es in Goethes „Faust", und das gilt sinngemäß für die Interpretation der eigenen künstlerischen Arbeit.

Zum Glück gibt es einen Fixpunkt, von dem man ausgehen kann: das sind die Bauten und Entwürfe. Sie stehen da, zum Teil schon über 20 Jahre, was heute auch in der Architektur eine lange Zeit ist. Diese Bauten sprechen zu uns – wie alle gebaute Umwelt. Das empfindet jeder, der sie sieht, gleich, ob er es sich bewusst macht oder nicht. Wir wollen versuchen – auch das eine „Krücke", weil sie Empfindungen rational zu erklären versucht – herauszuarbeiten, was sie „sagen", und daraus Rückschlüsse auf die Arbeit von Auer+Weber zu ziehen. Wobei eines von vornherein klar ist, aber dennoch gesagt werden muss: Architektenarbeit ist immer Arbeit einer Gruppe. Selbst wenn zwei Namen, zwei Personen für das Büro stehen: Es sind eine Vielzahl von kompetenten Gesprächspartnern und Mitarbeitern – nicht nur im eigenen Büro – notwendig, um aus einer Skizze auf dem

Introduction

Fritz Auer has just celebrated his seventieth birthday, while Carlo Weber turns seventy next year. Next year their joint architect's office celebrates 25 years of work. This has all the makings of an anniversary and a retrospective, especially since the first "real" book on their professional life's work is just being published.

When you meet the two men, all thoughts of their stopping work to enjoy their retirement are banished. They seem too curious about the future, too curious about what tasks it will bring, and too curious about how they will master them. You have the feeling they still contain a "store of creative potential" that needs to be worked off.

And yet – since life (according to Tucholsky) is tasteless enough to simply continue and the natural progression of things can be avoided only up to a point – this book automatically takes on the character of a retrospective, or shall we say, an interim stocktaking – of their almost 25 years of partnership. Looking back raises such questions as: What prompted them to team up? What objectives they have pursued? What detours they have taken along the way? What has been their motivation (apart from simply earning a living)? After all, architects work out of conviction.

Naturally, to a certain extent the answers to these questions are speculative. One's own thoughts, as well as those of the two partners, cannot always fully reflect what happens on an unconscious level. To quote Goethe's Faust: "You think you are pushing but you are being pushed." This phenomenon also applies to the understanding of one's own artistic work.

Luckily, in Auer+Weber's case, we have a point of reference in the form of their buildings and plans. Some of them have been around for over 20 years – a long period in contemporary architecture. Like all works of architecture, these buildings convey something to us. Everyone who has seen them senses this, although they may not be consciously aware of it. We want to try and work out what they "say", keeping in mind, of course, that this is an attempt to impose a rational explanation onto sensations, as a way of drawing conclusions about Auer+Weber's work. One thing is clear from the start, but needs to be clearly stated anyway: Architecture always involves a group of people. Even when there are two names representing an office, it takes a large number of competent partners and employees – including many who work outside the company – to create a building from a sketch. "Who built Thebes of the seven gates?" asked

Papier ein gebautes Werk zu machen. „Wer baute das siebentorige Theben?" fragte Bertold Brecht in seinen „Fragen eines lesenden Arbeiters". Er bedachte die Vielen, die an einem Werk arbeiten.

Umgekehrt würde es ohne die beiden, ohne Fritz Auer und Carlo Weber, diese Werke nicht geben.

Ge-Schichten bauen
Ein Schulbeispiel in der Baugeschichte der Moderne ist die Erweiterung des Rathauses Göteborg von Gunnar Asplund aus dem Jahre 1937. An ihm wird von den Historikern gern der Beweis geführt, dass das Formenrepertoire der Moderne keineswegs so radikal geschichtsfeindlich ist, wie ihr gern vorgeworfen wird: denn der Anbau nehme doch in seiner Fassadengliederung zahlreiche strukturelle Merkmale der alten Fassade auf.

Heute, nach der Phase der klassischen Moderne und der überstandenen Postmoderne, die den Rückgriff auf historische Formen zum Programm gemacht hatte, muss man das nicht mehr beweisen, und schon gar nicht am ziemlich untauglichen Objekt des Rathauses von Göteborg, dessen wirkliche Qualitäten nicht in den doch recht vordergründigen strukturellen Ähnlichkeiten der Fassade, sondern vielmehr in der unglaublichen Modernität der Innenräume liegen.

Der Gegensatz von alter und neuer Architektur, die Stein gewordene Auseinandersetzung zwischen beiden, taugt inzwischen nicht mehr recht zum ideologischen Streit. Es gibt zu viele herausragende Beispiele qualitätvollen Miteinanders von Alt und Neu, als dass man den Fall des Misslingens dem Gegensatz von alter und neuer Formensprache im Grundsätzlichen und nicht der mangelnden Qualität des jeweiligen Architekten zuweisen möchte. Und trotzdem, obwohl das Thema kaum Neues zu bieten scheint, geschieht auf diesem Gebiet bisweilen noch Überraschendes, wie beispielsweise beim Umbau und der Sanierung des Alten Rathauses in Pforzheim (Seite 174 ff.).

Die Hauptfassade zeigt den offenkundigen Gegensatz der traditionellen Lochfassade mit den Bogenstellungen im Erdgeschoss und einen streng dagegen gestellten, konstruktiv betonten Rahmen. Die Geschosshöhen wurden aufgegriffen – siehe Göteborg.

Über den alten und den neuen Bauteil greift ein neues „Dach", das aber eigentlich aus zwei normalen Vollgeschossen besteht, die filigran verglast und durch einen Lamellenvorhang zusammengefasst sind. Fassade und Dachaufbau nehmen Rücksicht

Bertold Brecht in his "Questions from a worker who reads" as a way of acknowledging the many people who are involved in creating a single piece of work.

While it takes a lot of people to construct a building, the buildings represented in this book would not exist without two specific individuals: Fritz Auer and Carlo Weber.

Building stories
A classic example of architectural history in the modern age is the extension of Gothenburg Town Hall by Gunnar Asplund in 1937. Historians like to cite it as evidence that the design repertoire of the modern age is not by any means as radically hostile to history as people like to think. After all, in creating an extension, numerous structural features from the old façade have to be included in the new one.

As we have now progressed beyond the classic modern and postmodern ages – which drew their inspiration from historical forms – it is no longer necessary to seek such evidence. There is no longer a need to cite the rather unsuitable subject of Gothenburg Town Hall either, whose true qualities lie not in the superficial structural similarities of the façade, but in the interior's incredible modernity.

Ideological battles can no longer be fought by citing the contrast between old and new architecture, or the confrontation between the two. There are too many excellent examples of high-quality alliances of old and new for anyone to assign a failure, except in the poor workmanship of the respective architect. While it would seem that this topic has been exhausted, surprising things are still continuing to happen in this area.

One example is the renovation and refurbishment of the Old Town Hall in Pforzheim (page 174 ff).

The main façade illustrates an obvious contrast between the traditional, punctuated façade with the positions of its arches on the ground floor, and the stark contrast of the framework, which stresses the design. The heights of the floors have been fully exploited.

Crowning the old and new sections is a new "roof", which actually consists of two normal, full stories with delicate glazing joined together through a curtain of blind slats. Façade and roof show regard for everything that is traditional; for example, the corner tower, which is one floor higher. In other words, the new features take into account what already existed without compromising the modern elements in any way.

Rathaus / Town Hall Göteborg, 1937
Gunnar Asplund

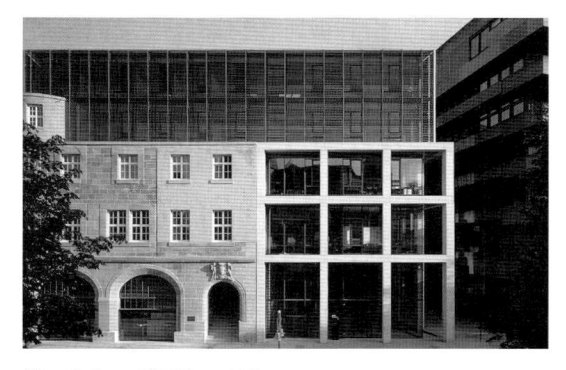

Altes Rathaus / Old Town Hall
Pforzheim, 2001

auf alles, was überliefert ist – wie man am Eckturm sieht, der ein Geschoss höher eingreift. Das Neue nimmt also erkennbar Rücksicht auf das Vorhandene, aber es kommt in sich kompromisslos modern einher. Der neue Bauteil soll zwar an das große Volumen des historischen Daches erinnern, aber er macht es „ohne Dach", ohne einen oberen Abschluss zu formulieren.

Die Fassade des Altbaus besteht wiederum aus zwei historischen Zuständen. Die traditionelle Natursteinfassade wurde bereits in den fünfziger Jahren, nach der teilweisen Zerstörung im 2. Weltkrieg, „geflickt" und mit glattem Putz geschlossen, unter Verzicht auf die Fensterlaibungen in Werkstein – ganz in der guten Tradition der damaligen Denkmalpflege: nicht Rekonstruktion, sondern Wiederaufbau plus Zeigen der historischen Veränderungen.

So setzt sich das Alte Rathaus aus mehreren Schichten der Erinnerung zusammen: Erinnerung an den Historismus, dem der Bau aus dem Jahre 1911 im Äußeren nachempfunden wurde, Erinnerung an die zerstörten Teile durch die vereinfachte Rekonstruktion in den fünfziger Jahren, die wiederum an die Zerstörung durch den Bombenkrieg erinnert, der fast die gesamte Stadt Pforzheim in Schutt und Asche legte.

Es geht also nicht mehr nur um „Alt" und „Neu", die zu einem Dritten zusammengefasst werden; es geht nicht mehr nur um Formales, sondern vielmehr um mehrere Schichten von Erinnerungen, die im Bau festgehalten werden und an ihm ablesbar sind. Und damit geht es um das Stein gewordene Gedächtnis der Menschen.

Die Kunst des Architekten besteht darin, ein Bauwerk zu schaffen, bei dem die Erinnerungsschichten auch von Nicht-Fachleuten verstanden werden, ohne über spezielle Kenntnisse und das architektonische Vokabular von Stilen und Formen verfügen zu müssen. Dieses Verstehen muss nicht rational sein; es muss nicht jedem Einzelnen bewusst werden. Auch der einfache Bürger einer mittelalterlichen Stadt verstand nicht sämtliche Konnotationen der Kathedrale – er empfand diese dennoch als etwas „Sakrales". Er „erfühlte" das Richtige mehr, als dass er es „verstand". Architektur behandelt genau das: das Fühlen, das Empfinden der Menschen noch vor dem verstandesmäßigen Begreifen.

Was können die Pforzheimer Bürger also instinktiv, ohne bauhistorische Kenntnisse, erfühlen? Ihr Altes Rathaus hat eine Ergänzung bekommen – das zeigt ihnen, dass „es das wert ist", dass das Alte auch heute noch taugt (insbesondere dann, wenn es das neue Bürgerzentrum beherbergt). Diese Ergänzung ist

Altes Rathaus / Old Town Hall
Pforzheim, 2001

The extension is intended to recall the considerable volume of the original roof but it does so "without a roof", and without formulating an upper limit.

The façade of the old building, by contrast, consists of two historical states. Following its partial destruction in World War II the traditional natural stone façade was already "repaired" in the 1950s, and covered with smooth plaster, forgoing intrados in hewn stone. This repair was totally in line with the tradition prevalent at the time of preserving historical buildings; a tradition not of restoration but of reconstruction that bears evidence of the historical changes.

Thus, the Old Town Hall is made up of several layers of recollection: historicism, on which the exterior of the building from 1911 is based; and memory of those parts destroyed by the reconstruction in the 1950s, which also reminds one of the destruction wrought by the air raids that razed almost the entire town of Pforzheim to the ground.

It is no longer about "old" and "new" being combined to create a third design; it is no longer (only) an issue of design, but rather the several layers of recollection that are captured in a building and that can be read from it. As such, what is at stake is human memory in stone form.

The architect's art consists of creating a building in which the layers of recollection can also be understood by the layperson, without needing them to have special knowledge or an architectural vocabulary of styles and forms. This understanding need not be rational; not every individual need be aware of it. It is not as if the lower orders in medieval cities understood every single con-notation of the cathedral – though they still had the feeling that there was something "religious" about it. They "felt" rather than "understood" what was right. This is exactly what architecture addresses: a person's feelings and senses, before rational understanding kicks in.

What then can Pforzheim's residents sense instinctively, without having any knowledge of architectural history? Their Old Town Hall has been given an extension and this shows them "it is worth it", that what is old is still valued today (especially when it is home to the new citizens' center). The extension is without a doubt contemporary and makes use of our technical means, for instance in the elegant roofing of the courtyard. Their town hall has undergone a change, and when using terms such as "layering" and "development" we indicate the temporal aspect of architecture and its ability to make history visible. It communicates the new identity of the old building to the

ganz unzweifelhaft gegenwärtig und nutzt unsere heutigen technischen Möglichkeiten, zum Beispiel mit der eleganten Überdachung des Lichthofes. Ihr Rathaus hat sich weiter entwickelt; und Begriffe wie „Schichtung" und „Entwickeln" zeigen den zeitlichen Aspekt: Bauen als Sichtbarmachen von Geschichte. Sie vermittelt dem Bürger die neue Identität des alten Gebäudes.

Bauen als das Sichtbarmachen von Geschichte – kein Zweifel, dass sich die Architektur darin nicht erschöpft. Aber es stellt eine wichtige Dimension dar; es verankert einen Bau in einer Gegenwart, die nicht voraussetzungslos ist, sondern auf den vorhergehenden Zeiten aufbaut. In der Architektur von Auer+Weber kann man an vielen Bauten die Sorgfalt ablesen, die im Umgang mit dem Vorhandenen waltet.

Das ist keine Frage nur des „Aufbewahrens", des bloßen Verwendens des Bestandes, weil er nun einmal da ist. Es zeugt vielmehr von Respekt. Die Sorgfalt, mit der die Schichten gezeigt werden, macht es den Menschen einfach, Emotion und Erkenntnis zu gewinnen.

Eigen, nicht gleich

In der Architektur von Auer+Weber spielt die Geschichte als „Schichtung" nicht nur, wenn es um Anbauten oder Erweiterungen geht, eine wichtige Rolle. Das Zeppelin Carré in Stuttgart (Seite 114 ff.), das Festspielhaus in Recklinghausen (Seite 102 ff.), aber auch der Umbau der Villa Bosch (Seite 38) zeigen dies. Dabei geht es nicht um die „Schichtung" als formales Element an sich, sondern im Kern darum, ein Gebäude von heute als Teil einer Geschichte zu zeigen. Das lässt sich nicht nur an der nahe liegenden Aufgabe, dem Umbau oder der Erweiterung, zeigen – auch jedes neu gebaute Haus ist Teil eines geschichtlichen Prozesses.

Dieses Bewusstsein kommt in den Bauten von Auer+Weber zum Ausdruck. Das führt gerade nicht zu einer einheitlichen formalen Herangehensweise, sondern heißt: Jeder Bau setzt sich mit seiner, der spezifischen Umgebung auseinander – der historischen wie der physischen. Fritz Auer hat in einem Gespräch 1992 gesagt: „Ein Grundsatz, den wir verfolgen, liegt darin, nicht zwei Dinge gleichzeitig zu verändern. Wenn sich zum Beispiel der Maßstab ändert, sollte man die architektonische Distanz nicht durch die Materialwahl noch einmal betonen. Ich glaube, unser Weg ist eher der, Entwicklungsfäden aufzunehmen". „Entwicklungsfäden aufnehmen" ist nur ein anderer Begriff dafür, ein Bauwerk als Teil einer Geschichte darzustellen. Diese Anknüpfung an das Vergangene geschieht dadurch, dass citizens. It goes without saying that architecture is not limited to making history visible. But it does represent one of architecture's important dimensions, which is to anchor a building in the present while recognizing the influences of earlier ages. In the architecture of Auer+Weber, you can see in many of their buildings the care taken in dealing with what is present.

This is not a question of conservation, or of merely using what has survived because it is there. No: it is a sign of respect. The care taken to reveal the various layers makes it easy for people to understand the architecture on both an emotional and a rational level.

Special – not identical

In Auer+Weber's architecture, history as "layering" plays an important role, and not just in annexes and extensions. It is evident in the Zeppelin Carré in Stuttgart (page 114 ff), the Ruhrfestspielhaus in Recklinghausen (page 102 ff), and the Villa Bosch conversion (page 38). In each instance the major concern is not the "layering" as a formal element per se, but a present-day building as part of a past story. This is demonstrated not only by the conversion or extension of an old building, because even newly built houses are part of an historical process.

This awareness is evident in Auer+Weber's work, but it does not result in a uniform, formal approach. On the contrary, every building comes to terms with its own unique historical and physical environment. In an interview in 1992 Fritz Auer said: "One principle we pursue is not to change two things simultaneously. For instance, if the scale changes you should not stress the architectural distance again by the choice of material. I believe our approach is about taking up threads of development". "Taking up threads of development" is just another way of saying that you present a building as part of history. This link to the past is made not just by replacing everything with something new, or altering "two things simultaneously". What things are altered should be left open, and will vary depending on the project. In the end, whatever has proved its worth in the past, and continues to stand the test of time should not be changed without reason.

In other words, every building is "special", but nobody can re-invent the architecture itself. It would be pointless, especially when you are producing architecture that is in line with market requirements. People like to be able to recognize things immediately, like the brand of a handbag, the radiator grille on a specific make of car, or an architect's handwriting. One

Ruhrfestspielhaus Recklinghausen, 1998

nicht alles neu gemacht wird, nicht „zwei Dinge gleichzeitig" verändert werden. Welche das sind, bleibt offen und wird sich je nach Bauaufgabe ändern, aber was sich in der Vergangenheit und auch heute noch bewährt, wird nicht unnötig geändert.

Es gilt also: Jeder Bau ist „eigen", aber keiner erfindet die Architektur neu. Das ist im Sinne einer marktgerechten Architekturproduktion nicht zweckmäßig. Die Menschen haben es gern, wenn sie die Dinge auf Anhieb erkennen: Die Marke einer Handtasche, den Kühlergrill, der für eine Autofirma steht. Oder eben die Handschrift eines Architekten. Der eine baut im Quadrat – immer –, der andere im Zickzack – immer –, der dritte bemüht in Form und Material den Expressionismus der Zwanziger Jahre: Das gibt ein *branding*, ein Markenzeichen. Auch in der Architektur hat man den größten Erfolg, wenn man eine „Marke" vertritt, die im übrigen, man kann das durchaus positiv sehen, auch Sicherheit in einer zunehmend schnell sich verändernden Umgebung bietet. Auer+Weber gehen einen anderen Weg; die jeweils eigene Herangehensweise an einen Entwurf lässt sich nicht auf eine schnell erkennbare Marke reduzieren. Weswegen die beiden nicht zu den „Stars" der Szene gehören. Sie wollen es auch nicht.

Die Altenwohnanlage in Lemgo (Seite 32 ff.), das Landratsamt in Starnberg (Seite 40 ff.), das Subzentrum Flughafen München (Seite 58 ff.), oder der Zentrale Omnibusbahnhof in München (Seite 226 ff.) – was haben sie schon äußerlich gemeinsam? Formen und Materialien wechseln zwischen High Tech und Regionalismus, was manchen Kritiker verzweifeln läßt: Er findet keine Schublade, in der diese Architektur abgelegt und etikettiert werden kann.

Übrigens behandeln die Kritiker die einzelnen Bauten durchaus wohlwollend; aber mit ihrer Suche nach dem *label* haben sie Unrecht. Es gab immer große Architekten, die nicht unter einen formalen Hut zu bringen waren. Eero Saarinen gehörte in den fünfziger und sechziger Jahren dazu, auch Pier Luigi Nervi oder auf nationaler Ebene Bernhard Hermkes. Eigenartigerweise sind es meist Architekten, die sich auch stark mit der konstruktiven Seite des Berufes befasst haben – was auch für Auer+Weber zutrifft.

Öffentliche Wege. Wege zum Öffentlichen
Wie beschreibt man eine Architektur, die nicht durch augenscheinlich formale Einheitlichkeit geprägt ist? Sie als „unterschiedlich" zu kennzeichnen, ist nicht hinreichend, weil es nur das Gegenteil von „formal einheitlich" bezeichnet. Ich meine,

person always favors a rectangular design, another always uses a zigzag arrangement, the third strives in form and material to match the Expressionism of the 1920s. This produces a branding, a trademark. In architecture you also have the greatest success when you represent a "brand", which offers familiarity in an environment that is always changing. Auer+Weber have a different strategy; their adoption of an individual approach to each design cannot be reduced to an easily recognizable brand. Which is why the two men are not part of the in-crowd. Nor would they want to be.

What do the following share in terms of appearance: The retirement home complex in Lemgo (page 32 ff), the District office in Starnberg (page 40 ff), the Subcenter at Munich Airport (page 58 ff), and the Central Bus Station in Munich (page 226 ff)? Forms and materials alternate between high-tech and regionalism, which makes some critics despair because they cannot find a convenient pigeonhole or label for the architecture.

Incidentally, critics usually take a more than favorable view of the individual buildings, but they are mistaken if they are looking for a label. After all, there have always been great architects who eluded formal classification. Take Eero Saarinen in the 1950s and 1960s, or Pier Luigi Nervi, not to mention German architect Bernhard Hermkes. Strangely enough, such architects typically have a strong interest in the structural aspect of architecture – which also holds for Auer+Weber.

Public paths and paths to the public
How do you describe a form of architecture that is not characterized by obvious formal unity? Describing it as "varied" is inadequate, since that merely defines the opposite of "formal unity". As well as its relationship to a place, I believe the most important aspect of Auer+Weber's architecture is the public nature of the buildings. In many cases they direct their efforts toward allowing people to experience this public aspect through the use of paths.

The term "public" embraces more than merely the question of whether the public has access to a building. Ultimately, it addresses the importance of the respective buildings in relation to all others in the city.

There are two main considerations when looking at urban architecture. We have already discussed how adding another new "layer" continues the story. Another consideration is how the new building presents itself with respect to all the others around it: Does it brag or boast? Does it fit in? Does it conceal

Altenwohn- und Pflegeheim / Retirement and Nursing Home Lemgo, 1986

Landratsamt / District Office Starnberg, 1987

Zentraler Omnibusbahnhof / Central Bus Station München, 2002

als den wichtigsten Kern der Architektur von Auer+Weber neben der Bindung an einen Ort die Frage nach der Öffentlichkeit des Bauens zu erkennen. In vielen Fällen wird versucht, über das architektonische Mittel des „Weges" diese Öffentlichkeit erlebbar zu machen.

Der Begriff der „Öffentlichkeit" umfasst dabei mehr als nur die Frage, ob ein Gebäude von der Allgemeinheit betreten werden darf. Er behandelt letztlich das Thema der Bedeutung, der Wichtigkeit des jeweiligen Hauses im Zusammenhang aller anderen einer Stadt.

Es geht dabei um die beiden Seiten des Städtischen: Zum einen hatten wir die Fortschreibung einer Geschichte durch das Hinzufügen einer weiteren, neuen „Schicht" betrachtet. Zum anderen wird die Repräsentanz des jeweils neuen Hauses im Zusammenhang aller anderen, bereits vorhandenen, betrachtet: Trumpft es auf? Fügt es sich ein? Versteckt es sich? Welche Aussage trifft es über seinen Bauherrn? Und schließlich: Wie bietet es sich den Menschen in der Stadt an, also: Wie öffentlich ist es?

Nehmen wir zum Beispiel das Ortszentrum von Germering (Seite 80 ff.), über das ich bereits in einem früheren Text geschrieben habe: „Der Ort liegt in der Nähe von München und wird überwiegend von Berufspendlern bewohnt. Die S-Bahnstation ist vermutlich die wichtigste öffentliche Einrichtung – jedenfalls, bis die Stadt beschloss, ein neues Zentrum mit verschiedenen Nutzungen vom Rathaus über eine Halle für Theater und gesellschaftliche Veranstaltungen bis hin zur Stadtbibliothek zu bauen. Die beiden letzten sind 1994 fertig gestellt worden, wogegen das Rathaus noch auf sich warten lässt.

Die städtebauliche Ordnung der zukünftigen Gesamtanlage, Ergebnis eines Wettbewerbserfolges, geht von einer im Grunde einfachen Wegeverbindung zwischen Bahnhof und den Wohngebieten aus; der Weg teilt das Zentrum diagonal und die Baukörper orientieren sich in ihrer Richtung daran.

Sie stellen sich aber nicht ‚in den Weg'. Sie fordern zum beiläufigen Eintritt auf; der Haupteingang der Stadthalle liegt an einem kleinen quadratischen Platz mit einer offenen Sitzmulde – ein ‚Amphitheater' möchte man es trotz seiner Form nicht nennen –, an dessen Rand der Weg entlangführt. Wenn man der Aufforderung folgt (und hoffentlich stehen die Türen nicht nur für Veranstaltungen offen!), dann setzt sich der Weg unter einem Glasdach in eine dreigeschossige Halle fort, an der Foyer und Restaurant liegen – öffentliche Bereiche."

itself? What does it say about its developer? And, finally, how accessible is it for people living in the city? In other words: How public is it?

Let us take as an example the Germering town center (page 80 ff), which I already wrote about in an earlier article: "The town is not far from Munich, and most of its residents are commuters. The suburban train station is presumably the most important public facility – at least it was until the town decided to build a new multipurpose center whose uses range from town hall via a hall for theater performances and social events through to a town library. The latter two were completed in 1994, but the town hall has yet to be built.

The urban planning arrangement of the future group of buildings, which was the outcome of a successful competition entry, is based on what is essentially an obvious connecting path between the station and the residential areas. The path divides the center diagonally, and the location of the buildings follows this diagonal design.

The buildings are not "in the way", rather, they invite people to drop in. The main entrance to the town hall is located on a small rectangular square with an open seating hollow – despite its shape, "amphitheater" is not quite the right word – whose border is edged by the path. For those who take up the invitation (and hopefully the doors will be open on days when no events are on as well!), the path continues under a glass roof into a three-story hall that is joined by foyer and restaurant – public spaces."

There are other examples, of course. The public aspect of the District office in Starnberg (page 40 ff) is not expressed primarily through paths, but rather through areas and urban "spaces" reserved for the public. We are all familiar with those long and stuffy corridors in local authority buildings where the clients sit like petitioners on benches outside the offices. Buildings like this convey the feeling that, if you cannot avoid dealing with the public altogether, you should at least give them somewhere to wait.

Not so in Starnberg. Here the building was constructed for the public. What is more – since the public was awarding the contract, and the project was funded with the help of taxpayers' money – it was taken seriously! The Japanese-style pavilions blend well into their surroundings – there is no trace of the state bragging, or trying to impress people. On the contrary, it presents itself as a service provider and both the people waiting and those working there are treated like human beings, not just as people who perform certain functions.

Ortszentrum / Town Center
Germering, 1993
Luftaufnahme / Arial View

Landratsamt / District Office
Starnberg, 1987

PRISMA-Haus / PRISMA Building
Frankfurt am Main, 2001

Es gibt andere Beispiele. Das „Öffentliche" beim Landratsamt in Starnberg (Seite 40 ff.) erschließt sich nicht in erster Linie über Wege, sondern eher über Flächen, städtische „Plätze", die für das Publikum reserviert sind. Wir kennen doch zur Genüge jene Flure von Behördenbauten, die normalerweise lang und muffig sind, wo auf den Bänken vor den Amtsstuben die Klientel als Bittsteller sitzt. Sie vermitteln das Gefühl, irgendwo müsse man das Publikum doch warten lassen, wenn man es schon nicht vermeiden könne.

Anders in Starnberg: Dort hat man für dieses Publikum gebaut, man hat es als virtuellen Auftraggeber des Gebäudes, notabene auch als dessen Finanzier mit Hilfe von Steuergeldern, ernst genommen! Die japanisch anmutenden Pavillons fügen sich in die Umgebung ein – hier trumpft nicht ein Staat auf, um die Menschen zu beeindrucken. Stattdessen artikuliert er sich als „Dienst"leistungsunternehmen, Wartende wie dort Arbeitende werden als Menschen behandelt, nicht als Funktionsträger.

Man muss sich vor allem die Erschließungstreppen in den verschiedenen Bauten von Auer+ Weber einmal ansehen, um das Öffentliche, das über Wege vermittelt wird, zu begreifen. Warum zieht sich eine Treppe als „Himmelsleiter" (der Ausdruck stammt von den Architekten) an der Fassade eines Bürohauses entlang, obwohl doch die Menschen darin in der Regel den Aufzug benutzen? Und warum wird bei diesem, dem „Prisma"-Haus in Frankfurt (Seite 168 ff.), ein Atrium als „Park" und „Stadt im Kleinen" gebaut, wenn nicht, um das Thema städtischer Öffentlichkeit auch in einem Bürohaus wirksam werden zu lassen? Dass diese Architektur einen „Zuschauer" zulässt, also jemanden, der von außen die Vorgänge im Inneren betrachtet (weswegen die Treppe auch von außen sichtbar ist), belegt, dass es nicht um die reine Bedürfnisbefriedigung, um die rein funktionale Verbindung zweier Geschosse geht: Diese „Himmelsleiter" bietet ein Stück städtisches Theater, indem Menschen diese Treppe hinauf und hinunter gehen können. Fast möchte man ihnen zurufen: „Schreitet – ihr seid Teil einer Inszenierung von Öffentlichkeit!"

Darstellen, wie etwas gemacht ist
Die „Schichtung" und das „Öffentliche", die Repräsentation als Darstellung dessen, was das jeweilige Haus im gebauten Kontext ausdrücken soll, bilden den Kern der Architektur von Auer+Weber. Sie drückt das – ein weiterer Punkt – aber auch auf eine bestimmte Art aus, indem sie die Frage „Wie ist das gebaut?" auf besondere Weise ernst nimmt und beantwortet.

In order to understand the public aspect that is presented through paths, you should make a point of viewing the access stairs in Auer+Weber's various buildings. Why does a flight of stairs run like a Jacob's Ladder (the architects' term) along the façade of an office building when its occupants generally use the lift? And why in this same building – the PRISMA building in Frankfurt (page 168 ff) – is an atrium built into a park and miniature city if not to express something about the subject of public access in urban environments, particularly in the form of office buildings? The fact that this architecture allows for spectators (i.e. people who observe what is going on inside, which explains why the stairs are also visible from outside), proves this is not just about satisfying a need, or fulfilling a practical purpose like providing a link between two floors. No, this "Jacob's Ladder" provides a piece of urban theater, since people can walk up and down it. You almost feel tempted to call out to them: "Keep walking – you're part of a production on public involvement!"

Showing how something is done
The core features of Auer+Weber's architecture are the "layering", the "public aspect", and the presentation of what each house is designed to express within its building context. However, another feature is that the architecture expresses its context in a specific manner, by asking the question "How is it built?" In other words, we can add a third aspect to the relationship with the past and the urban surroundings in the impact of the design and material employed.

Originally awarded first prize in the competition for the German pavilion at the World Expo in Seville (page 50 ff), but not built owing to a number of protests, the pavilion's four main subjects are highly conspicuous (perhaps for the very reason that the design works best as a pure concept). The two latter subjects address the impact of design and material. At the time I wrote the following article on these issues:

"The house as a stage (apparent in the transparency of the rooms, the expression of movement in ramps, stairs and slanting rooms). This is an architectural attempt to render the topic of the 'Self-presentation of Germany'. The public is treated simultaneously as spectator and as an actor, the building becomes a stage, the exhibition, an example of the very Spanish concept of openness to the city. This congruence of (Spanish) city and building is emphasized in the second element.

Zur Beziehung zu Geschichte und zum Städtischen kommt also als Drittes die Wirkung von Konstruktion und Material hinzu.

Im seinerzeit als 1. Preis im Wettbewerb prämierten, dann aber trotz vieler Proteste nicht gebauten Projekt für den Weltausstellungspavillon in Sevilla (Seite 50 ff.) treten die den Entwurf besonders eindringlich prägenden vier Hauptthemen hervor (vielleicht auch deshalb, weil der Entwurf noch eher reine Idee sein kann). Die beiden letzten befassen sich mit der Wirkung von Konstruktion und Material. In einem Beitrag beschrieb ich diese Themen damals:

„Das Haus als Bühne (in der Transparenz der Räume, der Bewegungsarchitektur aus Rampen, Treppen und schrägen Platzräumen). Das ist der architektonische Versuch, das Thema ‚Selbstdarstellung der Bundesrepublik' auszudrücken. Das Publikum wird gleichzeitig als Zuschauer und Schauspieler behandelt, der Bau wird zur Bühne, die Ausstellung zum Requisit einer sehr spanischen Beziehung von Öffentlichkeit zu Stadt. Diese Kongruenz von (spanischer) Stadt und Bau wird im zweiten Element betont.

Der Bau als Stadt: Gemeint ist damit die bauliche Struktur aus einzelnen geometrischen Elementen in einem festen Gerippe, einem Rahmen (der Kreis des Restaurants, das Oval des Vortragssaales, das Quadrat des Freirestaurants). Jeder dieser Teile behält seine Individualität, alle stehen in einem unterschwelligen Spannungsverhältnis zueinander, alle sind durch den Rahmen des konstruktiven Gerippes gehalten wie die Stadt durch ihr Straßennetz. Das dritte Thema ist daher dieses Gerippe aus den konstruktiven Einheiten plus dem Schattendach. Das ist dem leichten Pavillon buchstäblich angemessen, der ja auch so etwas wie ein ‚Fliegender Bau' ist und möglicherweise nach dem Ende der Ausstellung abgetragen werden wird. Er ist neutral für jede Art von Ausstellung, er erfüllt darüber hinaus auch die Forderung nach Signifikanz.

Das führt zu dem vierten und wichtigsten Element, das den Bau zum legitimen Nachfolger der großen Weltausstellungsbauten der Geschichte macht: sein Ausdruck von Technik. Weltausstellungsbauten sollten, so die Ausschreibung, ‚irgendwie signifikant und futuristisch' sein – was auch immer das heißen mag. Tatsächlich wirkt das Modell auf den ersten Blick so, als könne es diese Forderung erfüllen. Und es sieht ‚technisch' aus. Es wirkt allerdings auch ‚etwas unordentlich'. Und ich meine: das ist seine größte Qualität.

Denn hier wird Technik nicht als Kraftakt gezeigt, sondern als etwas, mit dem man spielerisch umgeht (und Spiel heißt: unge-

The building as a city: What this means is the architects' employment of individual geometric elements in a fixed framework (the circle of the restaurant, the oval of the lecture hall, the square of the outdoor restaurant). Each of these areas retains its individuality, yet all exist in a subliminally strained relationship with each other. In the same way a city is held together by its road network, and all areas are contained within the framework the structure provides. Consequently, the third topic is the framework of structural elements plus the canopy. This really is suited to the light pavilion, which is, after all, something of a temporary or mobile structure and might possibly be removed when the Expo is over. It is neutral, and therefore suited to every type of exhibition, while also meeting the requirement for appearing significant.

This leads to the fourth and most important element that makes the building a legitimate successor to the great Expo buildings of the past: The way it expresses technology. According to the brief, World Expo buildings are supposed to look somehow significant and futuristic – whatever that means. And indeed, at first glance, the model looks as if it could indeed meet this requirement. What is more, it has a 'technological' look about it. You could also say it comes over as 'a little untidy'. However, in my opinion, that is its greatest quality.

After all, technology is not presented here as a tour de force but rather as something treated in a playful manner (and playing implies unconstrained, but according to established rules). But only this can define our present relationship to technology: An eco-pavilion made of jute and clay would not be appropriate here, nor a high-tech building demonstrated by the British pavilion next to the German one. High-tech is about finding brilliant technical solutions for problems that would not exist without the architecture: Technology as an end in and of itself. Instead, in the rationality of its primary construction, the German pavilion shows a framework that is transparent in both senses of the word.

This is not an operational machine but rather an object made for people to use. This architecture says we cannot manage without technology; even the solution of our ecological problems can only be achieved in tandem with, and not by working against, technology. But we take our use of technology for granted, in the same way that ten-year-olds handle computers today, or we older people handle bicycles. This building would have become a bicycle – and been understood immediately."

EXPO '92 Sevilla, 1990

EXPO '92 Sevilla, 1990

EXPO '92 Sevilla, 1990

Altenwohn- und Pflegeheim
Retirement and Nursing Home
Lemgo, 1986

zwungen, aber nach festen Regeln). Nur das aber kann unser heutiges Verhältnis zur Technik bestimmen: Nicht der Öko-Pavillon aus Jute und Lehm wäre hier angemessen, nicht der High-Tech-Bau, wie er unmittelbar neben dem deutschen mit dem britischen Pavillon vorgeführt wird. Dort werden brillante technische Lösungen für Probleme entwickelt, die man ohne diese Architektur gar nicht hätte: Technik als Selbstzweck. Stattdessen zeigt der deutsche Pavillon in der Rationalität der Primärkonstruktion ein im doppelten Sinne einsehbares Gerippe.

Das ist keine funktionierende Maschine, sondern ein für Menschen zum Gebrauch gemachter Gegenstand. Wir können nicht ohne Technik auskommen, sagt diese Architektur; selbst die Lösung unserer ökologischen Probleme kann nur mit, nicht gegen die Technik erreicht werden. Wir gebrauchen sie aber mit der Selbstverständlichkeit, mit der heute Zehnjährige mit Computern umgehen und wir Älteren mit einem Fahrrad. Dieser Bau wäre ein Fahrrad geworden: sofort verständlich."

Material und Konstruktion übernehmen also nicht nur die Aufgabe, ein Raumvolumen technisch sicher und möglichst energiesparend zu umhüllen. Sie zeigen darüber hinaus auch einen Inhalt. Sie haben Bedeutung. Sie werden zu Mitteln des Ausdrucks, so, wie es die Form ebenfalls ist.

Das kann man auch an den Altenwohnungen in Lemgo (Seite 32 ff.) sehen, die in mehreren Bauabschnitten realisiert wurden. Kann es ein schöneres Kompliment geben, als wenn eine Bewohnerin dem die Bauten besichtigenden Kritiker zuruft, es seien die schönsten Häuser von Lemgo, und man möge das doch bitte den Architekten ausrichten?

Bei diesen Bauten aber geht es nicht um die Darstellung von anspruchsvoller Technik, sondern um eine eher bescheidene Einfügung in den Bestand – vertraute Dachneigung, vertraute Dachpfannen, vertrauter Putz. Dennoch sind die Bauten als neu zu erkennen; Balkone, zwischen die Häuser geschaltete Wintergärten, Materialien wie Holz, Metall und Glas sind Ausdruck einer Haltung, nicht (nur) reine Zweckerfüllung.

Dieser Ausdruck ist der von Leichtigkeit. Das bezieht sich nicht nur auf die Altenwohnungen oder den projektierten Expo-Bau in Sevilla (Seite 50 ff.); Leichtigkeit ist ein weiteres typisches Merkmal der Architektur von Auer+Weber. Viele ihrer Bauten scheinen „den Boden nur auf Zehenspitzen zu betreten", als ob sie nicht auf Dauer dort stünden. Die Eingriffe der Architektur werden nicht zu Verletzungen, sondern zu Ergänzungen, im besten Fall: zu Erweiterungen. So die Mensa der Offiziersschule des Heeres in Dresden (Seite 122 ff.): „Unterm Dach im

As we can see, material and structure not only have the task of covering a volume of space in a manner that is technically sound and as energy efficient as possible; they also say something about content. They are of significance. They become a means of expression, just as form does.

This is also evident in the retirement apartments in Lemgo (page 32 ff), which were realized in several construction phases. Can there be a nicer compliment than having a resident call to the critic who is inspecting the buildings, to say that these are the most beautiful houses in Lemgo, and would he please pass that on to the architect?

Yet these buildings are not concerned with presenting sophisticated technology; rather, they seek to merge modestly with what exists already – a familiar roof incline, familiar pantiles, familiar plasterwork. But the buildings are still recognizable as new; balconies, conservatories are inserted between the houses, and materials such as wood, metal and glass become an expression of attitude, and not (only) a means to an end.

Furthermore, the expression is one of lightness. This applies not only to the retirement homes but to the planned Expo pavilion in Seville, as well (page 50 ff). And indeed, lightness is another typical feature of Auer+Weber's architecture. Many of their buildings appear "to walk on tiptoe", as if they were not planning to stay permanently. The incisions this architecture makes are not damaging, but act as complements, and in the best instance as extensions. Take the mess in the Officer Training School in Dresden (page 122 ff): "Sitting under cover of a roof in the open", is how Carlo Weber refers to the design featuring a canopy and floor slab, which appears to hover above the ground – following the architectural principles developed by Mies van der Rohe. This is particularly evident when you contrast it with the pre-World War I mess, which has a solid, heavy look, small window openings, and its façade is structured using relief work (here, too, stressing the base area), while the former hovers above the ground and emphasizes the horizontal layers.

The prospects for this architecture, which has so little in common with the principles of traditional architecture up to the start of the twentieth century, arise from the materials available today and their adaptability. It is an uncompromisingly contemporary architecture employing every available technical means to achieve the intended effect. One consequence of this is that the chosen designs are not an end in themselves but rather serve architecture as consumer art. They enable architecture to be treated in a certain way, and express this outwardly, making it

Freien sitzen" nennt Carlo Weber die Konstruktion aus Dach- und Bodenplatte, die vom Erdboden losgelöst erscheint – eine Fortsetzung von architektonischen Prinzipien, wie sie Mies van der Rohe entwickelt hat. Im Gegensatz zum Casino aus der Zeit vor dem 1. Weltkrieg wird das besonders deutlich: Hier das massige, fest auftretende Volumen mit kleinen Fensteröffnungen, dessen Fassade nach Steinmetzart plastisch gegliedert ist (übrigens auch beim Casino eine Sockelzone betonend), dort die über dem Boden schwebenden, die Horizontale betonenden Ebenen.

Die Chance für diese Architektur, die mit den Prinzipien der traditionellen Architektur bis zum Beginn des 20. Jahrhunderts so wenig verbindet, ergibt sich aus den heute zur Verfügung stehenden Materialien und deren Fügung: Das ist kompromisslos zeitgenössisch und nutzt jedes technische Mittel, die beabsichtigte Wirkung zu erzielen. Daraus folgt aber: Die gewählten Konstruktionen sind nicht Selbstzweck, sondern dienen der Architektur als Gebrauchs-Kunst. Sie machen eine bestimmte Art des Umgangs mit ihr möglich und drücken diese nach außen hin aus, machen sie verständlich und im wörtlichen Sinne begreifbar. Der Selbstzweck der so genannten High-Tech-Architektur der neunziger Jahre war dagegen ein anderer: Sie feierte Technik. Die Architektur von Auer+Weber nutzt Technik.

Miteinander umgehen

Aus der Art des Umgangs mit der Technik, aus Schichtung und dem Prinzip des Städtischen auch in den scheinbar privaten Bauten entstehen Orte für Menschen, die „miteinander umgehen". Dieser Begriff enthält zwei Komponenten – einmal das Bewegungselement, zum anderen die Frage nach der Art des Umgangs, und beide sind gemeint.

Auf die Treppen als Elemente einer Bewegung wurde bereits hingewiesen; es geht aber darüber hinaus: Es entstehen Räume, in denen ein Publikum gleichzeitig Zuschauer und Akteur ist. So entstand aus bautechnischer Notwendigkeit beim Theater in Hof (Seite 94 ff.) aus einem besseren Hinterhof mit Treppe eine wintergartenähnliche Halle, die auch den sonst eher stiefmütterlich behandelten Bühnenarbeitern, Technikern und Schauspielern einen attraktiven Ort der Kommunikation bietet. Wie gut tut dem Festspielhaus in Recklinghausen (Seite 102 ff.), diesem monumentalen Bau der sechziger Jahre, der den Arbeitern im Zechenrevier einen schon damals etwas verstaubten, spätbürgerlichen Kulturbegriff vermitteln sollte, das neue Foyer, das über die Festspielwiese hinweg durch seine Transparenz Verbindungen zur

understandable and tangible in the literal sense. This is not the case with the so-called high-tech architecture of the 1990s, which was an end in itself, and celebrated technology. The architecture of Auer+Weber makes use of technology.

Dealing with one another

Handling technology, layering, and the principle of the urban, even in seemingly private buildings, creates locations for people to "deal with one another". This term contains two components – the element of movement and a question about the kind of handling, and both are relevant.

We have already seen how stairs are employed as an element of movement; but the idea extends further: Spaces are created in which the public is simultaneously spectator and actor. Take the theater in the German town of Hof (page 94 ff). Construction requirements led to the transformation of what was little more than a backyard with stairs into a kind of conservatory, thereby providing stage-hands, technicians and actors – for whom little provision had been made – with an attractive place to meet and talk. What an improvement the new foyer in the Ruhrfestspielhaus in Recklinghausen is (page 102 ff), this monumental building from the 1970s intended to convey to workers in the coal-mining industry an idea about culture, which even then was somewhat antiquated and stuffy. Thanks to its transparency it now forms a link to the city way beyond the performance grounds. And architects must lay great store in connections, in both senses of the word, in order to accord importance to the customary beaten paths between the suburban railway and residential areas that define the shape and direction of the individual buildings, as in the case of the Germering Town Center.

And even in what, at first sight, amounts to an everyday task – namely a hotel for scientists and employees of the European Southern Observatory (ESO) in Chile – the principle emerges clearly: The connecting ramps between the various levels, the "urban squares" interspersed by oases, the central hall as a glazed city park – and all of it in an almost archaic formal severity which resists the amorphous, but at the same time archaic, looking surroundings. This was accomplished even with a very tight construction budget, since hotel buildings generally follow economic objectives rather than aiming to achieve a particular spatial and architectural impact.

These buildings were intended to be more than an end in themselves; you can read it in every element, and can assume a value added in terms of architectural intention that extends

Haus / House Farnsworth
Fox River, IL, USA, 1949–1951
Ludwig Mies van der Rohe

Casino und Mensa der
Offiziersschule des Heeres
Army Officers' Mess
at the Training School
Dresden, 1998

Ruhrfestspielhaus Recklinghausen, 1998

Hotel der ESO
Cerro Paranal, Chile, 2001

Stadt aufnimmt. Und für wie bedeutsam müssen die Architekten Verbindungen – im Doppelsinn des Wortes – halten, wenn sie die gewohnten Trampelpfade zwischen S-Bahn und Wohngebiet so ernst nehmen, dass diese die Kontur und Ausrichtung der einzelnen Baukörper bestimmen dürfen, wie in der neuen Ortsmitte von Germering!

Und selbst bei einer auf den ersten Blick so undramatischen Aufgabe wie dem Hotel für Wissenschaftler und Mitarbeiter des European Southern Observatory ESO in Chile (Seite 196 ff.) wird das Prinzip deutlich: Die verbindenden Rampen zwischen den Ebenen, die „städtischen Plätze" als Oasen dazwischen, die zentrale Halle als überglaster Stadt-Park – das alles in einer beinahe archaischen Formenstrenge, die sich gegen eine amorphe, aber gleichfalls archaisch anmutende Umgebung stemmt – und das, obwohl der Bauetat extrem eng war und Hotelbauten in der Regel eher ökonomische Zielsetzungen haben als einen räumlich-architektonischen Anspruch ausstrahlen.

In diesen Bauten ist mehr beabsichtigt als nur die bloße Zweckerfüllung; man kann es an jedem Bauteil ablesen, und man kann auf einen „Mehrwert" der architektonischen Intention schließen über den praktischen Teil einer vertikalen oder horizontalen Wegeverbindung von Flur und Treppe hinaus. Bei Auer+Weber geht es nicht um eindimensional gerichtete Räume – auch Straßenräume –, die nur eine Richtung der Bewegung zulassen. Kennzeichen ihrer Raum-Zusammenhänge ist vielmehr das Nicht-Gerichtete, das Ziellose, besser: diejenige Bewegung, die in der Verbindung zwischen Menschen ihr Ziel findet. Das unterscheidet diese Wegeverbindungen von den Prozessionsstraßen und Aufmarschplätzen, die jedem Glied einer Gesellschaft einen festen Platz zuweisen möchten.

Die Frage bleibt, ob ein solches Verständnis von Bewegung nach festen Regeln, die Offenheit und Spiel zulassen, einer heutigen gesellschaftlichen Realität angemessen ist, die immer weniger durch den Gegensatz von Öffentlichkeit und Privatheit gekennzeichnet ist, die immer mehr als feste Größen verschwimmen.

Als man sich noch umkleidete, um „in die Stadt zu gehen", war das anders; heute hingegen wird das Private zunehmend zum Öffentlichen, zumindest zum Veröffentlichen. Folgerichtig werden unsere Städte zunehmend zu Ansammlungen privatisierter Räume, in denen das Öffentliche nicht mehr stattfinden soll – das Öffentliche, dessen Kennzeichen der Umgang prinzipiell Gleicher miteinander war, die sich nicht kannten, aber nach gleichen Regeln „zivilisiert" miteinander umgingen.

beyond the practical function of providing a vertical or horizontal connecting link in the guise of corridor or stairs. Auer+Weber's architecture is not concerned with spaces – streets included – having a single dimensional arrangement, or allowing movement in one direction only. What characterizes their use of space is that their choice of directions is determined by the desire to provide connections between people. That is what distinguishes these connecting links from the streets clearly designed for processions or squares that look fit for rallies, the object of the latter being to assign every member of society a set place.

The question remains whether an understanding of movement, according to predetermined rules described above, allows the openness and experimentation appropriate to contemporary social reality, characterized as it is by a dwindling contrast between the public and private, and a blurring of the distinction between these two domains.

Back when people still got dressed up to "go into town", things were different. Today, by contrast, private areas are increasingly becoming public, or at least advertise themselves as such. As a consequence, our cities are increasingly becoming collections of privatized spaces from which the public is excluded. By "public", I mean the behavior used towards those who are equal in principle, do not know each other, and yet deal with one another in a "civilized" manner according to the same set of rules.

But privatized urban space or "city" is merely presented as the epitome of public space that is accessible to everyone: You need only look at the signs prohibiting this and that, or the private security guards installed in front of and inside shopping malls to see this. Conversely, "true public", that which treats every person as being of equal importance, no longer seems to stand a chance. Many citizens are relieved precisely when they realize those false public places they frequent cannot be entered by everyone. People prefer to indulge in consumption amongst their own, but this attitude prevents our looking at another reality, a more complete image of society.

The works of Auer+Weber address this contradiction in urban life. This is done not only by making political statements (for one thing that does not work in architecture), but is also conveyed through architectural design; for example, using the direction of buildings and spaces to connect people. Or by taking the public aspect as seriously as the aforementioned examples do.

Der privatisierte Stadtraum aber stellt „Stadt" als Inbegriff des Öffentlichen, für alle Zugänglichen nur dar; die Verbotsschilder und die private Polizei vor und in den Einkaufsmalls beweisen es. Dagegen scheint eine tatsächliche Öffentlichkeit, die jeden Menschen gleich wichtig nimmt, keine Chance mehr zu haben: Viele Bürger sind froh, wenn die von ihnen frequentierten „schein-öffentlichen" Räume eben nicht von allen Menschen betreten werden können; man ist gern unter sich konsumfreudig – das verhindert aber den Blick auf eine andere Wirklichkeit, ein vollständigeres Gesellschaftsbild.

Dieser Widerspruch im städtischen Leben wird in den Arbeiten von Auer+Weber thematisiert. Das geschieht nicht mit dem politischen Zeigefinger (schon weil das in der Architektur gar nicht funktioniert), sondern wird über die architektonische Gestalt vermittelt – zum Beispiel im Nicht-Gerichteten der Räume. Oder darin, dass diese Architektur „das Öffentliche" so wichtig nimmt, wie die genannten Beispiele zeigen.

Schule machen

Die Art des Umgangs mit Material und Konstruktion und mit der Leichtigkeit aus der Bewegung, wie sie Auer+Weber pflegen, ist nicht einmalig in Deutschland; es gibt so etwas wie eine „Süddeutsche Schule" des Bauens der letzten Jahrzehnte, die diese Architektur prägt. Sie ist durch Exponenten wie Fritz Auer und Carlo Weber entscheidend mit entwickelt worden – eine Art „Weiterentwicklung von Mies van der Rohe, gesehen durch die Brille Hans Scharouns": konstruktive Stringenz bei räumlicher Vielfalt.

Diese Architektur kommt nicht „mit dickem Hintern" einher. Sie ist sich ihrer selbst so sicher, dass sie nicht aufzutrumpfen braucht. Sie stellt sich dar als Teil eines Spiels – Spiel aber heißt: feste Regeln, deren Einhaltung eine neue Freiheit des Umgangs gewähren.

Der historische Bezugspunkt dieser Architektur ist ganz sicher der Entwurf für die Bauten der Olympischen Spiele 1972 in München, an dessen Entstehen und Realisierung Fritz Auer und Carlo Weber als Partner von Günter Behnisch wesentlichen Anteil hatten. Der Olympiapark mit seinen Sportanlagen war für die architektonische Selbstdarstellung der Bundesrepublik in mehrfacher Hinsicht ein Markstein und ist es bis heute: als Ausdruck eines anderen Deutschland gegenüber demjenigen der Spiele von 1936, als neuartige Verbindung zwischen Sportbauten und Landschaft zu einem „Gesamtkunstwerk". Heute gilt die Anlage, nach einer Publikumsumfrage der Zeitschrift „Häuser",

Setting a style precedent

This particular handling of material and design, together with the lightness of movement, as practiced by Auer+Weber, is not unique in Germany. Over the last decades, what might be termed a "South-German School" of architecture has evolved, which informs this architecture. Exponents such as Fritz Auer and Carlo Weber have had a decisive influence on this style, which might be described as an "advancement of Mies van der Rohe, as seen through the spectacles of Hans Scharoun"; in other words, design stringency combined with spatial diversity.

This architecture does not come with a swaggering gait. It is so confident that it does not need to brag. It presents itself as part of a game, but a game relies on fixed rules, and abiding by them grants you greater latitude in dealing with things.

Without doubt the historical reference point for these structures is the design of the buildings for the Olympic Games in Munich, in whose conception and realization Fritz Auer and Carlo Weber, in their capacity as Günter Behnisch's partners, played a highly influential role. In several respects, the Olympic Park and its sports facilities was, and still remains, a milestone in Germany's architectural self-image. It was an expression of Germany that was very different from the country that hosted the Games in 1936; there was a new kind of link between the sports complexes and landscape that formed a *Gesamtkunstwerk*. According to a survey by architectural journal *Häuser*, it is considered the most beautiful ensemble ever built in Germany and is a listed building.

The Olympic Park's design marks a key position in the work of everyone involved, because it opened up a new freedom of thinking. The idea underlying this architecture is also evident in buildings with a totally different function – the idea of a utopia, of a better world, and a society based on equal rights for everyone.

Auer+Weber's work is very definitely critical of society. However, social criticism in architecture does not work when you present what you are criticizing. It only works when you present a better alternative, the image of a better world, from which you realize that today's world can be improved. But from the aspects of Auer+Weber's work outlined here, one can also see that there is also a level of social criticism present. A criticism of certain regulations that are restrictive rather than opening up new options; a criticism of the city that is increasingly becoming divided into separate, private spaces; a criticism of a structuring of society based on fitting into categories; a criticism of the

Olympiapark / Olympic Park
München, 1972

Behnisch & Partner, 1970
Olympiastadion / Olympic Stadium, 1972

als das schönste je in Deutschland gebaute Ensemble und steht unter Denkmalschutz.

Dieser Entwurf markiert eine Schlüsselposition im Werk aller damals Beteiligten, weil er eine neue Freiheit des Denkens erschloss. Die Idee dieser Architektur ist auch in anderen Bauten ganz anderer Funktion spürbar – es ist die Idee, die Utopie einer besseren Welt, einer Gesellschaft, die auf der Grundlage der Gleich-Berechtigung aller basiert.

Insofern sind die Arbeiten von Auer+Weber sehr wohl gesellschaftskritisch. Gesellschaftskritik in der Architektur aber funktioniert nicht durch die Darstellung des Kritisierten, sondern nur durch die Darstellung von etwas Besserem, nur durch das Bild einer besseren Welt, aus dem folgt, dass die heutige Welt verbessert werden kann. In diesem Sinne allerdings – das zeigen die beschriebenen Komponenten der Arbeiten von Auer+Weber – findet in der Tat eine Gesellschaftskritik statt: Kritik an bestimmten Ordnungen, die einschränken anstatt zu erweitern; Kritik an einer Stadt, die immer mehr in separate, private Räume zerfällt; Kritik an einer gesellschaftlichen Organisation, die auf Einordnung basiert; Kritik an einem Technikfetischismus, der in der Darstellung von Technik bereits die Lösung sieht.

So verstanden, stellt die Architektur von Auer+Weber tatsächlich eine Art Freiheitsversprechen dar. Analog zu den „heiteren Spielen" 1972, deren schlüssige architektonische Übersetzung wir heute noch bewundern, bauen sie für eine ideale, eine zwangsfreie Gesellschaft.

Damals wurden die „heiteren Spiele" mit dem Anschlag auf die israelische Olympiamannschaft beendet. Ein solches Ende droht jederzeit – auch heute. Das darf aber die Architekten nicht daran hindern, das Freiheitsversprechen in ihren Arbeiten immer wieder zu formulieren.

Jede Aufgabe neu
Fast 25 Jahre lang haben Fritz Auer und Carlo Weber mit Günter Behnisch zusammengearbeitet, am Anfang als Praktikanten, später als Mitarbeiter und schließlich 14 Jahre lang als Partner. In diesem langen Zeitraum haben sie die Architektur des Büros wesentlich mitbestimmt. Die Gründung ihres eigenen Büros führte zu einer Weiterentwicklung dessen, was den beiden „eigen" war und was man heute, über fast 25 Jahre gemeinsamer Tätigkeit hinweg betrachten kann.

obsession with technology that is expressed in the mere showcasing of technology.

Seen in this light, Auer+Weber's architecture really does represent something akin to a promise of freedom. In the spirit of the 1972 "Cheerful Games", whose logical architectural realization we still admire today, they build for an ideal society free of constraints.

In 1972, the "Cheerful Games" were abruptly ended by the attack on the Israeli Olympic team. There is always a danger of such an ending – even today. But that should not stop architects from repeatedly formulating the promise of freedom in their works.

Treating each task as something new
Fritz Auer and Carlo Weber worked with Günter Behnisch for almost 25 years, initially as trainees, later as employees and finally, for 14 years as partners. Over this long period, they had a significant influence on the architecture that emerged from the Behnisch & Partner office. Their work was productive and setting up their own office allowed them to further develop their own characteristic style, a development that can be traced through almost 25 years of self-employment.

They have adhered to their strategy of regarding every commission as something new. When you ask Fritz Auer why he and his employees constantly develop new forms, rather than follow the trend of developing a uniform brand, he explains: "That would mean producing many identical versions of me." This is obviously the worst thing he can imagine. He sees restriction as consciously limiting the diversity that design offers.

As such it is hardly surprising that neither the company, nor Fritz Auer and Carlo Weber, have ceased in their evolution; naturally, this will result in some surprises in the future. I find it remarkable that they are developing in a new direction. If you look at their latest works, which are documented in this publication, you are struck by a new constructional rigidity.

That does not, however, apply to all recent buildings; Magdeburg University Library (page 244 ff) still seems to belong to another epoch. Nor does it apply only to the archaic-looking building of the ESO Hotel (page 196 ff), which is situated in an archaic landscape. There, the severity results from dealing with an equally strict yet amorphous environment, in the same way that the pyramids respond to the desert – the whole crystalline element, and the pure geometrical form against formless nature.

Konstant geblieben ist der Ansatz, jede Bauaufgabe neu zu betrachten; „ich müsste mich vereinfältigen" meint Fritz Auer, wenn man ihn fragt, warum er und seine Mitarbeiter immer neue Formen entwickeln, anstatt sich eines marktgängigeren „Zeichens" zu bedienen; und das ist offenbar das Schlimmste, was ihm geschehen kann. Er sieht die Beschränkung, die bewusste und vorgegebene Reduktion von Vielfalt der entwurflichen Möglichkeiten als das, was sie zunächst einmal ist: nämlich eine Einschränkung.

Insofern verwundert nicht, dass die Entwicklung des Büros, die Entwicklung von Fritz Auer und Carlo Weber nicht abgeschlossen ist und auch in Zukunft Überraschungen bereithält. Bemerkenswert jedoch scheint mir die Richtung einer neuen Entwicklung zu sein. Wenn man sich die jüngsten Arbeiten ansieht, die in diesem Band dokumentiert werden, dann fällt eine neue Strenge der Bauten auf.

Das betrifft nicht alle Bauten der jüngsten Zeit; die Universitätsbibliothek in Magdeburg (Seite 240 ff.) scheint noch einer anderen Epoche anzugehören. Es betrifft aber auch nicht nur den archaisch anmutenden Bau des ESO-Hotels (Seite 196 ff.) in einer archaischen Landschaft. Dort ist die Härte Ergebnis der Auseinandersetzung mit einer ebenso harten, aber amorphen Umgebung, vergleichbar der Pyramide in der Wüste: Das ganz Kristalline, die reine geometrische Form gegen die gestaltlose Natur.

Neben einigen Hochhausentwürfen betrifft es, überraschenderweise, auch ein Ensemble wie die Schlossbergbebauung in Böblingen (Seite 220 ff.), eine multifunktionale Nutzung aus Bürgerforum, Ausstellung, Kindermalschule und kommerziellen Nutzungen, alle in einem strengen, orthogonalen Kubus zusammengefasst – und das in einem Stadttypus mit einem verwinkelten mittelalterlichen Stadtkern.

Schon im Stich von Matthäus Merian aus dem Jahr 1643 nehmen Stiftskirche und Schloss die prominentesten Plätze der Stadt ein und dominieren sie. Heute tritt ein Gebäude an die Stelle des Schlosses, das weitgehend öffentliche Funktionen hat. Das erlaubt aus Sicht der Architekten überhaupt erst, den prominenten Ort zu bebauen; eine rein private, kommerzielle Nutzung hätte „sich hier nicht gehört".

Warum aber in einer verwinkelten mittelalterlichen Stadt diese ungewöhnliche Form? Im Gegenteil: hätten vordergründig die Anpassung an eine vielgestaltige Bebauung ebenso wie die Komplexität des Raumprogramms nicht eine ebenso vielgestaltige Komposition nahe gelegt?

Along with several high-rise designs, it also applies surprisingly well to a group such as the Schlossberg ensemble in Böblingen (page 220 ff), which is a multipurpose space where a civic forum, exhibition venue, children's painting school and commercial venues, are all combined into a strict, orthogonal cube – all that in a town with a medieval core of narrow winding streets!

In the engraving Matthäus Merian produced of Böblingen, the collegiate church and castle occupy, and dominate, the town's most prominent locations. Today the building that stands where the castle once stood has a largely public function. And it is this, from the architect's perspective, which makes it possible to develop this imposing site; a purely private, commercial utilization would not have been appropriate.

But why use this unusual form in a medieval town with narrow, winding streets? On the contrary, would not adapting to a variform development and the complexity of the spatial arrangement not have suggested an equally variform composition?

At first sight this severe design appears somewhat strange, but it is this very severity that serves as an historical analogy for the castle. After all, it would be a historical falsification to see the castle (and the church, to which, in principle, the same applies) as something that melded with its surroundings. On the contrary, its construction was an expression of power; the prince's political and economic power enabled him to build in a manner that was strikingly different from the forms that were available to normal citizens. The latter were obliged – for economic reasons, and not, say, because they were satisfied with them – to use the material available locally, despite all the restrictions that came with it. This was not the case with the ruler: He could afford an architect and more sophisticated designs; he could have the building plastered or use natural stone; he could employ relief work or artistic embellishment. In short, he was in a position to display his wealth, as was his wish, and he wanted to set himself apart.

But why do that today, when today's utilizations no longer suggest the "castle as instrument of power" but, in the spirit of democracy, the will of all citizens articulated in the civic forum? In effect, not much has changed from the time when the castle stood here. The term "democracy" also refers to rule and national and local governments, town halls as well as civic forums, are designed to show a nation's constitution and what is considered most important to its community.

Universitätsbibliothek
University Library
Magdeburg, 2001

Matthäus Merian
Böblingen, 1643

Schlossberg Böblingen
Wettbewerb/Competition, 2002

Die strenge Form hingegen mutet auf den ersten Blick fremd an – aber sie bildet gerade dadurch die historische Analogie zum Schloss. Denn es wäre eine historische Verfälschung, das Schloss (und die Kirche, für die im Grundsatz das Gleiche gilt) als etwas zu sehen, das sich der Umgebung angepasst hätte. Ganz im Gegenteil war sein Bau Ausdruck von Herrschaft; die politische und wirtschaftliche Macht des Fürsten erlaubte, betont anders zu bauen als es den Bürgern möglich war. Diese mussten aus ökonomischen Gründen – nicht etwa, weil sie damit zufrieden gewesen wären – das am Ort vorhandene Material verwenden, mit den Begrenzungen, die sich daraus ergaben. Der Herrscher hingegen konnte Architekten und aufwendigere Konstruktionen bezahlen, den Bau verputzen lassen oder Naturstein verwenden, plastischen oder malerischen Schmuck anbringen, kurz: er konnte und wollte seinen Reichtum nach außen hin zeigen, das heißt: er wollte sich abgrenzen.

Warum aber sich heute abgrenzen, wenn doch die Nutzungen nicht mehr das „Schloss als Herrschaftsinstrument" nahe legen, sondern in demokratischen Zeiten den im Bürgerforum artikulierten Willen aller Bürger? Eigentlich ändert sich gegenüber dem Schloss nicht viel: Auch der Begriff der „Demokratie" erzählt von Herrschaft, und Bundes- oder Landtage, Rathäuser oder eben Bürgerforen sollen zeigen, welche Verfassung sich das Volk gibt und was es für das Wichtigste in seiner Gemeinde hält.

Die strenge Form ist also, zumindest im Falle Böblingens, historisch begründet. Die Tatsache aber, dass sie mehrfach in den letzten Jahren vorkommt, mag mit einer altersweisen Reduktion auf das Wesentliche zu tun haben. Heißt es, zu viel hinein zu lesen, in der Strenge nicht die Abkehr vom „Heiteren", vom Spiel zu sehen, sondern nur strengere Regeln, innerhalb derer man freier, aber auch verantwortlicher miteinander umgehen kann?

Fragen zum Schluss
„Architekten sind Überzeugungstäter" hatten wir eingangs gesagt und im folgenden versucht, die Überzeugungen im Werk von Auer+Weber aufzuspüren. Das Ergebnis der Suche erfasst nicht die gesamte Breite dessen, was ihre Architektur ausmacht. Es benennt aber wichtige Themen und die Prinzipien, diese in gebaute Räume und Körper zu übersetzen. Dies kann nur erfassen, wer mit ihr direkt umgeht. Wer in ihr wohnt oder arbeitet. Diese Architektur macht es den Menschen leicht, darin zu leben.

In other words, the strict form is historically justified at least in Böblingen's case. However, as this style has been used several times in recent years it might indicate the architects are favoring a reduction to the essential at this late stage in their careers. Would it be going too far to interpret this severity not as turning away from the "cheerful" and playful, but merely as the setting of stricter rules that require people to act more responsibly towards one another?

Final questions
"Architects work out of conviction", we said by way of introduction, before attempting to trace the convictions in Auer+Weber's work. The outcome of this search not only encompasses the entire spectrum of their architecture, but also identifies important topics and the principles employed to translate them into architectural spaces and volumes. It is only by dealing with the architecture directly – by working or living in it – that you really understand this. This architecture makes it easy for people to live in it.

This has been a consistent feature in this company's work over the past 25 years. The architecture has undergone formal changes and has achieved greater severity in the more recent buildings. This is a reflection of their experience with people, their willingness to listen to them, and their awareness of why people in certain social, historical, climatic conditions want this style rather than another.

Referring to his company's view of architecture, Fritz Auer once spoke of the "beauty of the ordinary". But it is also about the "beauty of the unusual", the great buildings and the great models. "You should not study what the old masters did, but what they sought to do." This wonderful saying by Confucius applies to Auer+Weber, when they cite Frank Lloyd Wright, Ludwig Mies van der Rohe or Le Corbusier as influences.

Auer+Weber face considerable challenge in coming years, especially its first project in China (page 234 ff). Once again the care with which the architects are approaching new territory is evident. Both in conversation with them and in their design, you sense the questions that automatically arise when you work for people in an unfamiliar environment and within a foreign culture: Can you use the cultural image of a city in Central Europe to deal with the totally different conditions in China? What does the client expect? What can a German architecture office export to the Far East? A planning service alone, or cultural understanding as well?

Das ist ein durchgehender Zug in der Arbeit dieses Büros, obwohl sich die Architektur auch in formaler Hinsicht über 25 Jahre verändert hat, bis hin zur größeren Strenge in den jüngsten Bauten. Darin spiegelt sich Erfahrung mit Menschen, die Bereitschaft, ihnen zuzuhören: die Kenntnis dessen, warum Menschen in bestimmten sozialen, historischen, klimatischen Gegebenheiten so und nicht anders gebaut haben.

Von der „Schönheit des Gewöhnlichen" hat Fritz Auer einmal im Zusammenhang der Architekturauffassung des Büros gesprochen. Aber es geht genauso um die „Schönheit des Ungewöhnlichen", um die großen Bauten, die großen Vorbilder. Diese müssen sich nicht direkt in den eigenen Arbeiten widerspiegeln: „Man soll nicht studieren, was die alten Meister machten, sondern was sie suchten" – der schöne Satz von Konfuzius gilt auch für Auer+Weber, wenn sie sich auf Frank Lloyd Wright, Ludwig Mies van der Rohe oder Le Corbusier beziehen.

In den nächsten Jahren steht eine große Herausforderung an für das Büro – mit dem ersten Projekt in China (Seite 234 ff.), zu dem sie eingeladen wurden. Auch hier erkennt man wieder das vorsichtige Auftreten auf neuem Terrain – man spürt im Gespräch, aber auch im Entwurf, die Fragen, die sich zwangsläufig stellen, wenn man für Menschen in einer nicht vertrauten Umgebung, in einer fremden Kultur arbeitet: Kann man mit dem kulturellen Selbstverständnis der zentraleuropäischen Stadt an die so ganz anderen Bedingungen in China herangehen? Was erwartet der Auftraggeber? Was exportiert ein deutsches Architekturbüro in den Fernen Osten – nur eine Planungsdienstleistung oder auch ein Kulturverständnis?

Das Schöne ist: Das Werk von Auer+Weber verändert sich, es stellt sich den neuen Fragen. Es öffnet sich für andere Wege. Die beiden Architekten werden Dinge neu sehen und uns lehren, sie neu zu sehen. Die Architektur verstehbar, anfassbar, öffentlich zu machen – darin sehen sie ihre Aufgabe, sicher auch ganz eigennützig ihr Vergnügen, denn ohne die Lust am Entwerfen täten sie es nicht. Die Frage, wie das Büro weiterlebt, wird zunehmend aktuell und wird zur neuen Herausforderung.

Als Beobachter bleibt man neugierig, weil die beiden Architekten und ihr Büro es geblieben sind.

The beautiful thing is that Auer+Weber's work will also undergo changes and address new questions. It is willing to consider alternatives. The two architects will see things differently and teach us to see them differently, too. They see their task as making architecture understandable, tangible, public, and they do it for their own pleasure. If they did not enjoy it, after all, they would not work as architects. The question of how the office will continue in the future is becoming more pressing and will also present them with new challenges.

It is because the two architects and their staff have retained their own curiosity that you remain curious as an observer.

Gert Kähler, Jahrgang 1942, hat Architektur in Berlin studiert. Nach sieben Jahren im Architekturbüro hat er über zehn Jahre an verschiedenen Hochschulen als Architekturhistoriker gewirkt.
Seit 1988 ist er als freiberuflicher Publizist und Wissenschaftler tätig.

Gert Kähler was born in 1942 and studied Architecture in Berlin. After working in an architect's studio for seven years, he was employed for over ten years at various universities as an architectural historian. Since 1988 he has worked as a freelance journalist and academic.

Bauten und Projekte/Buildings and Projects **1980 – 2003**

Kurgastzentrum Bad Salzuflen
1983
Wettbewerb 1976   1. Preis
(in Behnisch & Partner)

Bad Salzuflen Spa Center
1983
Competition 1976   1st prize
(in Behnisch & Partner)

Das Kurgastzentrum bildet die Nahtstelle zwischen Innenstadt und Kurpark. Es vereint die Kurverwaltung mit allen Abteilungen, die Kurgasthalle als zentralen Anlaufpunkt für die Betreuung des Kurgastes, ein Gesundheitsstudio, Werk- und Bastelräume, Läden und ein Café unter seinem Dach. Das Bauwerk zusammen mit dem Eingangsbereich gestaltet das Gebiet zwischen Bleichstraße, Kurpark und den Gradierwerken neu.

Vom klaren geometrischen Baukörper an der Bleichstraße ausgehend löst sich das Gebäude über die ein- und zweigeschossige Kurgasthalle und den Quellenhof bis zum Kurpark allmählich auf. Die Kurgasthalle entsteht durch die Anordnung pilzartiger Stützen, deren Teller sich nur an einzelnen Punkten berühren. Mit Seiten- und Oberlichtern erscheint sie weniger als „Haus" denn als beschützter Teil des Platzes; Innen und Außen durchdringen sich.

Im Mittelpunkt des Eingangs – und damit der gesamten Anlage – befindet sich die Quelle, deren inhaltliche Bedeutung durch die gärtnerische und architektonische Gestaltung der Freifläche unterstrichen wird.

Freistehende Betonpilze und glasgedeckte Wandelgänge bieten wettergeschützte Verbindungen zwischen Kurgastzentrum, Konzerthalle und Kurhaus.

The spa center forms the interface between the downtown area and the spa park. It unites under one roof the spa administration and its various departments: the spa hall, which focuses on patient welfare; a health studio; workshops and hobby rooms; stores and a café. The building – including the entrance area – redefines the area between Bleichstrasse, the spa park and the refining works.

Beginning with a distinct geometrical structure on Bleichstrasse, the building gradually loses its clear-cut appearance, becoming less structured as it continues through the one- and two-story hall and the courtyard with the spring, until it ends at the spa park. Here, the spa hotel lobby is entirely created by the arrangement of toadstool-shaped supports whose "caps" touch at only a few points. With lateral and overhead lighting it appears less like a house and more like a secluded section of the square: the inside and outside meld with one another.

At the center of the entrance – and thus of the entire complex – is the spring, its importance emphasized by the landscaping and architectural design of the open space.

Free-standing concrete toadstools indicate the glazed, covered walkways, which provide connections between the spa center, concert hall and casino.

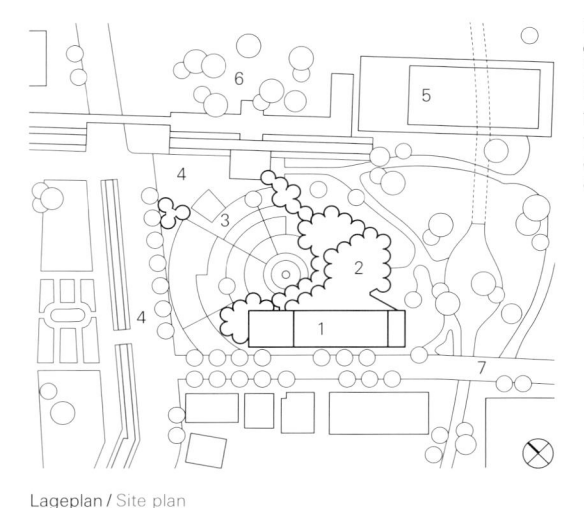

Lageplan / Site plan
1:3000

1 Verwaltungstrakt
   Administration wing
2 Kurgasthalle
   Hall for spa guests
3 Eingangsplatz mit Quelle
   Entrance area
   with the spring
4 Gradierwerke / Refining
   works
5 Konzerthaus / Concert hall
6 Kurpark
7 Bleichstraße

Die Quelle bildet das Zentrum der konzentrisch angelegten Freiraumgestaltung des Eingangsplatzes
The source of the spring forms the heart of the concentrically arranged open space designated as the entrance area

Johnson Wax Building
Racine, WI, USA, 1936–39
Frank Lloyd Wright

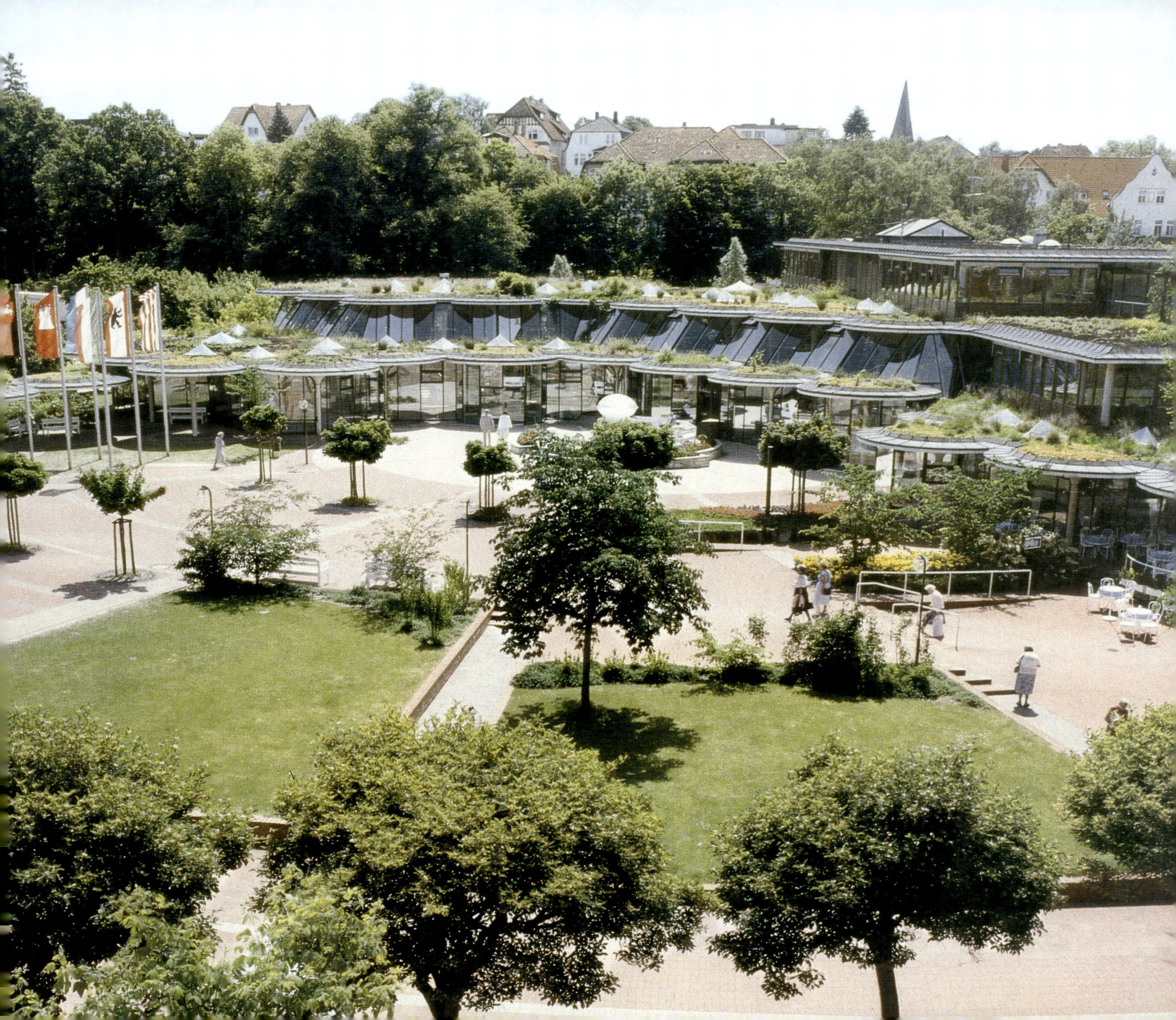

	Längsschnitt Longitudinal section 1:750	1 Salze
		2 Kurgasthalle Hall for spa guests
		3 Eingangsplatz Entrance area
		4 Gradierwerk Refining works

Freistehende Betonpilze leiten von der Halle in den Park über und bieten geschützte Aufenthaltsbereiche im Freien

Stand-alone concrete toadstools mark the transition from the hall to the park and provide welcome shaded areas outdoors

Erdgeschoss / Ground floor
1:750

1 Quelle / Spring
2 Kurgasthalle
  Hall for spa guests
3 Ausstellung
  Exhibition area
4 Café
5 Läden / Shops
6 Verwaltung / Administration
7 Bleichstraße

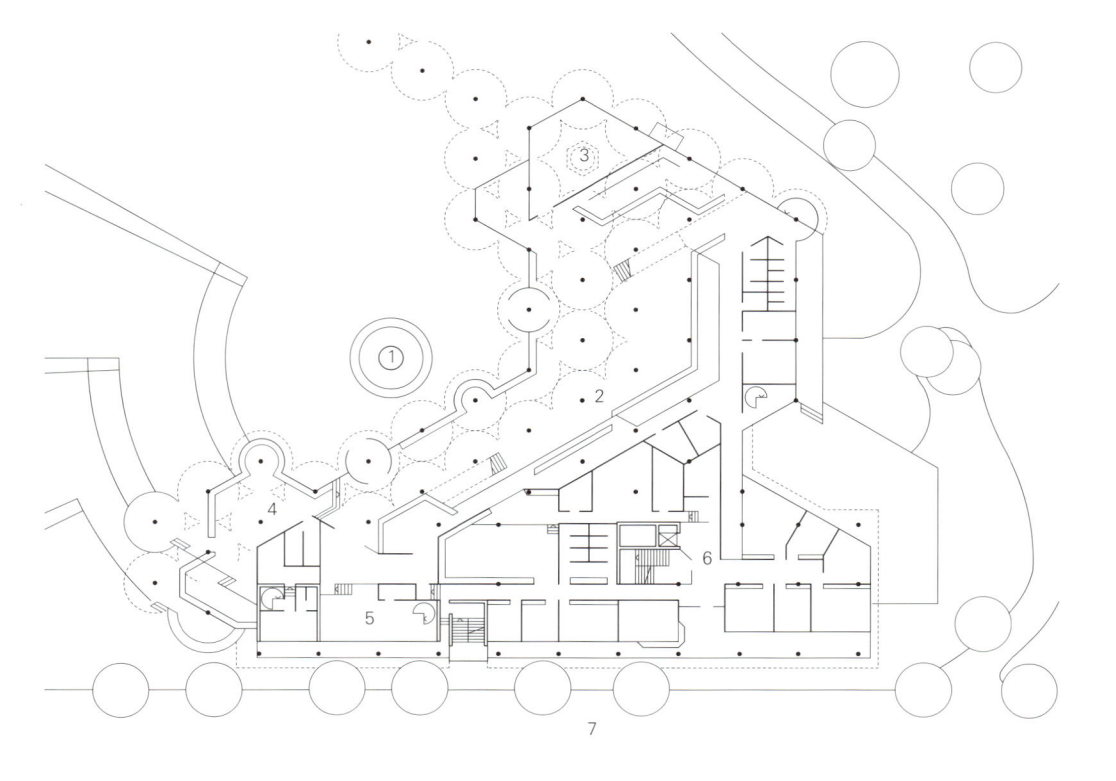

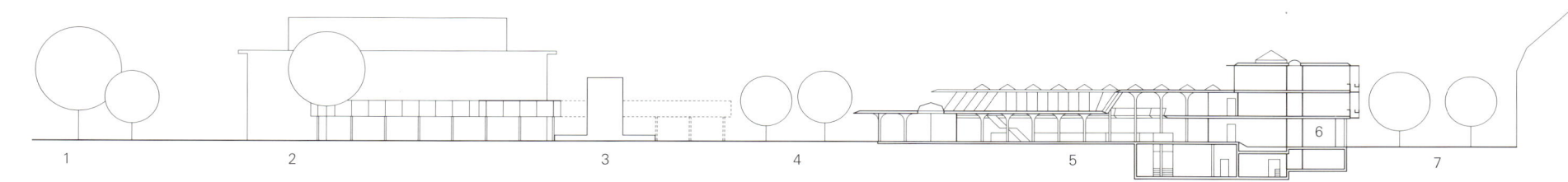

Querschnitt / Cross section
1:750

1 Kurpark / Spa park
2 Konzerthaus / Concert hall
3 Gradierwerk / Refining works
4 Eingangsplatz / Entrance area
5 Kurgasthalle / Hall for spa guests
6 Verwaltung, Läden / Administration, shops
7 Bleichstraße

Die tellerförmigen Aufweitungen der Pilzstützen bilden einen lichten begrünten Dachschirm über der Halle

Folgende Seiten:

Eingangsplatz und Kurgasthalle am Abend

Seiten- und Oberlichter lassen die Halle eher als beschützten Teil des Platzes erscheinen. Die Übergänge zwischen Innen- und Außenraum sind fließend

The plate-shaped spread of the toadstool supports forms a bright green roof covering the hall

Overleaf:

Evening: the entrance area and hall for spa guests

Thanks to the sidelighting and transoms, the hall seems to be more a protected part of the square, with a flowing transition from indoors to outdoors and vice versa

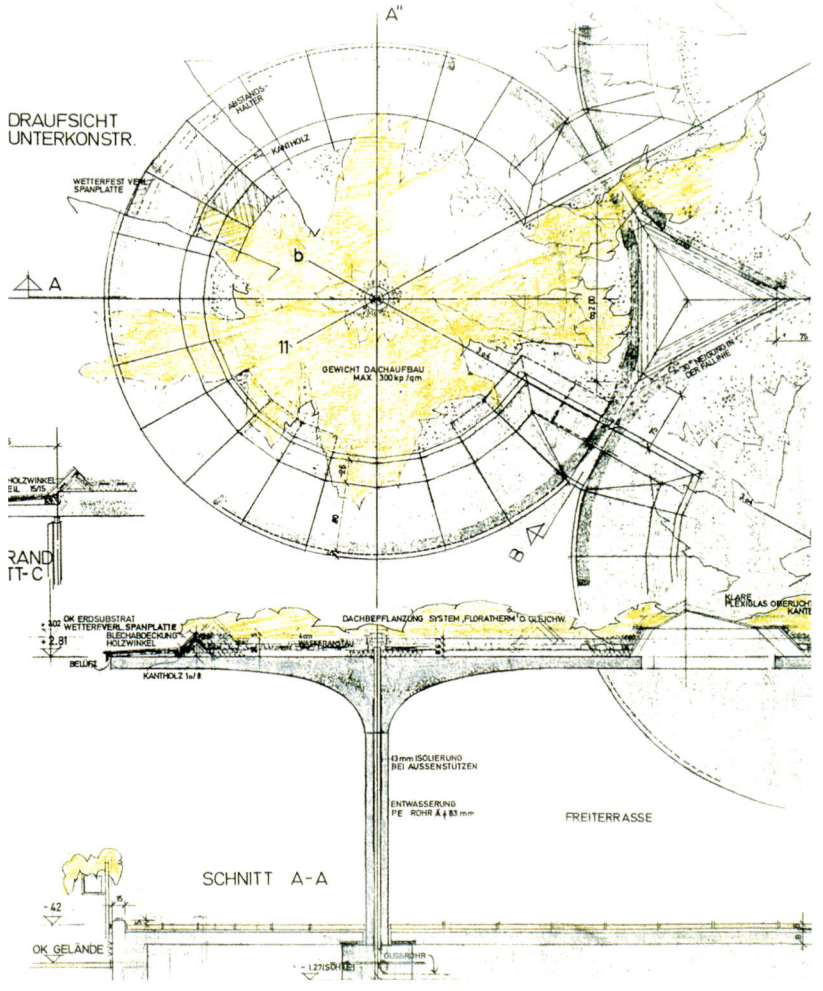

29   Kurgastzentrum / Spa Center Bad Salzuflen

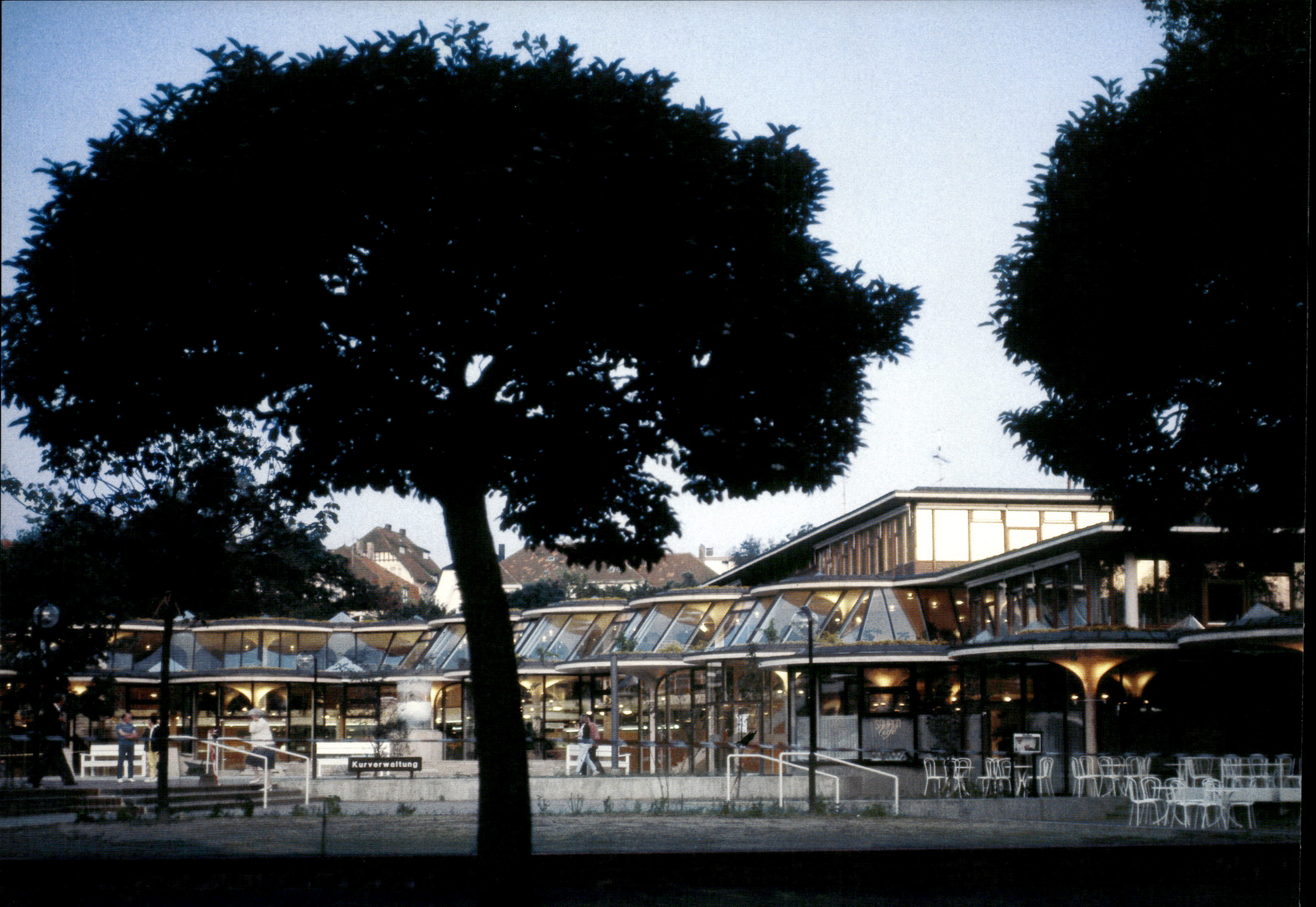
Kurverwaltung

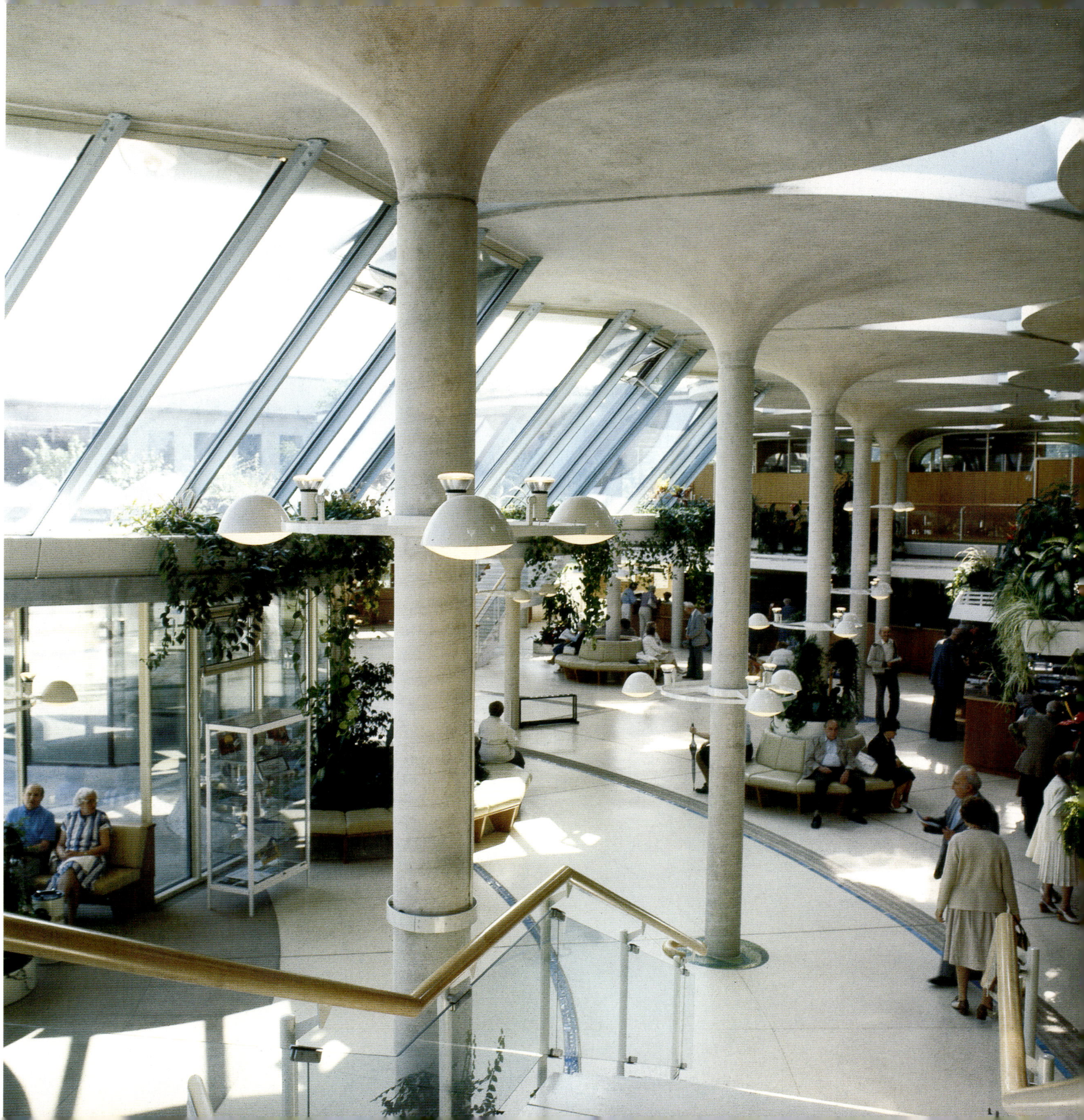

Altenwohn- und Pflegeheim St. Marien
Lemgo 1986
Wettbewerb 1982   1. Preis

Retirement and Nursing Home St. Marien
Lemgo 1986
Competition 1982   1st prize

Innerhalb des geschlossenen Stadtbildes der alten Hansestadt Lemgo greift das Alten- und Pflegeheim überlieferte Bauformen und -materialien seiner Umgebung auf und bietet damit einen vertrauten Lebensraum als neue Heimat für ältere Menschen. Sowohl baulich als auch sozial ist die Anlage eng in das Gefüge der Innenstadt einbezogen, um den Bewohnern die Teilnahme am städtischen Leben nahe dem Zentrum zu ermöglichen.

Die Giebelarchitektur lehnt sich an die Stadtgeschichte und das Stadtbild an: Einfache „Häuser", die selbstverständlich wirken und auch so angenommen werden; mit Wohnungen, die sich einerseits in die glasüberdeckten, halböffentlichen Zwischenräume der Hauszeilen, andererseits über Loggien und zweigeschossige Erker in private Gärten erweitern.

Der für diese Gegend typische Vorbau („utlught") ist an die Gartenseite verlegt. Zusammen mit den unter Glas geschützten Balkonen und farblich variiert, entwickelt sich daraus das die einfachen Hauszeilen belebende Motiv.

Um die Großzügigkeit und Schlankheit der Zeilen zu unterstreichen, verzichten die ruhigen Dachflächen auf Ausbauten und Gauben.

Die oberen Wohnungen greifen in den Dachraum hinein und vermitteln ein Gefühl der Geborgenheit. Jeweils zwei Giebelhäuser werden über dazwischen liegende „Grünhäuser" zu einer räumlichen Einheit zusammengefasst, die den Bewohnern auch bei schlechtem Wetter einen erweiterten Bewegungs- und Begegnungsraum außerhalb ihrer eigenen vier Wände bietet.

Set within the compact old Hanseatic city of Lemgo, this retirement and nursing home utilizes materials and forms of building that are typical of the region, and that offer senior citizens a familiar living space in which to establish their new home. In both building and social terms the complex is deeply ingrained in the inner city, enabling residents to participate in the city life close to its center.

The gabled architecture is consistent with the city's history and appearance; simple houses which look natural and are accepted as such. The apartments expand on one side into semi-open, glass-roofed spaces between rows of houses, and on the other side, open onto private gardens which are accessed via loggias and two-story bay windows.

The porches typical of this region ("utlught") are positioned on the garden side. With their variety of colors and glass-roofed balconies, they create lively motifs that liven up the simple rows of houses.

To accentuate the generous and slim proportions of the rows of houses, the subdued roof surfaces have no extensions or dormer windows.

The upper apartments extend into the attic space and convey a feeling of seclusion. Two gabled houses are always connected into one unit by a "greenhouse" in between, which offers residents additional space in which to meet and participate in activities outside their own four walls, even when the weather is bad.

Die Anlage zeigt sich zum Straßenraum geschlossen, wirkt aber durch ihre Formensprache vertraut
From the street, the complex appears compact, and its formal language gives a feeling of familiarity

Lageplan / Site plan
1:2500

1 Pflegeheim
   Nursing home
2 Altenwohnungen
   Retirement apartments
3 Wallanlagen / Embankment
4 Echternstraße

Straßenzug in der Lemgoer Altstadt
Street in the old part of Lemgo

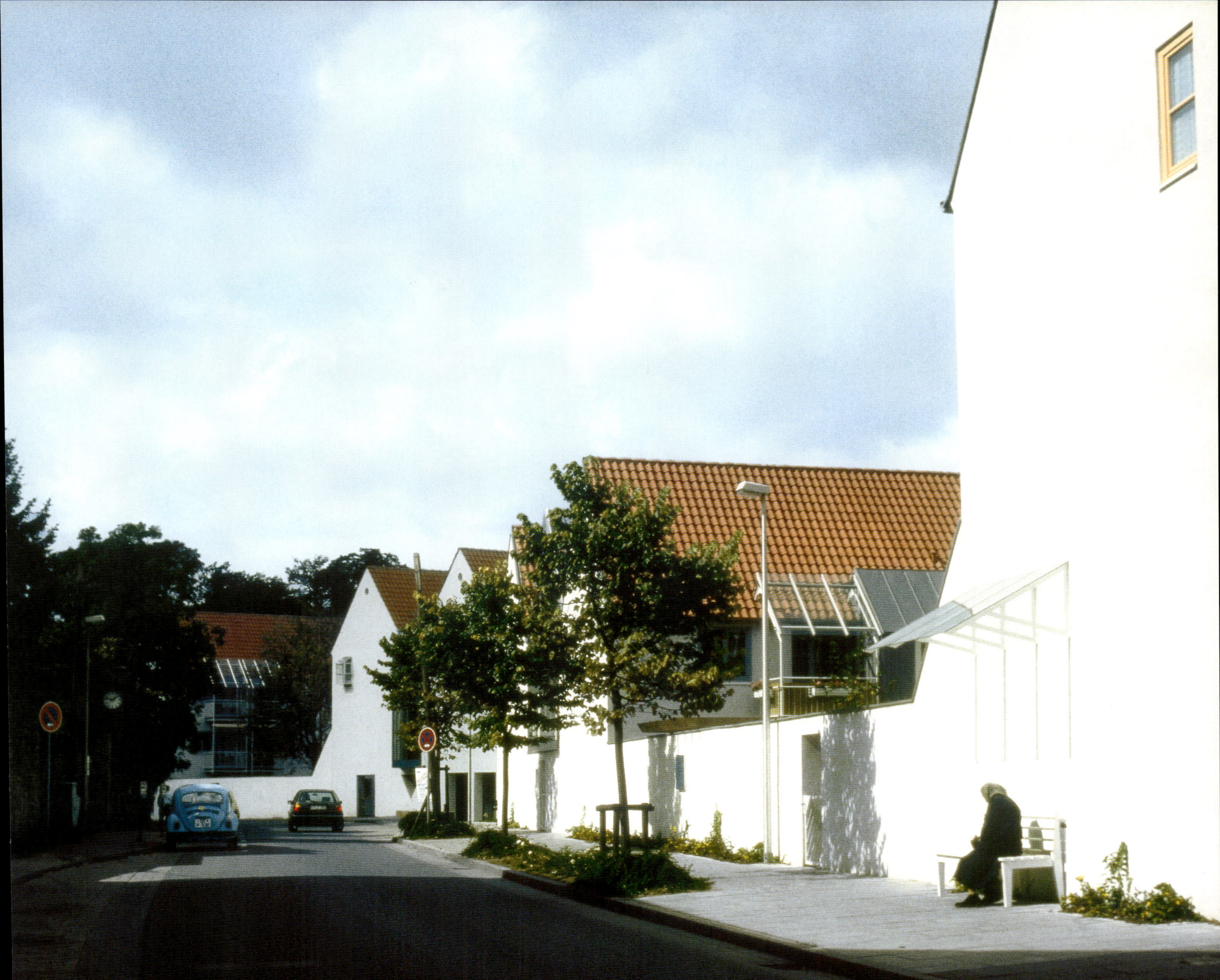

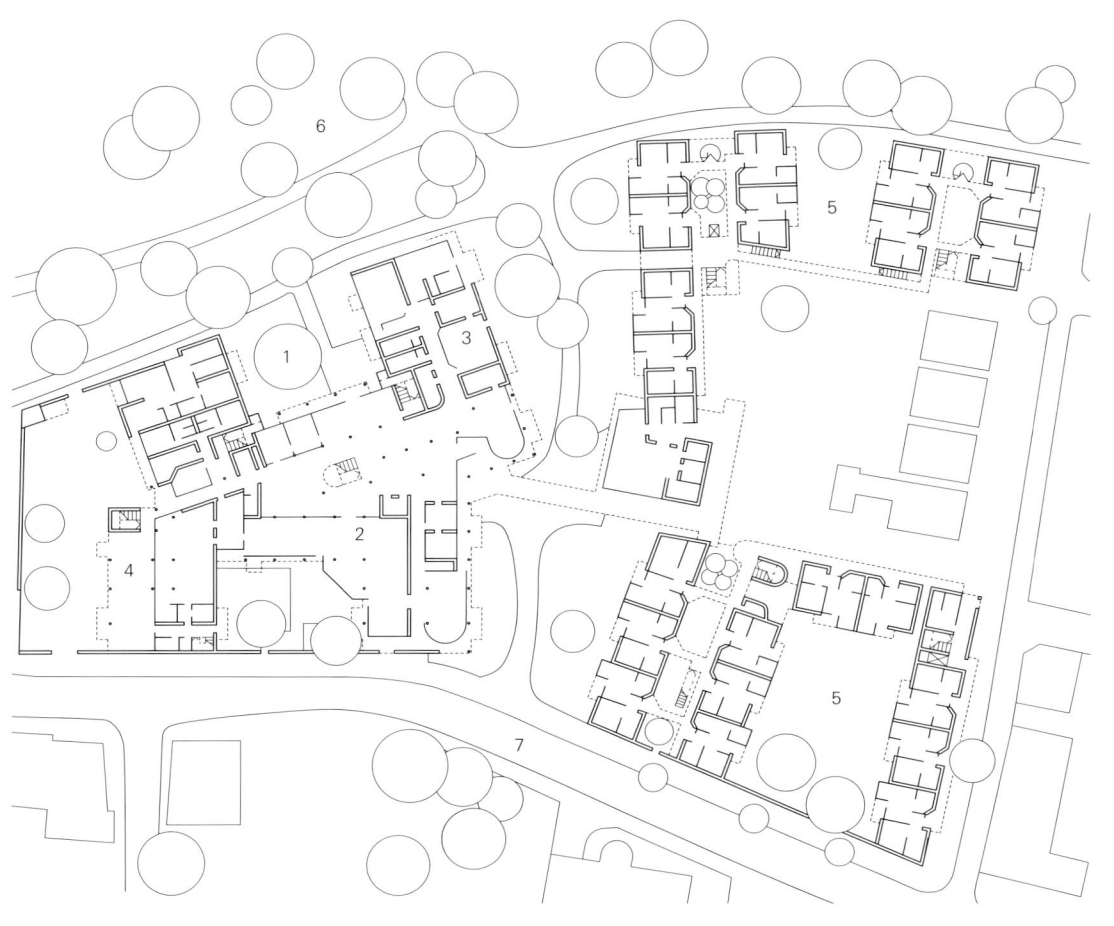

Erdgeschoss / Ground floor
1:1000

1. Pflegeheim / Nursing home
2. Gemeinschafts-einrichtungen
   Communal facilities
3. Therapie / Therapy facilities
4. Küche / Kitchen
5. Altenwohnungen
   Retirement apartments
6. Wallanlagen / Embankment
7. Echternstraße

Ansicht von der Echternstraße
View from Echternstrasse
1:500

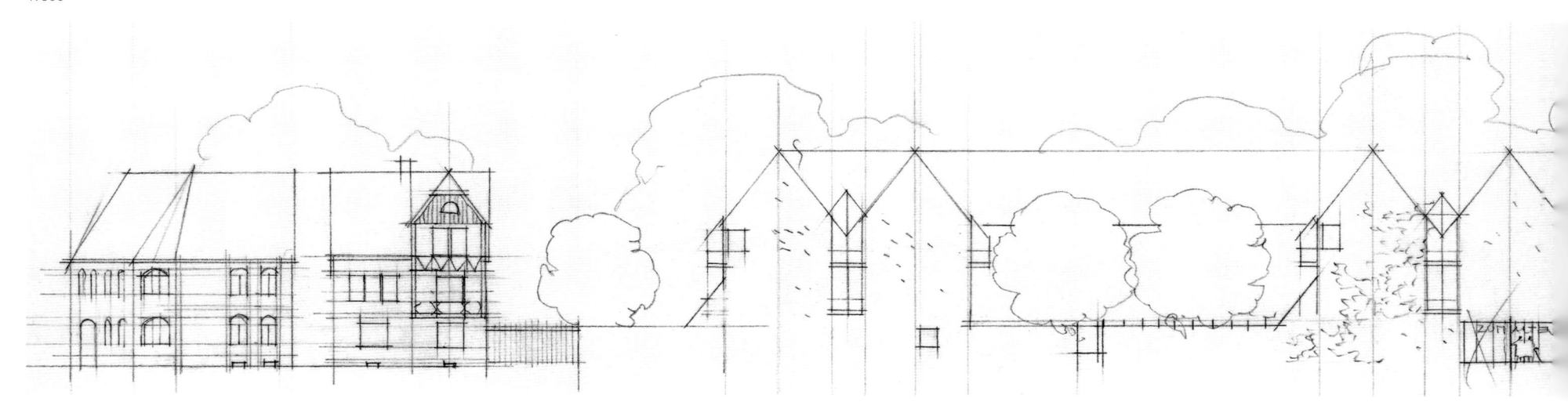

Links:
Wohnheim Teilbereich

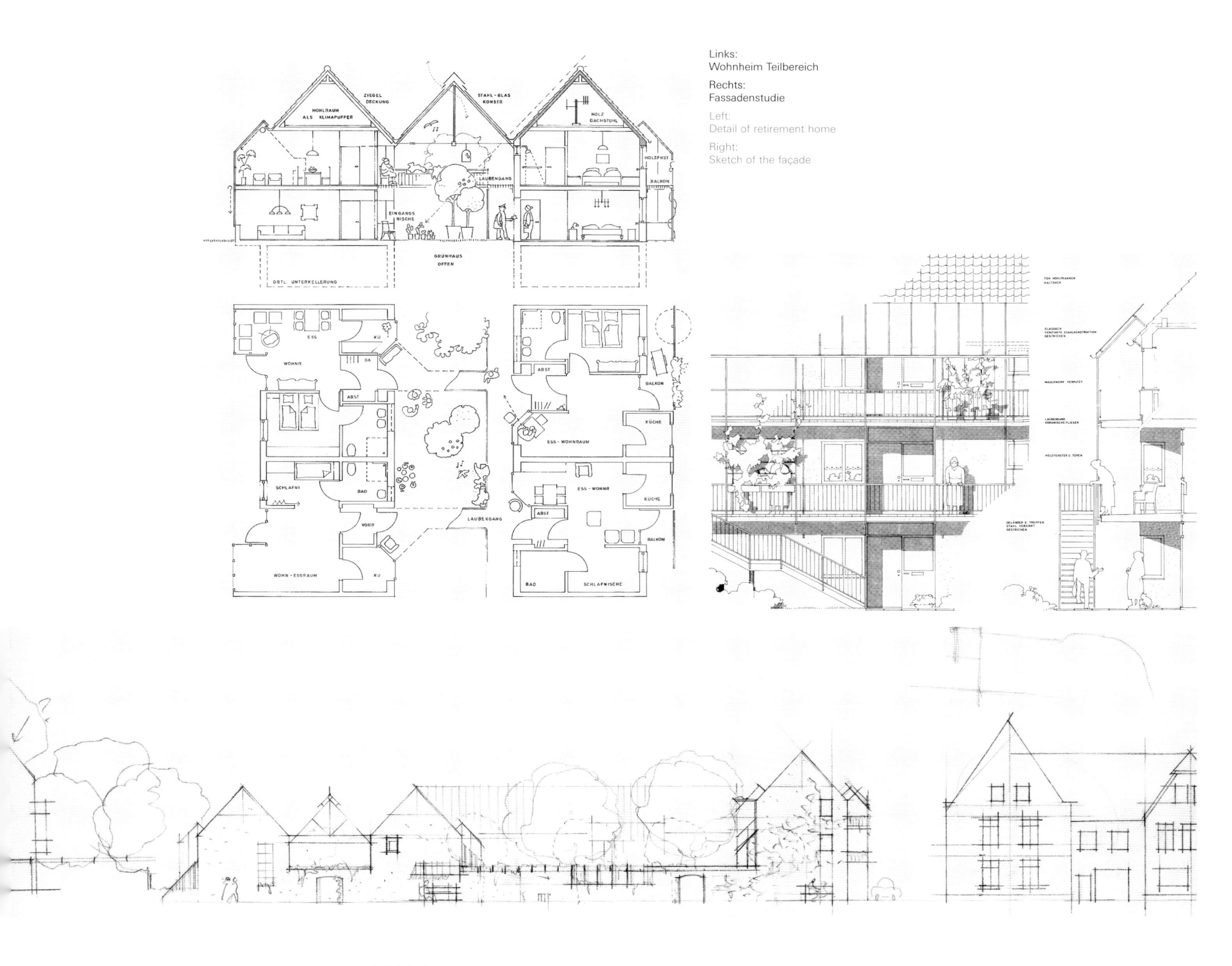

Rechts:
Fassadenstudie

Left:
Detail of retirement home

Right:
Sketch of the façade

35 Altenwohn- und Pflegeheim / Retirement and Nursing Home St. Marien Lemgo

Oben links:
Galerien in den „Glashäusern" als Spazierweg und Zugang zu den Wohnungen im Obergeschoss

Oben rechts:
Getrennt und doch verbunden

Links:
Im Pflegeheim wird die Flurzone zum sozialen Raum außerhalb des Zimmers

Rechte Seite:
Die glasüberdachten Zwischenräume bieten den Bewohnern wettergeschützten Freiraum und erweiterten Lebensbereich

Upper left:
Galleries in the "greenhouses" act as a walkway and provide access to apartments on the top floor

Upper right:
Separate yet linked

Left:
In the nursing home, the corridors form social areas outside the rooms

Right:
The glass-covered intermediate areas offer residents open space, which is protected from the elements and becomes an extension of their living space

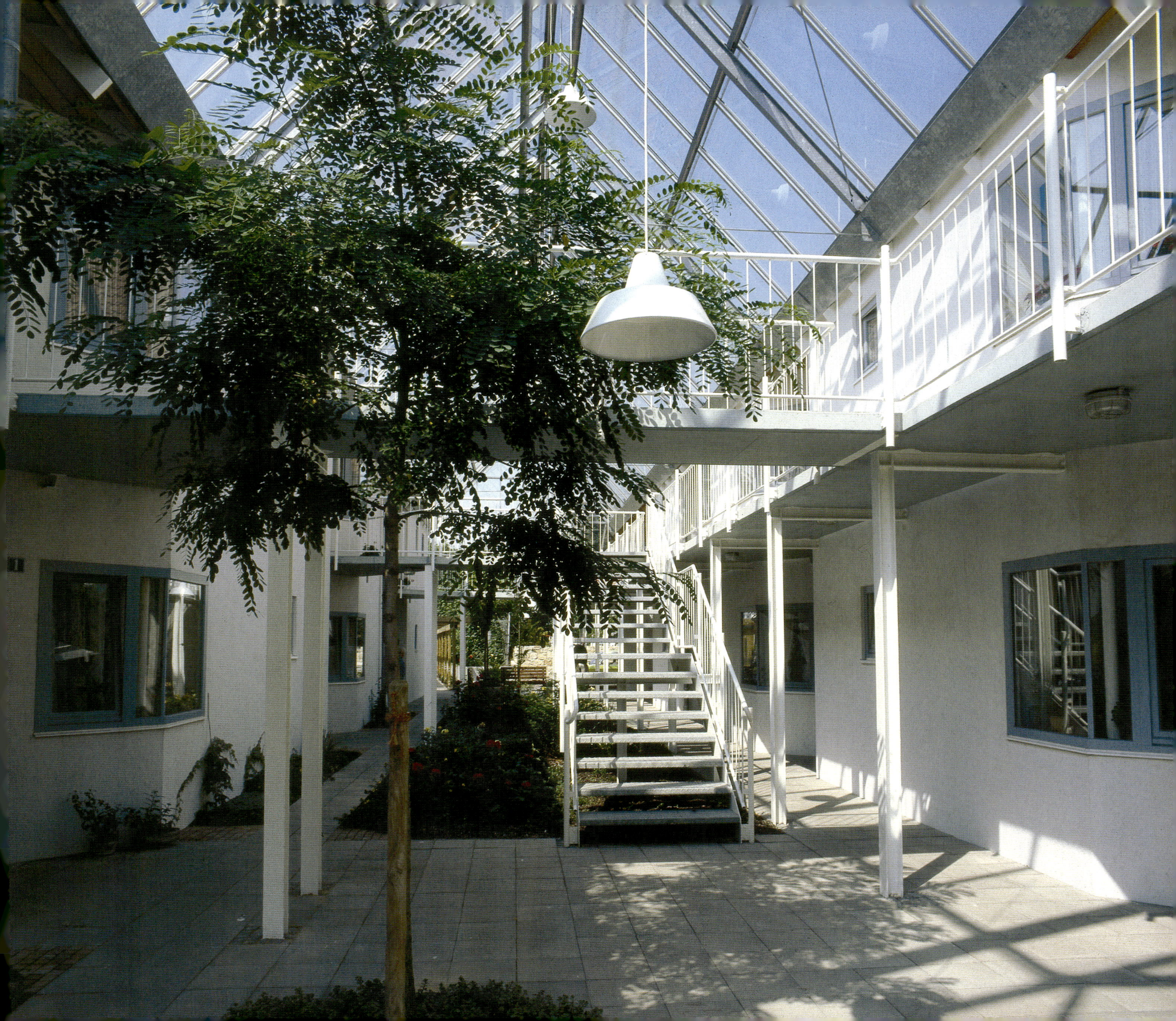

**Robert-Bosch-Haus Stuttgart
1986**

**Robert Bosch House Stuttgart
1986**

Die Villa Bosch, erbaut 1909 im Stil der Neorenaissance und über drei Jahrzehnte Wohnsitz des Unternehmensgründers, steht samt den alten Bäumen des Parks unter Denkmalschutz. Die Nutzung als Sitz der Robert-Bosch-Stiftung stellt neue Anforderungen an die alten Räumlichkeiten, welche die Gesichtspunkte einer zeitgemäßen Arbeitswelt ebenso berücksichtigen müssen wie die Belange des Denkmalschutzes. In enger und ständiger Abstimmung mit dem Landesdenkmalamt wurden der Park, das Äußere des Hauses und die Repräsentationsräume originalgetreu restauriert, während Sockelgeschoss, erstes und zweites Obergeschoss für die Belange der Stiftung umgestaltet wurden.

Die sorgfältige Wiederherstellung des Ensembles lässt ein Stück Unternehmerkultur aus der Frühzeit der Industrialisierung wieder aufleben und verbindet die Anschaulichkeit eines historischen Rahmens, der auf besondere Art und Weise mit der Geschichte des Unternehmens verwachsen ist, mit gegenwartsbezogener Nutzung.

Like the trees on the surrounding grounds, the Bosch villa is a listed building. Built in 1909 in the neo-Renaissance style, it served for more than thirty years as the home of the company's founder. Its conversion for use as the headquarters of the Robert Bosch Foundation created many challenges for the old rooms. Up-to-date workstations had to be designed and had to take into account all the restrictions imposed on a listed building. Working in close cooperation with state preservation authorities, the grounds, the house's exterior and its prestigious rooms have all been restored to their original state, while the ground, first and second floors have all been redesigned to accommodate the needs of the foundation.

Careful reconstruction of the building allowed a piece of entrepreneurial culture from the beginning of the industrial era to be resurrected. The vividness of the historical setting, which has a special significance in the company's history, has now been united with a function that is firmly embedded in the present.

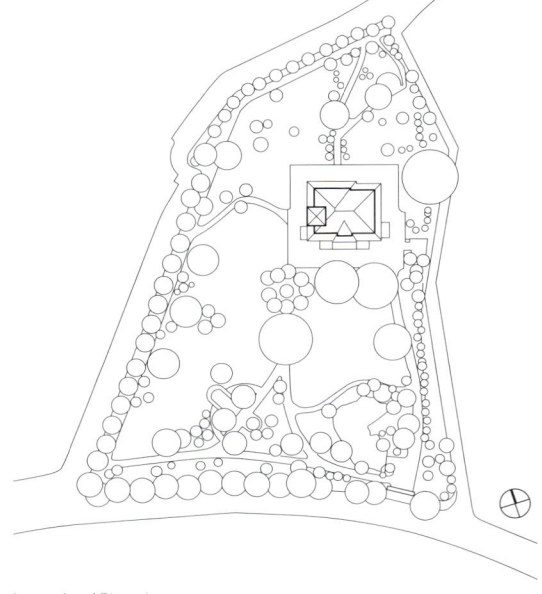

Lageplan / Site plan
1:2500

Beletage
1:250

1 Entrée / Foyer
2 Vorhalle / Entrance hall
3 Treppenhalle / Main stairs

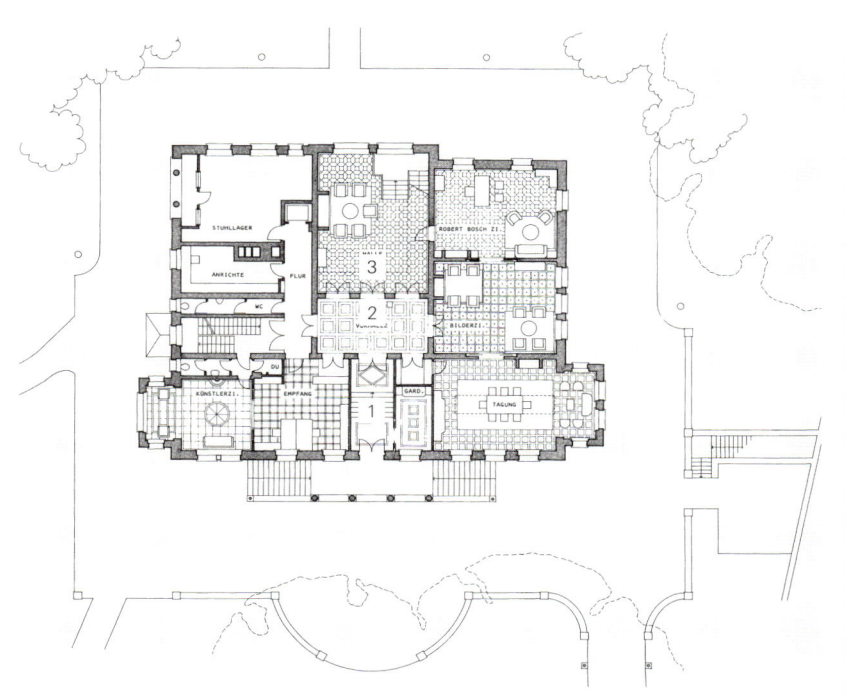

Die Hauptfassade der Villa nach der Renovierung

The main façade of the villa after renovation

Links:
Blick vom Turm über Stuttgart

Left:
A view of Stuttgart from the tower

Rechts:
Entrée, Vorhalle und Treppenhalle

Die Treppenhalle mit rekonstruiertem Glockenleuchter und Ledersesseln nach Entwurf von Walter Gropius

Right:
Entrance hall, foyer and main stairs

The hall with the main stair with a reconstructed bell candelabra; leather chairs based on a design by Walter Gropius

Landratsamt Starnberg
1987
Wettbewerb 1982   1. Preis

Starnberg District Office
1987
Competition 1982   1st prize

Das Haus des Landkreises ist kein üblicher Verwaltungsbau, sondern – durch seine Anlage und Ausstrahlung einladend, offen und kommunikativ – mehr „Haus des Bürgers" als Behörde. Im Zusammenspiel von Bedingungen aus Aufgabe und Eigenart des Ortes fügt sich Vorhandenes und Dazugekommenes zu einem neuen Ganzen.

Klarheit, Ursprünglichkeit, Leichtigkeit und Durchlässigkeit sind die bestimmenden Kriterien dieser Architektur: durch spannungsvolle Wechselbeziehungen zwischen innen und außen, Baulichem und Landschaftlichem, Künstlichem und Natürlichem gehen gefühlsmäßig Erlebbares und verstandesmäßig Begreifbares ineinander.

Die Anlage zeigt sich als flächig ausgreifende Struktur, deren Körperlichkeit unter schützenden Dachschirmen weitgehend aufgelöst ist und sich ohne Härten mit der Umgebung verbindet: Landschaft kommt zu Gebautem und umgekehrt. Obwohl nicht unmittelbar am Ufer des Starnberger Sees gelegen, reicht das Wasser doch über Kanäle und Becken bis ans Gebäude. Land, Wasser und Himmel sind folglich diejenigen Elemente, die in den Materialien, Konstruktionen und Farben des Bauwerks „reflektiert" sind.

Mit diesen Wesensmerkmalen steht die Anlage in der Tradition der europäischen Moderne; sie erinnert darüber hinaus an die großen Vorbilder fernöstlicher Baukultur.

Die modulare Konstruktion bestimmt die Gestalt des Bauwerks, das mit einfachen, handwerklichen Mitteln errichtet ist.

The building that houses the Rural District Offices is somewhat unusual for an administrative building: as a result of its layout and the general atmosphere that it radiates, it is inviting, open and communicative, more a "Citizens' Center" than a local authority building. Through the interplay of requirements dictated by its function, and the unique character of the place, new and existing elements meld into a new ensemble.

Clarity, originality, lightness and permeability are the architecture's defining features: what can be experienced through feelings and what can be understood through reasoning are joined together through the interplay between interior and exterior, buildings and countryside, artificial and natural.

The complex appears as an extensive two-dimensional structure, the body of which is largely broken down beneath protective screens on the roof, and which fits in with the surroundings without conflict: the countryside meets up with a built-up area and vice versa. Although it does not sit directly on the banks of the lake in Starnberg, canals and basins bring the water right up to the building. Consequently, land, water and sky are the elements reflected in the materials, constructions and colors used for the building.

These main characteristics place the complex firmly in the tradition of the European Modern Age; furthermore, it is evocative of the great examples of building tradition in the Far East.

The design of the building is determined by modular construction, and is constructed using basic craftsmen's skills.

Lageplan / Site plan
1:5000

1. Landratsamt / District office
2. Wasserflächen und Kanal / Water basins and canal
3. Parken / Parking lots
4. Festwiese / Festival grounds
5. Münchner Straße
6. Bootshäuser / Boathouses
7. Starnberger See / Lake

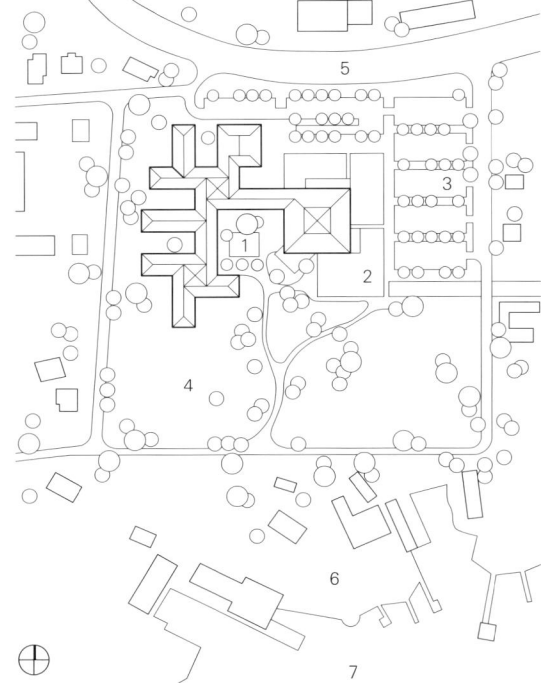

Rechts:
Die Anlage ist räumlich eng mit Umgebung und See verwoben. Sie zeigt sich als flächig ausgreifende Struktur unter einem alles verbindenden Dachschirm

Right:
The complex is spatially closely interwoven with the immediate surroundings and the lake. It appears as an extensive two-dimensional structure with a roof landscape that connects all the sections

Katsura-Palast, Kyoto, Japan
17. Jh.

Katsura palace, Kyoto, Japan
17th century

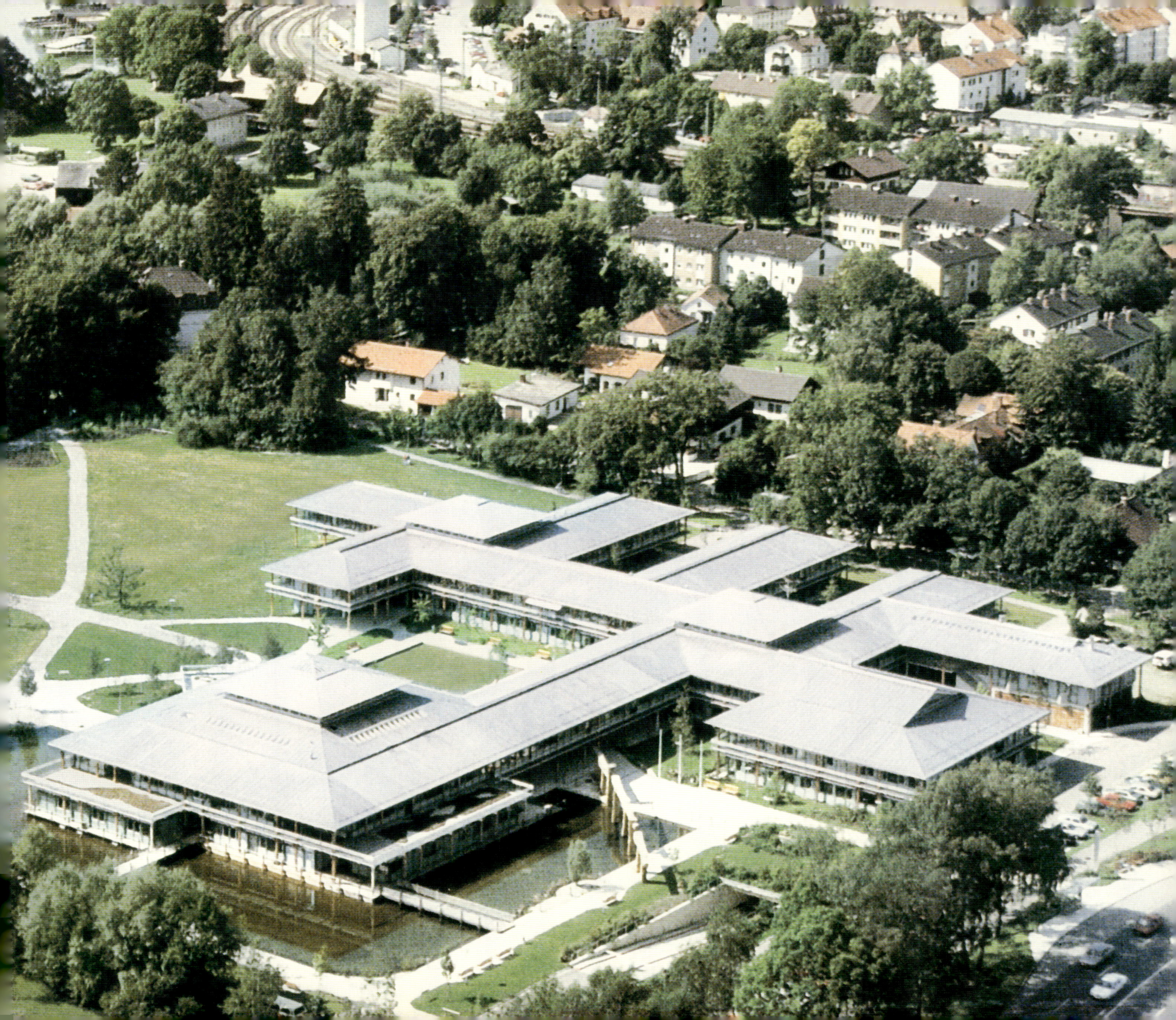

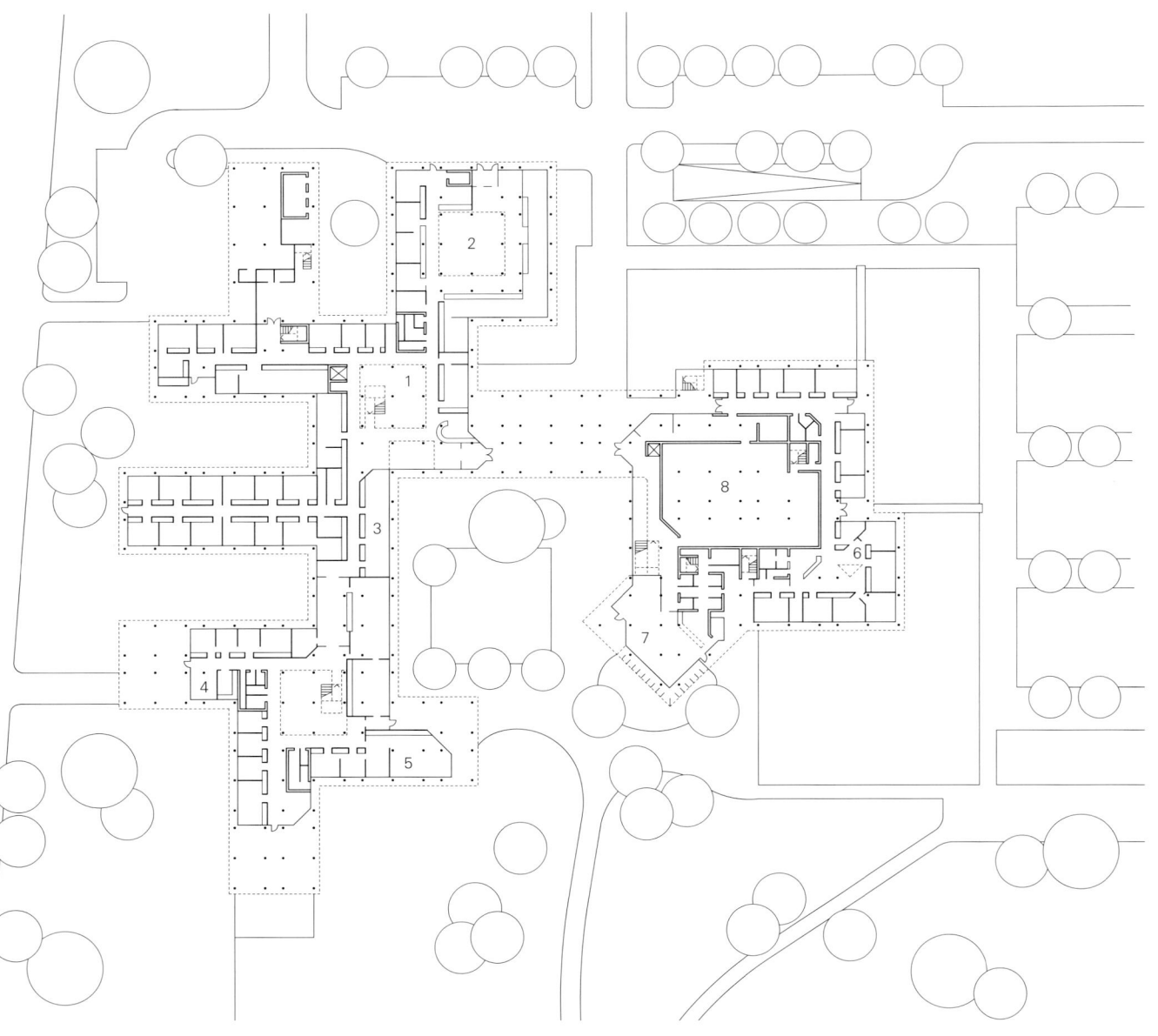

Erdgeschoss / Ground floor
1:1000

1. Eingangshalle
   Entrance hall
2. Kfz-Zulassungsstelle
   Vehicle registration office
3. Pass- und Meldewesen
   Registration and passport office
4. Veterinäramt
   Veterinary affairs
5. Schulamt
   School authority
6. Jugend und Familie
   Youth and family affairs
7. Cafeteria
8. Archiv / Archive

Obergeschoss / Upper floor
1:1000

1. Sozialamt / Welfare office
2. Jugend und Sport / Sporting and youth affairs
3. Kreishochbau / Regional building office
4. Umweltamt / Environmental affairs
5. Hauptamt / Main office
6. Leitung / Management
7. Sitzungssaal / Conference room

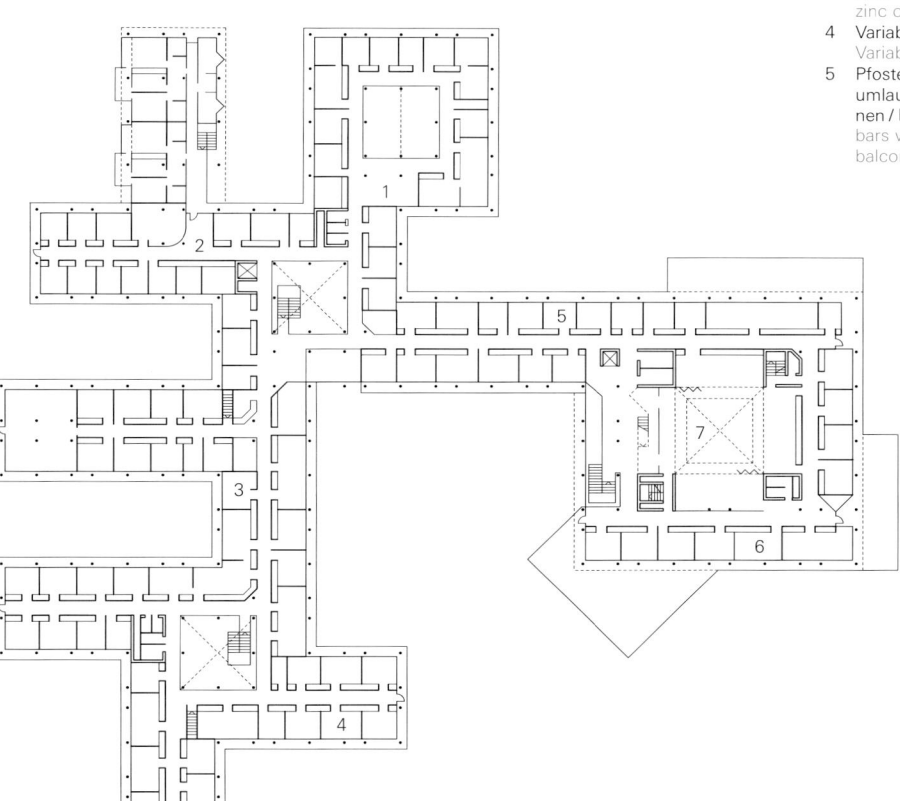

Konstruktiver Aufbau
Construction

1. Primärkonstruktion als kombiniertes Stahlbeton-Holzskelett / Primary construction of combined reinforced concrete and wooden skeleton
2. Geschossdecken Trapezblech mit oberseitigem Betonverguß / Ceilings made of trapezoidal corrugated sheet with a concrete cast on the upper side
3. Holzsparrendach mit Zink-Stehfalzdeckung / Wooden rafter roof with a folded zinc covering
4. Variables Ausbausystem / Variable fittings
5. Pfosten-Riegel-Fassade mit umlaufenden Stahlbalkonen / Façade of stakes and bars with surrounding steel balconies

Regelschnitt Gebäudeflügel
Wing standard section
1:300

1. Fundamentkasten / Foundation
2. Büroebenen / Offices
3. Dachraum für Installationsführung / Roof space for services
4. Wartungsbalkone mit Sonnenschutz / Balconies for maintenance with sunshades

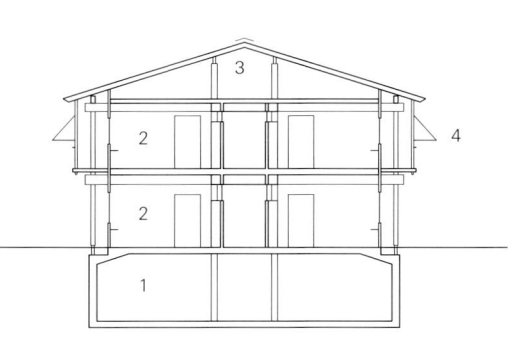

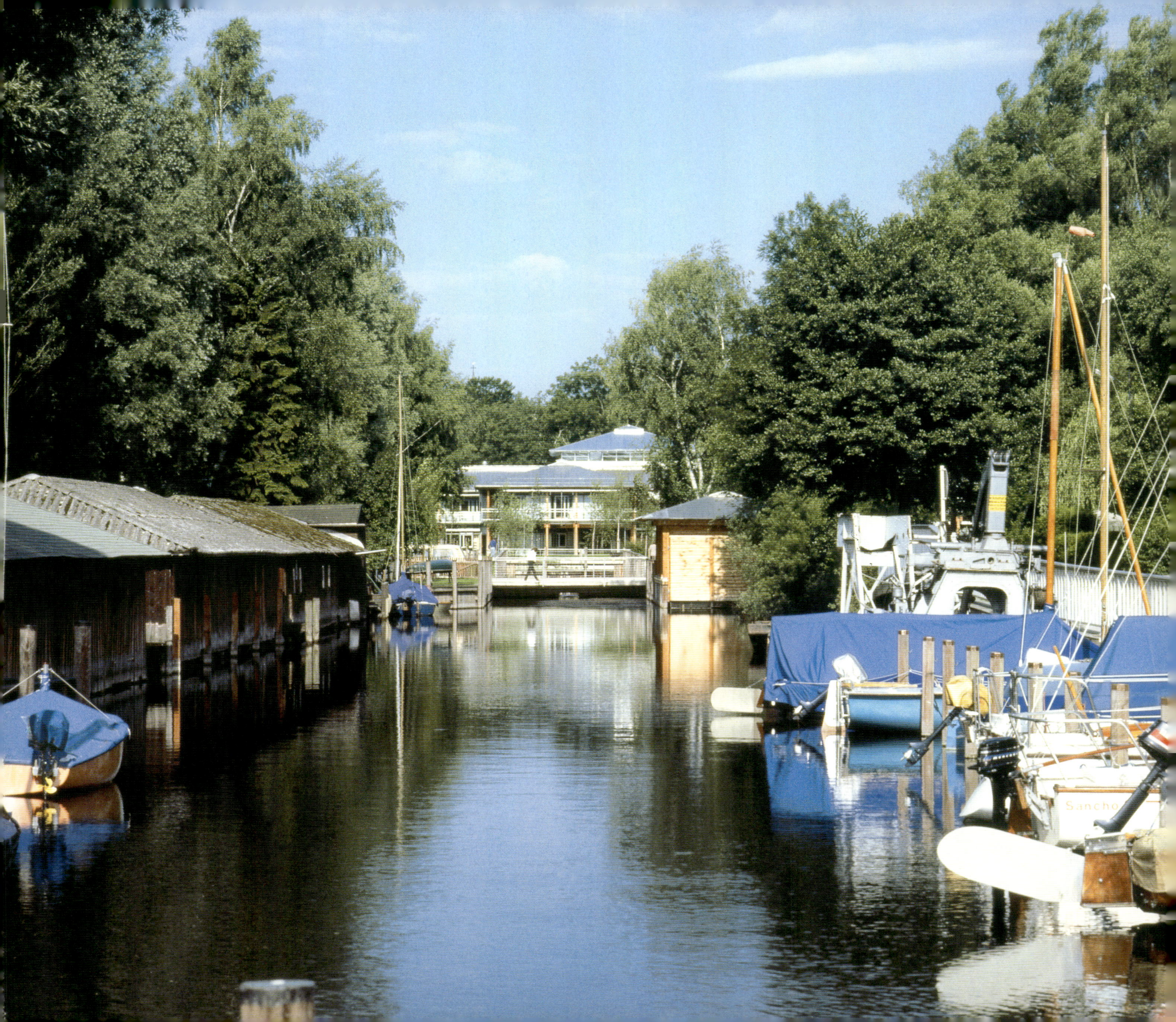
Sancho

Links:
Über Kanäle verbindet sich die Architektur mit der benachbarten Wassersport-siedlung und dem See

Rechts:
Zugangsstege „verankern" das Gebäude und lassen an Wasser und Freizeit denken

Left:
The architecture is connected to the neighboring watersports complex and the lake by canals

Right:
The building is "anchored" by access jetties, which are evocative of water and leisure time

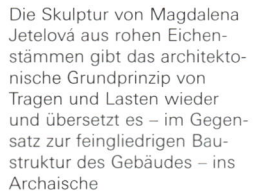

Die Skulptur von Magdalena Jetelová aus rohen Eichenstämmen gibt das architektonische Grundprinzip von Tragen und Lasten wieder und übersetzt es – im Gegensatz zur feingliedrigen Baustruktur des Gebäudes – ins Archaische

Magdalena Jetelová's sculpture, made of oak tree trunks, reflects architecture's basic principle of supporting and loadbearing and, set in opposition to the slender structure of the building, lends it a hint of the archaic

Überlagerung von Primärkonstruktion und Ausbau im Fassadenbereich – das modulare Prinzip bleibt durchgehend erkennbar

Seen in the overlayering of the primary construction and the extension in the façade area, the modular principle is clearly recognizable throughout

Wie in der Eingangshalle bewirkt horizontale und vertikale Transparenz eine ständige Wechselbeziehung zwischen Innen und Außen.
Bei größeren Stützweiten, wie im Sitzungssaal, wechselt das Konstruktionsmaterial von Holz zu Stahl

As in the entrance hall, horizontal and vertical transparency create a permanent interplay between the inside and the outside. Where larger areas require support, as in the conference room, the material used for construction is steel rather than wood

Besonders am Abend vermittelt sich das innere Gefüge der Anlage. Unterschiedliche Lichtfarben definieren unterschiedliche Räumlichkeiten und Nutzungen

Evening is a particularly good time of day to appreciate the interior of the complex, when varied colors denominate different areas and uses

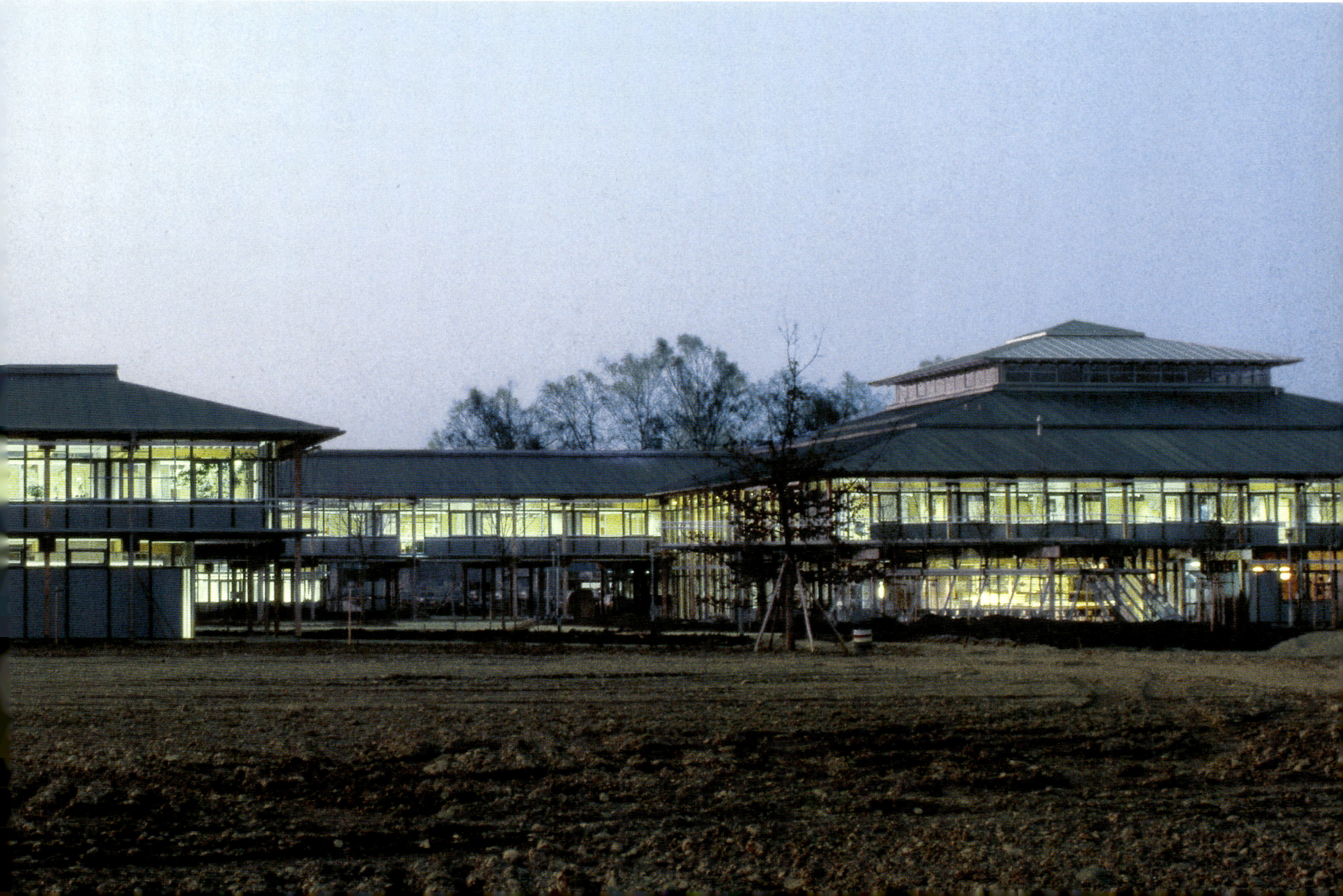

**Weltausstellung EXPO '92 Sevilla
Pavillon der Bundesrepublik Deutschland
1990**
Wettbewerb 1990 1. Preis
(nicht ausgeführt)

**EXPO '92 Seville
German Pavilion
1990**
Competition 1990 1st prize
(not built)

Weltausstellungen boten schon immer Gelegenheit und Chance zu einmaliger, experimenteller Architektur, zu ungewohnten Sehweisen und zu Ausblicken in unbekannte Epochen. Erinnert sei an die deutschen Architekturbeiträge – Barcelona 1929: Klassische Moderne und anspruchsvolle Materialwahl im Pavillon von Ludwig Mies van der Rohe; Brüssel 1958: sympathische Bescheidenheit in der Gebäudegruppe von Egon Eiermann und Sep Ruf; Montreal 1967: beschwingte Dynamik der Zelt-Konstruktion von Frei Otto und Rolf Gutbrod als Vorbild des Münchner Olympiadachs.

Der Beitrag für die EXPO '92 Sevilla stößt in eine neue Dimension vor: Integration baulicher Struktur und freier Skulptur zu einem Bau-Kunst-Werk, das für sich schon ein Exponat ist, jedoch offen bleibt für die Inszenierung der Ausstellung. Die Aufgabenstellung ist vielschichtig: räumliche Disposition mit Einladungscharakter, Selbstdarstellung ohne Überheblichkeit, Klimatologie und Bauphysik mit möglichst sanfter Technologie, Konstruktion, Logistik und Fertigung auf Zeit und unter Zeitdruck. Der Entwurf spiegelt und spielt mit dieser Komplexität: keine vorgefasste und gewollte Form, sondern überraschende Antwort auf die gestellte Herausforderung – undoktrinär, unprätentiös, unideologisch.

Zum eigentlichen Teil der Ausstellung im Inneren der frei im Raum hängenden Großskulptur „Deutschlandschaft" des Bildhauers Albert Hien gelangt der Besucher auf Stegen und Wegen, um dort das angekündigte Thema zu vertiefen. Aus dem Spannungsverhältnis zwischen architektonischer Struktur, die sich als Schirm und Schaubühne präsentiert, und der Großskulptur der inneren Ausstellungshülle soll Anziehungskraft, Unverwechselbarkeit und Erinnerungswert des deutschen Pavillons entstehen.

World exhibitions have always offered opportunities and chances for unique, experimental architecture, unusual perspectives and fast-forwards into as-yet-unknown eras. We need only think of the following German contributions – Barcelona 1929: Ludwig Mies van der Rohe's pavilion married the classic modern age with a discerning choice of material. Or Brussels 1958: pleasing modesty in the ensemble by Egon Eiermann and Sep Ruf. Montreal 1967: spirited dynamism in the tented construction by Frei Otto and Rolf Gutbrod, on which the Olympic roofing in Munich was modeled.

The contribution for EXPO 1992 in Seville explores a new dimension: Integration of architectural structure and free sculpture to form an architectural work of art that is an exhibit in itself, and yet remains open for the exhibition arrangement. The architects' brief incorporates many aspects: spatial arrangement to give a welcoming atmosphere, self-presentation without arrogance, the use of low-key technology for air-conditioning/ventilation and structural physics, design, logistics and manufacturing according to a tight schedule. The design both reflects and plays with this complexity: rather than choosing a preconceived, specific form, it offers a startling answer to the architectural challenge – flexible, unpretentious, free of ideology.

Visitors use a variety of walkways to reach the exhibition proper inside – sculptor Albert Hien's suspended large-scale sculpture "Deutschlandschaft" (Germanscape), which explores the aforementioned topic more deeply. The tension between architectural structure, which presents itself as both covering and showcase, and the large-scale sculpture displayed inside is intended to render the German pavilion fascinating, unmistakable and highly memorable.

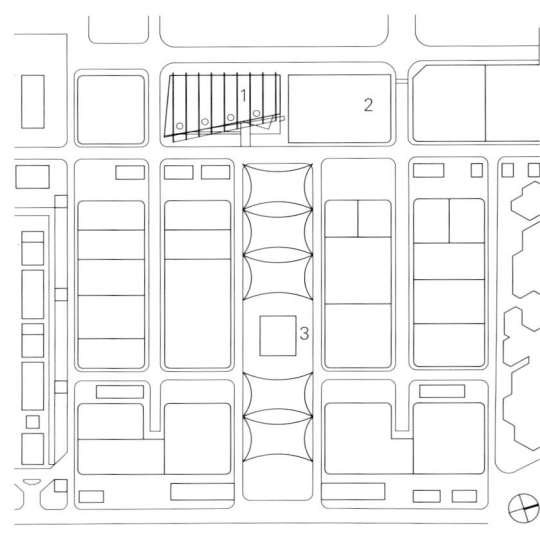

Lageplan / Site plan
1:6000

1 Pavillon Bundesrepublik Deutschland
   German Pavilion
2 Pavillon Großbritannien
   British Pavilion
3 Achse der Pavillons der Europäischen Gemeinschaft
   Axis of the European Union Pavilions

Im Gesamtbild des Pavillons verbinden sich Struktur und Skulptur zur „Deutschlandschaft"

Inside the German Pavilion, external structure and indoor sculpture merge to form "Deutschlandschaft" (Germanscape)

Skizzen zum „Drehbuch"
aus der Wettbewerbsphase

"Script" sketches from the
competition phase

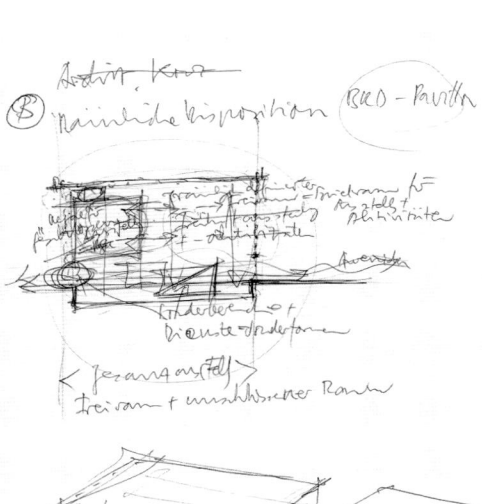

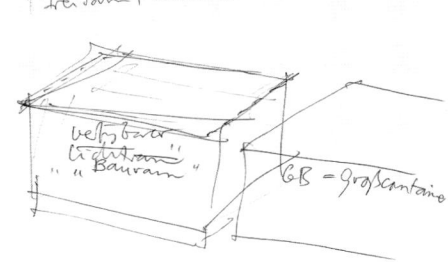

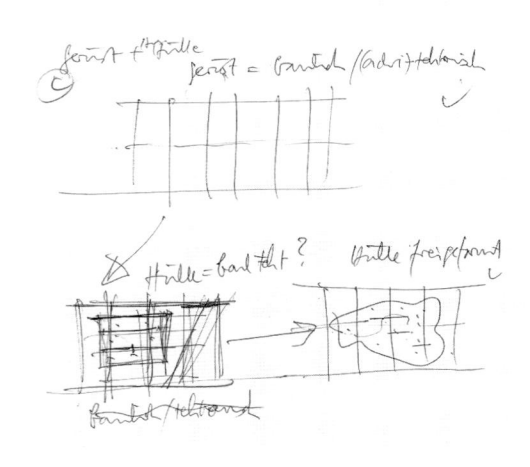

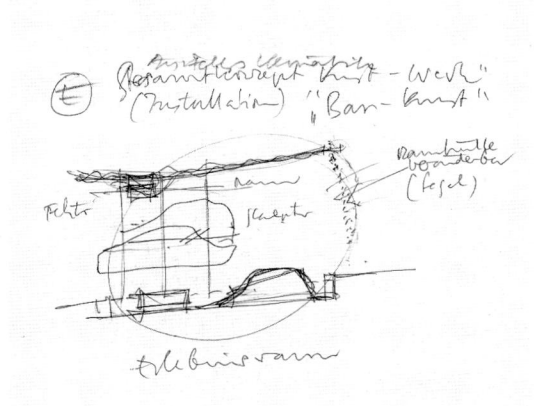

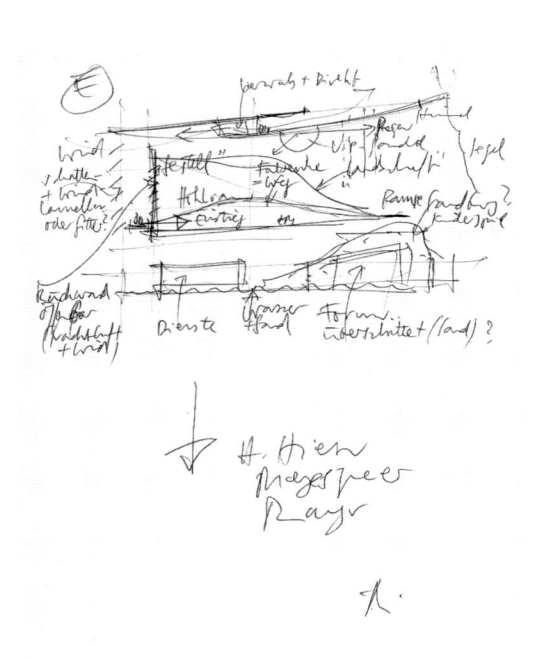

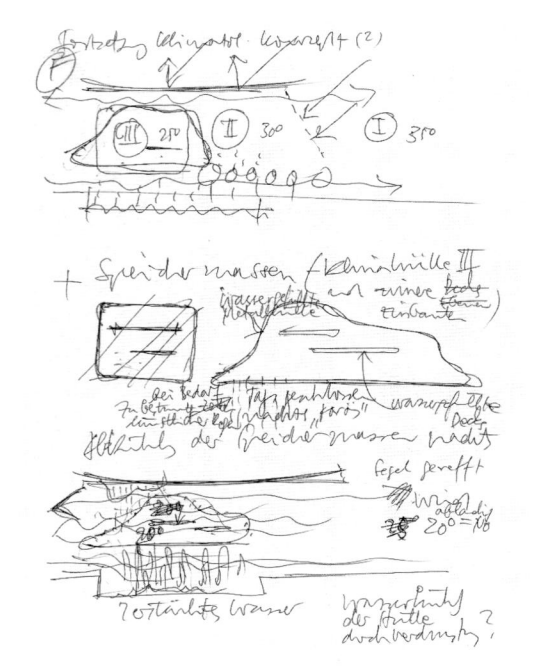

Entwurfsskizze von Albert Hien
zur Ausstellungshülle

Albert Hien's design sketch
for the exhibition casing

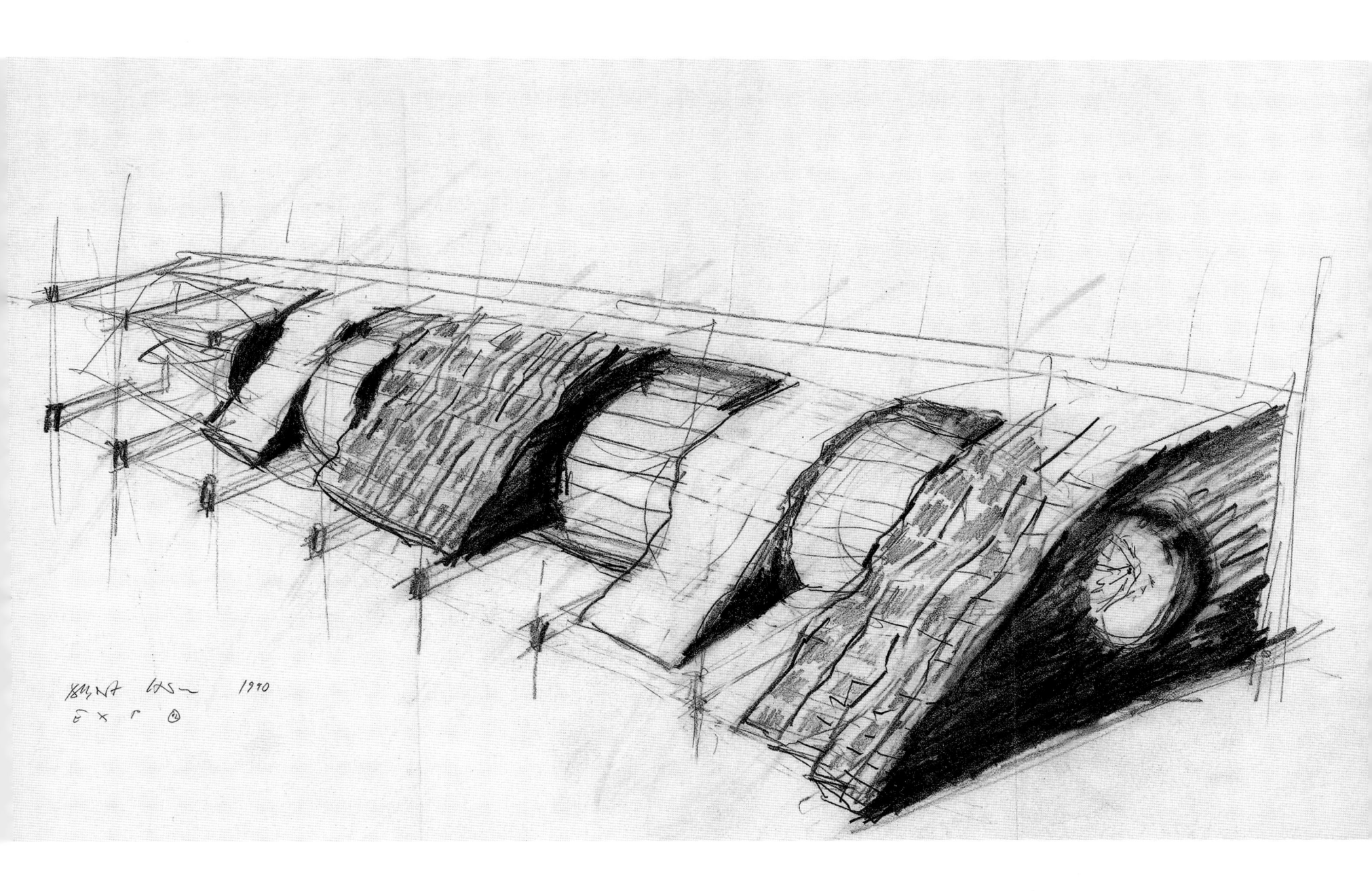

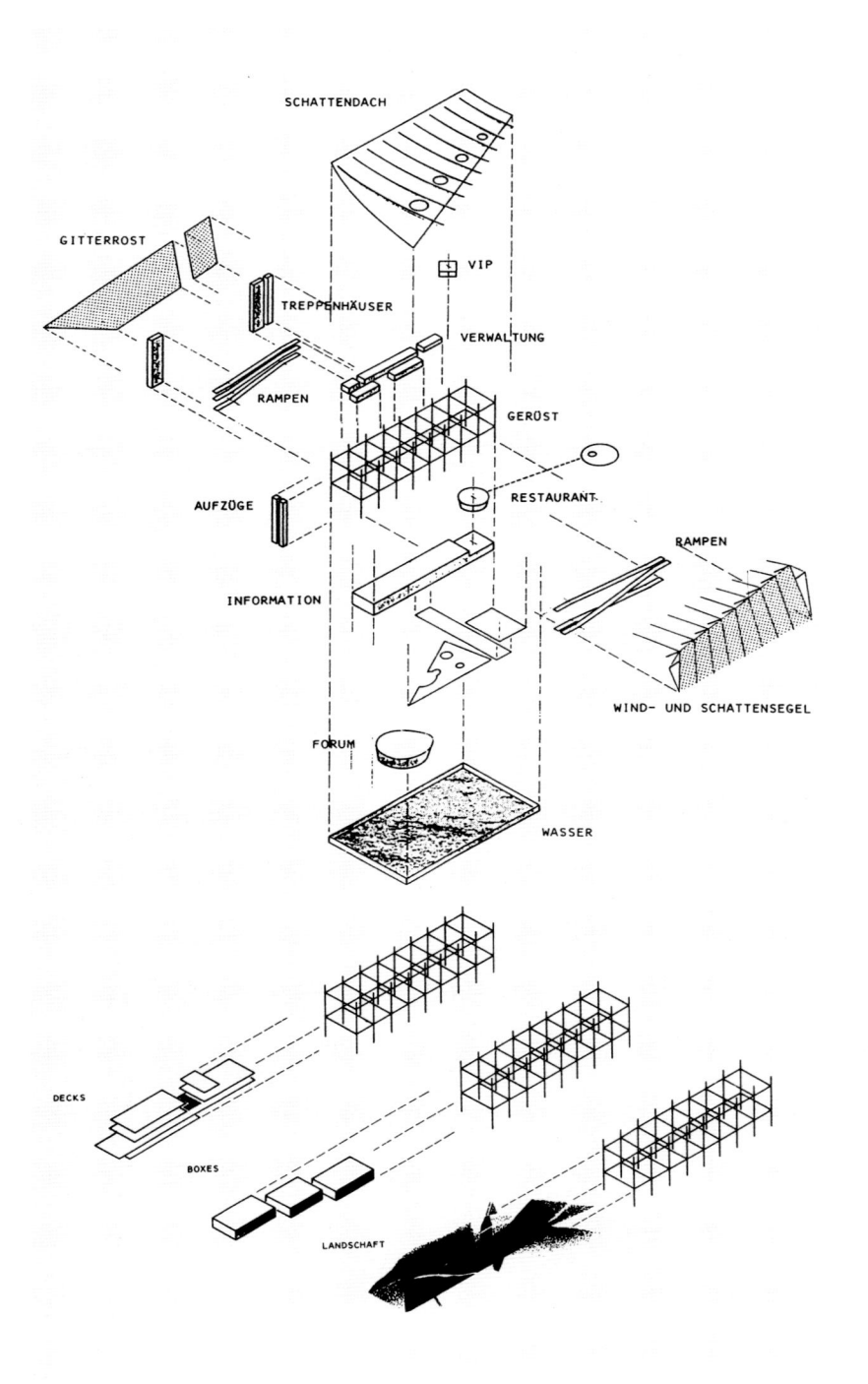

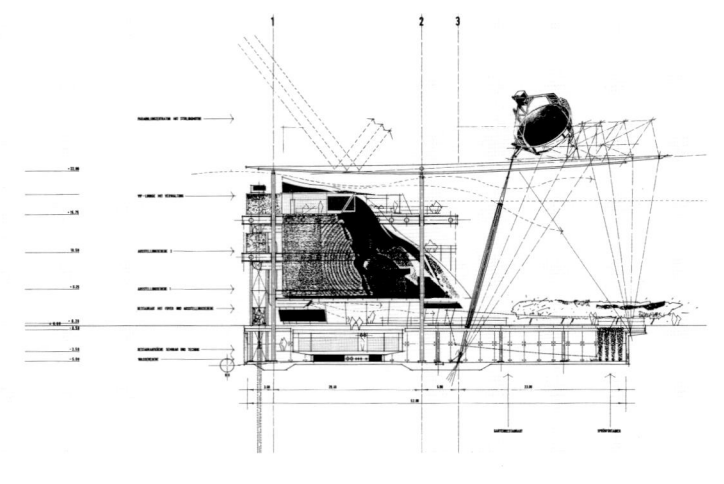

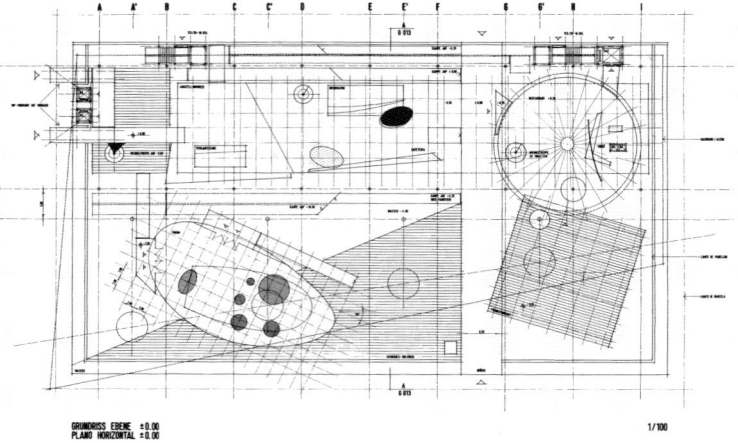

Links:
Die Konstruktions- und Ausstellungselemente als das Ganze konstituierende Teile

Left:
The construction and exhibition elements as parts making up a whole

Rechts oben / Upper right:
Querschnitt / Cross section 1:850

Unten / Below:
Eingangsebene / Entrance level 1:1000

Rechte Seite:
Der Pavillon empfängt den Besucher im Schatten seines weit ausladenden Dachschirmes. Bewegliche Segel schützen zusätzlich vor Sonne und fangen den Wind ein, dämpfen das grelle Licht und sorgen zusammen mit der großen Wasserfläche für angenehme Kühle

Right:
Visitors enter the German Pavilion in the shade of an extensive cantelevering canopy. Moving sails provide additional protection from the sun, catch the wind, soften the bright light, and, in combination with the large water surface, create an atmosphere of pleasant coolness

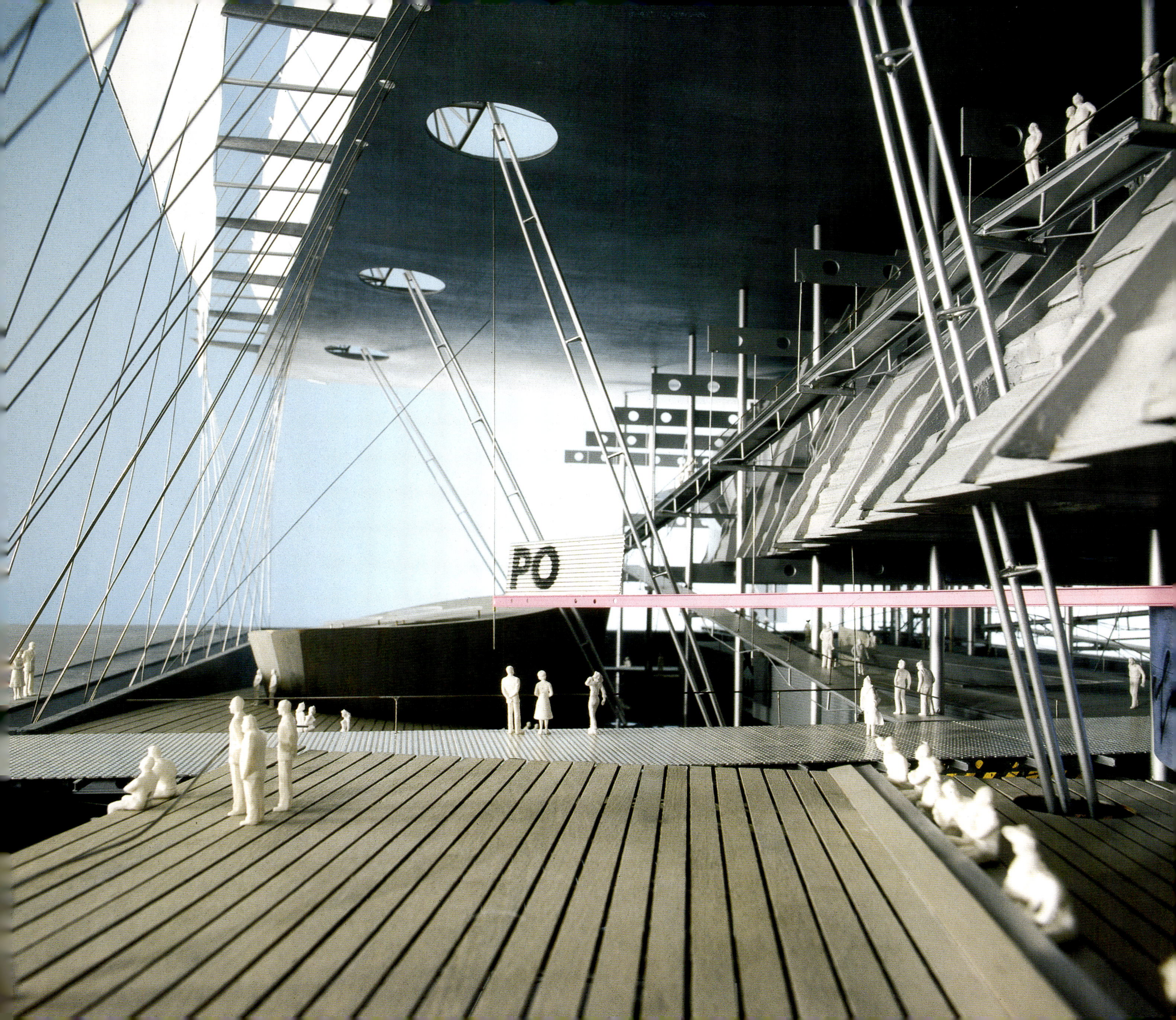
PO

Stadtportalhäuser Frankfurt am Main
1990
Wettbewerb Ankauf

City Portal Buildings Frankfurt/Main
1990
Competition Acquired

Ein unverwechselbares, weithin sichtbares Zeichen auf beiden Seiten der Einfahrt zur Frankfurter Innenstadt: Zwei Hochhäuser treten in eine äußere und innere Beziehung. Die Gebäudekomposition erhöht den Stadteingang zur anspruchsvollen Stadtpforte und liefert darüber hinaus einen Beitrag zur architektonischen Kultur des Bürohochhauses.

Anstelle einer monumentalen oder skulpturalen Interpretation wird das Innenleben des Gebäudes betont und nach außen hin sichtbar gemacht. Die Aufzugs- und Treppenkerne sind peripher angeordnet und die Geschossebenen in eine abgehängte, mit Seilen stabilisierte Konstruktion eingefügt. Dadurch entsteht ein über die gesamte Gebäudehöhe durchlaufender Hallenraum mit konstruktiv frei wählbaren Decks und Arbeitsplätzen, die von Wintergärten durchdrungen werden. Außen wie innen erkennbar findet die urbane Betriebsamkeit innerhalb des Hauses ihre Form in Gestalt von „Zimmern", „Häusern", „Plätzen".

Visible from afar, two high-rises form a distinctive image on both sides of the road into downtown Frankfurt. The composition of the buildings provides a unique entrance into the city and are significant contributions to the architectural history of office high-rises.

Instead of a monumental or sculptural interpretation, the emphasis is placed on the building's interior, which is made clearly visible on the outside. The elevators and stairwells are positioned on the periphery and the floors are set into a suspended construction, which is stabilized with cables. Thus, an atrium extends the whole height of the building allowing a free arrangement of decks and workstations penetrated by conservatories. Recognizable on both the outside and the inside, the urban activities that take place in the building find expression in the form of "rooms", "houses" and "squares".

Links / Left:
Lageplan / Site plan
1:4000

Rechts / Right:
Schnitt / Section
1:1250

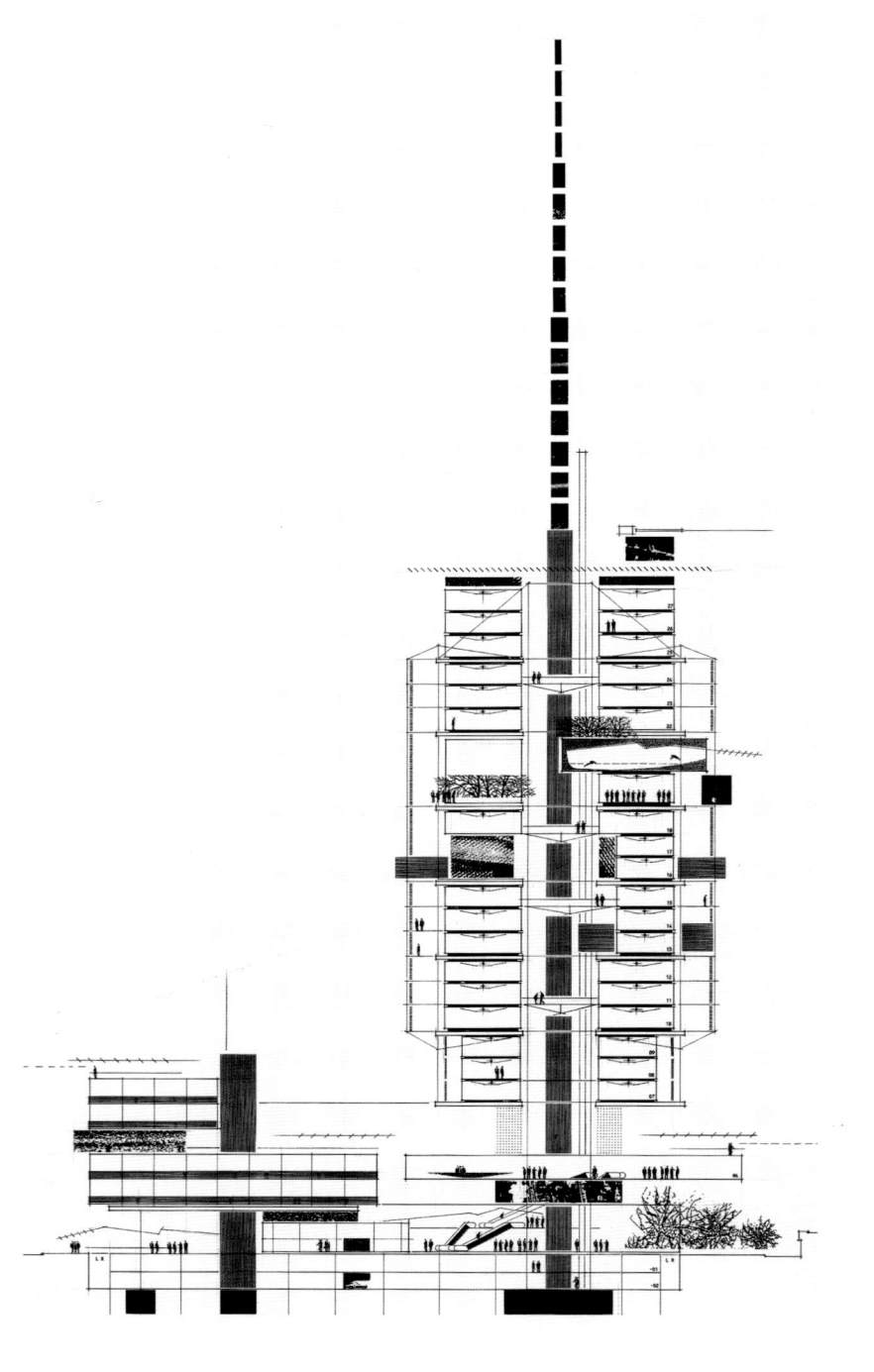

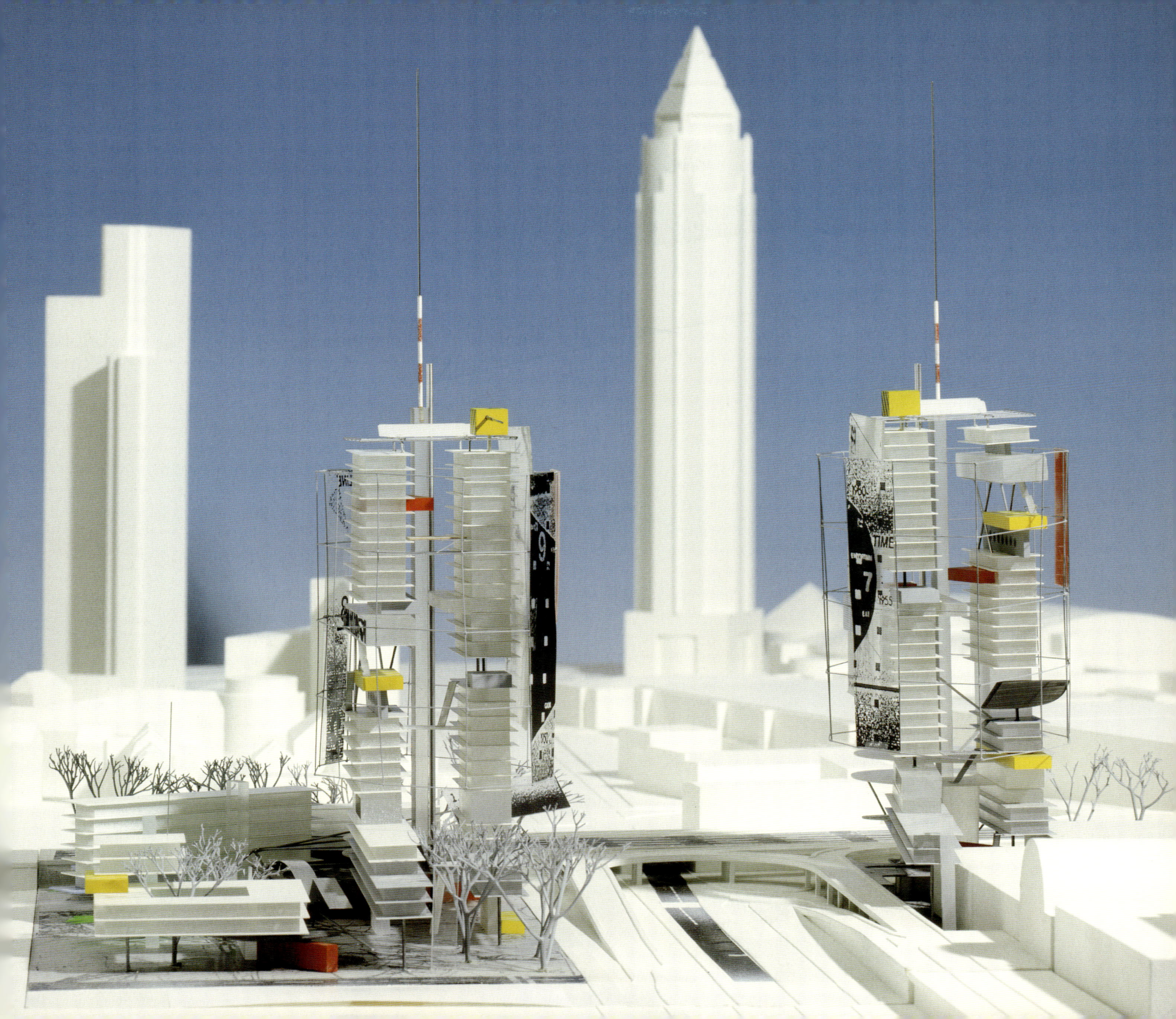
1960
TIME
7
1955

Subzentrum Flughafen München
1991
Wettbewerb 1978   1. Preis
(in Behnisch & Partner)

Subcenter at Munich Airport
1991
Competition 1978   1st prize
(in Behnisch & Partner)

Die verschiedenen Bauten des Subzentrums – Gebäude der Hauptverwaltung, Kantine mit Zentralküche und Freizeiteinrichtungen und Fußgängersteg zur S-Bahn – sind ein Teil der Gesamtanlage des Münchner Flughafens und stehen somit als technisches Projekt im Dialog mit der Ebene und der Offenheit des Landschaftsraums Erdinger Moos. Die Weite der agrarisch geprägten Landschaft wird durch die flächige Ausdehnung der Baulichkeiten, die Betonung der Horizontalen und eine überwiegend transparente Ausbildung der Gebäudehülle beantwortet.

Das Verwaltungsgebäude und die Baugruppe der Kantine ordnen sich in Ausdehnung und Erscheinung dem Terminal unter. Vorgehängte Wartungs- und Beschattungsvorrichtungen schaffen abgestufte Übergänge zwischen Innen und Außen und verändern je nach Jahreszeit und Sonnenstand das Erscheinungsbild.

Die Bereiche für Verwaltung, Schulung und Konferenzen sind beidseitig an eine gläserne, über 110m lange Erschließungshalle „angedockt", welche sich räumlich durch gegeneinander versetzte Innenhöfe erweitert.

The various buildings that make up the subcenter – main administrative building, a canteen with the main airport kitchen, leisure facilities, and a pedestrian walkway to the suburban railway platform – are all part of the overall Munich Airport complex. As such, as a technical project, they are at one with the plains and the open spaces that make up the Erding marshland. The expanse of this farming country is reflected in the two-dimensional spread of the buildings, the emphasis on horizontal structures and the predominantly transparent form of the building sheaths.

In their spread and appearance the administrative building and the group of buildings around the canteen are subordinate to the terminal. The horizontal aspects stress the layering of the utilization levels; they seem to hover over the flat landscape. Shading and maintenance facilities in front of the building create a staggered transition from outside to inside and alters the appearance of the building according to the time of year and the position of the sun.

The administration, training and conference areas are "docked" on both sides of a glass access hall, which is over 110 meters long and is extended even further by interior courtyards, which face each other.

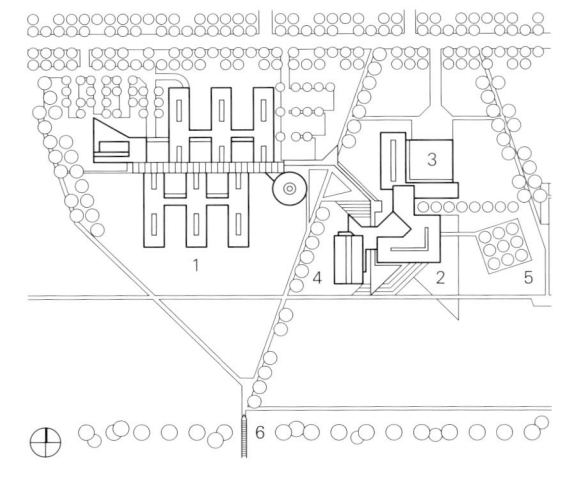

Lageplan / Site plan
1:5000

1   Hauptverwaltung
    Administration
2   Kantine / Staff canteen
3   Zentralküche
    Central kitchen
4   Sport und Freizeit
    Sports and leisure
5   Biergarten
    Beer garden
6   Fußgängersteg
    Footbridge

Rechts:
Die Weite der Landschaft und ihr Horizont spiegeln sich in der flächigen Ausdehnung der Bauwerke wider, die leicht vom Boden abgehoben erscheinen

Right:
The expanse of the countryside and the horizon are reflected in the two-dimensional spread of the buildings, which appear to be raised slightly above ground level

Deutsche Botschaft
German Embassy
Washington, DC, USA, 1964
Egon Eiermann

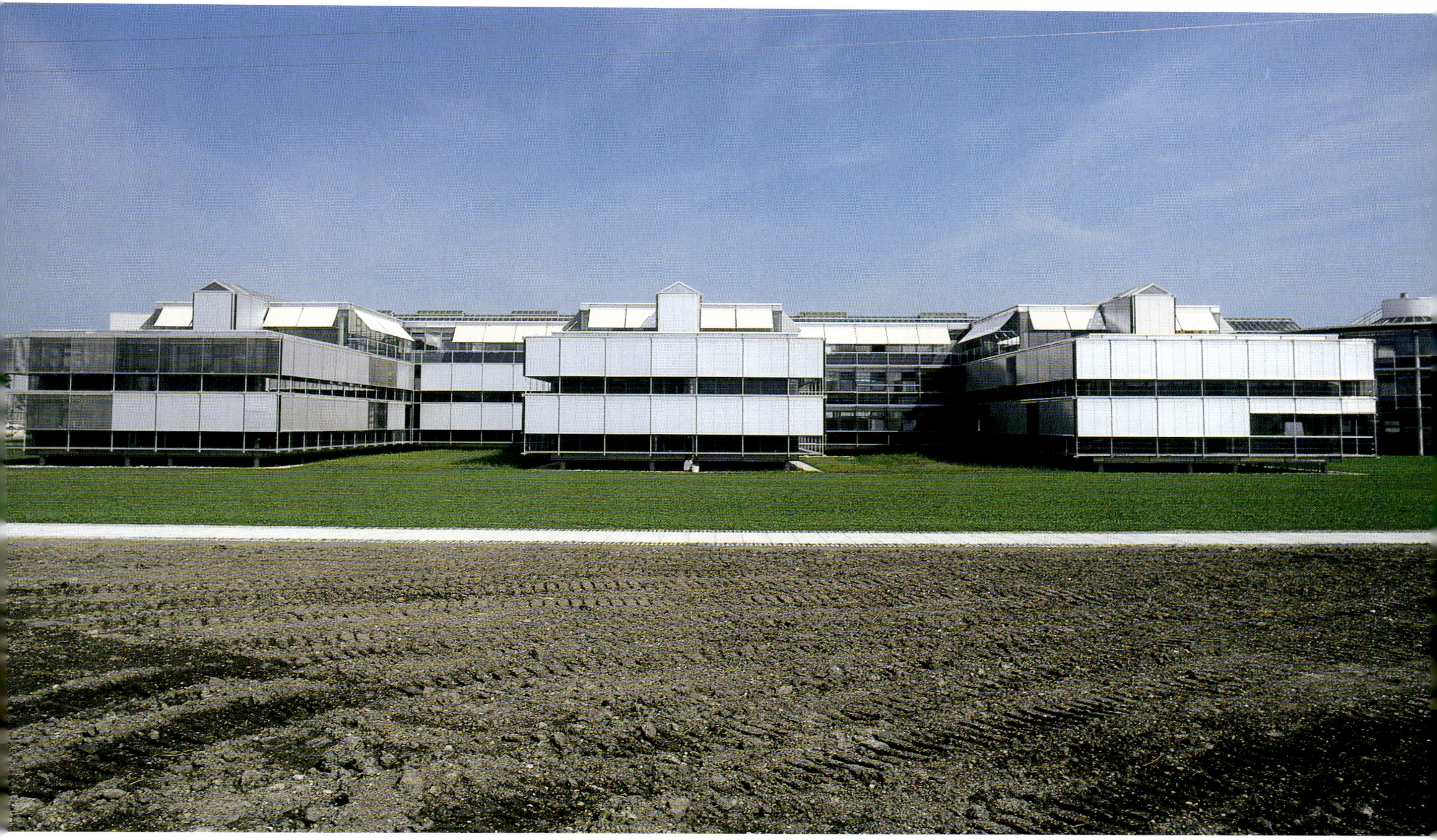

| Logisch und streng aufgebaut stellt sich die Architektur in den Dienst der Gesamtanlage Flughafen. Der vorgehängte Sonnenschutz als „äußerste Haut" verändert je nach Einstellung das Erscheinungsbild | Composed in a logical and stringent manner, the architecture serves the entire airport complex. Depending on which way it is set, the sun protection hung in front alters the appearance of the building |

Querschnitt / Cross section
1:750

1. Verwaltungsbereich / Administration
2. Halle / Hall
3. Innenhof / Inner courtyard

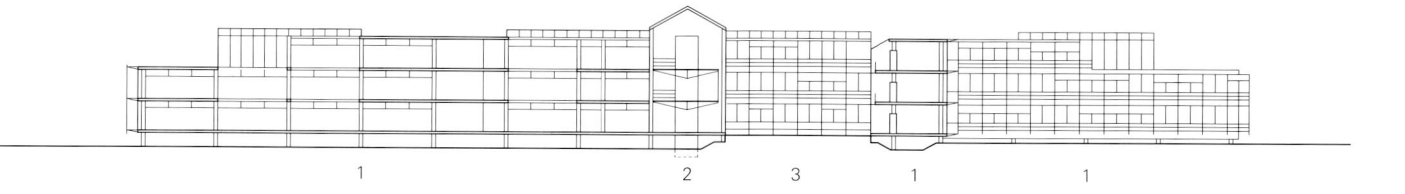

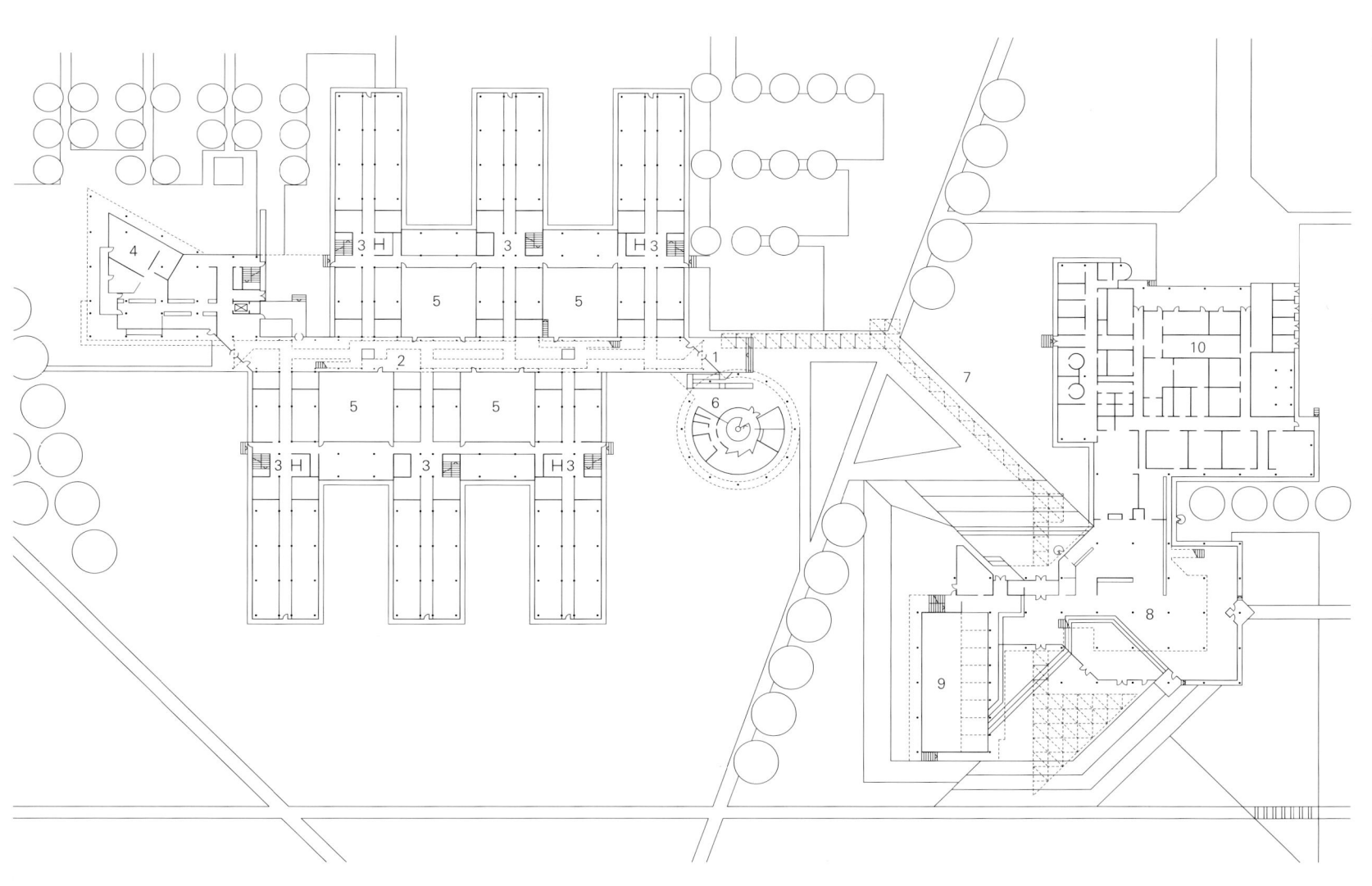

Erdgeschoss / Ground floor
1:1250

1. Haupteingang mit Empfang / Main entrance and reception
2. Halle / Hall
3. Verwaltung / Administration
4. Schulung / Training area
5. Innenhof / Inner courtyard
6. Sitzungsräume / Conference rooms
7. Gläserne Pergola / Glazed pergola
8. Kantine / Staff canteen
9. Mehrzweckhalle / Multifunctional hall
10. Zentralküche / Central kitchen

Oben:
Aus- und Einblicke zwischen Halle und Innenhöfen und abgestufte Übergänge zwischen Innen und Außen

Unten:
Der aufgeständerte, 263m lange Fußgängersteg zwischen Hauptverwaltung und südlichem Betriebsgelände überbrückt die Flughafenzufahrt und S-Bahnlinie. Der röhrenförmige Querschnitt minimiert die Konstruktion der transparenten Wetterschutzhülle, der Gang über den Steg wird so zu einem besonderen Erlebnis

Above:
Looking out and looking in between the hall and the inner courtyards and stepped transitions between interior and exterior

Below:
The raised, 263-meter-long pedestrian walkway between the main administrative building and the southern operational area bridges the airport approach road and the suburban railway line. Because of its tube-shaped cross section, the construction of the weather protection cover was reduced in size. As a result, strolling along the walkway becomes a special experience

Die Kantine als lichter Pavillon orientiert sich über vorgelagerte Wasserflächen zur Flughafenlandschaft

Like a pavilion of light, the staff canteen stretches across expanses of water towards the airport landscape

Roh- und Ausbau bleiben als Schichten deutlich ablesbar. Oberlichter und Glassteindecken leiten Tageslicht in die darunter liegenden Flure

The carcass and finishing layers remain visible. Skylights and glass block floors allow natural light to penetrate to lower levels

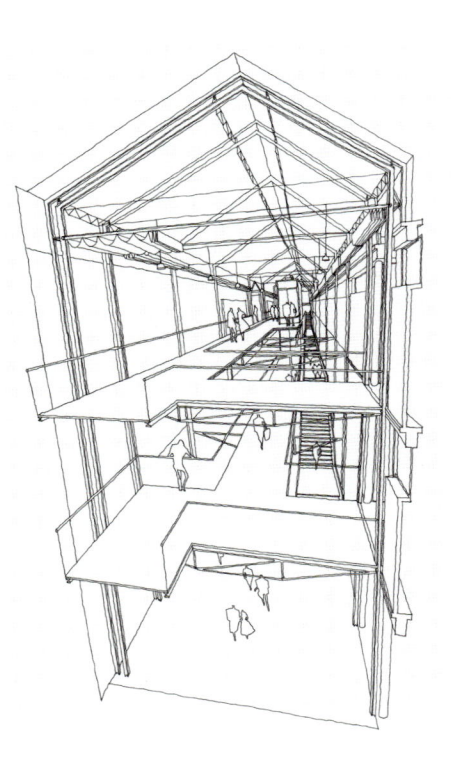

Die über 110m lange Halle mit hölzernen Verbindungsstegen und textilem Sonnenschutz unter dem Glasdach ist räumliches wie organisatorisches Rückgrat des Verwaltungsgebäudes

The hall, over 110 meters long, with its wooden connecting stakes and textile sun protection beneath the glass roof, forms the spatial and organizational backbone of the administrative building

Eiserne Brücke über die Donau
Regensburg
1991
Wettbewerb 1987   Sonderpreis

Iron Bridge over the Danube
Regensburg
1991
Competition 1987   Special prize

Die Eiserne Brücke über die Donau ersetzt die namensgebende Eisenkonstruktion eines langjährigen Provisoriums. Der Entwurf nimmt das Prinzip des Bogens auf und übersetzt es in die Sprache moderner Technik. Konsequent detailliert und mit filigraner Transparenz entsteht mit dem Baustoff Stahl und seiner ihm eigenen Gestaltsprache ein spannungsvoller Kontrast zur wuchtigen Masse der Steinernen Brücke aus dem Mittelalter und zum mächtigen Salzstadel. Ist die Steinbrücke ein homogener Körper, so ist die Stahlbrücke bestimmt durch die deutliche Trennung ihrer Konstruktionselemente. In ihrer Gegensätzlichkeit bereichern beide Bauwerke das Flusspanorama der Altstadt.

Die Brückenplatte ist als dünnes, aufs Notwendigste reduziertes Flächentragwerk ausgebildet, dessen Lasten über feine Bogenträger schubfrei auf die Pfeiler und Widerlager abgeleitet werden.

Die auf einem Werftgelände gefertigten drei Brückenabschnitte wurden per Schiff an die Baustelle transportiert und in kurzer Zeit mit hoher Präzision auf die vorbereiteten Auflager gesetzt.

The Iron Bridge over the Danube was built to replace a temporary solution that had stood there for many years, and derived its name from the use of iron in its construction. The design takes the principle of the arch and translates it into the language of modern technology. In using steel and its characteristic design language, there is an emphasis on detail and delicate transparency, which creates a fascinating contrast to the solid mass of the medieval Stone Bridge and the massive Salzstadel. While the Stone Bridge is a homogenous structure, the defining feature of the steel bridge is the clear division of its structural elements. This stark contrast between the two bridges serves to enrich the riverside panorama of the Old Town.

The thin bridge deck is reduced to the essentials, whose loads are deflected without shearing force via elegant arched supports to the piers and abutments.

The three sections comprising the bridge were manufactured at a shipyard and transported by ship to the building site, where they were placed with great precision onto the waiting supports.

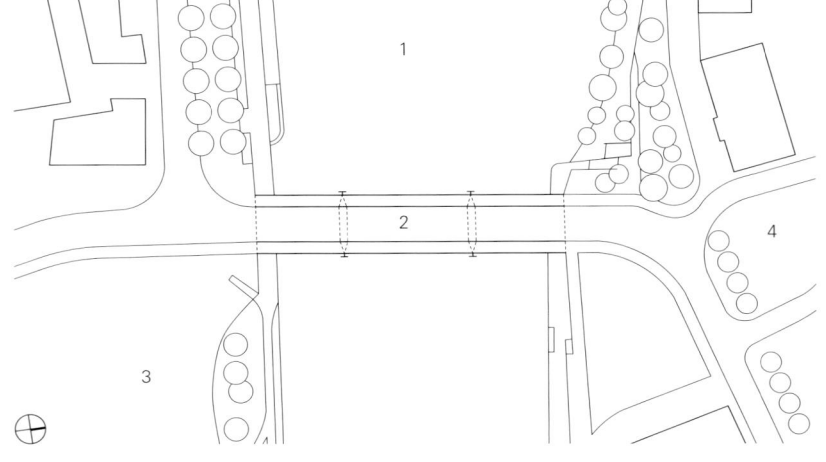

Lageplan / Site plan
1:2000

1   Donau / Danube
2   Eiserne Brücke / Iron Bridge
3   Donaumarkt / Market
4   Unterer Wöhrd

Die Brücke vor der Silhouette der Regensburger Altstadt mit dem alles überragenden Dom

The bridge, with the silhouette of old downtown Regensburg and the towering cathedral in the background

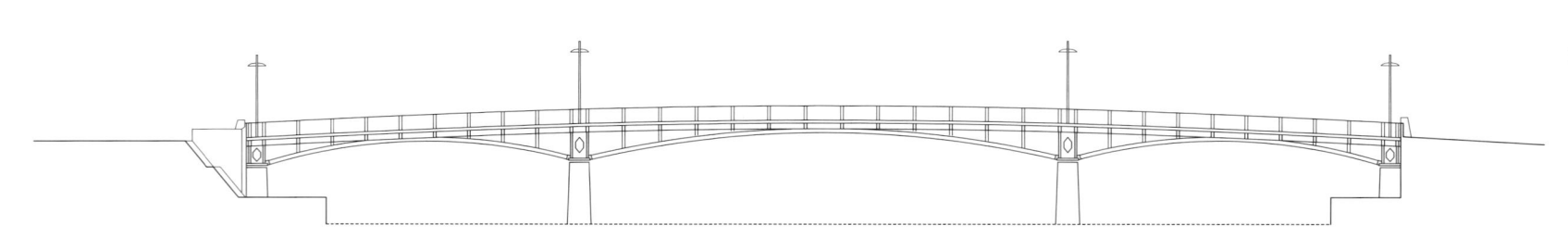

Ansicht / Elevation
1:500

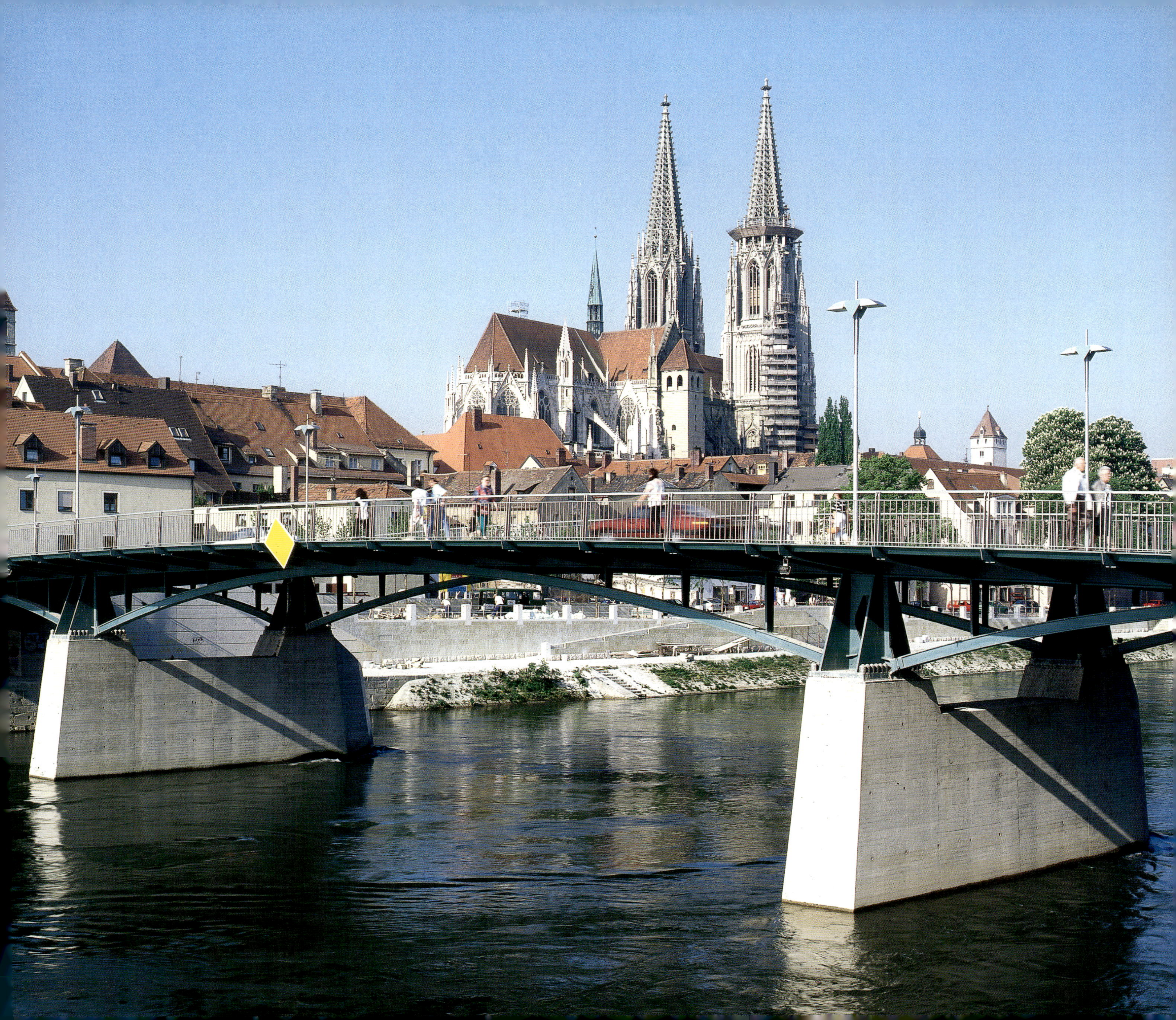

Das zierliche Bauwerk ruht auf mächtigen Strompfeilern und lässt auch in der Untersicht das aufgelöste Tragwerk erkennen

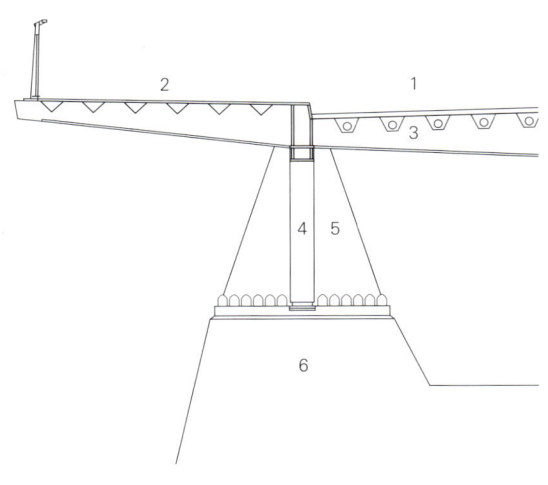

This fragile-seeming edifice rests on massive piles in the river and, even when viewed from below, reveals its multi-sectional support structure

Detailschnitt / Detail section
1:100

1 Fahrbahnplatte / Deck
2 Gehweg / Sidewalk
3 Querträger / Transverse girders
4 Bogenlängsträger / Longitudinal girders
5 Auflagerknoten / Abutment
6 Strompfeiler / River pier

Pont des Arts, Paris, 1803
Ing. de Cessart

Bei einer Fahrt auf der Donau treten die gegensätzlichen Charaktere der beiden Brücken am deutlichsten hervor

From the vantage-point of a boat on the Danube, the contrasting character of the two bridges becomes apparent

**Verwaltungsgebäude
der Stadtwerke Reutlingen
1991**
Wettbewerb 1987   1. Preis

**Administration Building
for Public Utilities Reutlingen
1991**
Competition 1987   1st prize

Das Verwaltungsgebäude fügt sich mit betonter Längsausrichtung in die lineare Struktur der Werksanlage aus den Anfangsjahren des zwanzigsten Jahrhunderts ein, welche durch den Wechsel von Bebauung und Grün gekennzeichnet ist. Seiner Bedeutung entsprechend überragt es die anderen Werksbauten und markiert so – von Bahn und Schnellstraße aus zu sehen – zusammen mit der Kugel des Gasbehälters das Werksgelände als Teil der traditionellen Industrie- und Gewerbestadt.

Der Neubau bildet mit seinem großzügigen, begrünten Vorfeld den stadtwärts orientierten Kopf des Areals. Im flachen Querbau befinden sich die publikumsorientierten Räume, im aufgeständerten Längsbau die allgemeinen Verwaltungsbereiche und im Dachgeschoss die Werksleitung mit dem Sitzungssaal.

Die verschiedenen Inhalte werden auch durch Material und Konstruktion unterschiedlich ausgeformt: der zweigeschossige Querbau, die Kundenhalle und das Dachgeschoss mit schöner Aussicht auf Altstadt und Schwäbische Alb sind in Stahlskelettbauweise ausgeführt, der Längsbau als schlankes Stahlbetonskelett mit metallischer Außenhaut. Dagegen beziehen die benachbarten Bauten der Werksanlage ihren Ausdruck aus der handwerklichen Qualität von Mauerwerk und Werkstein – Elemente, die als Einfriedungen auch die Verbindung zwischen Neubau und historischer Werksanlage herstellen.

With its emphasis on a longitudinal design, the administrative building blends in with the linear structure of the plant – which dates from the beginning of the twentieth century – and is characterized by the interplay of greenery and buildings. As is usual for a building of such importance, it towers over the other buildings on the site; it is visible from the railway and adjacent road and, together with the spherical gasometer, defines the utility complex as a firm fixture in the traditional industrial town.

The new building, with its green entrance area, forms the front of the site, which faces in the direction of the town. Sections open to the public are located in the flat transverse building, general administrative sections are to be found in the elevated longitudinal building, while the plant's management staff and conference room are located under the roof.

The interiors of the building are all designed differently using various materials and forms. In the two-story transverse building, the customer area and the attic area – with its splendid view over the old town and the Swabian hills – are constructed with a steel skeleton. The longitudinal building, on the other hand, has a reinforced concrete skeleton with a metallic exterior sheath. The neighboring buildings on the site stand out for the craftsmanship of their walls and hewn stone – elements that, as an enclosure, create a link between the new building and the historic site.

Lageplan / Site plan
1:5000

1   Verwaltungsgebäude
    Administration building
2   Werksanlage / Site
3   Gasbehälter / Gasometer

Der Querbau mit Eingangs- und Kundenbereich als Teil der kreuzförmigen Gebäudeformation wird vom Längstrakt des Verwaltungsbereichs überlagert. Das geschwungene Dach des Sitzungssaals nimmt Bezug auf den kugelförmigen Gasbehälter im Werksgelände

As part of a cruciform arrangement of buildings, the transverse building, housing the entrance and customer areas, is overlaid with the longitudinal tract of the administrative area. The curved roof of the conference room takes its cue from the spherical gasometers on the site

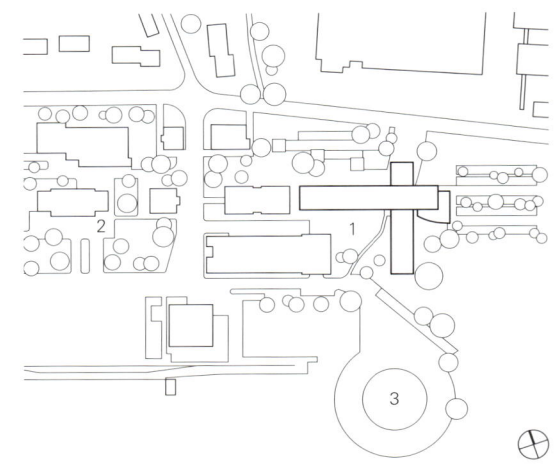

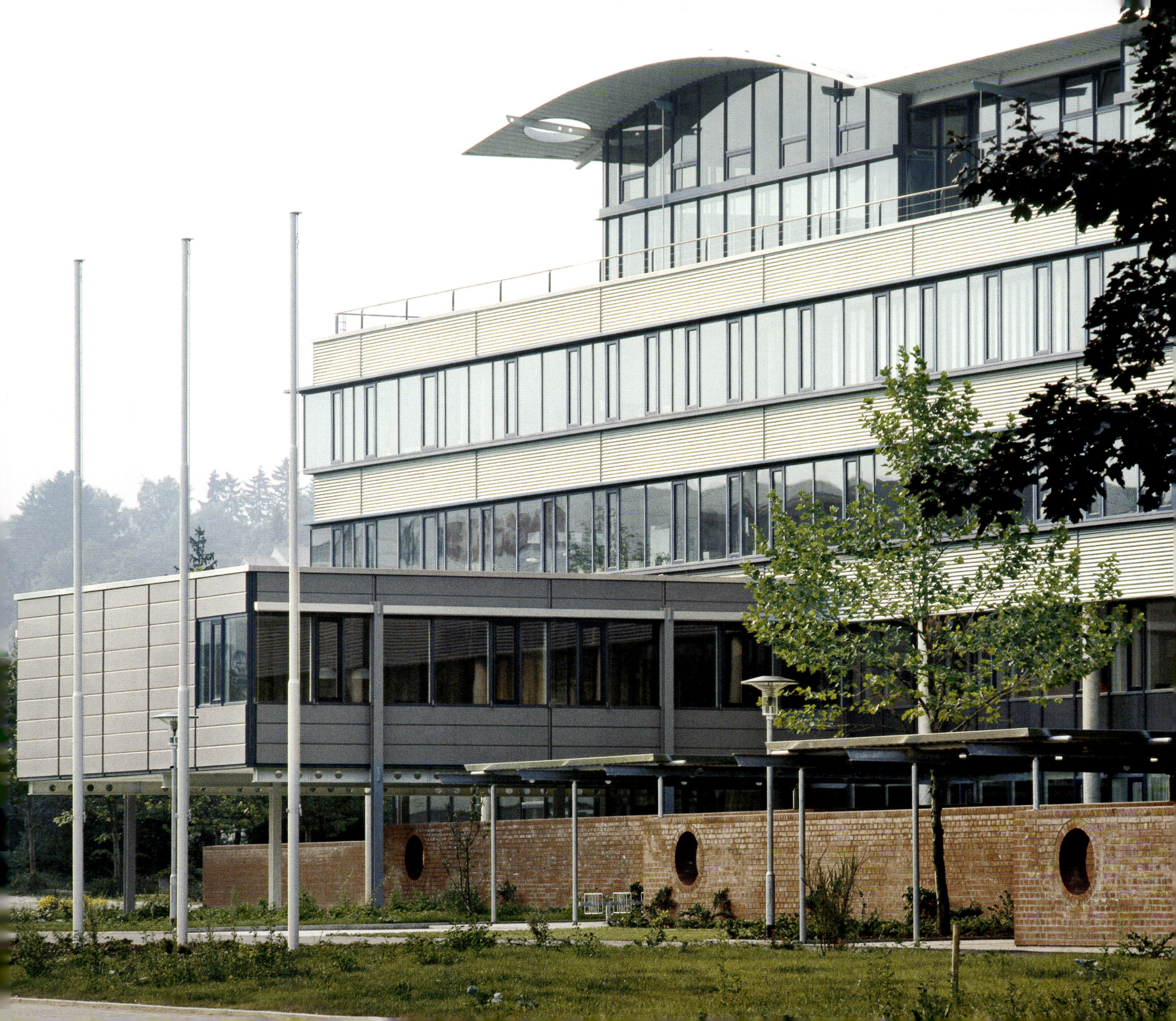

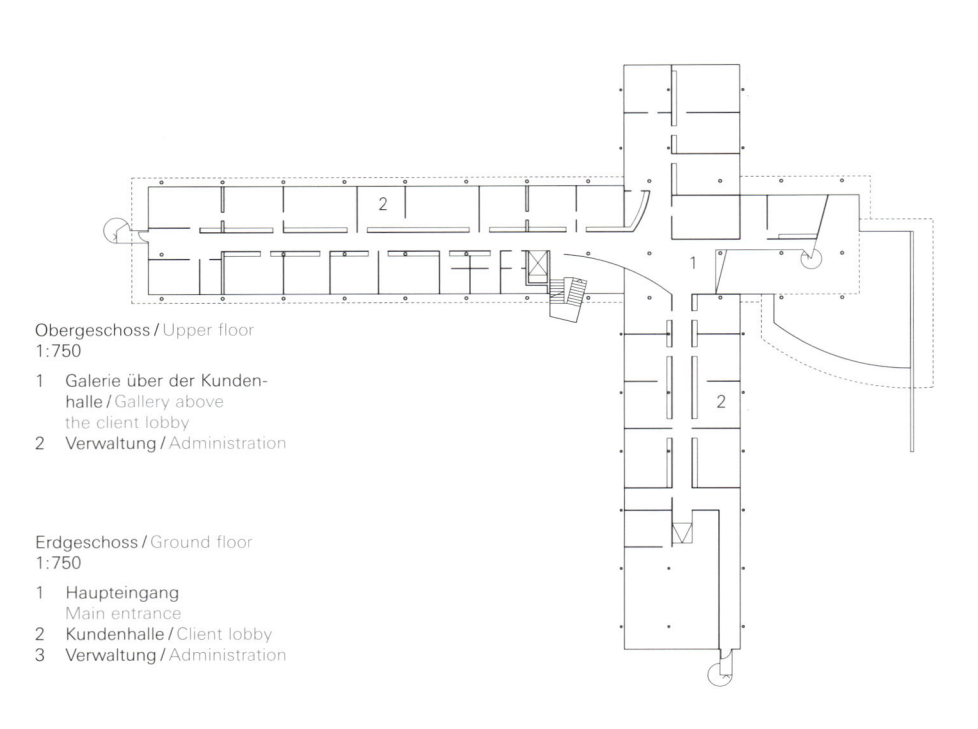

Obergeschoss / Upper floor
1:750

1. Galerie über der Kundenhalle / Gallery above the client lobby
2. Verwaltung / Administration

Erdgeschoss / Ground floor
1:750

1. Haupteingang / Main entrance
2. Kundenhalle / Client lobby
3. Verwaltung / Administration

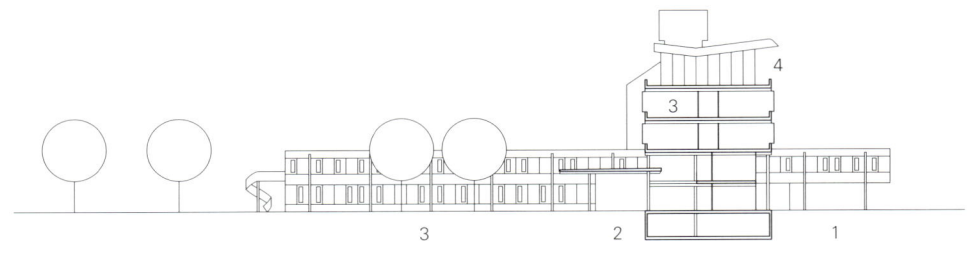

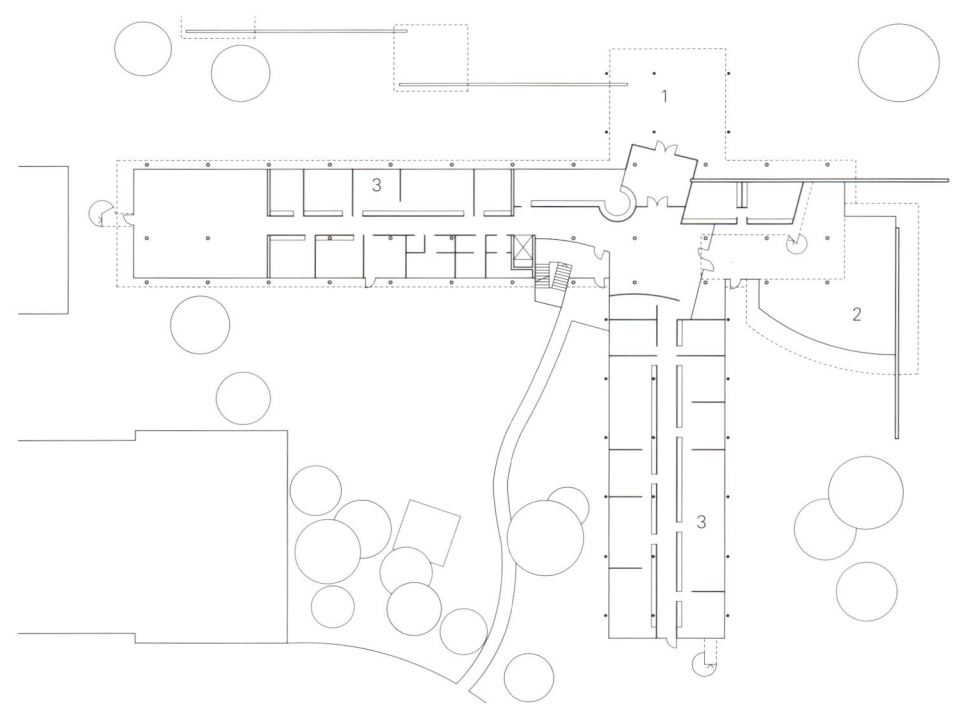

Links / Left:
Schnitt / Section
1:750

1 Haupteingang
  Main entrance
2 Kundenhalle / Client lobby
3 Verwaltung / Administration
4 Sitzungssaal
  Conference room

Links:
Die Stirnseite des Längstrakts zeigt die Überlagerung von publikumsorientierten und internen Verwaltungsräumen

Rechte Seite, links:
Die Kundenhalle von der Galerie: Roh- und Ausbau durchdringen sich und bleiben erkennbar

Rechts:
Das wechselnde „Licht-Bild" des Künstlers Günter Dohr in der Eingangshalle veranschaulicht das Thema Energie

Left:
The short end of the longitudinal tract shows the superimposition of the client and administrative sections

Right side, left:
The client lobby from the gallery; the shell and the extension intermingle and yet remain discernible

Right side, right:
The alternating "Light-Picture" by artist Günter Dohr in the entrance hall visualizes the subject of energy and power

73 Verwaltungsgebäude der Stadtwerke / Administration Building Reutlingen

Helen-Keller-Realschule
München-Johanneskirchen
1992
Wettbewerb 1987   1. Preis

Helen Keller Secondary School
Munich Johanneskirchen
1992
Competition 1987   1st prize

Die Schulanlage bildet den Übergang zwischen einem städtischen Wohngebiet und offenen Grünflächen. Da in dem Gebiet früher Ton abgebaut wurde, hat das Grundstück zwei Gelände-Niveaus: auf der „Stadtseite" die ursprüngliche, auf der „Landschaftsseite" die nach der Tongewinnung um etwa ein Geschoss tiefer liegende Ebene.

Diese städtebaulichen und topographischen Gegebenheiten bestimmen das räumliche Konzept der Schule: Der Eingangsplatz verbindet über einen offenen Durchgang zwischen Schule und Sporthalle die „städtische" Ebene mit der tiefer liegenden „Landschafts"-Ebene der Freibereiche. An den Längstrakt mit Fachklassen und Verwaltungsräumen, welcher die Schwelle zwischen den beiden Niveaus bildet, lagern sich auf der Landschaftsseite die Unterrichtsräume in pavillonartigen Klassenhäusern an. Das Spannungsverhältnis zwischen linearem Rückgrat und den dazu „geschwenkt" angeordneten Anbauten bestimmt Struktur, Bild und Erlebnis der Schulanlage im Äußeren wie im Inneren: zur Stadt hin Wand bildend und straff, zur Landschaft hin aufgefächert, nahezu improvisiert – verspielt, eher an Gartenlauben erinnernd.

Eine lang gestreckte, lichterfüllte und die verschiedenen Niveaus verbindende Halle bildet den inneren Begegnungs- und Gemeinschaftsraum der Schule, dessen rhythmische Raumfolge durch ein filigranes Kunstwerk von Michael Kramer als räumliche „Promenade" interpretiert ist.

The school complex forms a transition between an urban residential area and open green areas. Since clay was previously mined in the area, the ground has two levels: the side facing the town, which is the original level, and the landscape side, which is the level that lies one story lower due to the clay mining.

These two sets of conditions determine the school's spatial concept. Starting at the forecourt, an open passage between school and gymnasium links the town level with the lower-lying landscape level characterized by open spaces. Specialist classrooms and administration rooms line the intersection of the two levels, with classrooms on the landscape side arranged in pavilion-like houses. The suspense between the straight-line backbone and the annexes that effectively swivel towards it defines the school's design, appearance, and how it is experienced both inside and out. The school forms a solid wall to face the town, while fanning out towards the landscape side with an almost improvised, playful appearance more reminiscent of summerhouses.

An elongated hall suffused with light connects the various levels and forms the school's internal meeting and common room area. Its rhythmic arrangement is picked up in the delicate artwork by Michael Kramer, and is experienced as a spatial "promenade".

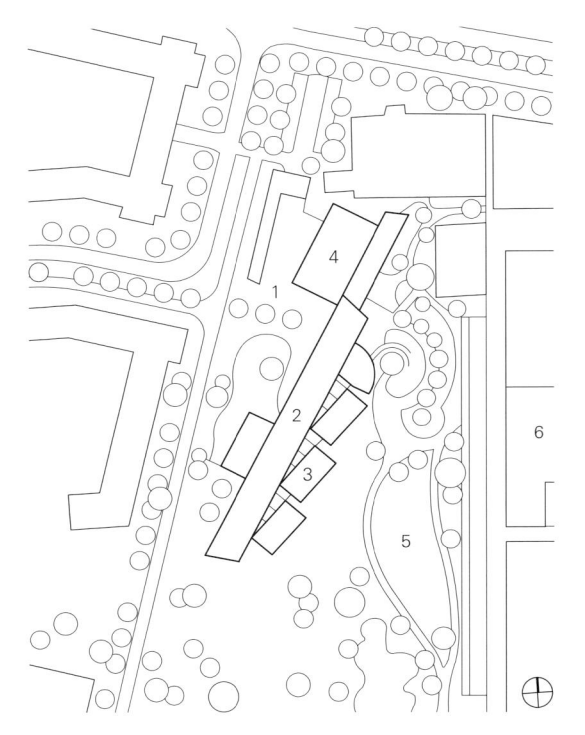

Lageplan / Site plan
1:2500

1 Eingangsplatz
   Entrance square
2 Fachklassen, Verwaltung
   Specialist classrooms, administration
3 Klassenhäuser
   Class houses
4 Turnhalle / Gymnasium
5 Schulgarten
   School garden
6 Spielplätze
   Playgrounds

Mit ihrer wandartigen „Stadtseite" antwortet die Schule auf die gegenüber liegende Wohnbebauung

On the "town" side, the school responds to the residential area opposite by presenting a solid wall

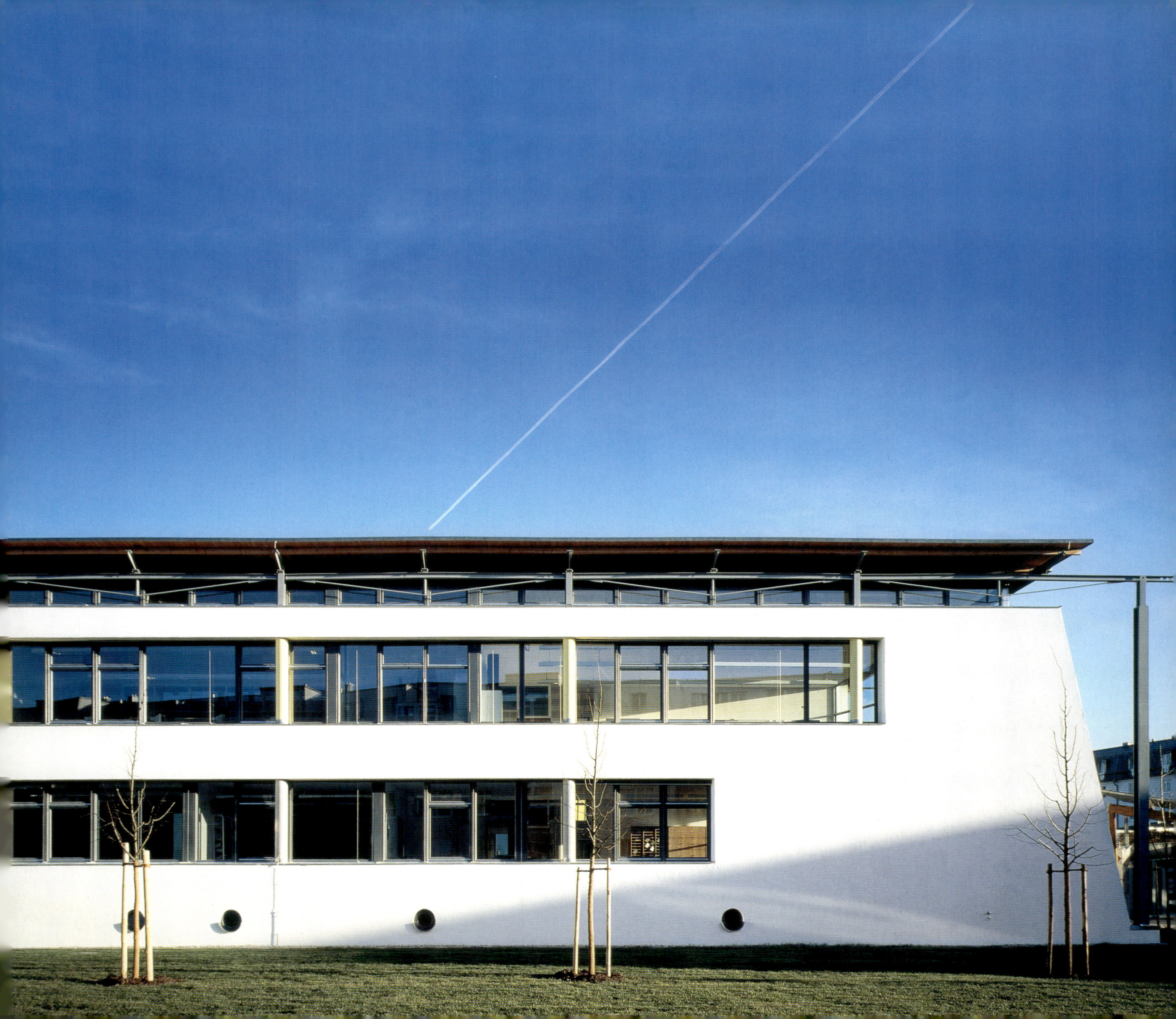

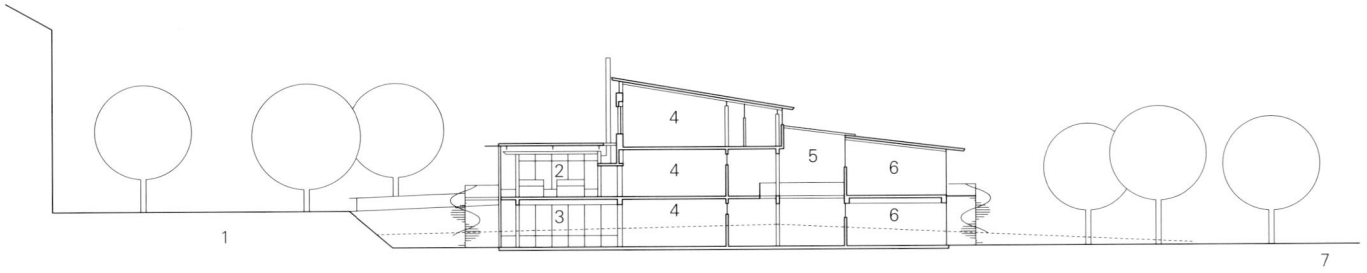

Querschnitt / Section
1:500

1 Eingangsplatz
  Entrance square
2 Lehrsaal / Lecture hall
3 Werken / Crafts
4 Fachklassen
  Specialist classrooms
5 Halle / Hall
6 Klassen / Classrooms
7 Schulgarten / Garden

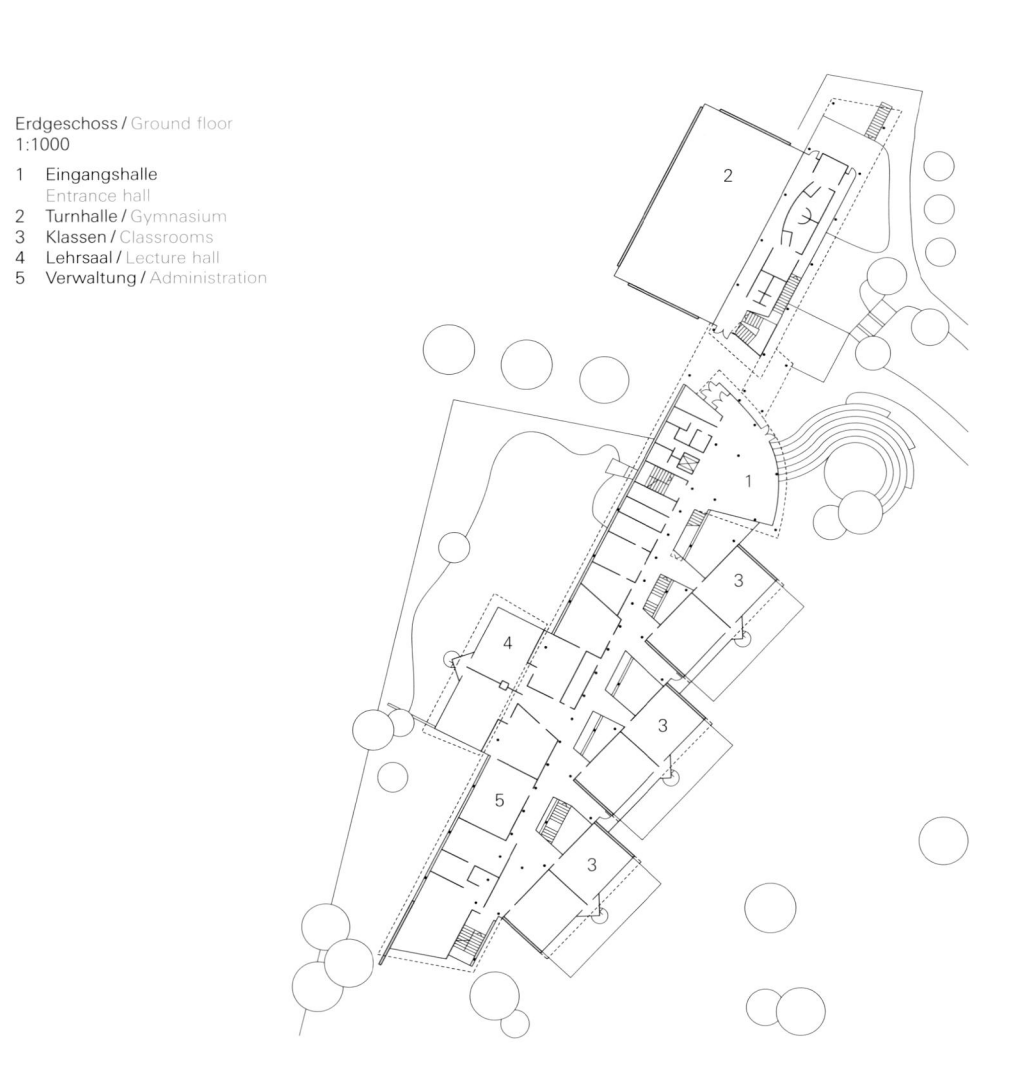

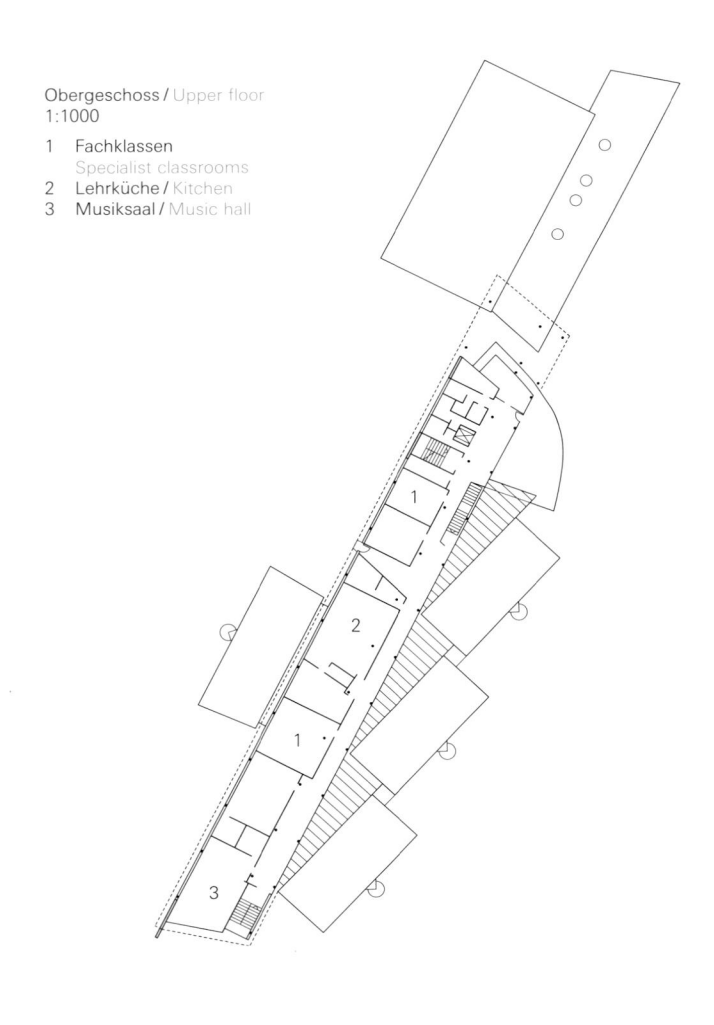

Erdgeschoss / Ground floor
1:1000

1 Eingangshalle
  Entrance hall
2 Turnhalle / Gymnasium
3 Klassen / Classrooms
4 Lehrsaal / Lecture hall
5 Verwaltung / Administration

Obergeschoss / Upper floor
1:1000

1 Fachklassen
  Specialist classrooms
2 Lehrküche / Kitchen
3 Musiksaal / Music hall

Die Halle als innere Promenade
mit der raumdurchdringenden
Skulptur von Michael Kramer

The hall with Michael Kramer's
pervasive sculpture

Helen-Keller-Realschule / Helen Keller Secondary School **München**

Über eine Freitreppe und einen offenen Durchgang sind „Stadt"- und „Landseite" der Schule miteinander verbunden

The "town" and "country" side of the school are connected via stairs and an open passage

Die „Landseite" der Schule mit den an den Längstrakt angedockten, pavillonartigen Klassenhäusern

The "country" side of the school with the pavilion-like classrooms adjoining the main section

**Ortszentrum Germering
Stadthalle und Bibliothek
1993**
Wettbewerb 1984   1. Preis

**Germering Town Center
Civic Hall and Library
1993**
Competition 1984   1st prize

Mit der Gemeindegebietsreform wurden im Jahr 1978 die Gemeinden Germering und Unterpfaffenhofen im Westen von München zusammengefasst und 1991 zur Stadt Germering erhoben.

Der Glücksfall, dass an der Nahtstelle der beiden Gemeinden ein noch freies Grundstück verfügbar war, machte es möglich, hier ein bauliches und kulturelles Zentrum für die junge Stadt zu verwirklichen, welches sich mit klaren äußeren Raumkanten aus seiner indifferenten Umgebung und den tangierenden Verkehrsadern abhebt.

Die städtebauliche Ordnung der Situation formuliert unterschiedliche Freiräume: den Marktplatz als Entrée, die „Agora" als geschützten Stadtplatz, einen parkartigen Grünraum als Überleitung zu den östlichen Wohngebieten sowie den Bahnhofsplatz als Bindeglied zum überörtlichen Nahverkehr.

Eine diagonale Wegebeziehung verbindet diese Freiräume miteinander und mit dem vorhandenen Gewebe des Ortes. Alle für das kulturelle Leben wichtigen Einrichtungen – Stadthalle, Bibliothek und künftiges Rathaus – öffnen sich zum Stadtplatz, der durch eine Ladenarkade und eine Wohn- und Geschäftshausbebauung im Süden flankiert und gegenüber der Bahnlinie abgeschirmt wird.

Die Stadthalle in ihrer Gesamtheit will weniger „Haus" sein sondern in erster Linie verfügbarer Raum, der die Begegnung unterschiedlicher, am gesellschaftlichen Leben beteiligter Gruppen ermöglicht. Die einzelnen Bereiche stehen horizontal und vertikal zueinander in Beziehung und sind je nach Bedarf separat oder gemeinsam nutzbar.

Eine alle Geschosse verbindende Halle zwischen Langhaus und Veranstaltungssaal bildet die „gläserne Fuge" zwischen den Funktionsbereichen. Der räumliche Organismus lebt – und wird erlebt – nicht allein im Saal, sondern im Zusammenspiel aller Nutzungen.

Die mehrere Ebenen übergreifende Leselandschaft der Bibliothek präsentiert sich unter einem weit auskragenden Dachschirm und lädt die Öffentlichkeit zur Begegnung mit Buch und Medien ein.

Following communal reforms in 1978 the local authorities of Germering and Unterpfaffenhofen, west of Munich, were united and were joined together in 1991 as the town of Germering.

It was a stroke of luck that an empty piece of and was still available on the boundary line between the two communities, making it possible to build an architectural and cultural center for the young town, which would set it apart from its indifferent surroundings and adjacent arterial roads through the use of distinctive exterior edges.

The design allows for a variety of open spaces: the market square as an entrance; the "Agora" as a protected town square; a park-like stretch of greenery as a point of transition between the eastern residential areas; and the station square as a connecting link to the suburban railway system.

Diagonal paths connect these open spaces with each other and integrate them into the existing fabric of the town. All those institutions that are of relevance to the cultural life of the town – the civic hall, library and future town hall – open onto the town square, which to the south is flanked by a shopping arcade and a retail and residential building, and is shielded from the railway line opposite.

Overall, the town hall sees itself less as a "building" and more of an accessible space, which provides the various groups of citizens with a place to interact. The individual areas are connected both horizontally and vertically and can be used separately or combined as necessary.

A hall between the main building and the civic hall, which connects all floors, creates a "glass joint" between the functional spaces. The spatial organism lives – and is lived – not in the room alone but in the way the various areas interact.

The library's reading landscape, which extends over several levels, is situated beneath an extended cantilevered roof, and inspires the public to engage with books and media.

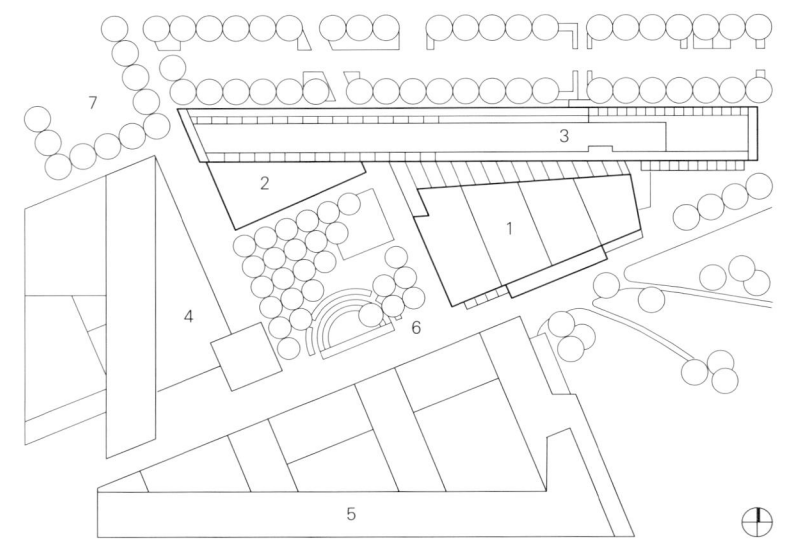

Lageplan / Site plan
1:4000

1 Stadthalle / Civic hall
2 Bibliothek / Library
3 Langhaus / Main building
4 Künftiges Rathaus
  Future town hall
5 Wohn- und Geschäftsbebauung mit Ladenarkade
  Retail and residential building with shopping arcade
6 Agora
7 Marktplatz / Market square

Hofgut Freiham bei Germering

The Freiham estate near Germering

Die 150m lange Fassade des Langhauses an der Landsberger Straße setzt als eindrucksvolle Großform einen eigenen Maßstab in dem kleinteilig bebauten Umfeld

The impressive scale of the 150-meter-long façade along Landsberger Strasse stands out in an area of otherwise small-scale development

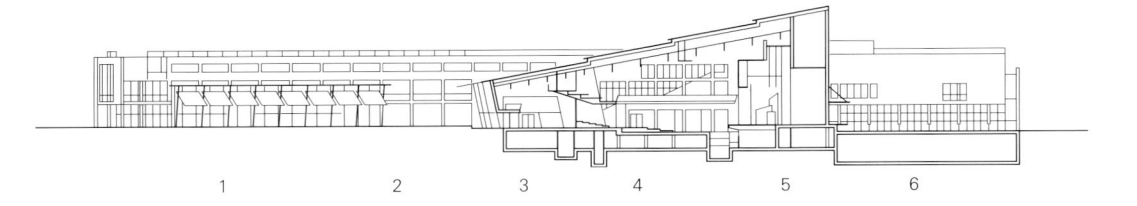

Schnitt / Section
1:1250

1. Bibliothek / Library
2. Langhaus / Main building
3. Saalfoyer / Foyer
4. Saal / Auditorium
5. Bühne / Stage
6. Technik / Equipment

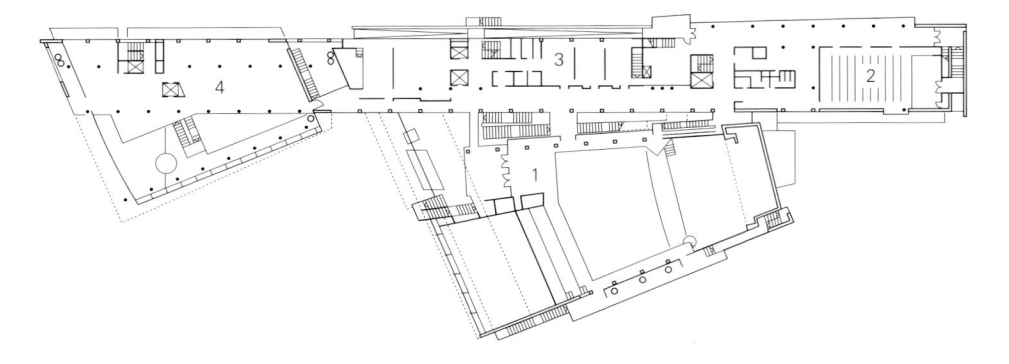

Obergeschoss / Upper floor
1:1250

1. Rang / Circle
2. Kleiner Saal
   Small auditorium
3. Tagungsbereich
   Conference area
4. Bibliothek / Library

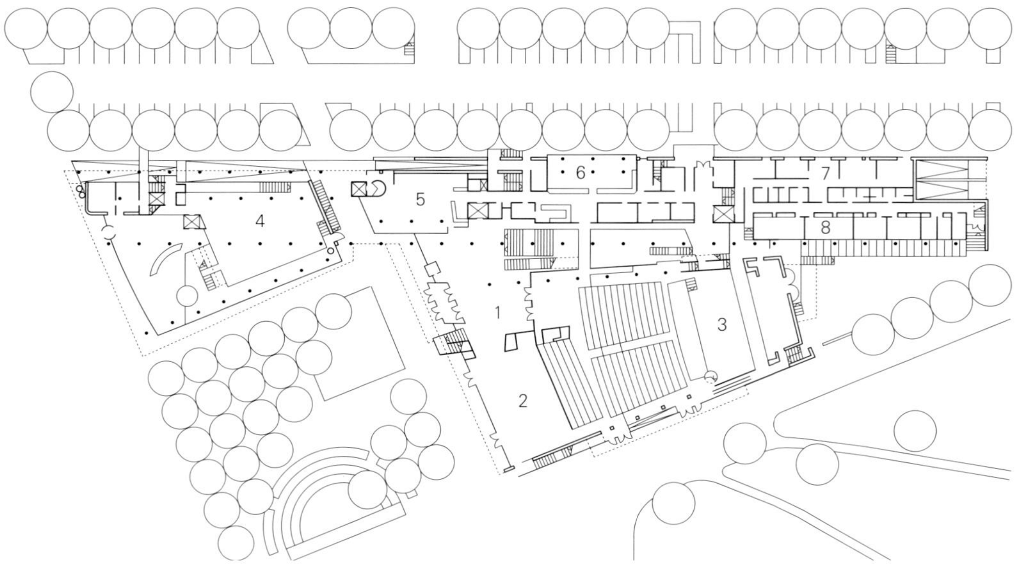

Erdgeschoss / Ground floor
1:1250

1. Eingang / Entrance
2. Saalfoyer / Foyer
3. Bühne / Stage
4. Bibliothek / Library
5. Restaurant / Restaurant
6. Küche / Kitchen
7. Verwaltung / Administration
8. Künstler / Artists

Rechts oben:
Die Straßenfassade ist in drei Schichten gestaffelt, die durch unterschiedliche Farbgebung voneinander abgesetzt sind

Unten:
Offene Baustrukturen bestimmen das Bild des Stadtplatzes mit Bibliothek, „gläserner Fuge" und Stadthalle

Right, above:
The street façade is divided up into three layers which are distinguishable through their different colors

Below:
Open structures dominate the town square where there is a library, "glass joint" and civic hall

Ortszentrum / Town Center Germering

Die „Gläserne Fuge" zwischen Langhaus und Saal verbindet als Eingangshalle und Foyer Orte, Funktionen und Ereignisse über alle Ebenen hinweg

Rechts:
Die Medienlandschaft der Bibliothek mit Rückzugsorten zum Lesen, Hören und Sehen

The "glass joint" between the main building and the auditorium functions as an entrance hall and foyer and unites the locations, functions and events on all levels

Right:
The library's media landscape with places for reading, listening and observing

85 Ortszentrum / Town Center Germering

Oben:
Die keilförmige Verjüngung in der „Gläsernen Fuge" erzeugt je nach Blickrichtung unterschiedliche Perspektiven

Mitte und rechts:
Der Große Saal lässt sich für die unterschiedlichsten Veranstaltungsformen nutzen. Seine Hülle ist zweischalig, außen teilweise verglast, innen mit wandelbaren Verdunkelungselementen ausgestattet, die auch für unterschiedliche akustische Anforderungen flexibel gesteuert werden können. Auszugspodeste schaffen optimale Sichtverhältnisse zur Bühne

Unten:
Gehobene und bodenständige Gastronomie in Restaurant und Bierkeller

Above:
The tapering staircase in the "glass joint" creates perspectives that vary according to the direction of view

Middle and right:
The main room can be used for a wide range of events. It has a double-shell sheath, which is partially glazed on the outside and is equipped on the inside with moveable blinds that can be adjusted to suit a variety of acoustic requirements. Retractable podiums provide optimum views of the stage

Below:
High-quality cuisine and down-to-earth cooking can be found in the restaurant and the bierkeller

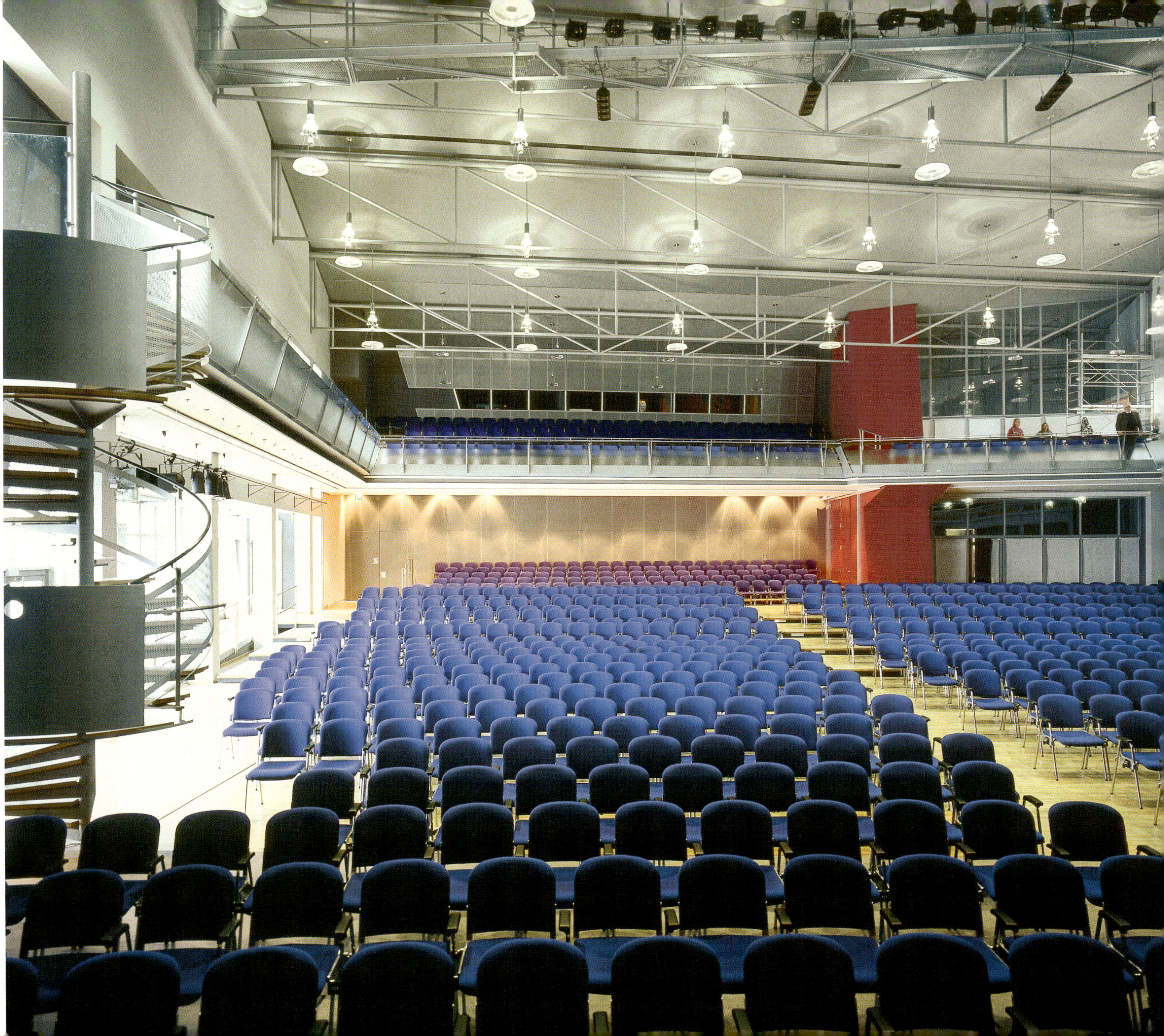

**Großvolière in der „Wilhelma" Stuttgart
1993**

**Large Aviary in the "Wilhelma" Stuttgart
1993**

Die Stuttgarter „Wilhelma", 1846 vom württembergischen König Wilhelm I. gegründet, nimmt durch ihre Verbindung von Botanik und Zoologie eine Sonderstellung unter den Tierparks ein. Als Programmpunkt der Internationalen Gartenbauausstellung 1993 sollte unter gleichzeitiger Berücksichtigung des wertvollen Baumbestands innerhalb einer bauhistorisch einmaligen Anlage die biotopgerechte Haltung und Zucht attraktiver Vogelarten gezeigt werden.

In zwölf Einzelgehegen mit dazu gehörigen Nebengebäuden sind verschiedene miteinander verträgliche Vogelfamilien untergebracht. Die Außenvolièren teilen sich den Raum unter dem ca. 3500m² großen, mit einem Feinnetz belegten Seilnetz, welches auch die seitliche Abgrenzung der Einzelvolièren bildet. Durch die größtmögliche Reduzierung der konstruktiven Elemente erlebt der Besucher auf seinem Gang durch die Vogelwelt das zierliche „Exponat Vogel" ungestört in seiner natürlichen Umgebung.

Zusammen mit den denkmalgeschützten Bauten der Wilhelma und der dominierenden Baumkulisse ist ein Ort von großer Leichtigkeit und Schwerelosigkeit entstanden, der mit seinen freischwingenden Formen das Thema Vogel und Fliegen aufnimmt und umsetzt.

As a result of its focus on both zoology and botany, the "Wilhelma" in Stuttgart – which was founded in 1846 by the king of Württemberg, Wilhelm I – enjoys a special reputation among zoological gardens. As part of the International Garden Exhibition in 1993, it showcased the way in which attractive species of birds are bred and kept in natural conditions, while respecting the valuable trees on the unique grounds.

Various compatible families of birds are housed in twelve individual enclosures, each with an adjoining building. Beneath a cable mesh that is covered with an even finer meshing, an area of 3,500 square meters is divided up into the outer aviaries. With construction elements reduced to an absolute minimum, visitors can experience birds undisturbed in their natural surroundings.

Together with the Wilhelma's listed buildings, and the imposing backdrop of trees, an area of tremendous lightness and ethereality has been created, which, along with its free-floating shapes, addresses and interprets the subject of birds and flying.

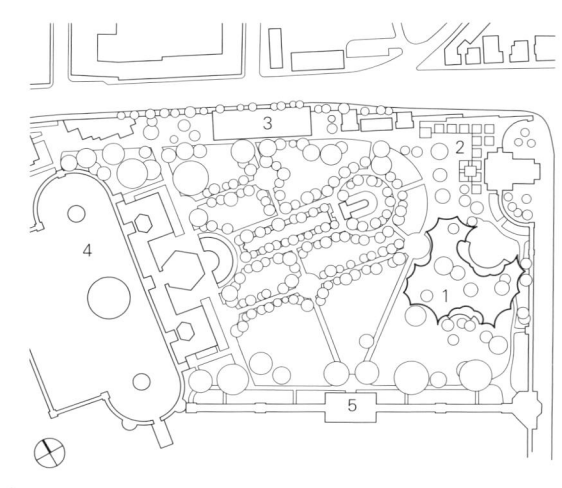

Lageplan / Site plan
1:5000

1 Großvolière / Large aviary
2 Restaurant
3 Amazonienhaus
  Amazonian House
4 Maurischer Garten
  Moorish garden
5 Gewächshäuser
  Greenhouses

Rechts:
Wie ein schimmerndes Gespinst erscheint die zarte Konstruktion zwischen dem alten Baumbestand der Wilhelma

Right:
Set among the old trees of the Wilhelma, the filigree structure looks like a shimmering web

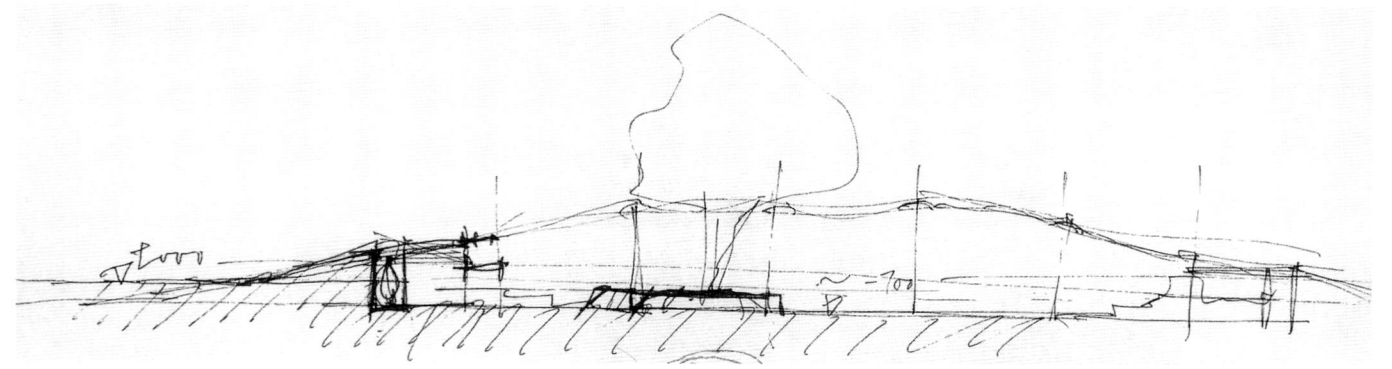

Spinnennetz / Spider web

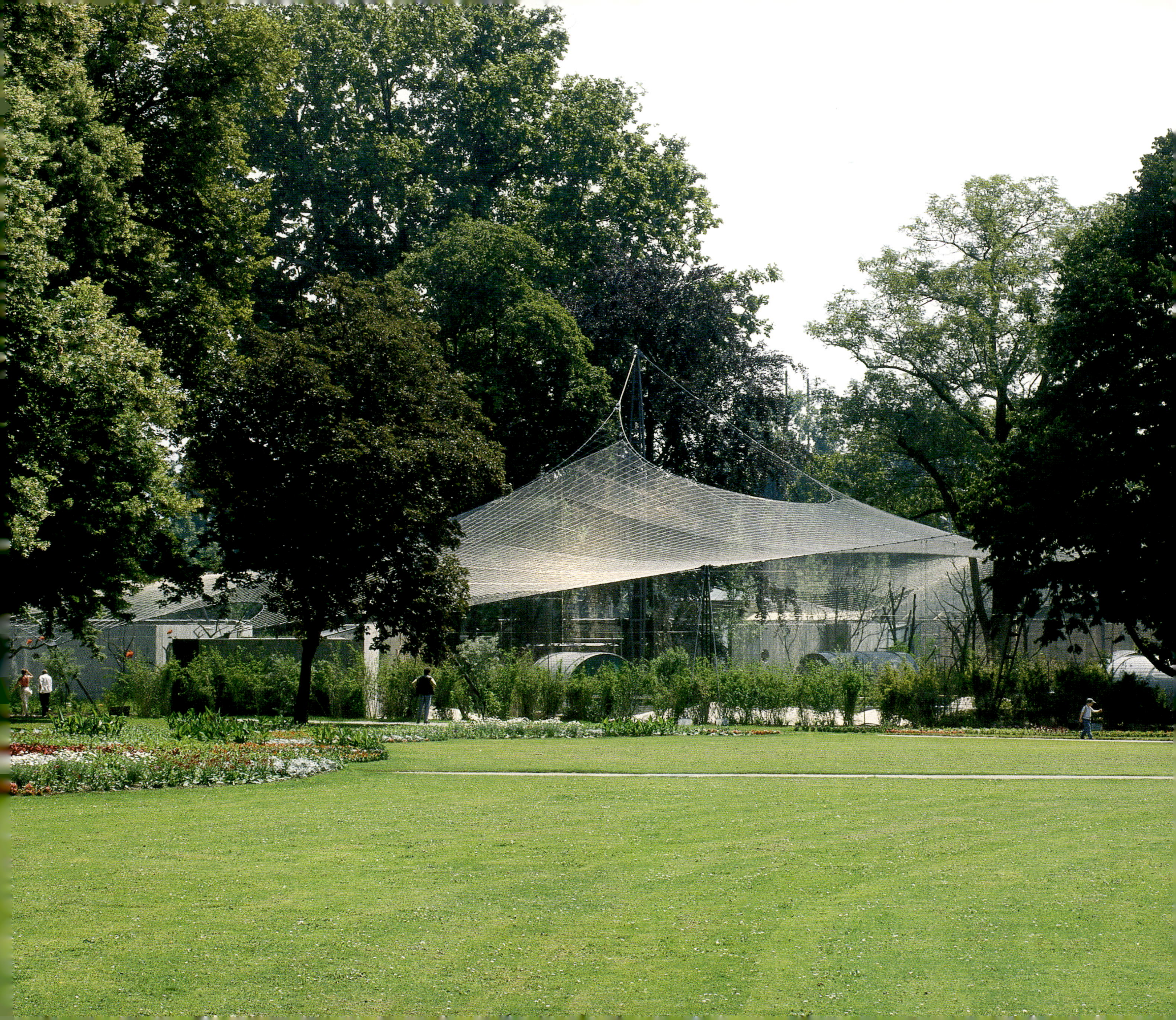

Computermodell

Das durch Randseile eingefasste Seilnetz wird in den Hochpunkten von abgespannten Stahl-Gittermasten gehalten; Feinnetze bilden die Gehege der Vogelfamilien

Die geschwungenen Linien der Netzkonstruktion spielen mit der maurisch anmutenden, historisierenden Architektur aus dem 19. Jh.

Computer model

The cable mesh, enclosed by edge cables, is secured at the top by suspended steel-grid masts; the enclosures for the bird families are made of fine mesh

The curved lines of the mesh construction hark back to the Moorish style historical architecture of the nineteenth century

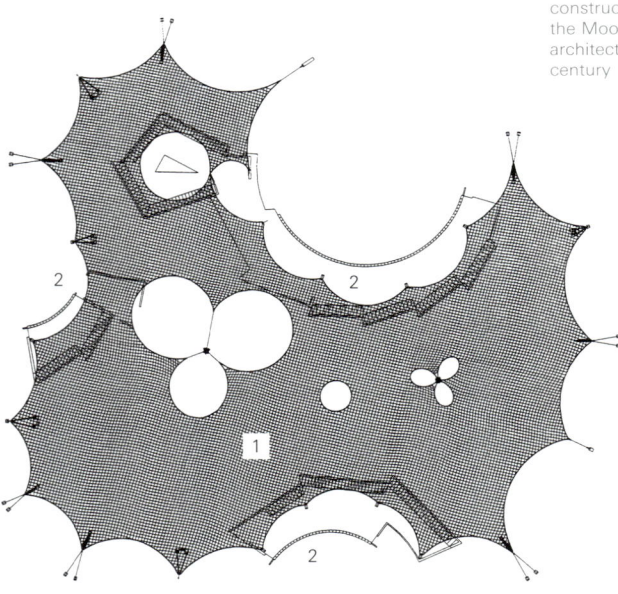

Grundriss / Plan
1:750

1 Seilnetz / Cable mesh
2 Vogelquartiere / Aviaries

Ingenieurskizze zu konstruktiven Knotenpunkten

Engineer's sketch for constructional nodes

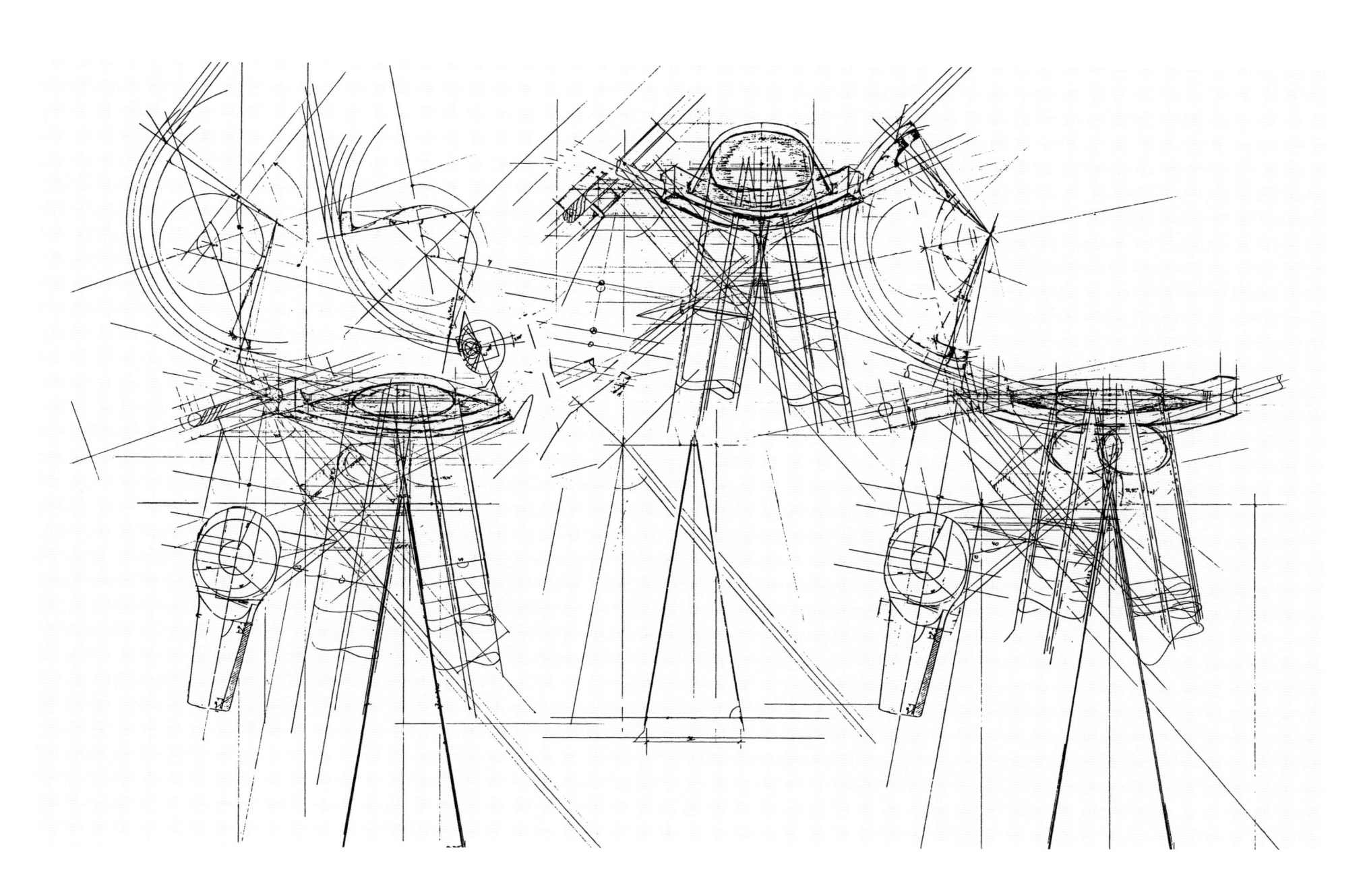

Großvolière in der „Wilhelma" / Large Aviary in the "Wilhelma" Stuttgart

Der Besucher begegnet auf seinem Weg durch die Gehege den Vögeln ohne trennende Zwischennetze

Visitors, on their way through the enclosures, encounter birds without any dividing mesh

Schwerelos umspielt die Netzfläche den alten Baumbestand. Frei geschwungene Wege leiten den Besucher durch die Gehegelandschaft. Jeglicher Eindruck eines Käfigs wird vermieden

Seemingly weightless, the mesh plays around the old trees. Meandering footpaths lead visitors through the enclosures. There is absolutely nothing of a cage about it

Theater Hof
1994
Wettbewerb 1987   1. Preis

Theater Hof
1994
Competition 1987   1st prize

Die architektonische Gestalt des Bauwerks zwischen einem Gewerbegebiet und dem parkartigen Freiraum, zwischen Theater und Freiheitshalle, entwickelt sich aus der baulichen Umsetzung der Inhalte eines Drei-Sparten-Theaters – Sprechtheater, Musiktheater und Ballett –, das neben Aufführungen im eigenen Haus zusammen mit den Hofer Symphonikern eine Vielzahl von Gastspielen in Theatern der Region Oberfranken und Vogtland gibt.

Der Theaterbau setzt sich aus dem Zuschauer- und dem Produktionsbereich zusammen. Diese Gliederung ist sowohl an der Anordnung der Baukörper als auch an der Gestaltung der Innenräume ablesbar. Über Bühne, Studio und Orchesterraum treten Schauspieler und Publikum in direkten Kontakt zueinander.

Der Produktionstrakt bildet die räumliche Grenze zwischen Gewerbegebiet und Theaterwiese, zu welcher sich der Zuschauerbereich über das Foyer und den Eingangsbereich hin öffnet.

Im Unterschied zum transparenten und einladenden Foyer, das dem Publikum gewissermaßen als Bühne dient, ist der Zuschauerraum mit 600 Sitzplätzen ganz auf den eigentlichen Ort des Geschehens, die Theaterbühne, ausgerichtet. Der Längstrakt mit Künstler- und Verwaltungsbereich, Großwerkstätten und Lager ist nach den betrieblichen Anforderungen der Produktion organisiert.

Zusammen mit der Freiheitshalle ist mit dem Hofer Theaterbau nicht nur für die Stadt selbst, sondern für die ganze Region ein kultureller Schwerpunkt entstanden, wofür der mit einem Metallgitter umkleidete und abends illuminierte Bühnenturm ein weithin sichtbares Zeichen ist.

The architectural design of this building – located between an industrial estate and a park-like stretch of open space, between the theater and the Freiheitshalle – derives from the constructional requirements of a tripartite theater for the spoken word, music and ballet. In addition to performing on its own premises, the ensemble makes a number of guest appearances, together with members of the Hof Symphony Orchestra, in theaters throughout the Upper Franconia and Vogtland regions.

The theater building is composed of the auditorium and the production area. This division is clearly recognizable both from the way in which the building elements are arranged and the design of the interior. Actors and the audience are in direct contact with each other via the stage, the studio and the orchestra pit.

The production tract marks the border between the industrial estate and the theater grounds, on which the auditorium opens out via the foyer and entrance area.

In contrast to the transparent and inviting foyer, which to a certain extent serves as a stage for the spectators, the 600-seat auditorium focuses on where the action really takes place: the stage. The longitudinal tract, with its administrative area, artists' quarters, large production workshops and storage rooms, is organized according to the theater's operational and production requirements.

Together with the Freiheitshalle, the theater in Hof has created a cultural focal point not only for the town but for the whole region; the stage tower, veiled with a metal grille, creates a highly visible symbol when it is illuminated at night.

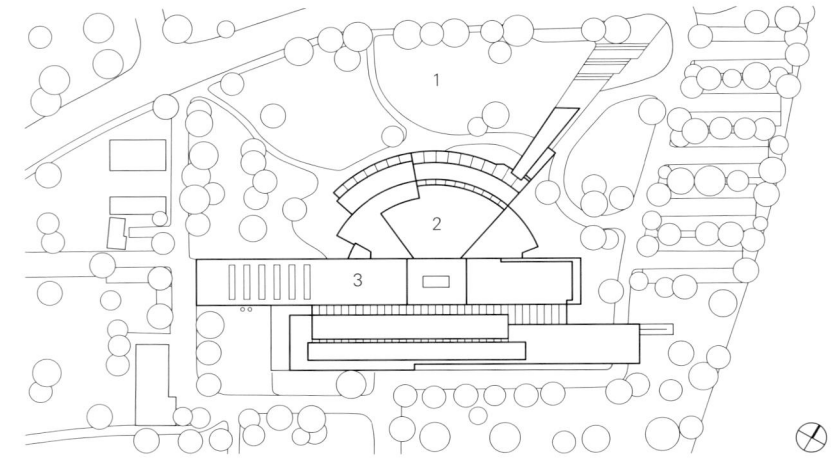

Lageplan / Site plan
1:2500

1 Theaterwiese
   Theater grounds
2 Zuschauerbereich
   Auditorium
3 Produktionsbereich
   Production area

Rechts:
Das Theater als festlicher und einladender Ort erhebt sich selbstbewusst über die Theaterwiese und setzt mit dem abends illuminierten Bühnenturm ein weithin sichtbares Zeichen

Right:
As a festive area and welcoming venue, the theater rises boldly above the theater grounds. The illuminated stage tower creates a clearly visible symbol at night

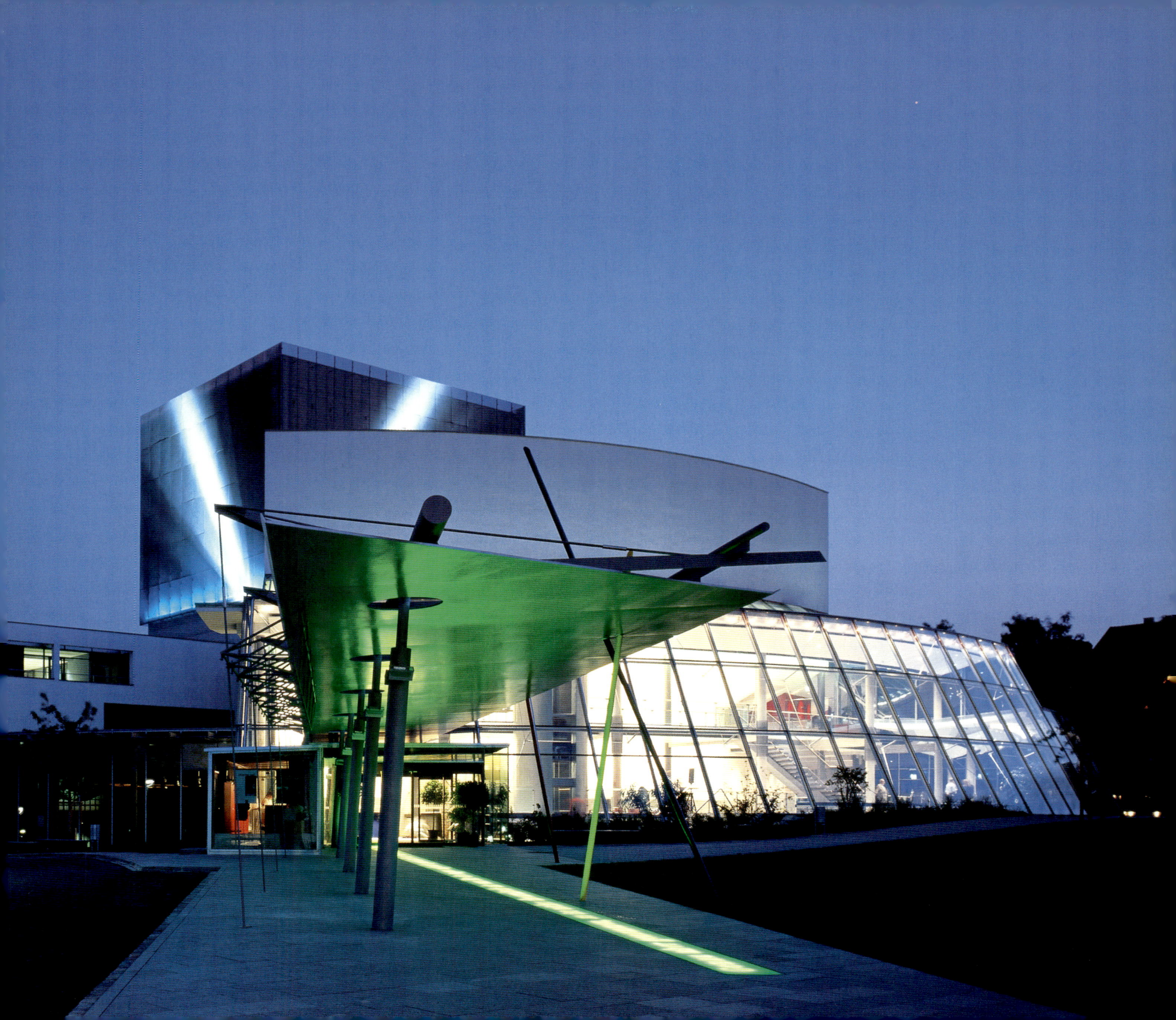

Querschnitt / Cross section
1:1000

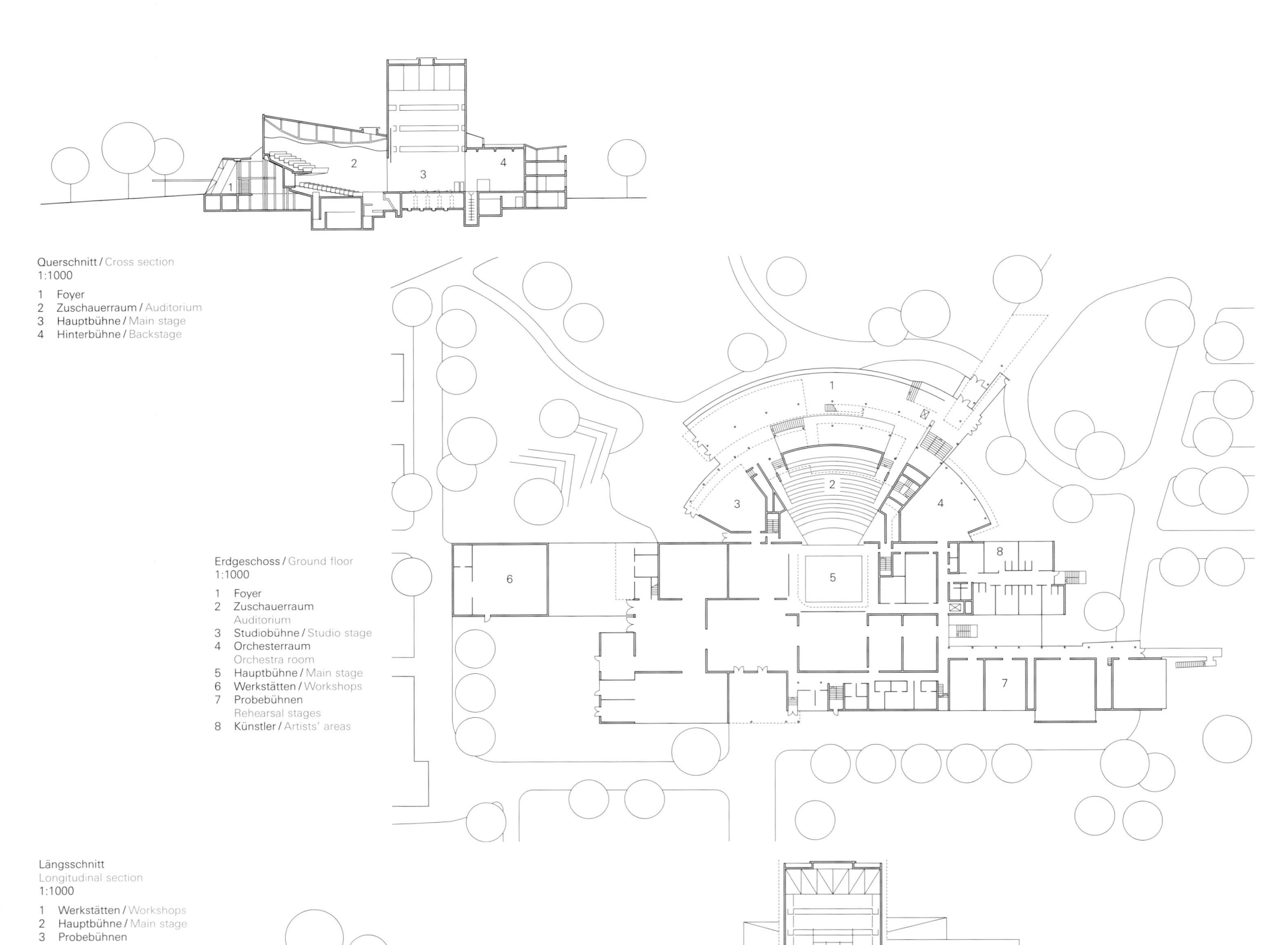

1 Foyer
2 Zuschauerraum / Auditorium
3 Hauptbühne / Main stage
4 Hinterbühne / Backstage

Erdgeschoss / Ground floor
1:1000

1 Foyer
2 Zuschauerraum
  Auditorium
3 Studiobühne / Studio stage
4 Orchesterraum
  Orchestra room
5 Hauptbühne / Main stage
6 Werkstätten / Workshops
7 Probebühnen
  Rehearsal stages
8 Künstler / Artists' areas

Längsschnitt
Longitudinal section
1:1000

1 Werkstätten / Workshops
2 Hauptbühne / Main stage
3 Probebühnen
  Rehearsal stages

96

Konzentrisch legt sich das transparente Hauptfoyer, welches alle Ebenen verbindet, um den keilförmigen Zuschauerraum. Das Rangfoyer als frei in den Raum eingehängte Galerie ist über Stege mit dem Saalkörper verbunden

Folgende Seiten:
Eine komplexe Bühnentechnik bestimmt die Welt hinter dem Eisernen Vorhang. Im Gegensatz dazu ist der Zuschauerraum auf das Bühnengeschehen konzentriert

Doppelseite:
Die Silhouette der Anlage entwickelt sich aus den funktionalen Zusammenhängen: Wege über die Theaterwiese, transparentes Foyer mit Ranggalerie, asymmetrischer Zuschauerraum, Bühnenturm, Shed-Halle des Malersaals, Schornsteine des Blockheizkraftwerks

A transparent main foyer connects all levels and wraps itself concentrically around the wedge-shaped auditorium. The circle foyer, a gallery that hangs freely in the foyer, is connected to the body via walkways

Following pages:
Complicated stage machinery determines what goes on behind the iron curtain. In contrast, what takes place on stage is the focus of the auditorium

Double page:
The silhouette of the complex is created by functional connections: paths across the theater grounds; the transparent foyer with circle gallery; an asymmetrical auditorium; the stage tower; the shed hall of the painting room; the chimneys of the district heating plant

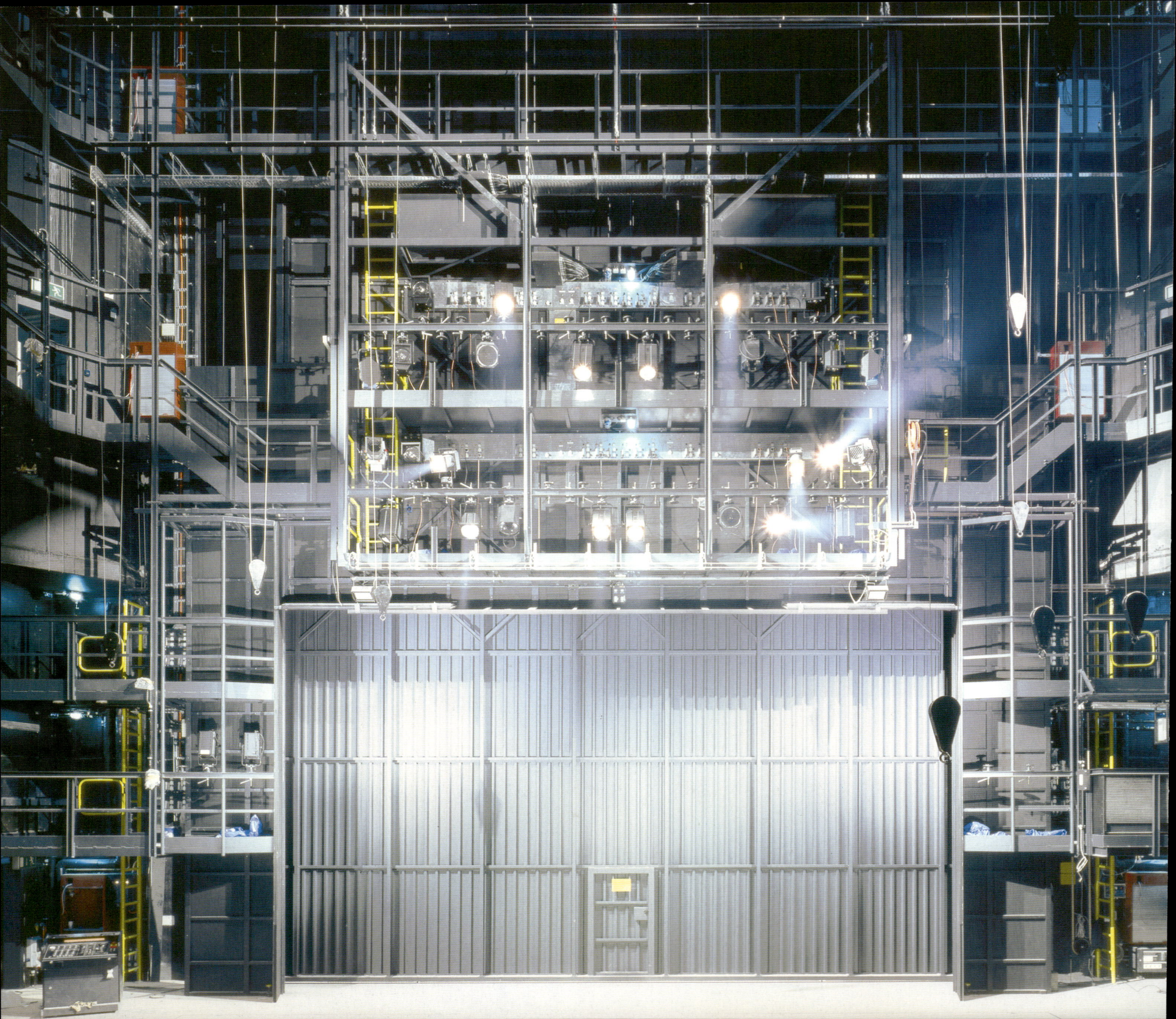

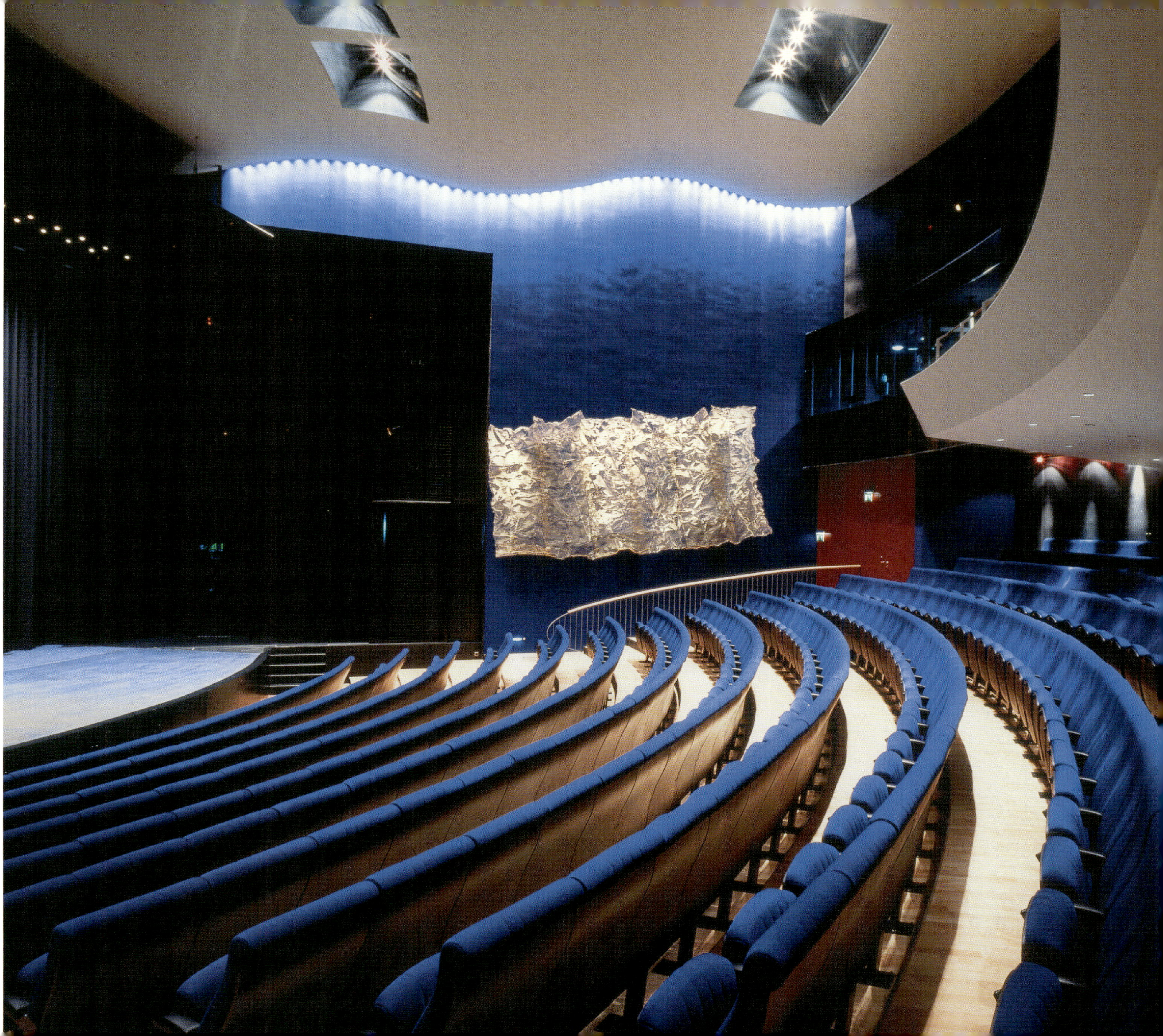

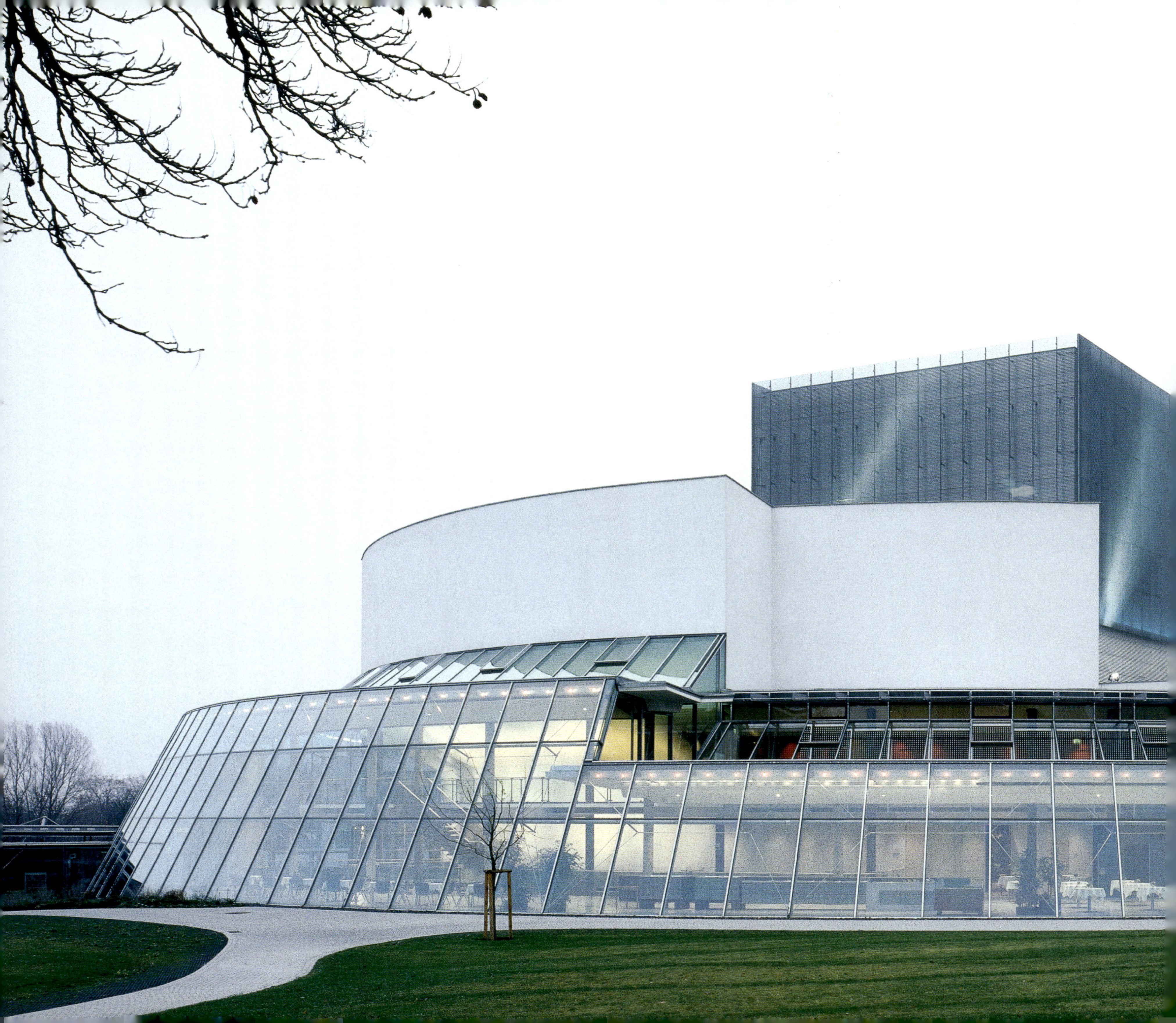

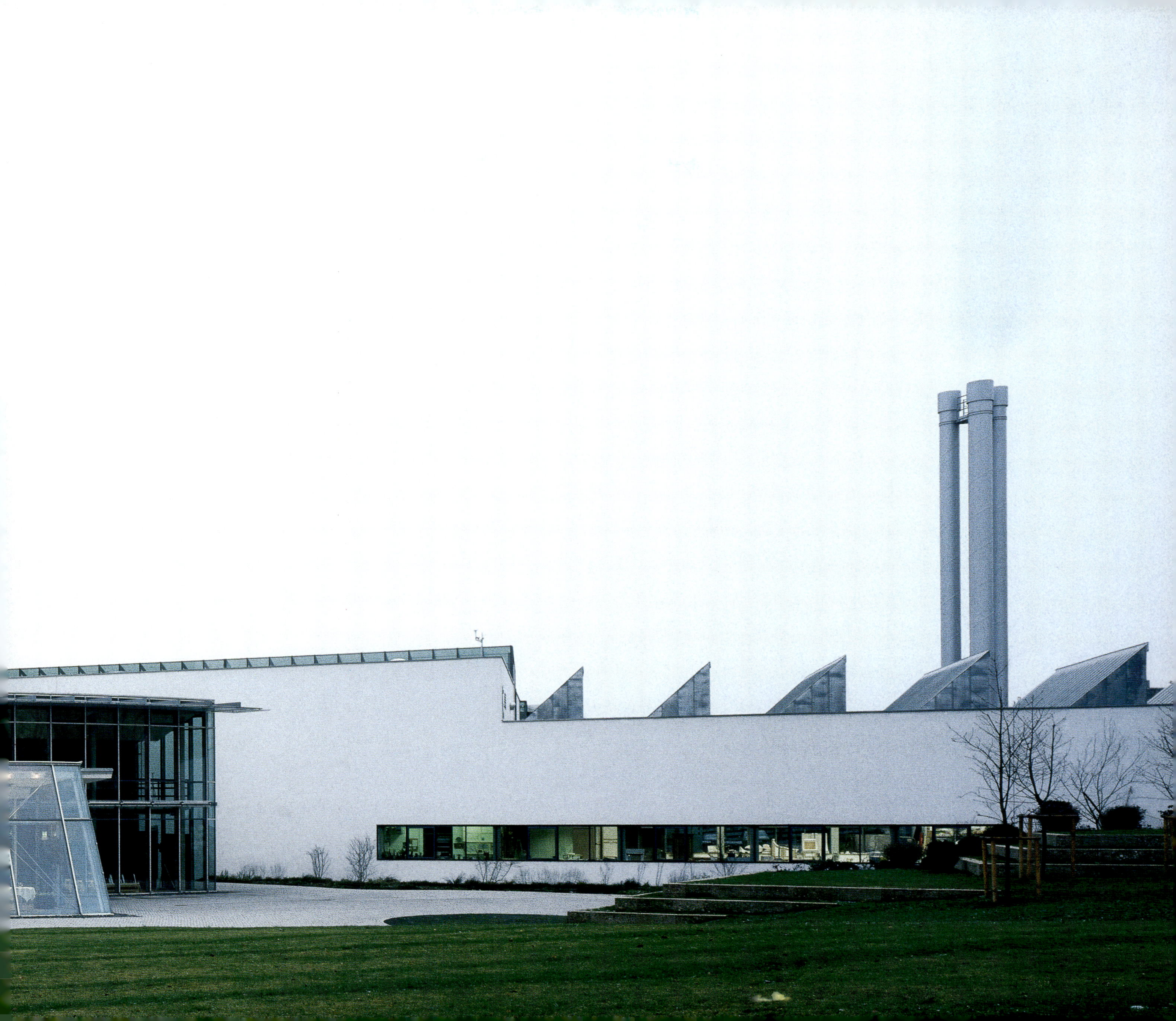

Ruhrfestspielhaus Recklinghausen
Umbau und Anbau
1998
Wettbewerb 1993   1. Preis

Ruhrfestspielhaus Recklinghausen
Conversion and extension
1998
Competition 1993   1st prize

Lageplan / Site plan
1:5000
1 Festspielhaus
2 Dachschirm über dem neuen Foyer / Covering roof screen above new foyer
3 Festspielwiese / Festival grounds

Nach Kriegsende im Jahr 1946 hatten Recklinghauser Bergleute Hamburger Schauspielern mit Kohle ausgeholfen. 1947 kamen diese zurück nach Recklinghausen, um sich zu bedanken: „Kunst gegen Kohle" – damit waren die Ruhrfestspiele geboren. Mit dem Umbau des 1965 eröffneten Ruhrfestspielhauses, eines mächtigen, mit Basaltstein verkleideten Betonkubus, der seither Stätte dieser renommierten Festspiele ist, wurden Funktionsprobleme behoben und Voraussetzungen für ein breites Veranstaltungsspektrum geschaffen. Das transparente, schaufensterartige Eingangsfoyer, das den bisherigen, schwer lastenden Eingangsbereich ersetzt, verbindet alle Ebenen und betont zusammen mit einem weit ausgreifenden, leichten Dachschirm über der „Festspielwiese" die optische und ideelle Verknüpfung mit der Stadt am Fuße des Festspielhügels.

Als räumliche Erweiterung des nach innen gerichteten Theatersaals wird der Stadt auf diese Weise ein bisher fehlender, attraktiver Verweil- und Kommunikationsraum geboten, – insbesondere für Tagungen und Kongresse. Mit 1050 Plätzen und einer Bühne von 1200m² ist der Theatersaal einer der größten in Nordrhein-Westfalen. Hinzugekommen sind ein neuer Veranstaltungssaal mit ca. 700m² Nutzfläche auf der gleichen Ebene und vier neue Tagungssäle mit je 185m² auf der Rangebene.

Das neue Foyer ist aus der Struktur der sechziger Jahre, ihren Proportionen und Linien entwickelt. Die Materialien sind bewusst kontrastreich eingesetzt, um diesen Dialog zu betonen. Aus dem Zusammenwirken von Alt und Neu, von Beton- und filigraner Stahl/Glas-Architektur, mit Respekt vor dem Überlieferten, bezieht das umgebaute Festspielhaus seine neue Identität.

In 1946, in the shortages after the end of the Second World War, Recklinghausen miners helped out Hamburg actors with coal. In 1947, the actors returned to Recklinghausen to say thank you and "Art for Coal," the Ruhrfestspiele festival, was born. In 1965 the Ruhrfestspielhaus was built, a massive concrete cube faced with basalt, which has housed the renowned Festspiele ever since. The 1998 conversion eliminated several practical problems with the theater, and created suitable conditions for presenting a wide range of events. The transparent, display-like entrance foyer, which replaces the former weighty entrance area now links all levels, and works with a light, extensive canopy above the festival grounds to provide the ideal optical and conceptual connection to the town at the foot of the festival hill.

By expanding the inward-facing theatre, the town has gained an attractive venue for various events, especially conferences and congresses, which it had lacked. Seating 1,050 and with a 1,200 square meter stage, the theater auditorium is one of the largest in North Rhine-Westphalia. Other additions include a new events room with some 700 square meters of usable area at the same level, and four new conference rooms, each of 185 square meters, at dress circle level.

The new foyer is developed from the design, proportions, and lines of the 1960s. This dialogue is further emphasized by the deliberate use of materials that create a stark contrast. The converted theater takes its new identity from the interplay of old and new, concrete and filigree steel/glass architecture, carried out with respect for the existing features.

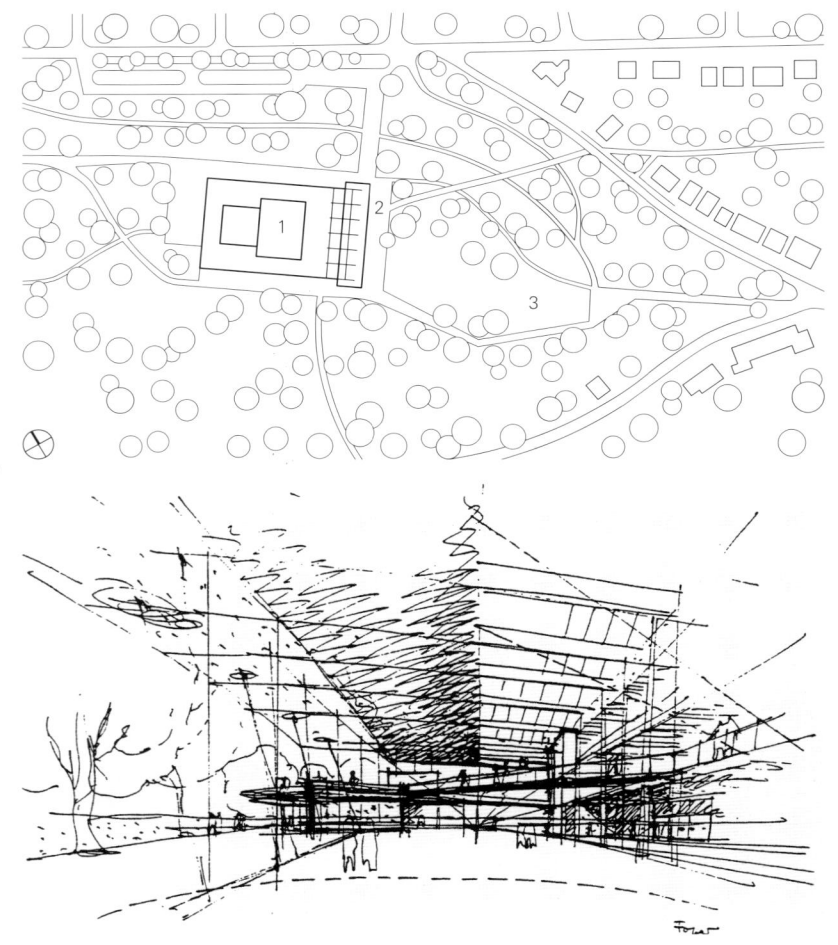

Oben:
Skizze aus der Konzeptphase des Wettbewerbs

Above:
Sketch from competition concept phase

Nach dem Umbau öffnet sich das Festspielhaus über seine filigrane Glasfassade zu Park und Stadt. Mit dieser Geste wird das erweiterte Veranstaltungsspektrum auch nach außen deutlich. Im Vordergrund eine Skulptur von Henry Moore

Following structural alterations, including the addition of an elegant glass façade and expansive canopy, the Festspielhaus now looks out towards the park and town. This gesture serves to reflect the expanded program of events. In the foreground a sculpture by Henry Moore

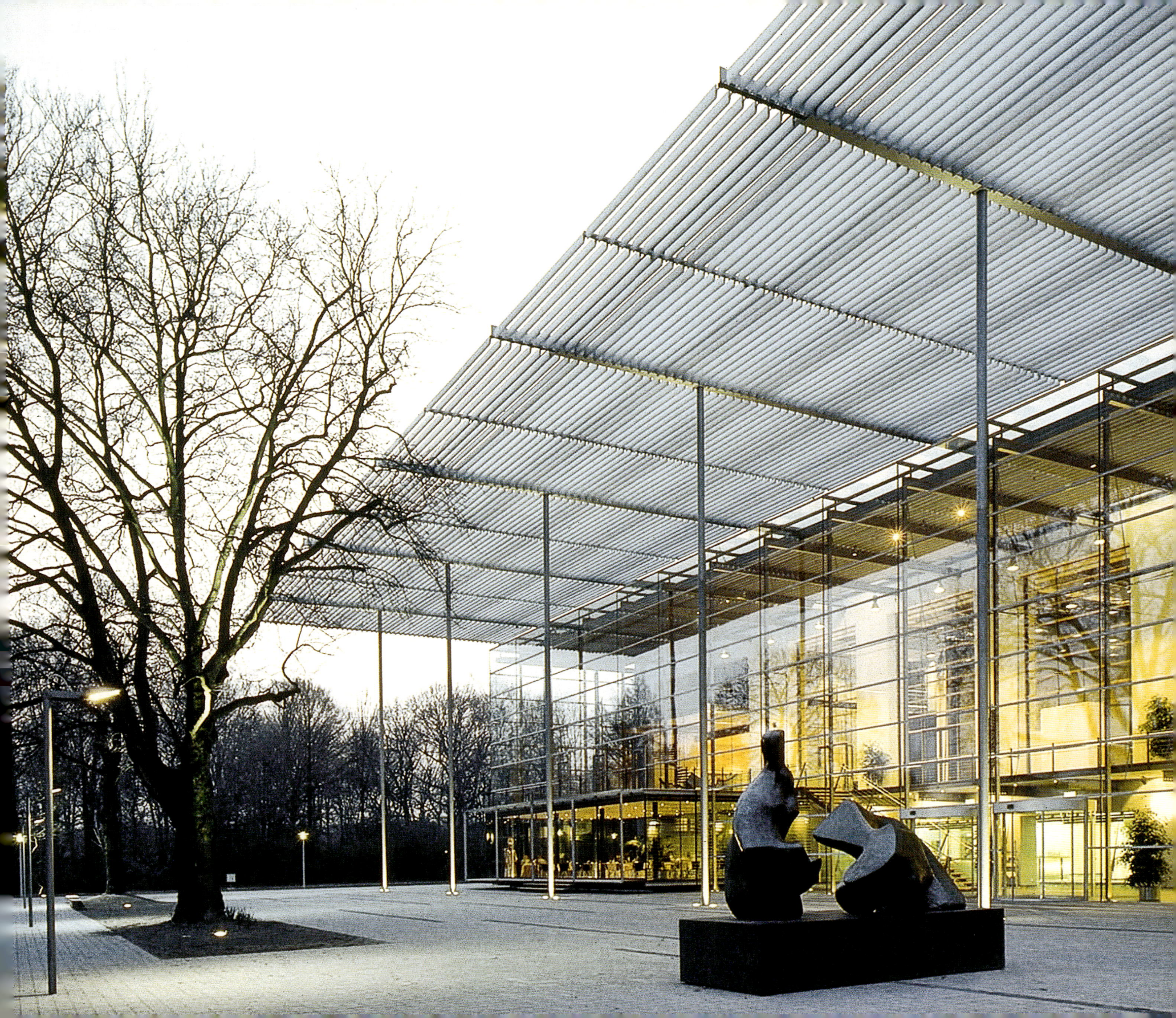

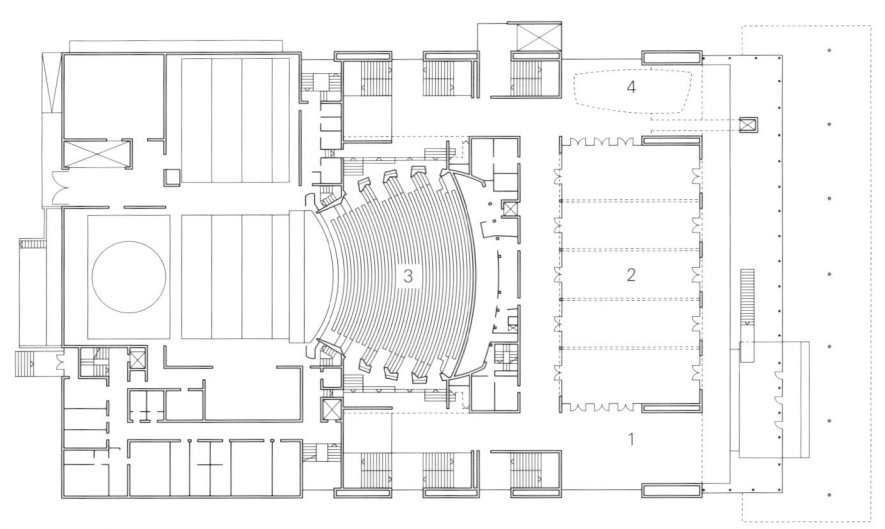

Obergeschoss / Upper floor
1:1000

1 Foyer
2 Mehrzwecksaal / Multi-purpose hall
3 Theatersaal / Theater auditorium
4 Seminarraum / Seminar room

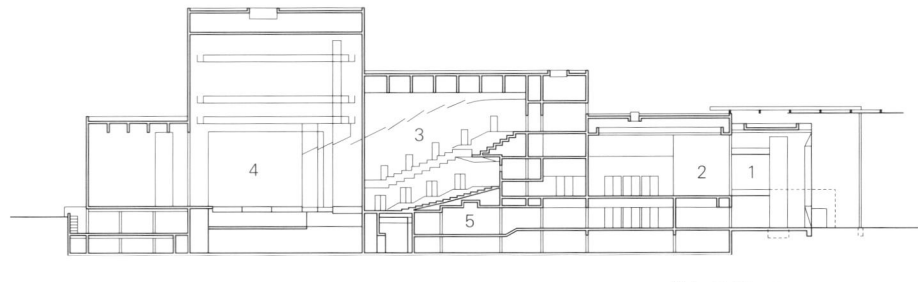

Schnitt / Section
1:1000

1 Foyer
2 Mehrzwecksaal / Multi-purpose hall
3 Theatersaal / Theater auditorium
4 Bühne / Stage
5 Garderobe / Cloakroom

Erdgeschoss / Ground floor
1:1000

1 Foyer
2 Garderobe / Cloakroom
3 Restaurant / Restaurant

Das Festspielhaus, erbaut 1956 bis 1965 von Ganteführer und Hannes, mit seiner wuchtigen Eingangsfront

The Festspielhaus, built between 1956 and 1965, with its massive front entrance

An der Nahtstelle zwischen
Alt und Neu begegnen sich
die beiden unterschiedlichen
Architektursprachen innerhalb
der Verbindlichkeit einer
gemeinsamen strukturellen
Geometrie

At the interface between
old and new, the two diverse
architectural languages also
converge, bound together
by a joint formal geometry

Links:
Aus dem Hintergrund schiebt sich der Seminarraum als plastisches Gebilde in die rechteckige Struktur des Foyers

Rechts:
Über das Foyer und den Mehrzwecksaal im Obergeschoss geht der Blick in die Tiefe bis zur roten Rückwand des Theatersaals

Left:
Like a sculptural element, the seminar room emerges from the background into the rectangular structure of the foyer

Right:
The gaze travels through the foyer and multipurpose hall on the first floor to the red wall at the back of the theater auditorium

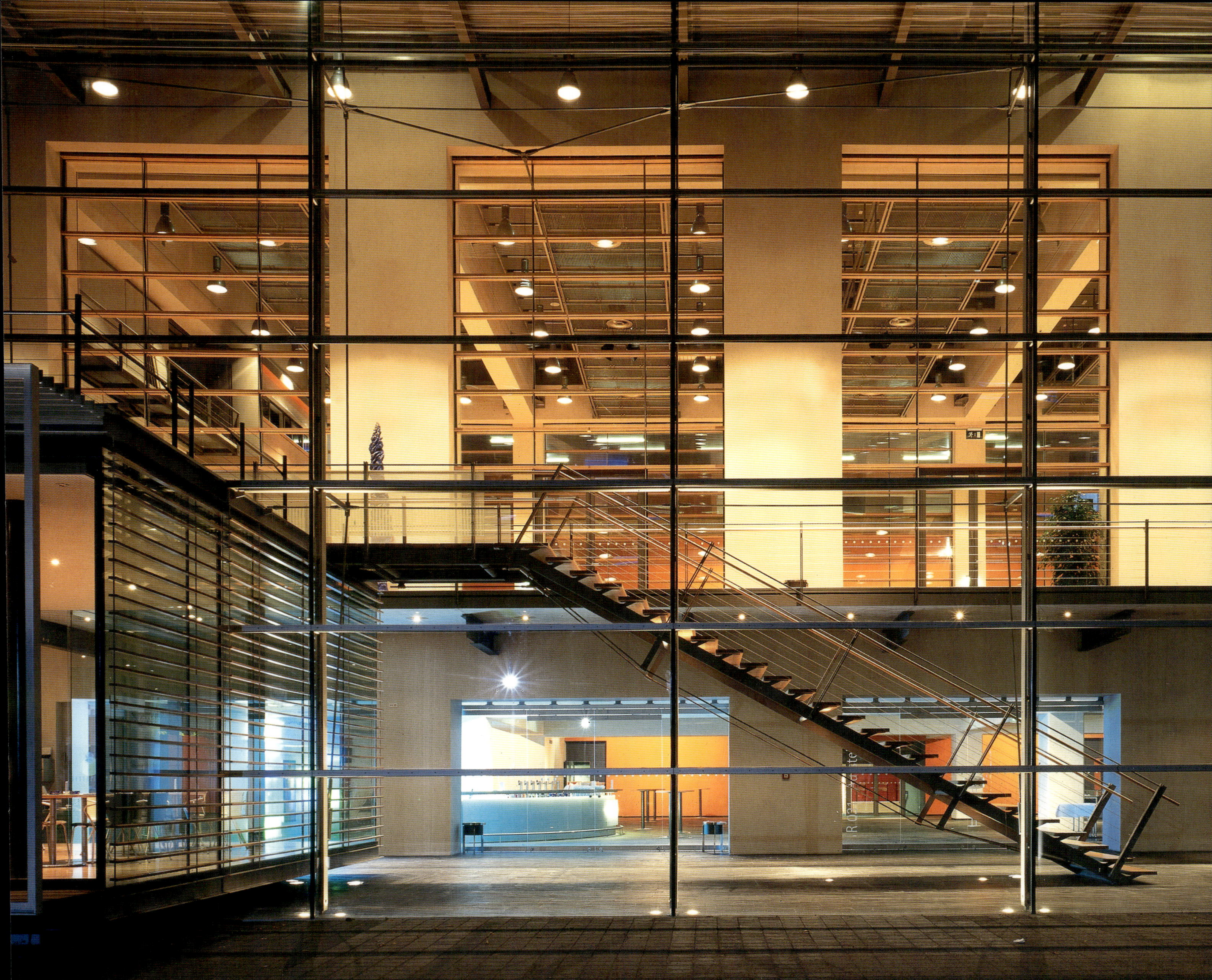

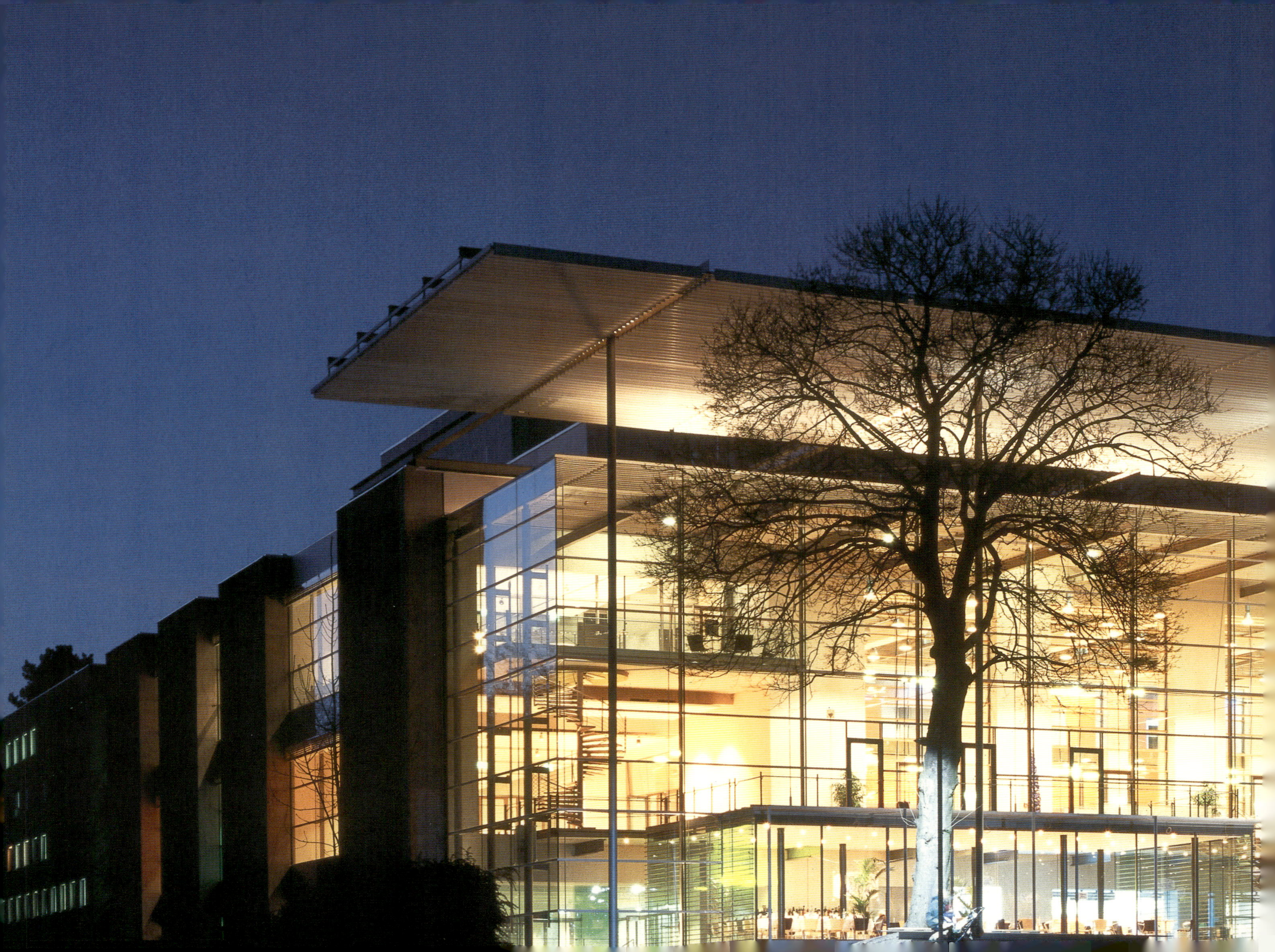

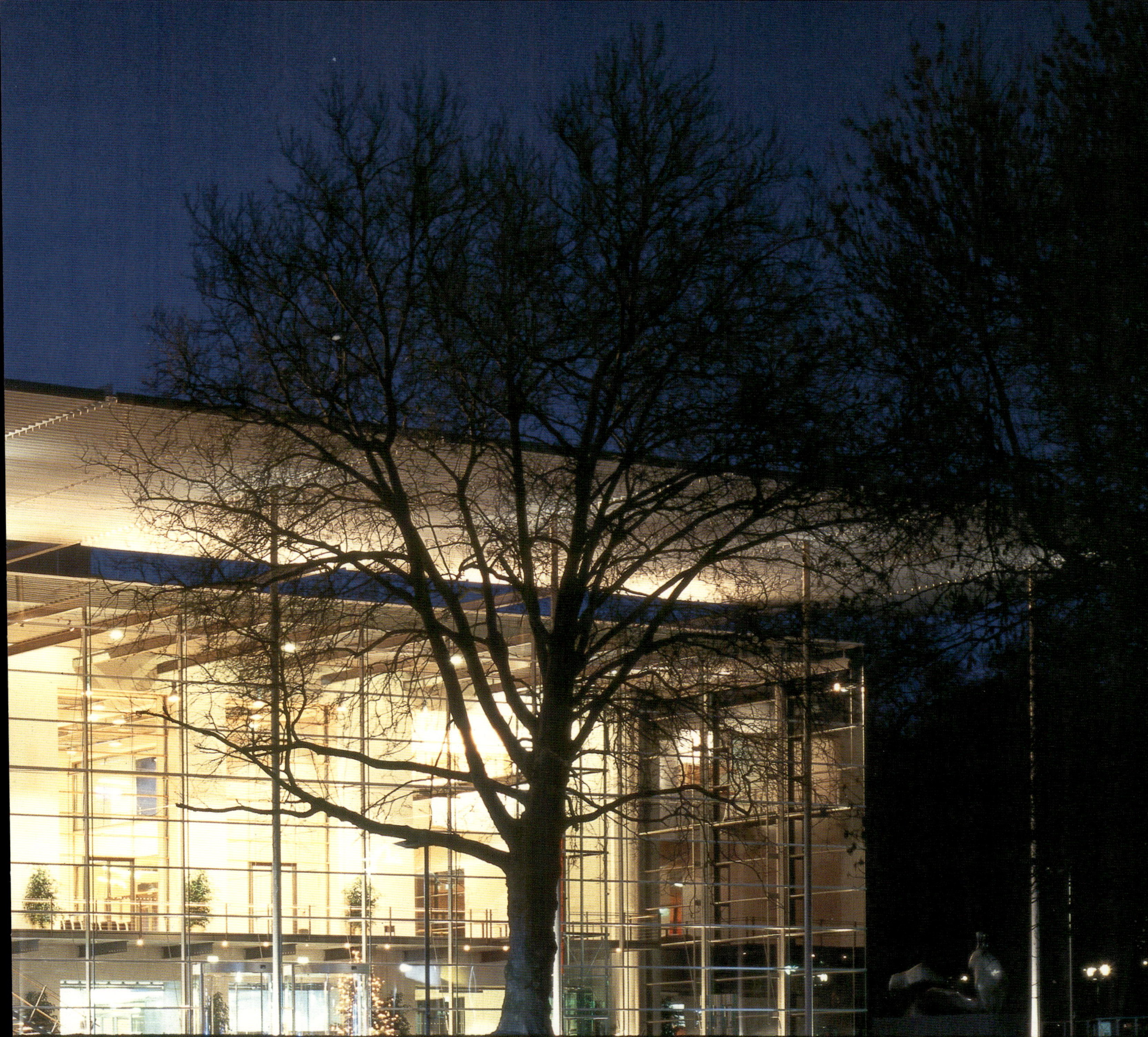

**Wohnen am Innenhafen Duisburg
1998**

**Living by the Inner Harbor Duisburg
1998**

Der städtebauliche Masterplan für den Innenhafen Duisburg, ein Projekt der Internationalen Bauausstellung „IBA Emscher Park", bot die Chance, ein städtisches Quartier mit hohem Wohnwert in unmittelbarem Anschluss an das Wasser und die Innenstadt zu entwickeln.

Die bislang realisierte Gebäudezeile ist gekennzeichnet durch ihre besondere Lage zwischen neuem Stadtpark im Westen und der Gracht im Osten, wie auch durch den großzügigen Grundstückszuschnitt, der einen parkartigen Grünraum im künftigen Blockinneren ermöglicht. Fußwege öffnen und vernetzen das Quartier mit seiner Umgebung, der Stadt und dem Hafengelände.

Die nach beiden Seiten orientierten, offenen Wohnungen profitieren sowohl von der sonnigen Straßenseite mit Blick auf die Gracht als auch über vorgelagerte Veranden, die wechselweise als Wintergärten oder Balkone ausgebildet sind, von der grünen Hofseite. Verglaste Treppenhäuser gliedern die Gebäudelänge und lassen das Flair dieser holländisch anmutenden „Wasserstraße" ins Gebäude hineinspielen.

The architectural master plan for the inner harbor in Duisburg, a project for the "Emscher Park International Building Exhibition", provided an opportunity to develop an urban area with superior living conditions right next to both the water and the downtown district.

The row of buildings constructed to date is characterized by its special location between the new city park in the west and the canal in the east. The buildings are also defined by their generous plots of land, which create a park-like area of greenery in the inner courtyard of the block. Footpaths open up the neighborhood and connect it to the surrounding area, the city and the harbor.

The open-plan apartments have views on two sides: The sunny street side looks out over the canal, while the courtyard side has extending verandas with alternating conservatories and balconies. Length-wise, glazed staircases divide up the building, allowing the flair of the Dutch-style "waterway" to intrude on the building.

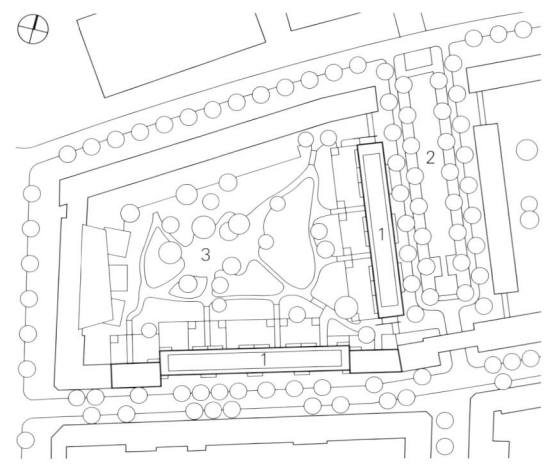

Lageplan / Site plan
1:3000

1 Wohnzeilen
  Row of buildings
2 Gracht / Canal
3 Gartenhof
  Garden courtyard

Schnitt / Section
1:500

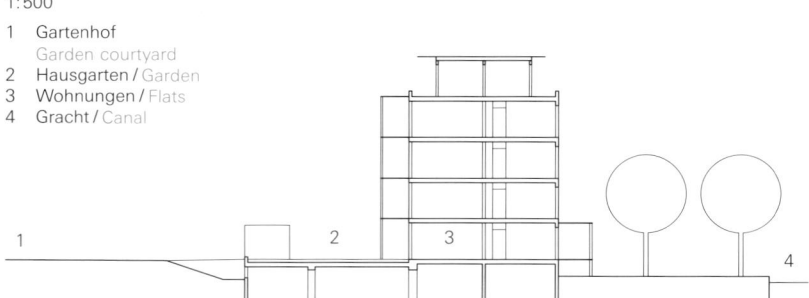

1 Gartenhof
  Garden courtyard
2 Hausgarten / Garden
3 Wohnungen / Flats
4 Gracht / Canal

Hiialankaari Apartmenthaus
Espoo, Finnland, 1983
Gullichsen Kairamo Vormala

Die Treppenhäuser korrespondieren mit der spiegelnden Wasserfläche der Gracht und betonen zusammen mit den vorgesetzten, leicht aufgeständerten Loggien die besondere Qualität des Wohnens am Wasser

The staircases harmonize with the reflecting surface of water in the canal and, together with the protruding, slightly raised loggias, emphasizes the unique quality of living by the water

Links:
Der aufgelockerte Gartenhof mit Spielmöglichkeiten bildet das Gegenstück zur eher ruhigen Straßenseite an der Gracht

Rechts:
Die Seite zum Gartenhof zeigt wechselweise Wintergärten, Loggien oder Balkone, welche die lebendige Gliederung der Zeile ausmachen

Left:
The open garden courtyard, with its opportunity for playing, is the antithesis of the more peaceful side, which looks out onto the canal road

Right:
On the courtyard side, alternating conservatories, loggias or balconies mark the lively division between the row of buildings

Erdgeschoss / Ground floor
1:1000

1   Wohnungen / Living area
2   Garten / Garden
3   Durchgang / Passage
4   Gracht / Canal
5   Gartenhof
    Garden courtyard

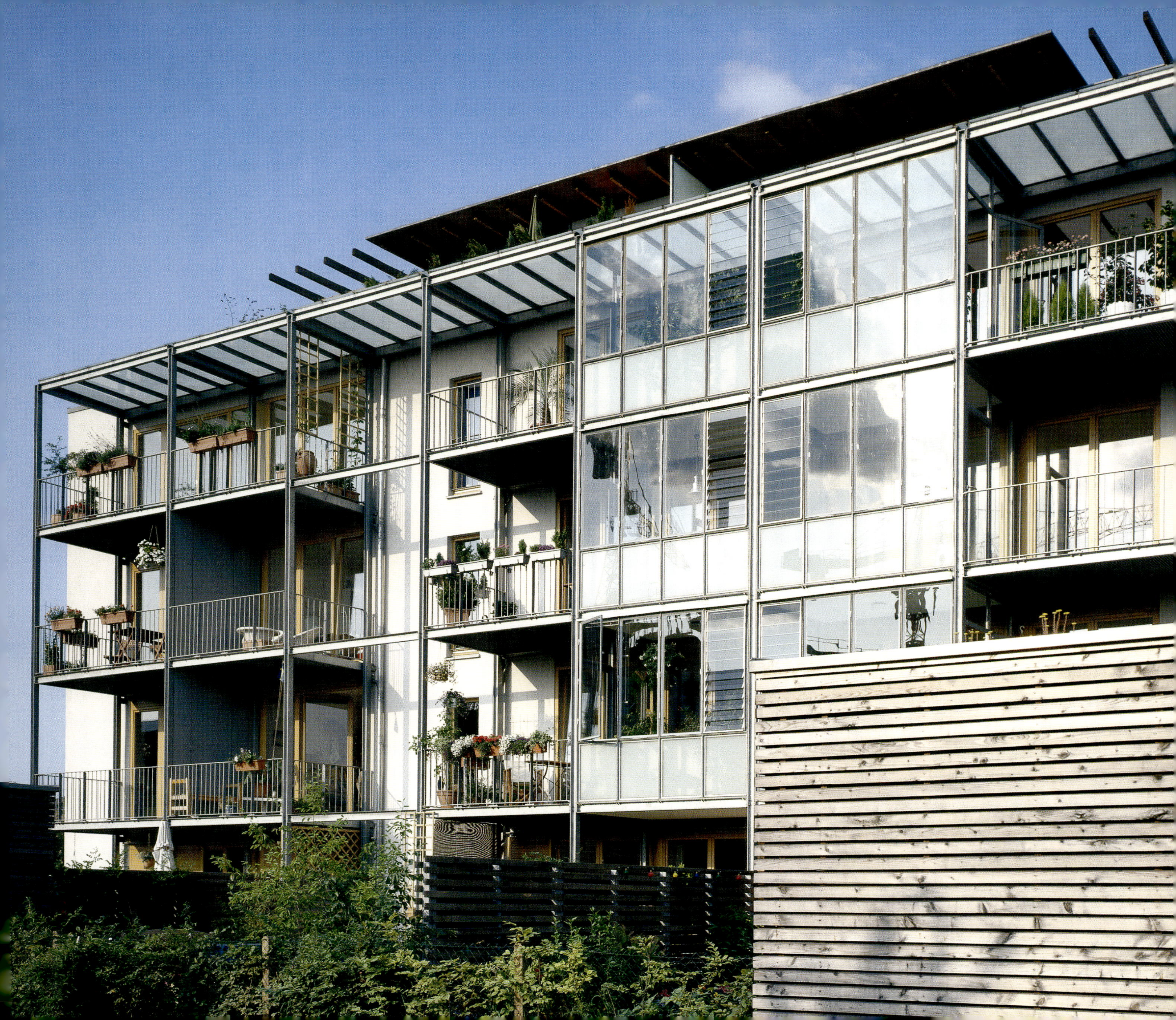

Zeppelin Carré Stuttgart
1998

Zeppelin Carré Stuttgart
1998

Lageplan / Site plan
1:2500

1 Arnulf-Klett-Platz
2 Lautenschlagerstraße
3 Kronenstraße
4 Friedrichstraße
5 Hotel Graf Zeppelin
6 Hauptbahnhof
  Main station

Obwohl unmittelbar gegenüber dem Stuttgarter Hauptbahnhof gelegen, war das Zeppelin Carré bis Ende der neunziger Jahre ein unattraktives und kaum zugängliches Stück Innenstadt.

Das Quartier, nun Eigentum einer Immobilienfonds-Gesellschaft, bietet nach umfassender Sanierung und Öffnung der früher geschlossenen Innenhöfe Spielräume für neues städtisches Leben mit hochwertigen Arbeitsplätzen und idealer Verkehrsanbindung an Stadt und Region.

Stadterneuerung ist in diesem Falle nicht durch Abriss und Neubau praktiziert, sondern – nach sorgfältigem Erkunden – durch den größtmöglichen Erhalt von Substanz und deren Erneuerung und Verwandlung zu einem stadträumlich und architektonisch attraktiven Ensemble. Einige Gebäude sind stark verändert, andere in ihrer ursprünglichen Gestalt und behutsam ergänzt wieder zur Geltung gebracht – wie beispielsweise der „Zeppelinbau" des Architekten Paul Bonatz aus den dreißiger Jahren. Städtebauliche und architektonische Schwächen, die aus den ideologischen Leitbildern der fünfziger Jahre herrühren, sind im Sinn einer „Stadtreparatur" behoben.

Konzeptionelle wie wirtschaftliche Leitlinie der Umgestaltung war das ständige Abwägen zwischen Erhalt, Rückbau und Veränderung. In der daraus resultierenden Vielfalt unterschiedlicher „Handschriften" und baulicher Charaktere liegt die Besonderheit dieses Ensembles.

Despite its location directly opposite the main station in Stuttgart, until the end of the 1990s, the Zeppelin Carré was a section of the downtown area that was both unattractive and inaccessible.

Following extensive refurbishing work, which included opening up previously enclosed interior courtyards, the area – which is now owned by a real estate company – provides an opportunity to create a new urban environment with high-quality workplaces and ideal transportation connections within the city and out to the surrounding areas.

In this case, rejuvenation of the area did not involve demolition and reconstruction but, following some careful exploratory work, the renewal and transformation of as much of the original buildings as possible, and developing them into an attractive architectural ensemble. Several buildings have been wholly transformed, while others, such as the 1930s Graf Zeppelin Hotel by the architect Paul Bonatz, stand out through careful additions onto the original form. The weaknesses in town planning and architecture that stem from the ideological models of the 1950s have all been eradicated through "urban repair work".

The conceptual and economic theme governing the redevelopment was an ongoing evaluation of each individual situation: whether to preserve, reconstruct or transform. It is the resulting variety of "signatures" and building characteristics that contribute to the unique features of the ensemble.

Das Carré als Teil der Stadt liegt unmittelbar gegenüber dem Hauptbahnhof. Außer einem kleinen Hotel sind alle Gebäude des Quartiers in unterschiedlicher, jedoch mit der Gebäudestruktur verträglicher Architektursprache umgebaut. Vier Höfe mit jeweils verschiedener Ausprägung laden ins Innere des Blocks ein. Die Dachflächen sind begrünt, zum Teil begehbar und mit Solaranlagen bestückt

The Zeppelin Carré is located directly opposite the main station. Apart from a small hotel, all the buildings have been renovated using different architectural languages, which are nonetheless compatible with the structure of the building. Four courtyards, different in appearance, entice one into the block's interior. Greenery adorns the rooftops, some of which can be walked on and are fitted with solar power installations

Die Öffnung der Höfe gegenüber dem bisherigen Zustand bietet die Chance, städtisches Leben und attraktive Adressen ins Quartiersinnere zu bringen

Opening up the courtyards provides an opportunity to bring urban life and attractive places together in the heart of the neighborhood

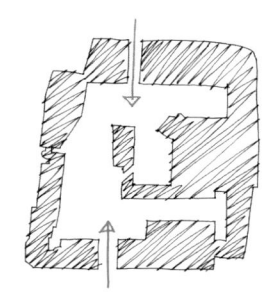

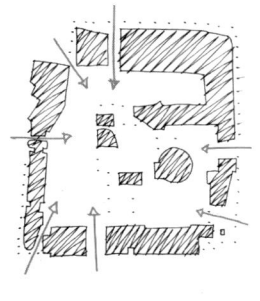

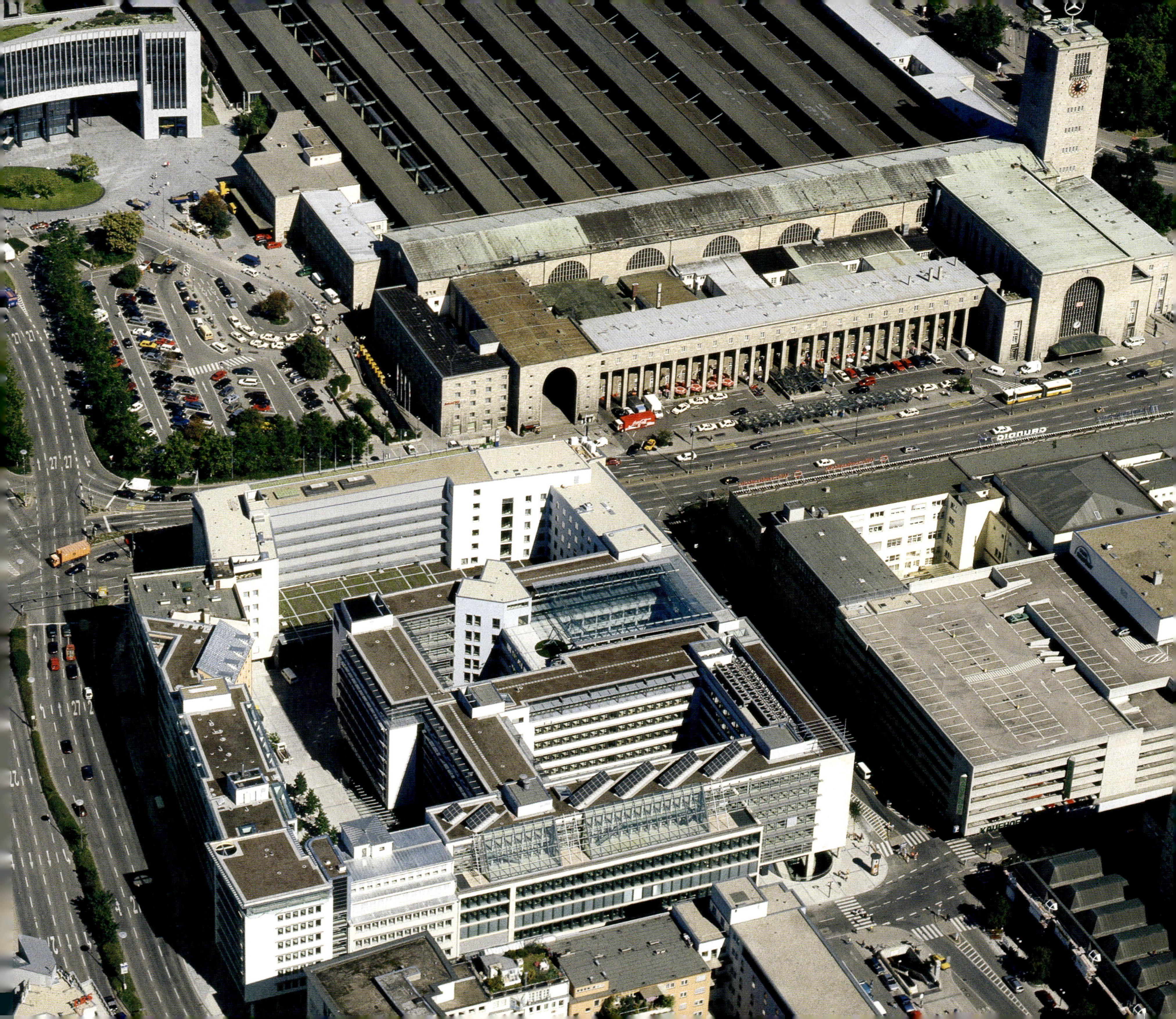

Obergeschoss / First floor
1:1500

1 Hotel Graf Zeppelin
2 Büroflächen
  Office space

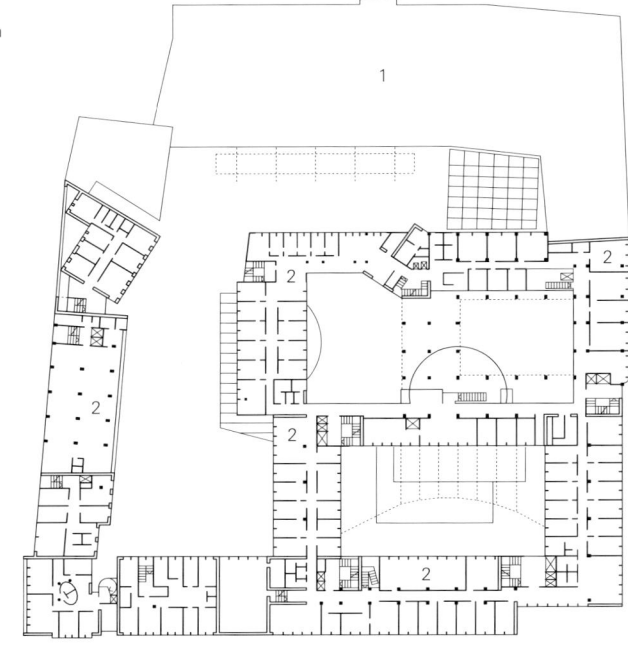

Erdgeschoss / Ground floor
1:1500

1 Bistro
2 Läden / Shops
3 Hotel Graf Zeppelin
4 Tiefgarageneinfahrt
  Entrance to basement garage
5 Höfe / Coutyards
6 Aufgang von der S-Bahn / Exit from the underground suburban railway

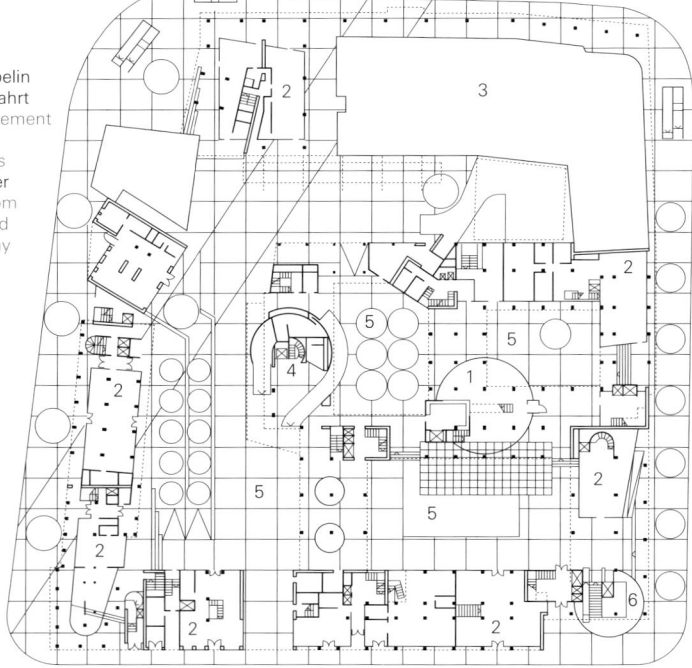

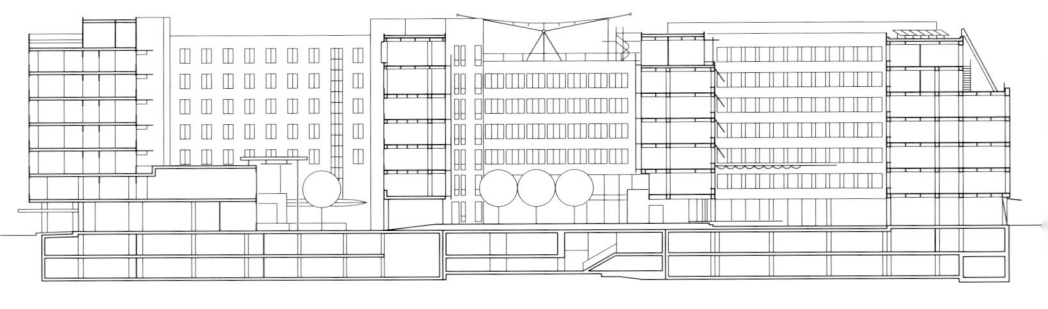

Schnitt / Section
Arnulf-Klett-Platz / Kronenstraße
1:1000

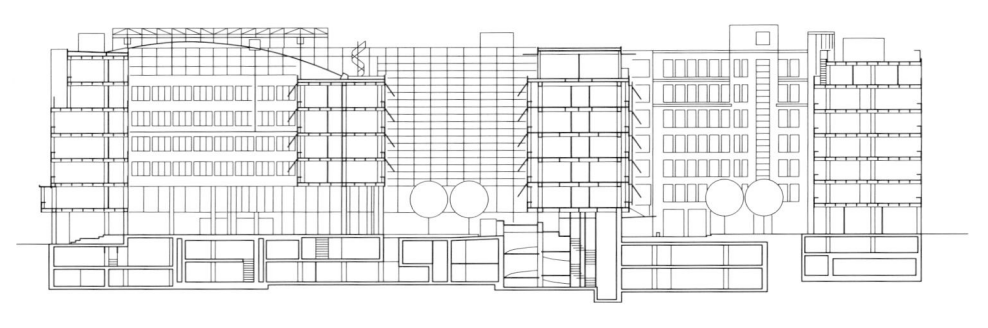

Schnitt / Section
Lautenschlager- / Friedrichstraße
1:1000

Links:
Gebäudefront an der Friedrichstraße vor dem Umbau

Rechts:
Eine durchgehende Wandscheibe entlang der stark befahrenen Friedrichstraße fasst mehrere Einzelgebäude zusammen; die verglaste dreieckige Loggia bezieht das älteste, sich am früheren Straßenverlauf orientierende Haus mit ein, das Gebäude mit Flugdach markiert die Quartiersecke an der Kronenstraße

Left:
The condition of the buildings before redevelopment

Rechts:
To enable the complex to fit in with the general town planning, the greatest changes were made on the busy Friedrichstrasse: A continuous wall unites several detached buildings; the glazed, triangular loggia integrates the oldest building, which used to follow the course of the street

Zeppelin Carré Stuttgart

Ein schützendes „Glassegel" überspannt den Atriumhof. Die über der ehemaligen Kassenhalle des Zeppelinbaus liegenden Geschosse zeigen die ursprüngliche, dreigeteilte Fensterform

A protective "glass sail" covers the atrium courtyard. The floors above the former cashier's hall of the bank display the old form of window, divided into three

Im „Bistrohof" spannt sich eine von unten beleuchtete Glas-Terrasse über eine grundwassergespeiste Wasserfläche. Der seilgeführte textile Sonnenschutz gibt dem Hof auch nach oben räumliche Fassung und lässt die Terrasse zeitweise zur Bühne werden

In the "Bistro Courtyard", above an area of water supplied with ground water, there is a glass veranda, illuminated from below. The canvas sunshades operate using cables, transforming the veranda at times into a stage; they also lend the courtyard some upward spatial structure

Unten rechts:
Zustand vor dem Umbau

Nach dem Rückbau bis auf die bauliche Substanz sind Büroarbeitsplätze mit überdurchschnittlichem Standard entstanden

Below right:
The condition of the buildings before redevelopment

By digging far down into building's original foundation, more high-quality office space was created

Schnitt durch die Doppelfassade an Lautenschlager- und Kronenstraße / Section of the double façade
1:50

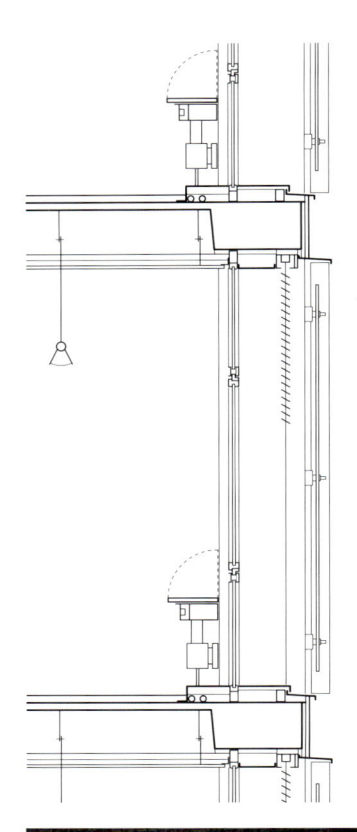

Der Gebäudeflügel an der Lautenschlagerstraße aus dem Jahre 1956 verbindet sich nach der Sanierung mit der leicht geschwungenen, entsprechend der originalen Fassung aus dem Jahr 1931 restaurierten Fassade des Zeppelinbaus

Following the redevelopment work, the wing on Lautenschlagerstrasse, dating from 1956, joins up with the restored, slightly curved façade of the Zeppelin building, which corresponds to the 1931 original

Casino und Mensa der Offiziersschule
des Heeres Dresden
1998

Army Officers' Mess at the Training College
Dresden
1998

Im Zuge der Verlegung der Offiziersschule des Heeres von Hannover an ihren ursprünglichen Standort Dresden wurde das ehemalige Offizierscasino, ein denkmalgeschützter Natursteinbau aus dem Jahr 1903, unter Wahrung seiner historischen Bausubstanz restauriert und zu seiner ursprünglichen Bestimmung zurückgeführt.

Der Mensa-Neubau für die Speise- und Clubräume ordnet sich in die rechteckige Struktur der Kasernenanlage ein, markiert die Hangkante des Prießnitztals und lässt, zusammen mit „Feldherrnhügel" und historischem Casino, einen geschützten Freiraum mit Biergarten entstehen. Das pavillonartige, eingeschossige Gebäude bildet einen zusammenhängenden, lichtdurchfluteten Raum, der sich über die transparente, zurückgesetzte Außenhülle mit dem parkartigen Umfeld verbindet. Klarheit des konstruktiven Gefüges, Mehrschichtigkeit der Übergänge zwischen Innen und Außen sowie die Leichtigkeit des weit ausgreifenden Dachschirmes kennzeichnen das Bauwerk. Mit den Baustoffen Stahl, Glas und Holz, seiner „Durchschaubarkeit" und Offenheit mutet das Gebäude in keiner Weise „militärisch" an.

As part of the Army Officer Training College's relocation from Hanover to its old base in Dresden, the former officers' mess underwent restoration. In returning the building – a listed natural stone building dating from 1903 – to its original function, the focus was on maintaining the building's historical structure.

The new mess building, complete with eating quarters and club rooms, is designed to blend in with the rectangular arrangement of the barracks. It also marks the drop to the Priessnitz Valley and, in conjunction with "Feldherrnhügel" and the historic canteen, creates a sheltered open space containing a beer garden. The pavilion-like one-story building, forms a continuous, light-filled room that, through its transparent, set-back outer skin, is connected with the park-like surroundings. The clarity of the structure, the multilayered transitions between indoors and outdoors, as well as the lightness with which an extensive canopy projects from the outside walls, all lend the building its characteristic features. By using materials such as steel, glass and wood, and with its transparency and openness, the building in no way appears to have a military function.

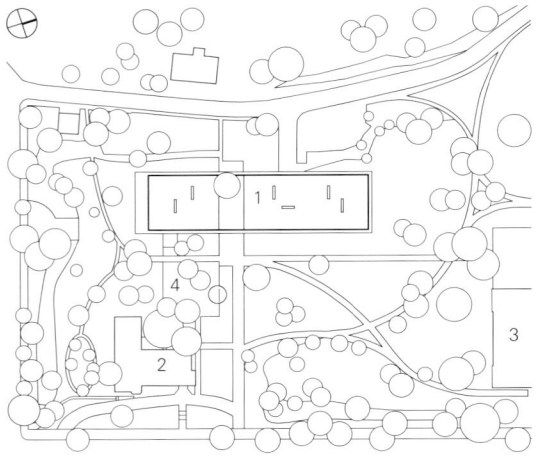

Lageplan / Site plan
1:3000

1 Casino und Mensa
  Canteen and mess
2 Offizierscasino
  Officers' mess
3 Kasernen / Barracks
4 Biergarten / Beer garden

Erdgeschoss / Ground floor
1:1000

1 Foyer / Foyer
2 Casinobereich / Mess area
3 Speisenausgabe
  Meal counter
4 Speisesaal / Dining room

Rechts:
Im Schutz eines Birkenwäldchens liegt das Casino auf dem Gelände der Albertstadt-Kaserne. Glas, Stahl und Holz sind Materialien, die das Gebäude zu einem „freien" Ort zwischen den Pflichten des Dienstes machen

Right:
Protected by a small birch forest, the mess is located on the Albertstadt barracks. Through the use of materials such as glass, steel and wood, the building becomes a "free" space for off-duty periods

Rechts / Right:
Festhalle / Festival hall
Seebad Rügen, 1936
Heinrich Tessenow

Festpavillon / Festival Pavilion
Udine, 1993
Pirzio Brioli

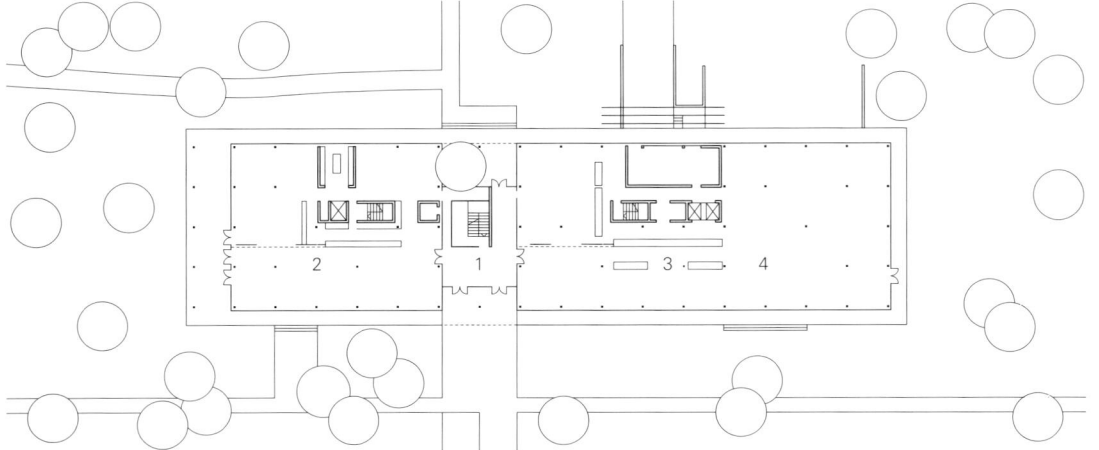

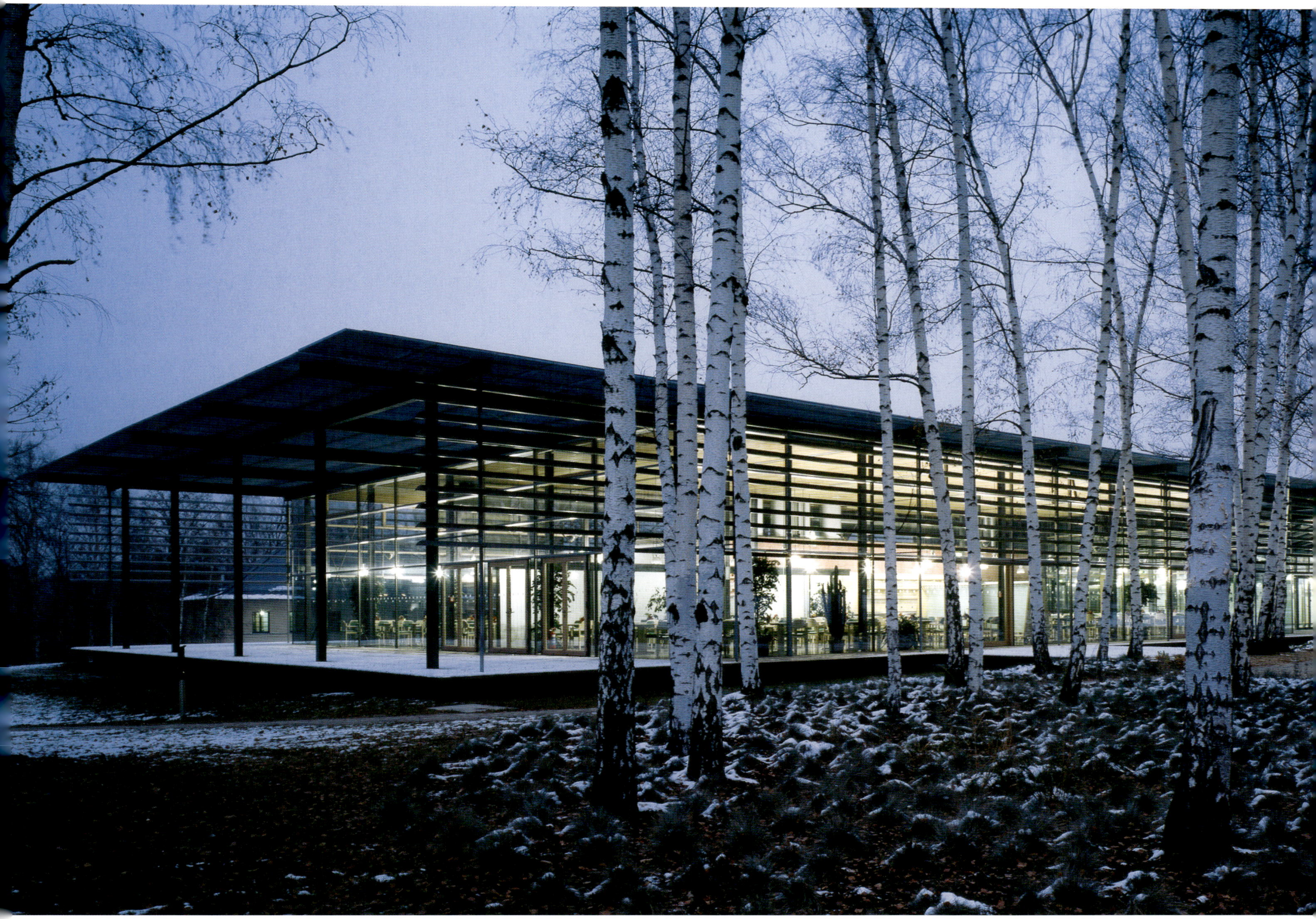

Das nahezu gläserne Gebäude stellt in seiner Transparenz die geläufigen Vorstellungen von Kasernenarchitektur in Frage. Die Schwerelosigkeit des Bauwerks wird durch seine Mehrschichtigkeit gesteigert

The transparency of the building, constructed almost entirely of glass, places a question mark over common ideas about the architecture of barracks. The many levels of the building serve to heighten its ethereal qualities

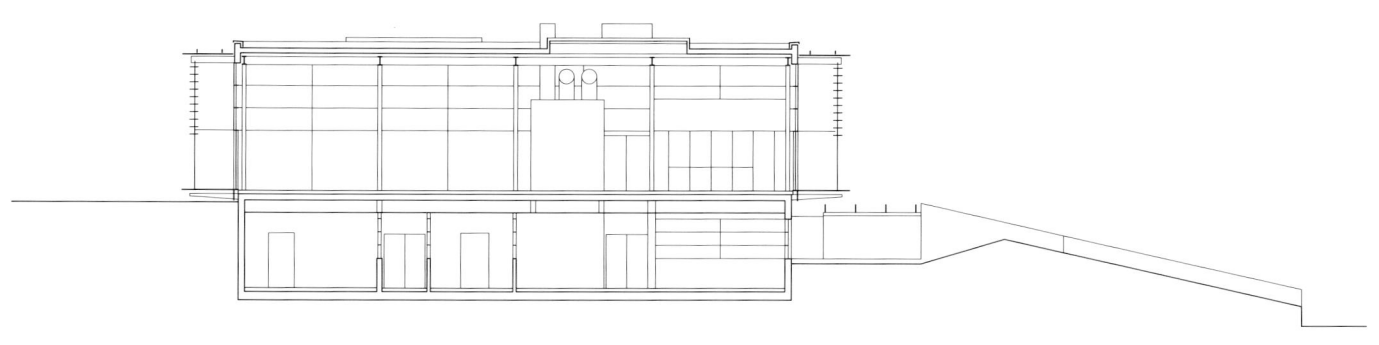

Schnitt / Section
1:300

Schnitt / Section
1:50

1. Gitterrostabdeckung
   Grid covering
2. Verstellbare Aluminium-
   lamellen / Adjustable
   aluminum blinds
3. Holzterrasse
   Wooden patio
4. Metall-Pfosten-Riegel-
   Fassade mit Öffnungs-
   flügeln aus Holz
   Metal post and stake
   façade with wooden
   opening wings
5. Sperrholzlamellendecke
   Plywood lamella ceiling

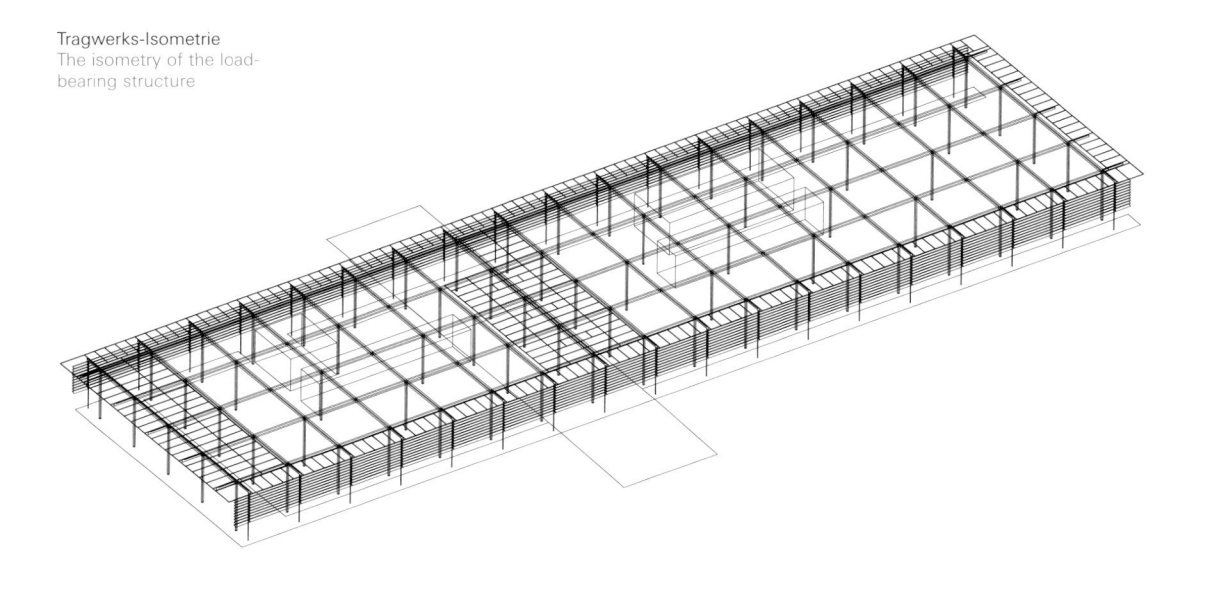

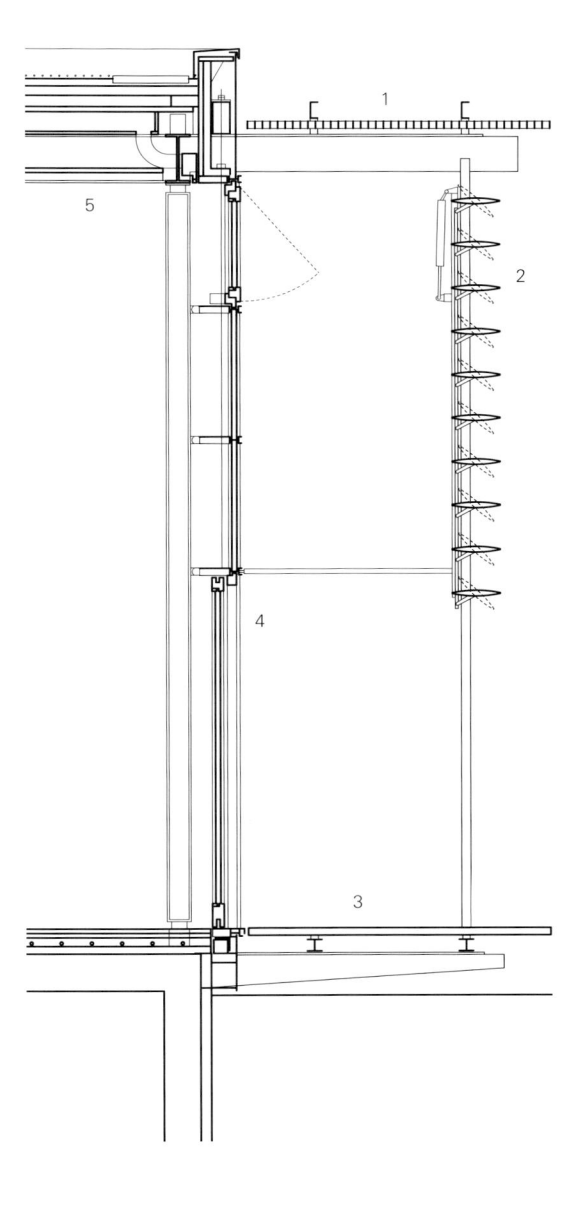

Tragwerks-Isometrie
The isometry of the load-
bearing structure

Der bewegliche Sonnenschutz lässt freie Blicke in die Landschaft und auf die Kasernenanlage aus dem Jahr 1903 zu

Der Dachrost greift weit über die gläserne Gebäudehülle hinaus; in Verbindung mit den hölzernen Decks und dem Sonnenschutz bildet er einen abgestuften Übergang zum Freiraum

The moveable sun protection permits open views of the surrounding countryside and the barrack grounds dating from 1903

The roof girder extends far beyond the glass sheath of the building; in conjunction with the wooden decks and the sun protection, it forms a gradual transition towards open space

Die Zurückhaltung in Form, Material und Ausstattung vermittelt den Eindruck eines freien Ortes unter einem schützenden Dach

The restrained shape, materials and fittings create the atmosphere of a tranquil open-air spot beneath a protective roof

U-Bahn-Station Westfriedhof München
1998

Westfriedhof Underground Station Munich
1998

Lageplan / Site plan
1:5000
1 U-Bahnabgänge
  Underground exits
2 Bushaltestelle / Bus stop
3 Westfriedhof
  Western Cemetery
4 Kleingartensiedlung
  Allotments

Das bestimmende Element der U-Bahn-Station Westfriedhof bilden die aus dem Herstellungsprozess in hoch entwickelter Tiefbautechnik felsartig anstehenden Oberflächen der Bahnsteigwände, deren archaische Rohheit in bewusstem Gegensatz zur Präzision des Ausbaus steht.

Das Lichtkonzept, in Zusammenarbeit mit dem Büro Ingo Maurer entwickelt, unterstreicht diesen Gegensatz, indem der Bahnsteig durch elf farbige „Lichtdome" von je 3,80m Durchmesser betont wird, während Wände und Decke in einem gedämpften, das Mystische des Raumes betonenden, bläulichen Licht erscheinen.

Die Schalterhallen vermitteln mit ihrer Auskleidung aus rötlichem Putz zwischen den Welten über und unter der Erde. Die transparenten und aufs Notwendigste reduzierten Wartedächer der Zugänge und Bushaltestellen setzen schließlich oberirdisch das Zeichen für diese außergewöhnliche unterirdische Welt.

The cliff-like surfaces of the platform walls are a defining element in the underground station at the western cemetery Manufactured using a high-tech process for underground construction, the platform walls possess an archaic roughness that stands in deliberate contrast to the precision of the design. The lighting concept, developed together with designer Ingo Maurer, underscores this contrast: The platform is highlighted by eleven colored "light domes", each measuring 3.80 meters in diameter, while the walls and the ceiling appear in a subdued, bluish light that emphasizes the mystical qualities of the space.

With their reddish plaster coating, the ticket halls mediate between the worlds above and below ground level. The transparent roofs over the waiting areas at the entrances and bus stops – which have been reduced to an absolute minimum – act as an above-ground symbol for this extraordinary underground world.

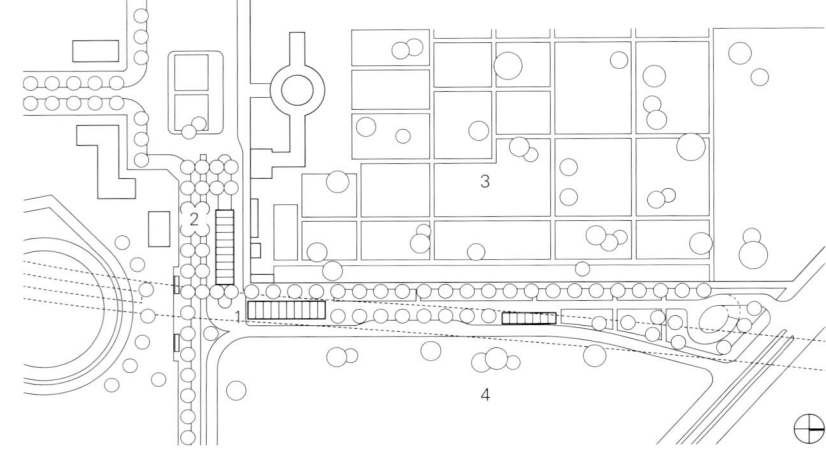

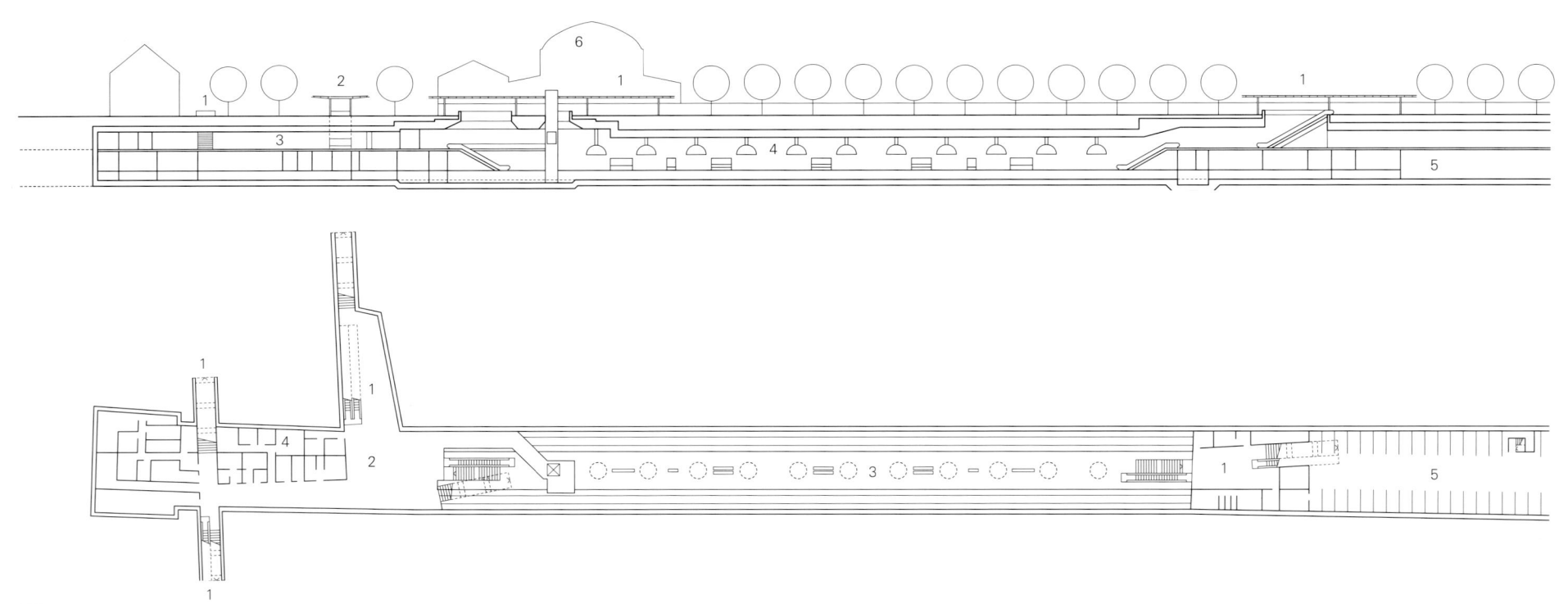

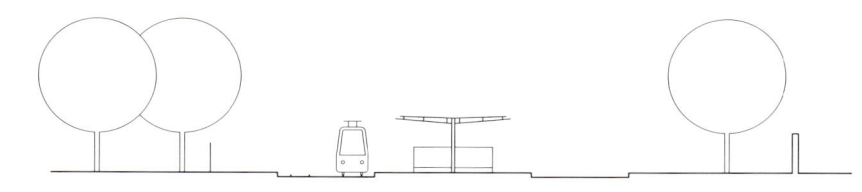

Querschnitt / Cross section
1:500

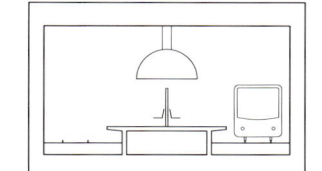

Tageslicht fällt durch das Glasdach der über der Station liegenden Bushaltestelle bis auf den Bahnsteig und vermittelt dem Fahrgast ein Gefühl der Sicherheit und das Erlebnis des Auf- und Abtauchens

Die felsartig rau belassenen Bahnsteigwände bilden in Verbindung mit farbigem Licht und den präzisen Ausbauelementen einen eindrucksvollen unterirdischen Raum

Daylight penetrates the glass roof of the bus stop above the station and reaches the platform, instilling the passengers with a sense of security and the illusion of breaking the surface or going underground

In conjunction with colored light and the precision-made elements in the construction, the platforms, which are cliff-like in appearance and have been left unfaced, create an impressive underground space

Längsschnitt / Longitudinal section
1:1250

1 U-Bahnabgänge
  Underground exits
2 Bushaltestelle / Bus stop
3 Schalterhalle / Booking hall
4 Bahnsteig / Platform
5 Parkgarage
  Basement garage
6 Friedhofskapelle
  Cemetery chapel

U-Bahn-Station in Stockholm, 1970

Underground station in Stockholm, 1970

Grundriss / Plan
1:1250

1 U-Bahnabgänge
  Underground exits
2 Schalterhalle / Booking hall
3 Bahnsteig / Platform
4 Technik- und Nebenräume
  Equipment and ancillary rooms
5 Parkgarage
  Basement garage

129

Die Wartedächer der Bushaltestellen aus Stahl und Glas kommen durch minimalen Materialaufwand zu Funktion und Wirkung

Using a minimal amount of material, the steel and glass roofs over the bus stops are both functional and effective

Der Bahnsteig ist durch farbige „Lichtdome" hell herausgehoben; der Tunnelraum dagegen erscheint in gedämpftem, mystischem Licht

The platform stands out as a result of colored "light domes"; the tunnel itself appears in a subdued, mystical light

Amazonienhaus in der „Wilhelma" Stuttgart
1999

Amazonian House in the "Wilhelma" Stuttgart
1999

Mit 66m Länge, 18m Breite und 14m Höhe präsentiert sich das Amazonienhaus in der Stuttgarter „Wilhelma" nach der Großvolière (S. 88 ff.) als ein weiterer filigraner Neubau. Innerhalb seiner hochtransparenten Hülle aus Stahl und Glas stellt er die Flora und Fauna des Amazonasgebiets naturnah zur Schau. Üppige Vegetation und feuchtwarmes Klima vermitteln dem Besucher auf seinem „Erlebnisweg" den Eindruck, sich inmitten des tropischen Regenwalds zu bewegen. Für diese Region typische Tierarten verstärken auch akustisch diese Illusion.

Zusammen mit dem Insektarium und der Schmetterlingshalle bildet das Amazonienhaus einen baulichen Rücken, der das Motiv der Einfriedung aus Terrakotta-Mauern weiterführt und den zoologisch-botanischen Garten der Wilhelma gegen die stark befahrene Pragstraße abschirmt.

Das exotische Innere des Glashauses fließt über die gebogene Hülle in den Park hinein, sodass sich überraschende Wechselbeziehungen zwischen einheimischer und fremder Pflanzenwelt ergeben.

Along with the large aviary (p. 88 ff), the Amazonian House – 66 meters long, 18 meters wide and 14 meters high – is another fine example of the new filigree buildings in the Stuttgart "Wilhelma". Inside its highly transparent sheath of steel and glass, it displays the flora and fauna of the Amazon region in a natural setting. The lush vegetation and a humid atmosphere combine to give visitors on the Amazon Experience Route the feeling of walking through a tropical rain forest. Animals that typically inhabit these regions heighten the illusion – acoustically, as well.

The Amazonian House, with the insectarium and the butterfly hall, forms a backbone or spine of buildings which continue the motif of terracotta wall enclosures and shield the Wilhelma's zoological and botanical gardens from the heavy traffic on Pragstrasse.

The exotic interior of the greenhouse appears to flow out over the curved glass sheath and into the park, resulting in a surprising interplay between the worlds of domestic and foreign plants.

Lageplan / Site plan
1:5000

1 Amazonienhaus
  Amazonian house
2 Maurischer Garten
  Moorish gardens
3 Gewächshäuser
  Green houses
4 Großvolière / Large aviary
5 Restaurant
6 Pragstraße

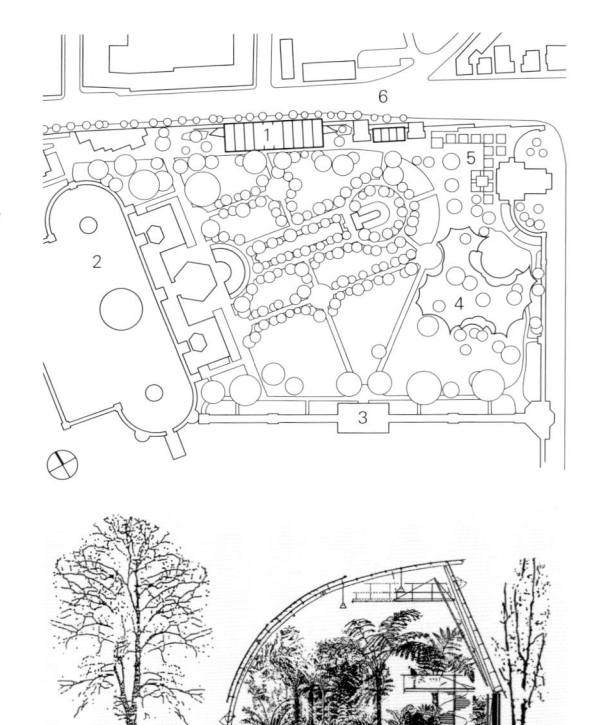

Querschnitt / Cross section
1:500

Zum Park hin gewölbt, zur Straßenseite abgeschrägt: so präsentiert sich das gläserne Schauhaus am Rande der „Wilhelma". Die Architektur greift Formen berühmter Vorbilder aus dem 19. Jahrhundert auf und übersetzt sie mit den heute verfügbaren technischen Mitteln in unsere Zeit

Curving outward on the park side, angled on the streetside – this is the glass display building on the edge of the "Wilhelma". The architecture takes its cue from famous 19th-century predecessors and transposes them into the present using contemporary technology

Grundriss / Plan
1:750

1 Amazonienhaus
  Amazonian house
2 Außengehege
  Outside cages
3 Insektarium und
  Schmetterlingshalle
  Insectarium and
  butterfly hall
4 Terrakottawand
  Terracotta wall

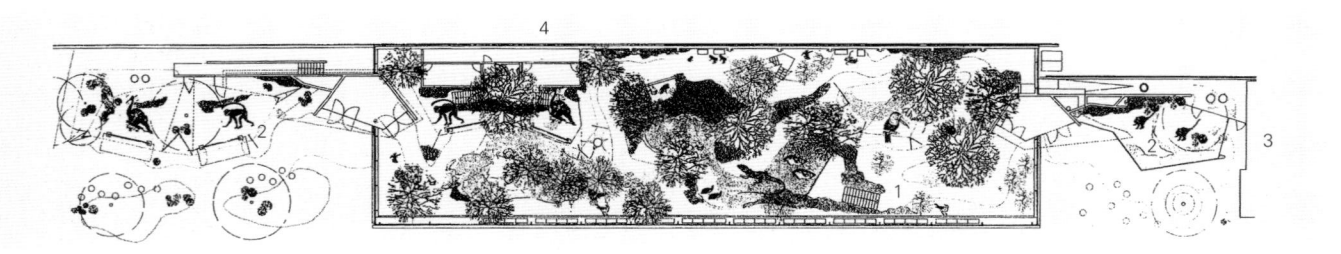

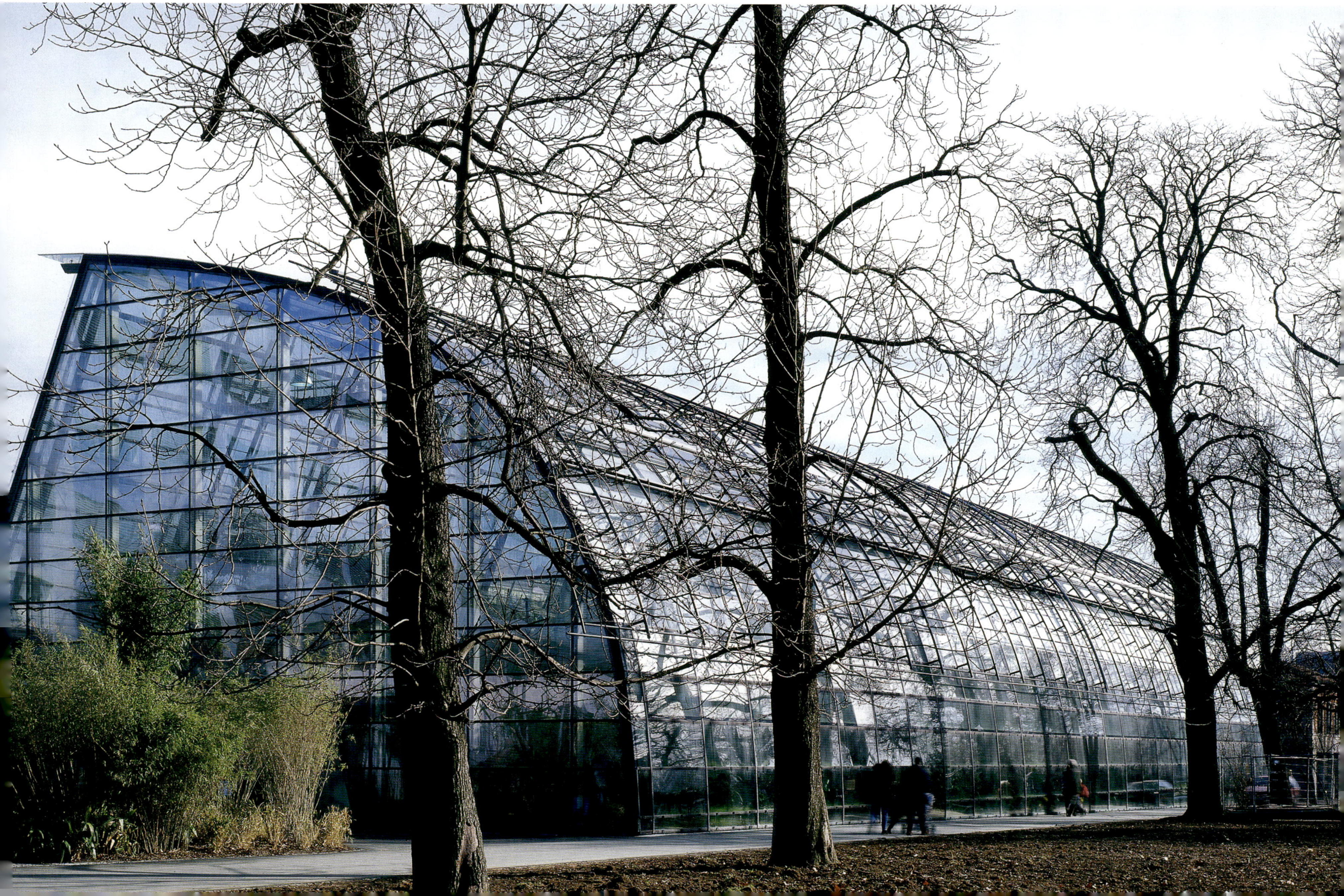

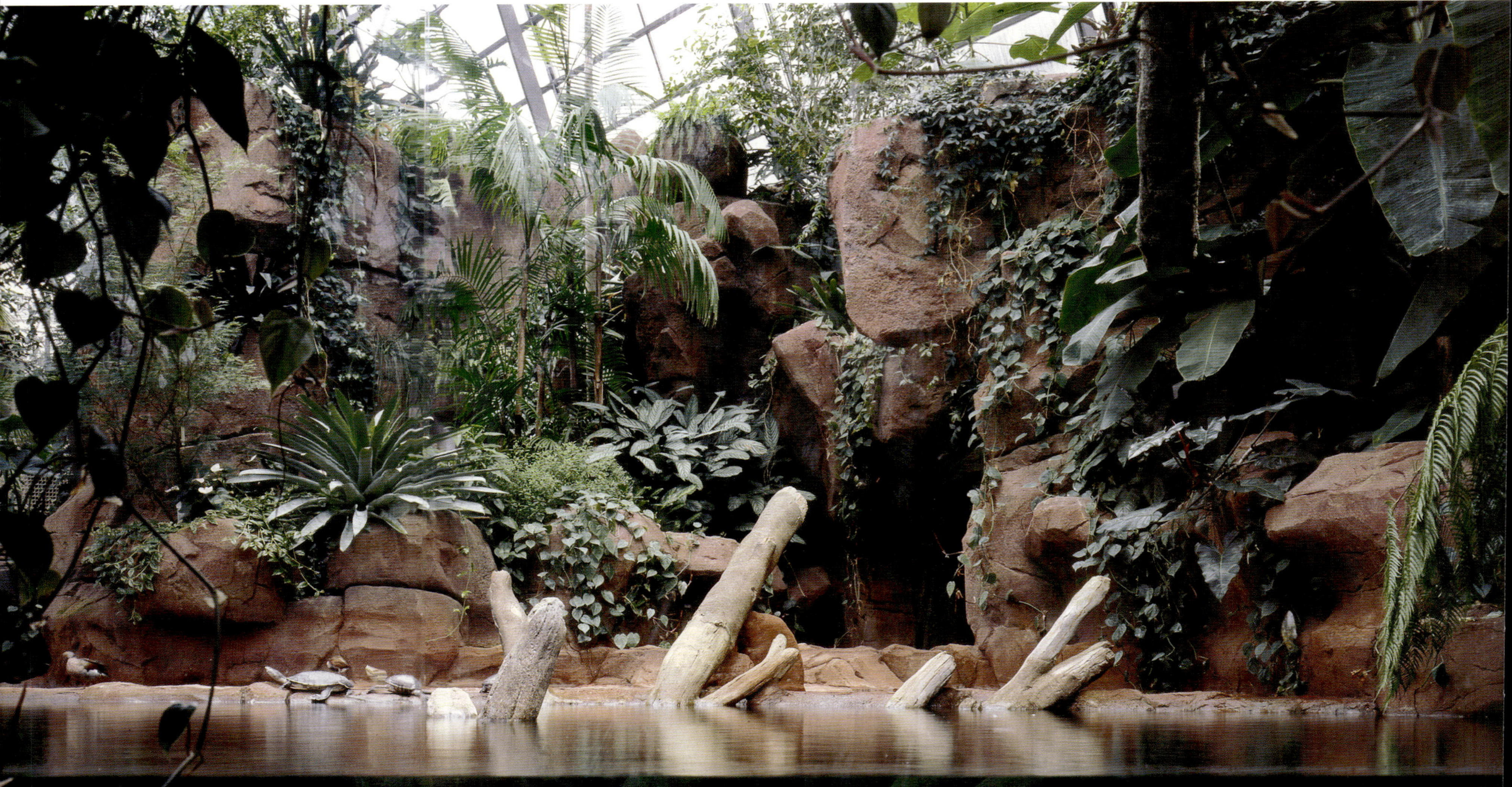

Die Anforderungen an ein Gebäude, das im mitteleuropäischen Klima die tropische Pflanzenwelt zur Schau stellen soll, sind vielfältig und teilweise widerspruchsvoll. Trotzdem bekommt der Besucher den Eindruck, sich inmitten der Flora und Fauna des tropischen Regenwalds zu bewegen

A building to present tropical plants in a Central European climate has to meet a variety of in part mutually contradictory standards.
Nevertheless, visitors get the impression that they are in the midst of the flora and fauna of a tropical rainforest

**adidas "World of Sports" Herzogenaurach
1999**
Wettbewerb   3. Preis

**adidas "World of Sports" Herzogenaurach
1999**
Competition   3rd prize

adidas, einer der größten Sportartikelhersteller der Welt, beabsichtigt, seinen Hauptsitz in Herzogenaurach weiter auszubauen. Hierzu soll auf dem Gelände eines ehemaligen Luftwaffenstützpunktes ein neuer Stadtteil entstehen, der außer der "World of Sports" eine Wohnsiedlung für ca. 2500 Einwohner, ein Gewerbegiet sowie großzügige landschaftliche Flächen umfasst – ein attraktiver Standort für Arbeit, Wohnen und Freizeit. Der Wettbewerbsbeitrag gliedert das ehemalige Flugplatzgelände in drei Bereiche, welche die Spuren früherer Nutzungen verdeutlichen: Die "World of Sports" als Ergänzung einer bereits umgenutzten Kasernenanlage; Gewerbe und ergänzende Einrichtungen auf dem Band der ehemaligen Start- und Landebahn; Wohnen in Verbindung mit der parkartigen Landschaft des Golfplatzes aus der Zeit militärischer Nutzung.

Für die "World of Sports" wird zeichen- und symbolhaft die Form des Stadions als Inbegriff für Sport und Spiele gewählt. Unter einer aufgeständerten „Teststrecke" sind die Funktionen für Verwaltung, Produktion, Forschung und Entwicklung zusammengefasst, die, ergänzt durch Freisportflächen im Inneren der Gesamtanlage, in direkter Wechselbeziehung miteinander stehen.

adidas, one of the largest manufacturers of sporting goods in the world, is planning to expand its headquarters in Herzogenaurach even further. In order to do this, a former air base is being transformed into an entirely new neighborhood, which, in addition to "World of Sports", will provide residential accomodation for 2,500 people, an industrial park and generous landscaped areas. Overall, the area will be an attractive place to work, live and pursue leisure activities. This particular entry for the competition divides the former air base into three areas, all of which clearly illustrate their former use. The "World of Sports" complements a barrack complex, which has already been put to alternate use; commercial and associated premises on the former runway; a residential area adjacent to the park-like landscape of the former golf course.

The shape of a stadium, the symbolic embodiment of sport and games, was chosen for the "World of Sports". The administrative, production, and research and development facilities are all grouped beneath the elevated "test track" which, complemented by the open sport areas in the interior of the whole complex, intermingle directly with each other.

Stadion Delphi, 5.Jh. v. Chr.

Delphi Stadium, built in the 5th Century B.C.

Fiatwerke Turin-Lingotto, um 1920, Mattéo Trucco

The Fiat plant at Lingotto, circa 1920, Mattéo Trucco

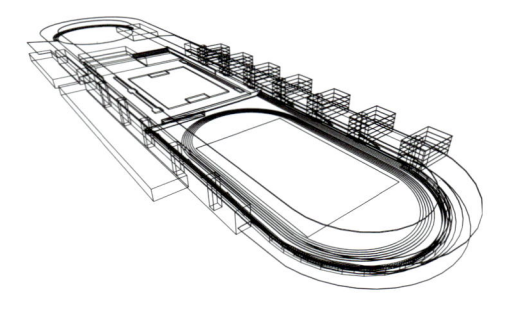

Die „Teststrecke" als ein weithin sichtbares Symbol für Dynamik, Wettbewerbsfähigkeit und technische Höchstleistung des expandierenden Unternehmens adidas

The "test track" forms a widely visible symbol of dynamism, of competitiveness, and of the high technical performance of the expanding company that is adidas

Rechts / Right:
Lageplan / Site plan
1:12 000

1   "World of Sports"
2   Hauptverwaltung / Main administration building
3   Cafeteria
4   Gewerbeband
    Commercial section
5   Wohnen / Residential accommodation

Haundorf
Kr ERH 3
Kr ERH 25
Mältelesäcker
Alte Gartenäcker
Hundswiesen
Langwiesenäcker
Schwarzholzäcker
Im Schwarzwald
Leitenäcker
Krohäcker
Stockweiheräcker
Schwarzweiher
Alten Beutelsdorfer Weg
Auf der Nutzung
Färbersäcker
Vereine
Gilgenweiheräcker
Popperleite
Im Steinknöglein
In der Breite
Lohhof
Reihenzach
1
2
3
4
5

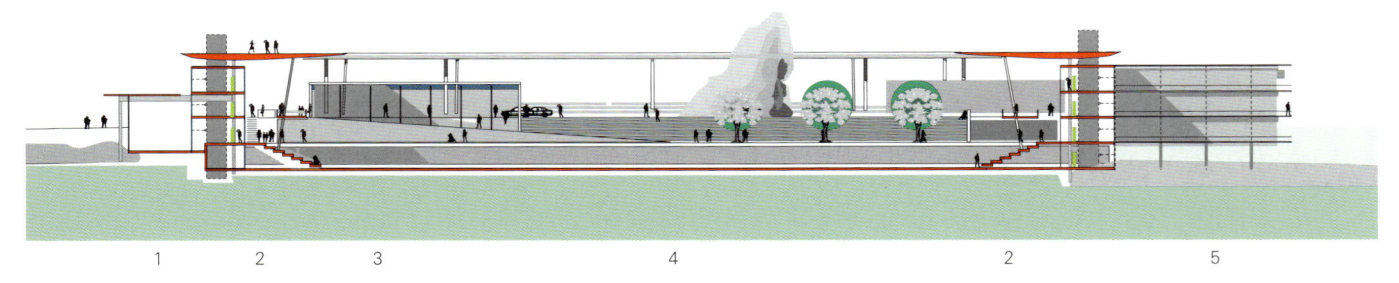

Querschnitt / Cross section
1:1000
1. Forschung und Entwicklung
   Research & development
2. Teststrecke / Test track
3. Multifunktionshalle
   Multipurpose hall
4. Sportflächen / Training area
5. Verwaltung / Administration

Grundriss / Plan
1:5000
1. Hauptverwaltung
   Company headquarters
2. Trainingsplatz
   Training area
3. Verwaltung / Administration
4. Multifunktionshalle
   Multipurpose hall
5. Konferenz- und Ausbildungszentrum
   Conference and training center
6. Forschung und Entwicklung / Research & development
7. Cafeteria

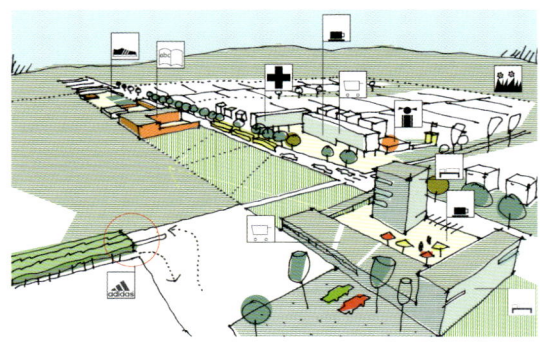

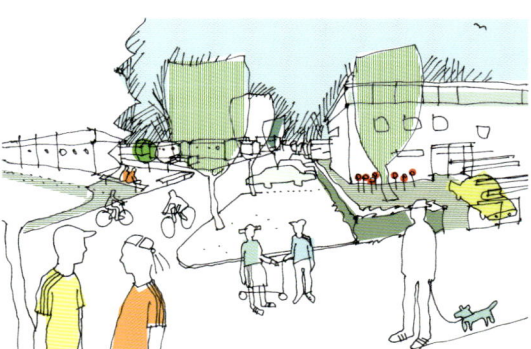

Oben:
Gewerbe / Commercial section

Unten:
Wohnen / Residential accommodation

139 adidas "World of sports"

Hochhauskomplex MAX Frankfurt am Main
1999
Wettbewerb   Engere Wahl

MAX High-rise Frankfurt/Main
1999
Competition   Short-listed

Lageplan / Site plan
1:5000

1 Stammhaus
  Parent building
2 Bestehendes Hochhaus
  Existing high-rise
3 Hochhaus MAX
  MAX high-rise
4 Neuer Stadtplatz
  New town square
5 Große Gallusstraße
6 Commerzbank-Hochhaus
  Commerzbank high-rise

Mit dem Hochhaus MAX will die Deutsche Bank in unmittelbarer Nachbarschaft zu ihrem Stammsitz und ihrem bereits vorhandenen Hochhaus ein neues, unverwechselbares Zeichen in der Stadtsilhouette des Frankfurter Bankenviertels setzen.

Der Wettbewerbsvorschlag lässt durch die Geometrie zweier gleichseitiger, um 120° gegeneinander verdrehter Dreiecke an Basis und Spitze eine skulpturale Großform entstehen, deren Erscheinungsbild je nach Standort zwischen Vertikalität und Neigung wechselt.

Sockel und Schaft bilden, anders als bei anderen Hochhäusern, eine auch formal homogene Einheit und unterstreichen damit die Verbindung von Stadtraum und Gebäude.

Zwischen Stammhaus, vorhandenem und neuem Hochhaus entsteht im Schnittpunkt der öffentlichen Wege ein großzügiger, zum Teil wettergeschützter Stadtplatz, der über die Große Gallusstraße hinweg mit dem Eingangsbereich des Commerzbank-Hochhauses in Verbindung steht.

Deutsche Bank intends the MAX high-rise, directly adjacent to the traditional headquarters and its existing high-rise, to set a new, unmistakable mark on the skyline of Frankfurt's central banking district.

The competition entry entails the geometry of two equilateral triangles, turned to each other at an angle of 120° at the base and peak, creating a large-format sculpture, the appearance of which varies from being vertical to tilted, depending on the location from which it is viewed.

Unlike most other highrises, the base and the shaft form a single homogenous unit, thus underscoring the connection between the urban surroundings and the building.

At the interface of public paths between head office, the existing high-rise and the new one, a generous city square would be created, which is protected from the elements and would connect to the entrance of the Commerzbank high-rise, via the Grosse Gallusstrasse.

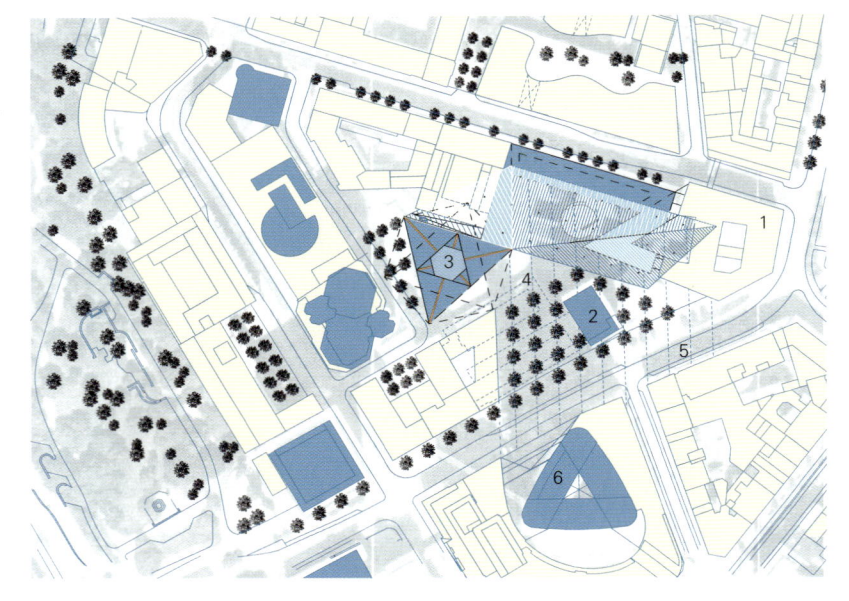

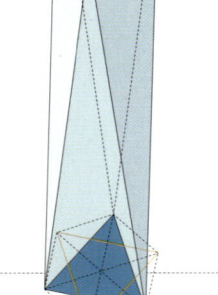

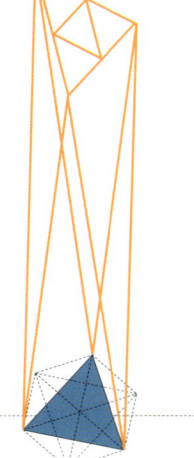

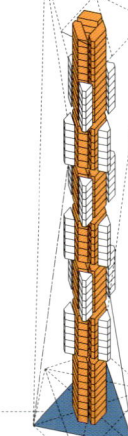

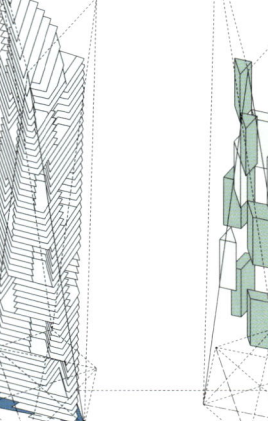

Links / Left:
Entwicklung der Gebäudeform und innere Organisation

Development of the building's form and internal arrangement

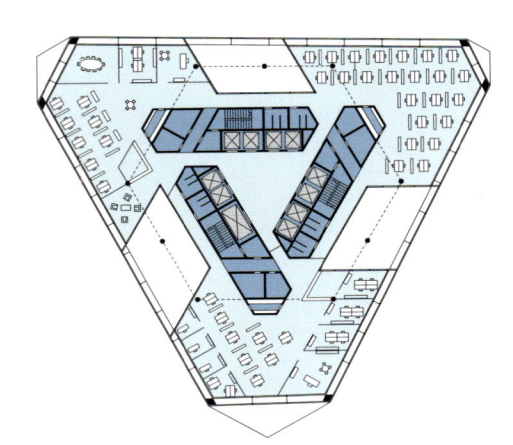

Jedes Geschoss ist in bis zu drei Mieteinheiten teilbar. Über interne Verbindungstreppen können auch größere mehrgeschossige Büroeinheiten entstehen

Each story can be divided up into three suites for renting out. Via internal connecting staircases large offices spread over several stories can be generated

Bürogeschoss / Office floor
1:1000

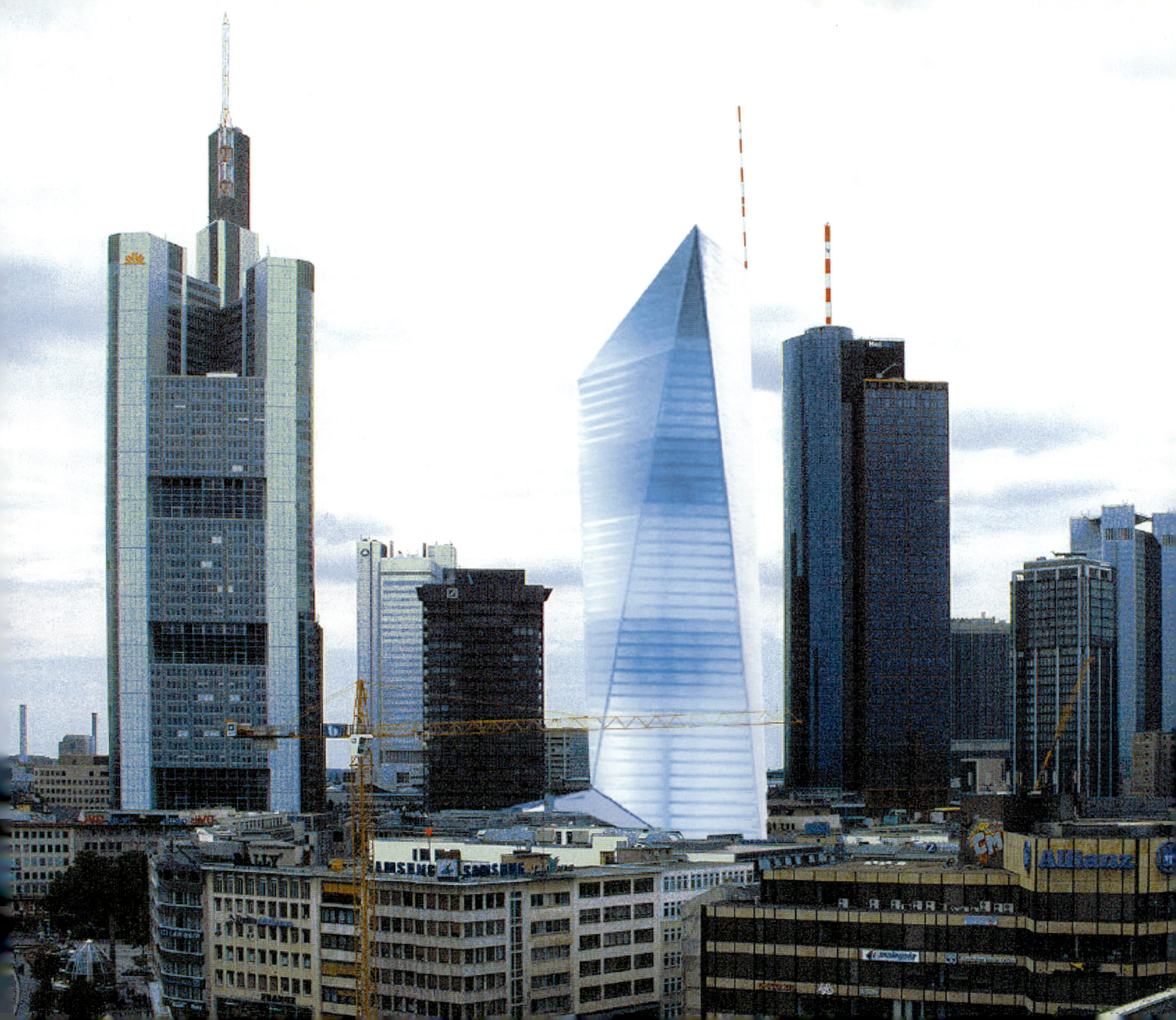

Allianz

Multifunktionales Sport- und Veranstaltungszentrum Stuttgart
1999
Wettbewerb   3. Preis

Sports and Events Center Stuttgart
1999
Competition   3rd Prize

Als Ergänzung der für Großveranstaltungen zu kleinen und in technischer Hinsicht nicht mehr ausreichenden Hanns-Martin-Schleyer-Halle soll zwischen dieser und dem Gottlieb-Daimler-Stadion eine neue Hallenarena für etwa 13000 Zuschauer entstehen, die mit der vorhandenen Halle zu einer funktionalen und räumlichen Einheit verbunden werden kann.

Anstatt in den begrenzten Raum zwischen Schleyer-Halle und Stadion einen weiteren Solitär einzufügen, zeigt der Wettbewerbsentwurf die Chance auf, alle drei Veranstaltungsorte in einen großzügigen stadträumlichen und inhaltlichen Zusammenhang zu bringen. Träger dieser Idee ist die „Grüne Welle", eine weit ausschwingende Landschaftsplatte, die, aufsteigend vom Daimler-Stadion, die neue Arena „umspült" und über der Schleyer-Halle ausläuft. Sie gleicht die durch Überbauung weggefallenen Freiflächen aus und bietet einen beeindruckenden Ausblick auf die Stuttgarter Hafen- und Hügellandschaft.

Unter der „Welle" entstehen zwischen den beiden Hallen foyerartige Bewegungsräume, die als Forum für verschiedene Service- und Marketingaktivitäten während der Veranstaltungen dienen.

To support the Hanns Martin Schleyer Hall – which is too small to handle large events and no longer has the proper technical facilities – plans were made to create a new covered arena between it and the Gottlieb Daimler Stadium that could house approximately 13,000 spectators and could be linked to the existing hall to form one functional and spatial unit.

Instead of creating a third stand-alone building in the limited space between the Schleyer Hall and the stadium, the design presents a way of combining all three venues to form one generously dimensioned entity, which would form a clear part of the town layout. The idea behind this is the "Green Wave", a generous landscape plateau that extends in a gradual slope from the Daimler Stadium, circles the new arena on both sides and continues until it ebbs around the Schleyer Hall. It compensates for the outdoor space that has been lost due to the buildings and provides an impressive view out across the Stuttgart inland harbor and the hills.

Beneath the "Wave", and between the two halls, a lobby-like, free space for movement would be constructed as a forum for various service and marketing activities during events.

Die Landschaftsplatte der „Grünen Welle" fasst die bestehende und die neue Halle räumlich zusammen. Unter der Platte entstehen großzügige Foyerzonen

The "Green Wave" landscape plateau unites the existing hall with the new hall. Generous foyers are located beneath the plateau

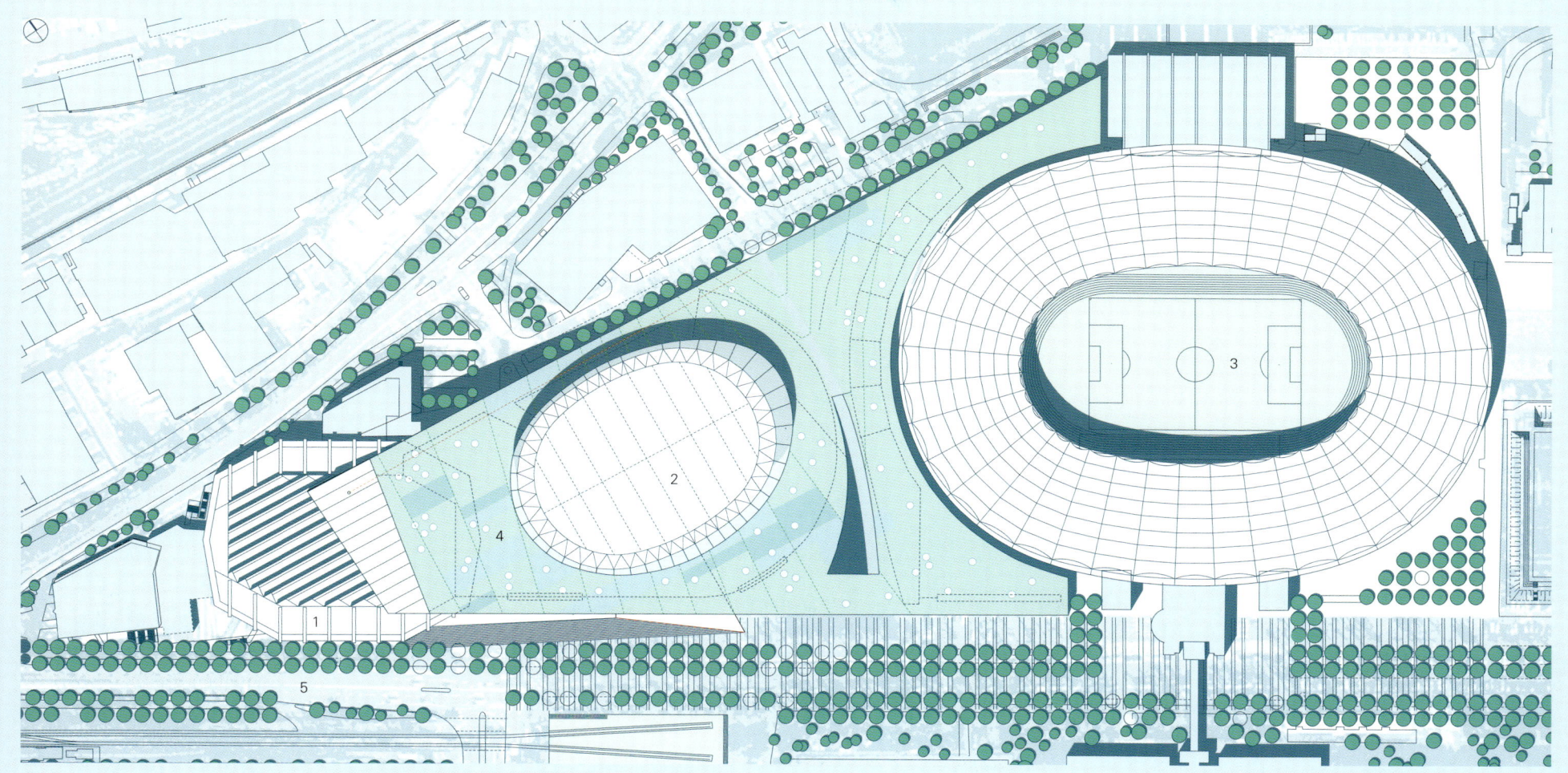

Lageplan / Site plan
1:3000

1. Hanns-Martin-Schleyer-Halle / Hall
2. Hallenarena / Hall arena
3. Gottlieb-Daimler-Stadion Stadium
4. „Grüne Welle"
   "Green Wave"
5. Mercedes-Boulevard

144

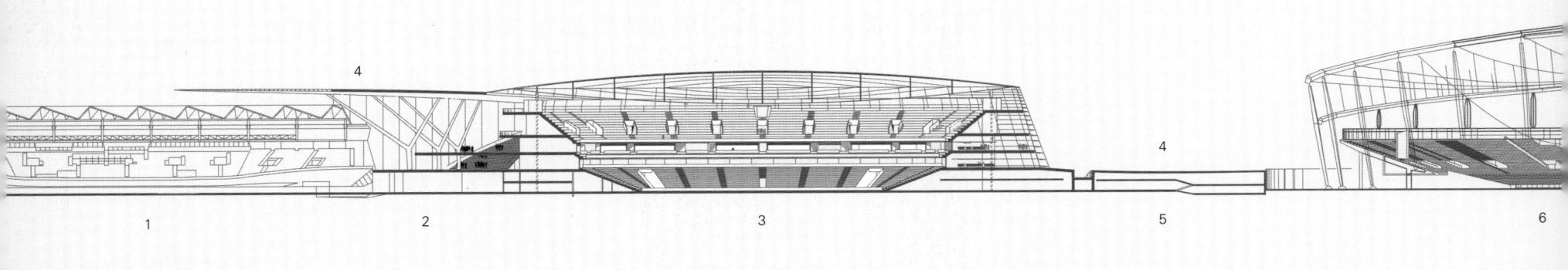

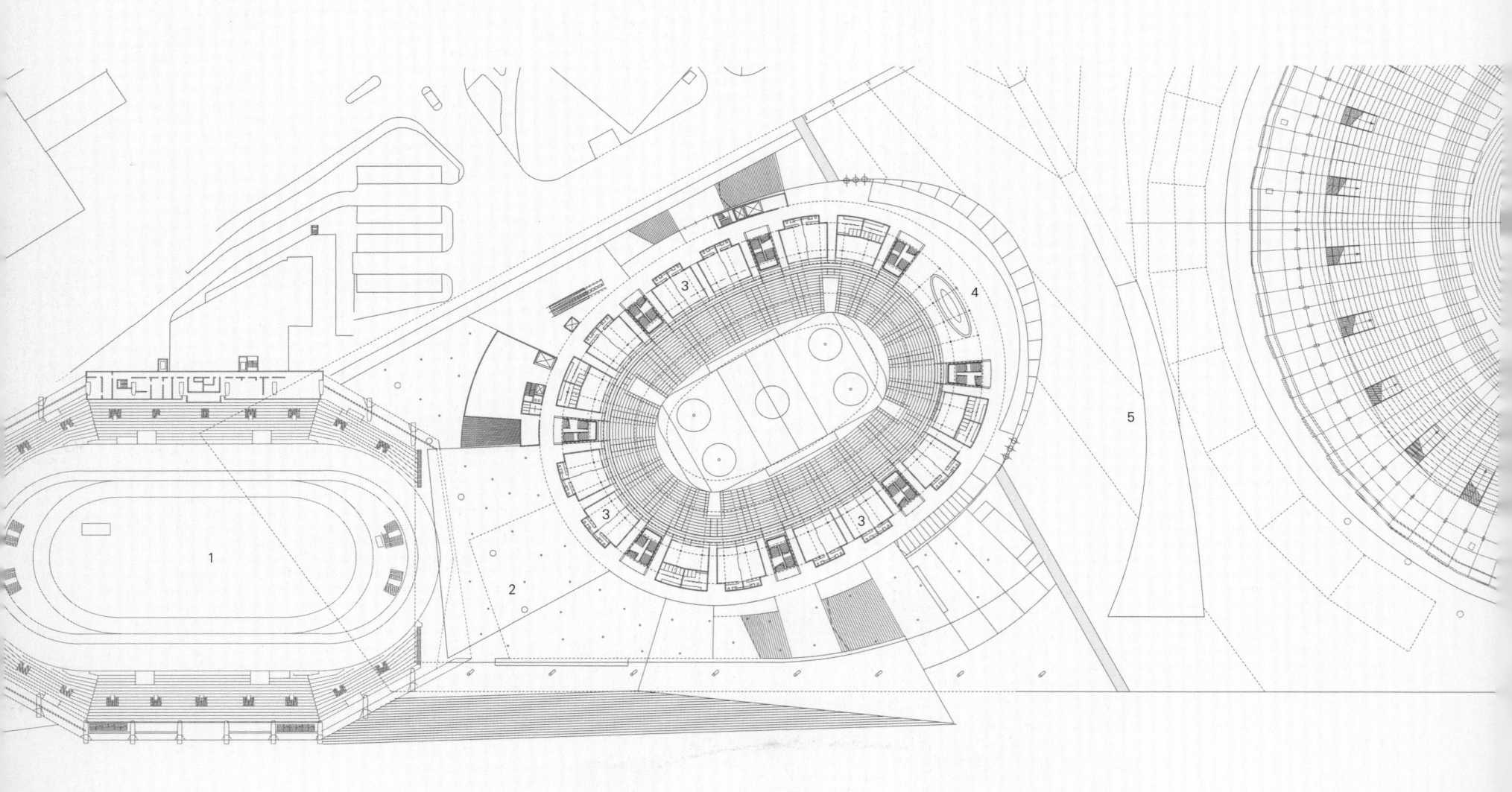

Längsschnitt
Longitudinal section
1:1500
1 Hans-Martin-Schleyer-Halle / Hall
2 Foyer / Foyer
3 Hallenarena / Hall arena
4 „Grüne Welle"
 "Green Wave"
5 Parken und Infrastruktur
 Parking and infrastructure
6 Gottlieb-Daimler-Stadion
 Stadium

Die neue Arena und die Schleyer-Halle werden über eine gemeinsame Foyerzone miteinander verbunden

The new arena and the Schleyer Hall are connected by the foyer area

Untere Rangebene
Level lower circle
1:1500
1 Hanns-Martin-Schleyer-Halle / Hall
2 VIP- und Multifunktionsflächen / VIP and multifunctional areas
3 Logen / Boxes
4 VIP-Lounge / VIP Lounge
5 „Grüne Welle"
 "Green Wave"
6 Gottlieb-Daimler-Stadion
 Stadium

Kurmittelhaus Bad Brambach
2000
Wettbewerb 1996   1. Preis

Spa Center Bad Brambach
2000
Competition 1996   1st prize

Der im oberen Vogtland am Dreiländereck Sachsen/Bayern/Tschechien gelegene Kurort bildet zusammen mit Bad Elster sowie den böhmischen Bädern Karlsbad, Marienbad und Franzensbad eine traditionsreiche Bäderregion.

Mit dem Neubau eines Kurmittelhauses hat sich das bisherige Kurangebot um eine großzügige Bade- und Saunalandschaft mit Außenschwimmbecken erweitert und ist damit auch gegenüber konkurrierenden Angeboten attraktiver geworden.

Das terrassierte, längs zum Hang orientierte Raumgefüge antwortet auf die topographischen und hydrogeologischen Gegebenheiten des Kurparks: die Parklandschaft geht über eine Badeterrasse mit Freibecken „fließend" in die Badehalle über, die in einem darüber aufgeständerten Therapietrakt ihre Erweiterung findet.

Mit seiner Transparenz und Offenheit, Materialität und Farbigkeit setzt das neue Kurmittelhaus ein nicht zu übersehendes Zeichen für eine neue Ära des Kurbetriebs in Bad Brambach.

The spa located in Upper Vogtland in the triangle where Saxony, Bavaria and the Czech Republic meet, is located in a health resort region steeped in tradition that includes Bad Elster and the Bohemian spas Karlovy Vary, Marianske Lazne, and Franziskovy Lazne.

The construction of the new Kurmittelhaus expands the existing range of facilities to include a spacious bathing and sauna landscape that incorporates an outdoor swimming pool. This makes it much more attractive in comparison with other resorts.

The terraced ensemble which follows the slope responds to the park's topographical and hydrogeologic conditions: a bathing terrace with outdoor pool makes for a smooth transition from the park landscape to the indoor bathing landscape; a raised therapy tract was added to the latter.

With its transparency and openness, materiality and use of color, the new Kurmittelhaus clearly points the way towards a novel era of health resorts in Bad Brambach.

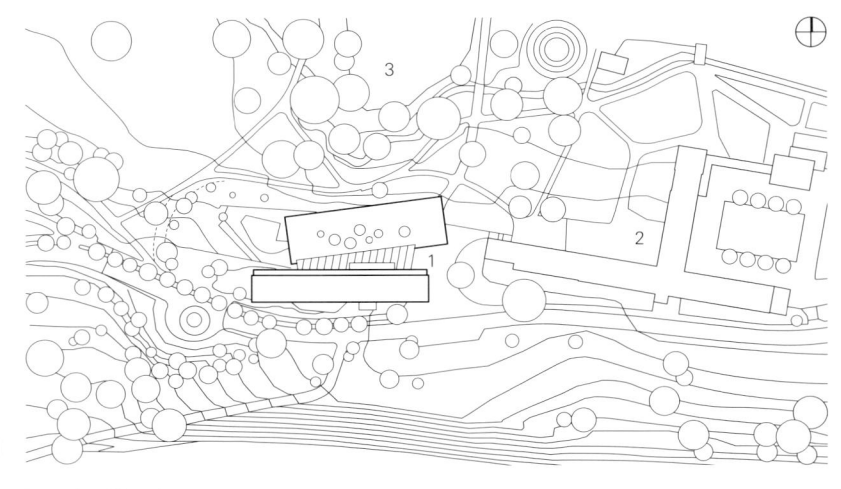

Lageplan / Site plan
1:2500

1   Kurmittelhaus / Spa center
2   Vogtlandhaus
    Vogtland house
3   Kurpark / Spa park

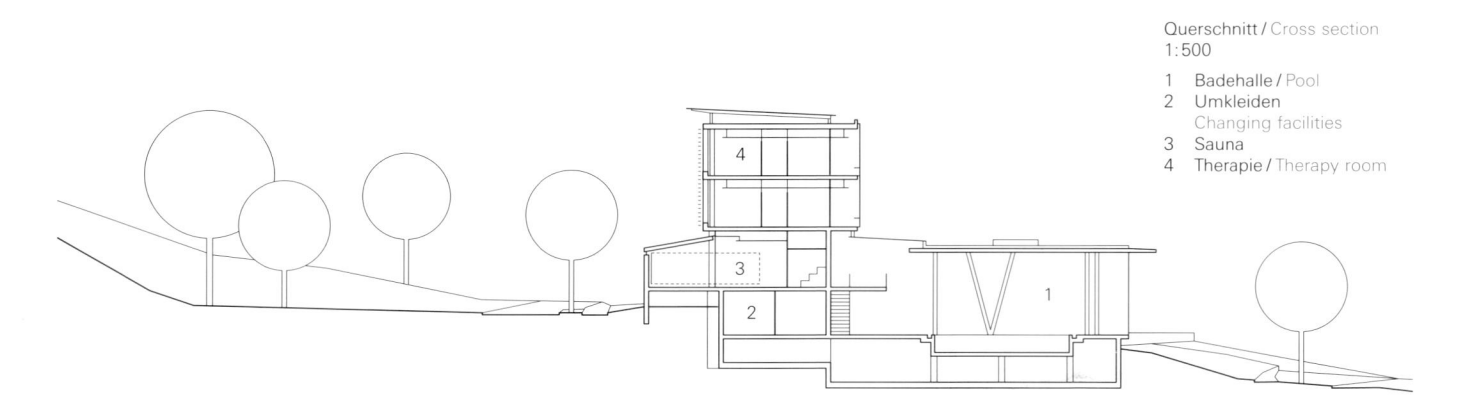

Querschnitt / Cross section
1:500

1   Badehalle / Pool
2   Umkleiden
    Changing facilities
3   Sauna
4   Therapie / Therapy room

Vor allem abends wird das terrassierte Raumgefüge vom Kurpark aus erlebbar: der ebenerdige Gymnastikbereich, die Badehalle mit vorgelagerter Badeterrasse, darüber das Therapiezentrum

Especially in the evening, the terraced ensemble is clearly visible from the spa park: the ground floor gymnastics section, the indoor pool with adjoining bathing terrace, and above that the center for therapy

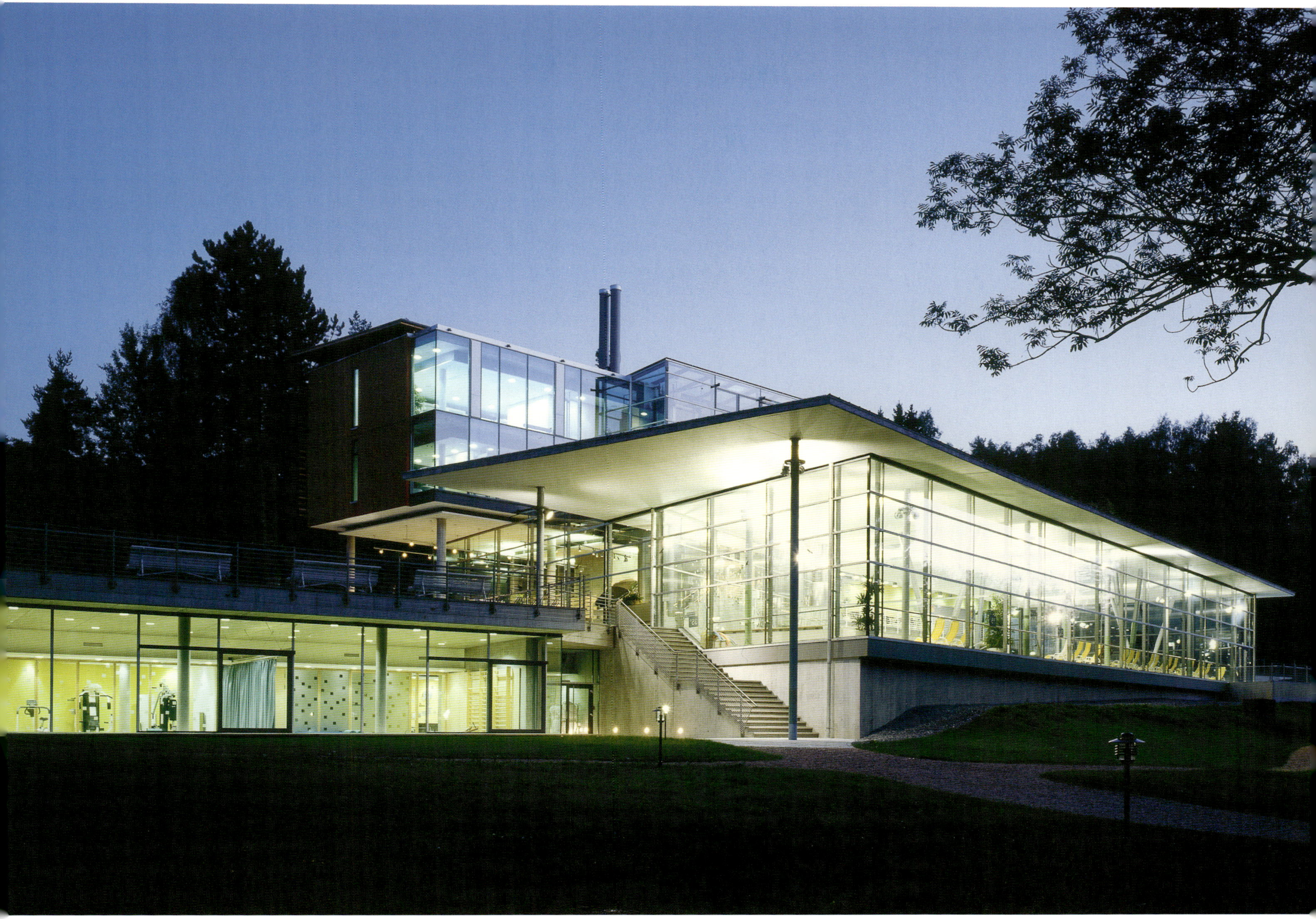

Schlanke, unregelmäßig angeordnete Stahlverbundstützen in V-Form bieten viel Bewegungsraum und erlauben eine freie Ausformung der Wasserfläche in der Badehalle

Narrow, V-shaped, steel composite beams arranged in an irregular pattern offer great flexibility of usage, allowing areas of the indoor pool to be cordoned off

Oben:
Ruhe- und Liegeraum mit freiem, ungestörtem Ausblick in die Parklandschaft

Unten:
Schon beim Empfang wird der Besucher auf das Badeerlebnis eingestimmt

Above:
The relaxation and resting room offers unobstructed views of the park landscape

Below:
Visitors are already given a foretaste of the spa experience at the reception area

Obergeschoss / Upper floor
1:750

1 Luftraum Badehalle
  Void above the pool
2 Sauna

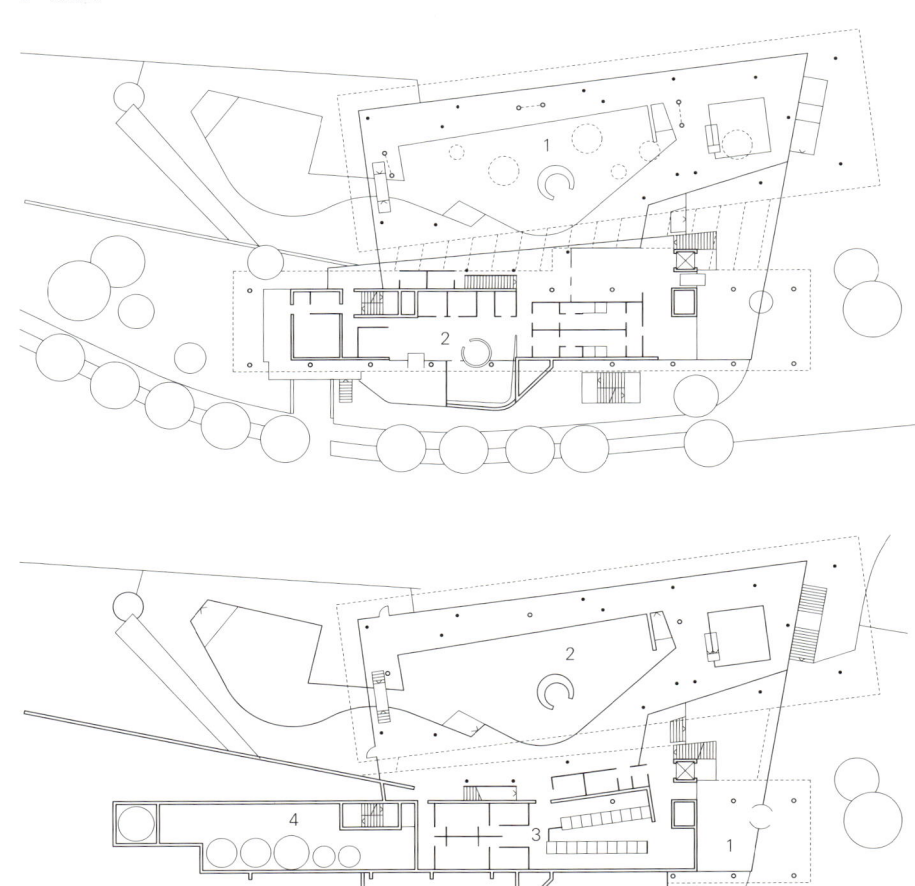

Erdgeschoss / Ground floor
1:750

1 Eingang / Entrance
2 Badeebene / Bathing level
3 Umkleiden
  Changing facilities
4 Technik / Technical equipment

Kurmittelhaus / Spa Center Bad Brambach

Aufgeständert liegt der Therapiebereich über der Eingangshalle. Freundliche, kräftige Farben signalisieren die neue Ära des Kurbetriebes

The section for therapy is raised above the entrance hall. Bright, friendly colors signalize a new era of spa services

Der „fließende" Übergang zwischen Badehalle und Badeterrasse, der leichte Dachschirm sowie die horizontale Fassadengliederung betonen den Bezug zum Park

The smooth transition between indoor and outdoor pools, as well as the horizontal organization of the façade emphasize the relation to the park

Überdachung Niedersachsenstadion
Hannover
2000
Wettbewerb 2. Preis

Roofing over the Niedersachsen Stadium
Hanover
2000
Competition 2nd prize

Das Niedersachsenstadion Hannover ist in Form eines Erdstadions in einen aufgeschütteten Trümmerberg eingegraben. Dabei ist die von einem begrünten Hügel gefasste Westseite nahezu doppelt so hoch wie die vom Tribünengebäude begrenzte Ostseite.

Diese unterschiedlichen Niveaus des Stadions werden unter einem verbindenden Dach zusammengefasst, das als Überhöhung des künstlichen Hügels konzipiert ist und die Asymmetrie der Anlage unterstreicht.

Die Grundidee des stählernen Dachtragwerkes ist eine druckbeanspruchte Schale. Seine Dachhaut aus lichtdurchlässigen Kunststofftafeln erhellt das Stadioninnere bei Tag und lässt es bei abendlichen Veranstaltungen weithin leuchten.

The Niedersachsen stadium in Hanover is embedded in a mound of ruins in the form of a natural stadium. The western side, framed by a hill of greenery, is almost twice as high as the eastern side, where the stand building is located.

The different levels of the stadium are joined together by a connecting roof, which is conceived as the camber of the artificial hill and underscores the asymmetrical shape of the ground.

The basic idea behind the steel loadbearing structure of the roof is a compression stressed shell. The roof sheath is made of translucent polycarbonate panels and lights up the interior of the stadium by day and glows during events at night.

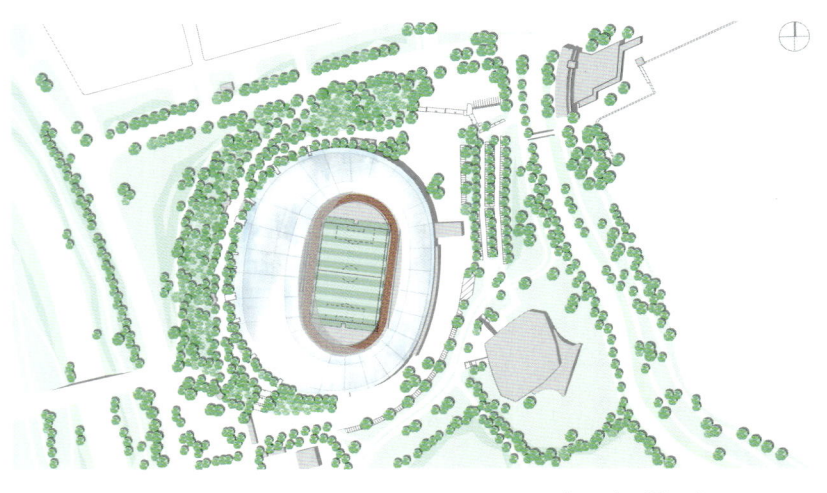

Lageplan / Site plan
1:8000

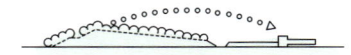

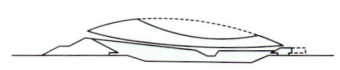

Entwicklung des Konzeptes
von oben nach unten:

Bisheriger Zustand des
Stadionhügels

Überhöhung zur eindeutigen
Form

Kalotte mit ansteigendem
unterem Rand

Ausschnitt über dem Spielfeld

Development of concept,
top to bottom:

Previous condition of the
stadium hill

Camber to the distinctive
shape

Spherical segment with rising
lower edge

Sectional view above the
playing field

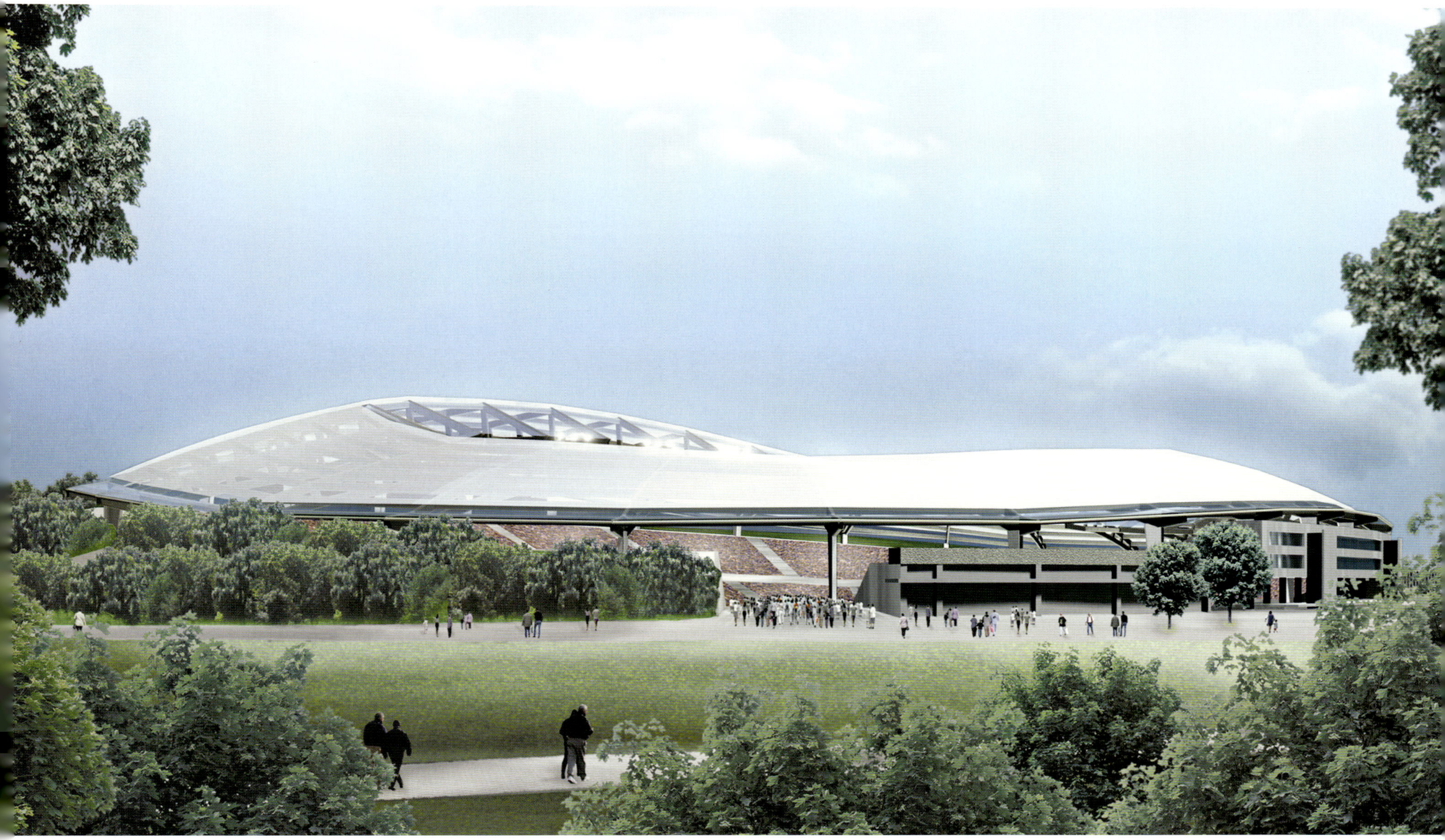

Entwicklung des Dachtragwerks aus der Grundgeometrie einer druckbeanspruchten Schale
Development of the load-bearing structure of the roof using the basic geometry of a compression stressed shell

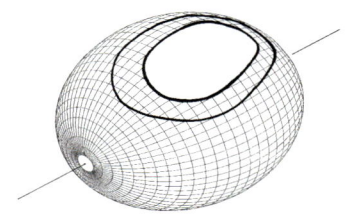

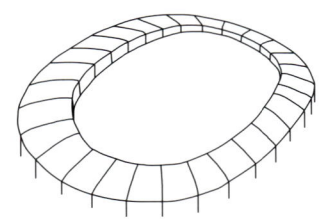

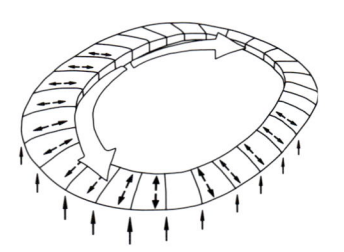

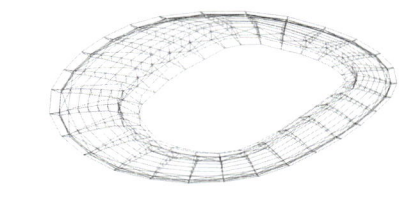

Querschnitt / Cross section
1:1000

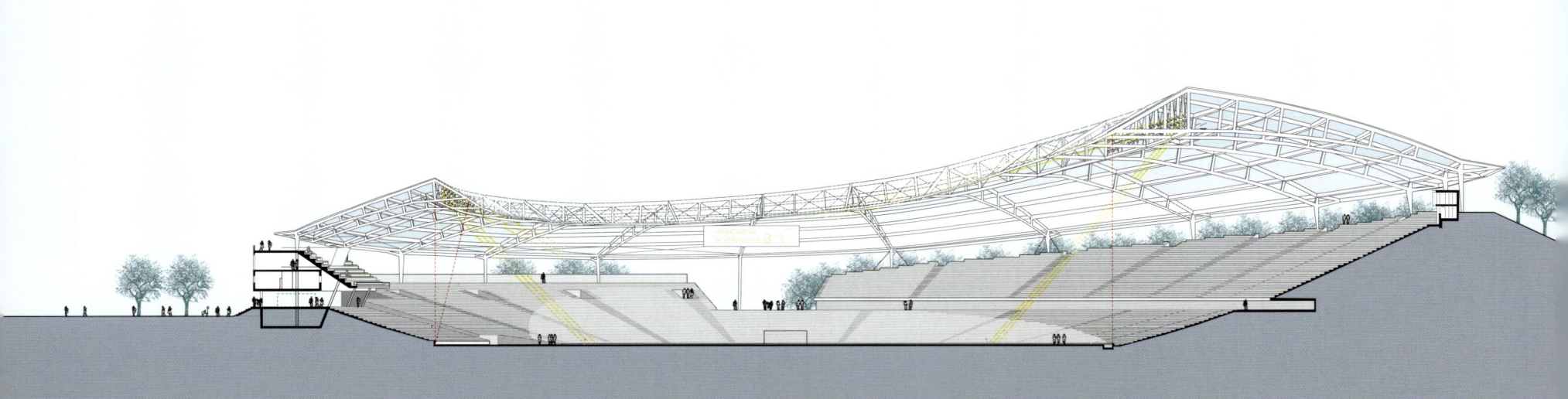

Überdachung / Roofing Niedersachsenstadion Hannover

Hochhausensemble „Münchner Tor" München
2000
Wettbewerb   1. Preis

"Münchner Tor" (Twin Towers)
High-rise Complex Munich
2000
Competition   1st prize

Das Twin Tower Ensemble am Anschlussknoten Mittlerer Ring–Autobahn Nürnberg bildet den Auftakt der neuen Parkstadt Schwabing.

In seiner klaren Zeichenhaftigkeit markiert es den nördlichen Stadteingang durch die Gegenüberstellung zweier in Höhe und Abmessung unterschiedlicher und bis zu 140m hoher Türme. Dimension und Anordnung minimieren die Verschattung der Nachbarschaft und erzeugen je nach Blickrichtung eine wechselnde Silhouette. Das horizontale Bebauungsband der Parkstadt Schwabing entlang der Autobahn wird in einer fünf- bis siebengeschossigen Sockelbebauung aufgenommen und unmittelbar in die Vertikale der Türme übergeleitet.

Der als gemeinsames Entrée für das Verlagshaus Langenscheidt und den Twin Tower vom Verkehr freigehaltene Vorplatz wird durch einen Schirm aus Bäumen gegen den Mittleren Ring geschützt.

Die Gebäudehülle, ein engmaschiges Gitter aus schlanken horizontalen und vertikalen Betonfertigteilen, verstärkt den Gesamteindruck des „Monolithischen". Die eingesetzten Fassadenelemente übernehmen Lüftungs-, Lärm- und Sonnenschutzfunktionen und betonen Porosität und Transparenz. Nach oben geht das Volumen der Türme über offene Dachgärten, die der Erholung und Aussicht dienen, in den Himmel über.

The Twin Tower complex at the intersection where the Mittlerer Ring and Nuremberg motorway converge, forms the threshold of the new Schwabing Garden City.

With striking symbolism, it marks the northern entry to the town by contrasting two towers of different height and dimensions, the taller one rising up 140 meters. Intelligent choice of dimensions and arrangement minimize loss of light to neighboring buildings, and create an imposing silhouette that varies according to the line of vision. The horizontal strip of development lining the autobahn that makes up the Schwabing Garden City is reflected in a base course five to seven stories high, before joining up with the vertical lines of the towers.

The traffic-free forecourt, which forms a joint entrance to Langenscheidt publishing company and the Twin Towers, is planted with trees that screen off the Mittlerer Ring.

The building's shell, a fine-meshed network of slim horizontal and vertical precast concrete elements, reinforces the overall impression of monolithic structures. By contrast, the façade elements assume ventilation, noise reduction and sun protection functions, and also emphasize the porous, transparent appearance. Open roof gardens incorporated into the towers for relaxation purposes and as viewing terraces form a direct transition to the open skies.

Lageplan / Site plan
1:5000

1   Twin Tower-Ensemble
    Twin Towers
2   Langenscheidt-Verlagshaus
    Langenscheidt publishing
    company
3   Vorplatz / Entrance square
4   Parkstadt Schwabing
    Schwabing Garden City
5   BAB-München – Nürnberg
    Motorway Munich –
    Nuremberg
6   Mittlerer Ring

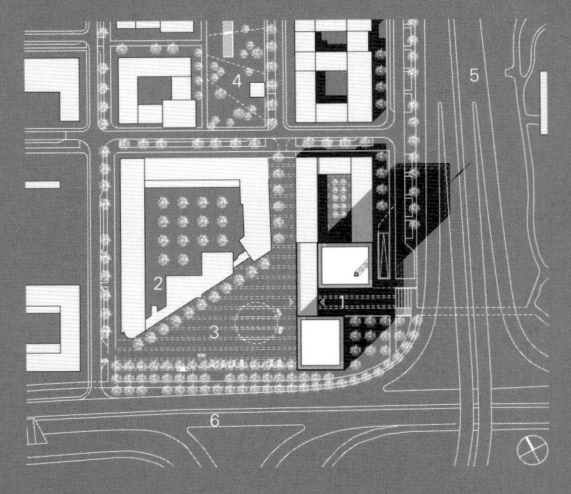

Lake Shore Drive Apartments
Chicago, USA, 1951
Ludwig Mies van der Rohe

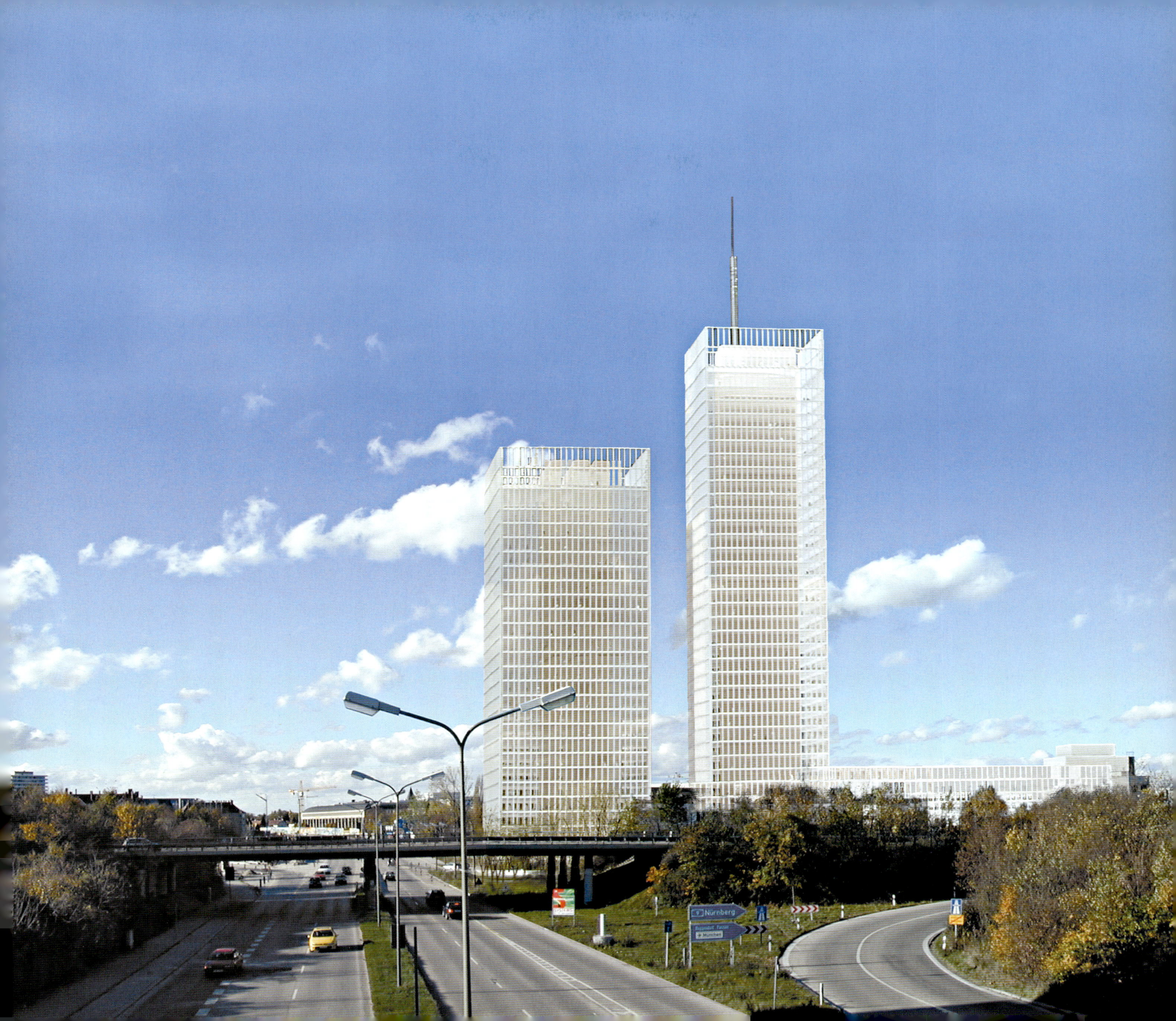
Nürnberg

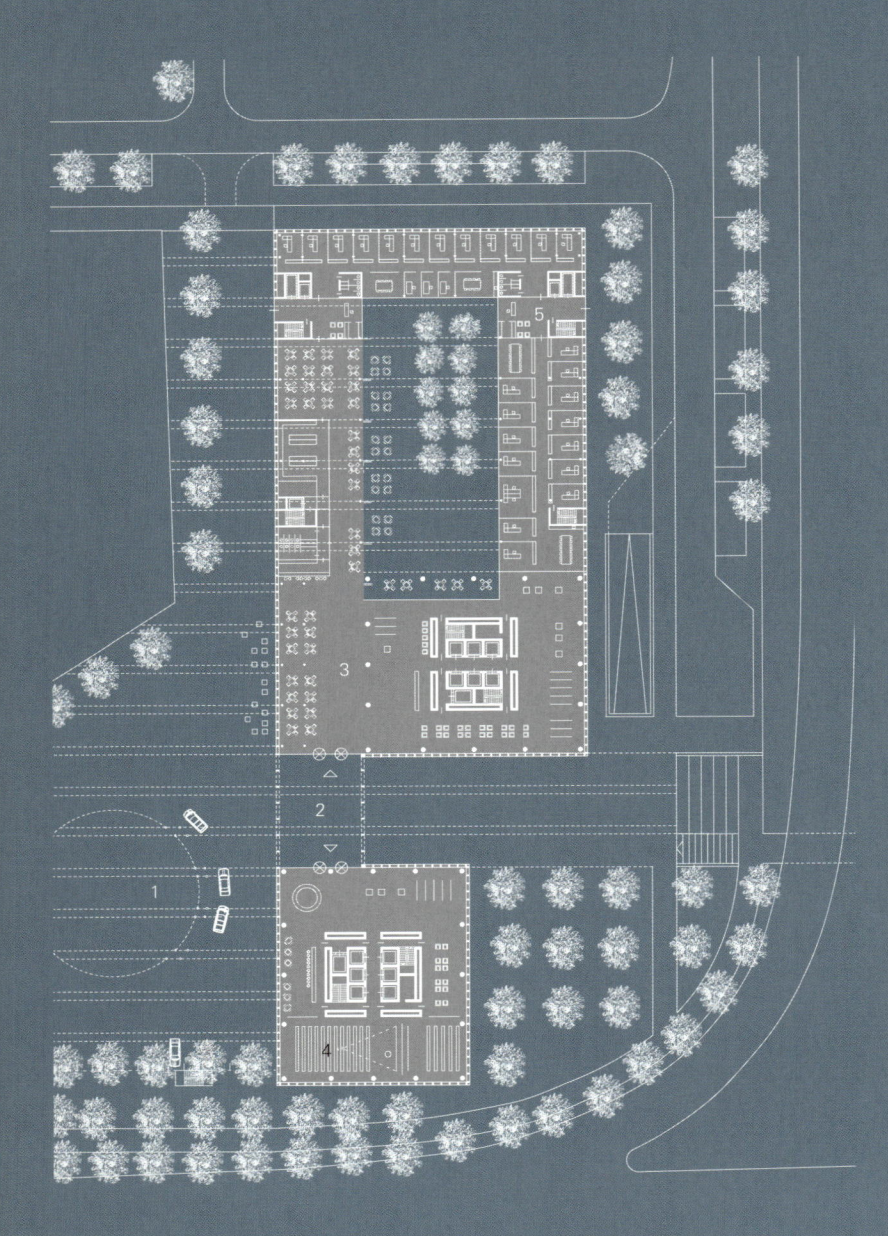

Erdgeschoss / Ground floor
1:1250

1. Eingangsplatz
   Entrance square
2. Eingangshalle / Entrance hall
3. Café, Empfangsbereich
   Café, reception area
4. Veranstaltungszone
   Event zone
5. Büroflächen / Offices

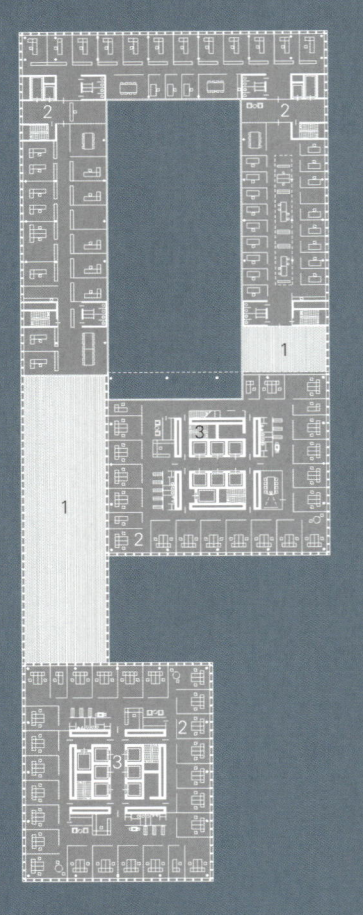

Obergeschoss / Upper floor
1:1250

1. Dachterrasse / Roof terrace
2. Büroflächen / Offices
3. Erschließungs- und Service-
   kerne / Access and service
   points

Schnitt / Section
1:1250

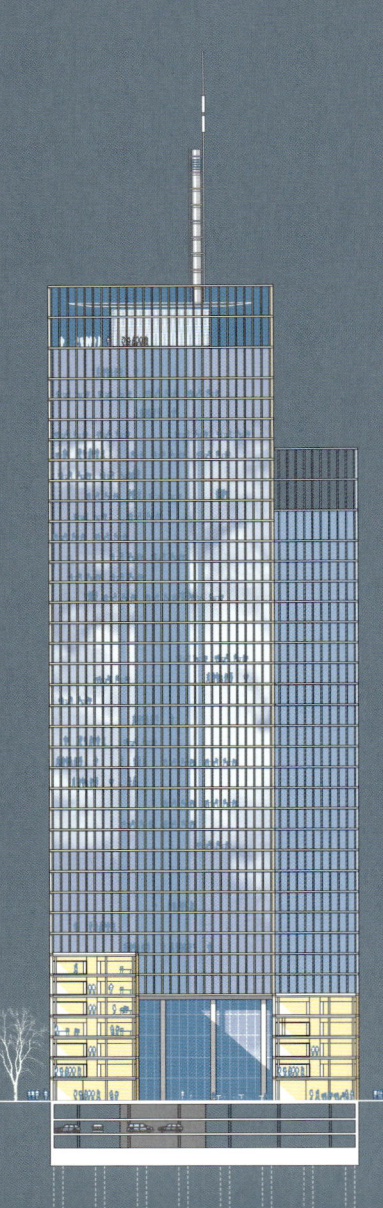

Die gitterartige Außenhaut setzt sich je zur Hälfte aus wind- und lärmgeschützten Kastenfenstern und Einfachfassaden-Elementen zusammen

Anders als in den meisten Hochhäusern können Fenster zur Regulierung des Raumklimas manuell geöffnet werden

The network-like appearance of the shell is a synthesis of single façade and countersash windows

In contrast to typical highrises, windows can be opened manually to regulate the indoor climate

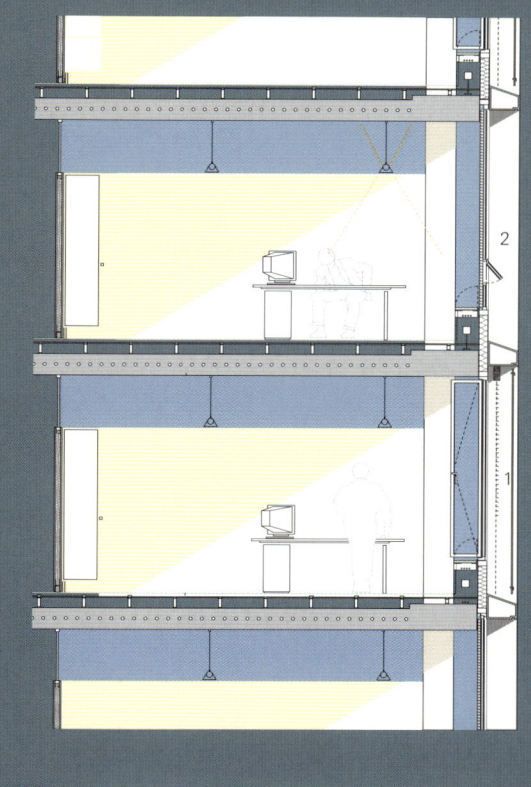

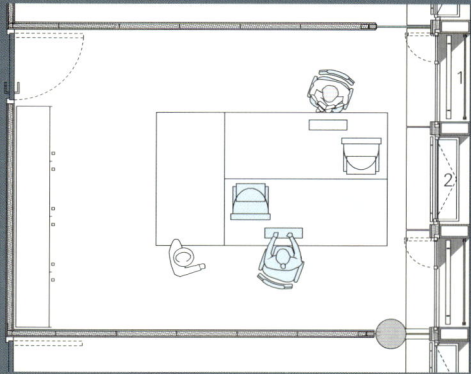

Schnitt / Section
1:1250

Fassadenausschnitt
Façade section
1:100

1 Kastenfenster mit Prallscheibe und windgeschütztem Fensterflügel Countersash window with wind-protected wing

2 Einfachfassade mit Lüftungsflügel für direkte Außenluftzufuhr / Single façade with ventilation flap for direct air intake

Kronen Carré Stuttgart
2001
Wettbewerb 1997   1. Preis

Kronen Carré Stuttgart
2001
Competition 1997   1st prize

Lageplan / Site plan
1:5000

1 Kronen Carré
2 Zeppelin Carré
3 Hauptbahnhof / Station
4 Hahn-Haus
5 Arnulf-Klett-Platz
6 Friedrichstraße
7 Kriegsbergstraße
8 Kronenstraße

Das Kronen Carré ist, nach dem benachbarten Zeppelin Carré (Seite 114 ff.), das zweite Quartier der Stuttgarter Innenstadt, das unter Erhaltung wesentlicher Bausubstanz der fünfziger und sechziger Jahre umfassend neu gestaltet wurde.

Bestand und neue Ergänzungsbauten definieren das Quartier auf neue Weise nach außen und innen, indem die Eck- und Zugangssituationen architektonisch hervorgehoben sind und sich zu einem offenen Gartenhof orientieren, an den sich auf Straßenniveau Läden und Gastronomie anlagern. Bewusst sind umgewandelter Bestand und Neubau in Wechselbeziehung gesetzt. Charaktervolle Bauten, wie das „Gelbe Haus" aus den fünfziger Jahren, kommen neu zur Geltung. Fassaden sind unterschiedlich ausgeformt und gegliedert. Die Arbeitswelt der Büros wird zu den Straßen durch kühle, zur Hofseite durch wärmere, wohnliche Farben vermittelt.

Durch die entsprechende Ausbildung der Fassaden sind trotz stark befahrener Stadtstraßen Arbeitsplätze von hoher Qualität entstanden.

Following the adjacent Zeppelin Carré (page 114 ff), the Kronen Carré is the second area of downtown Stuttgart that was extensively re-designed, involving buildings that mostly dated from the 1950s and 1960s.

By highlighting corners and access points that lead to an interior garden, where at street level there are shops and restaurants, the combination of new and original buildings redefines the area looking both inward and outward. Refurbished original buildings and new constructions were deliberately positioned in juxtaposition with each other. Buildings full of character, such as the "Gelbes Haus" (yellow house) dating from the 1950s, come into their own again. Various designs and structures are used for the façades. Looking out onto the street, cool colors hint at work being performed efficiently, while on the courtyard side they are warmer and more inviting.

Despite the heavy traffic thundering along the neighboring city streets, high-quality workplaces have been created by integrating sound insulation into the design of the façades.

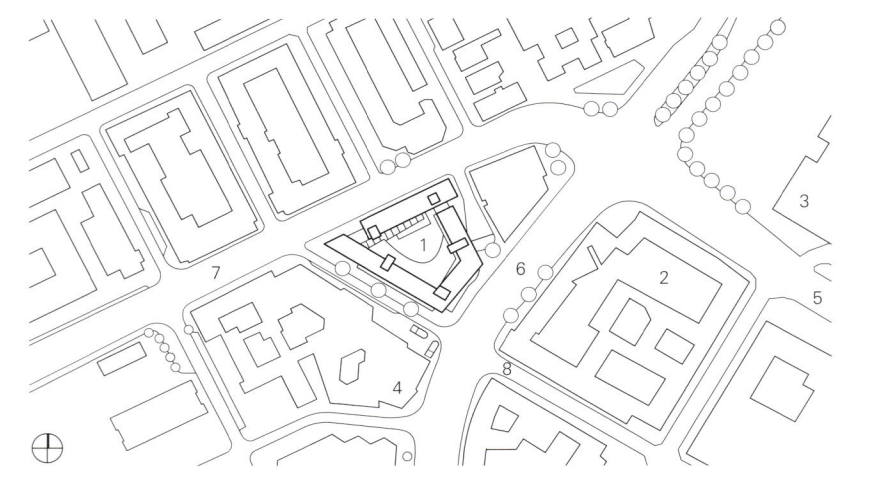

Die neue Quartierecke Kronen-/Kriegsbergstraße markiert den Zugang zum Innern des Carré; links das „Gelbes Haus", ein aus den fünfziger Jahren stammendes, renoviertes Bürogebäude

The new corner where Kronenstrasse and Kriegsbergstrasse meet marks the point of access to the Carré's interior. The "Gelbes Haus" (yellow house), a renovated office building dating from the 1950s, is on the left

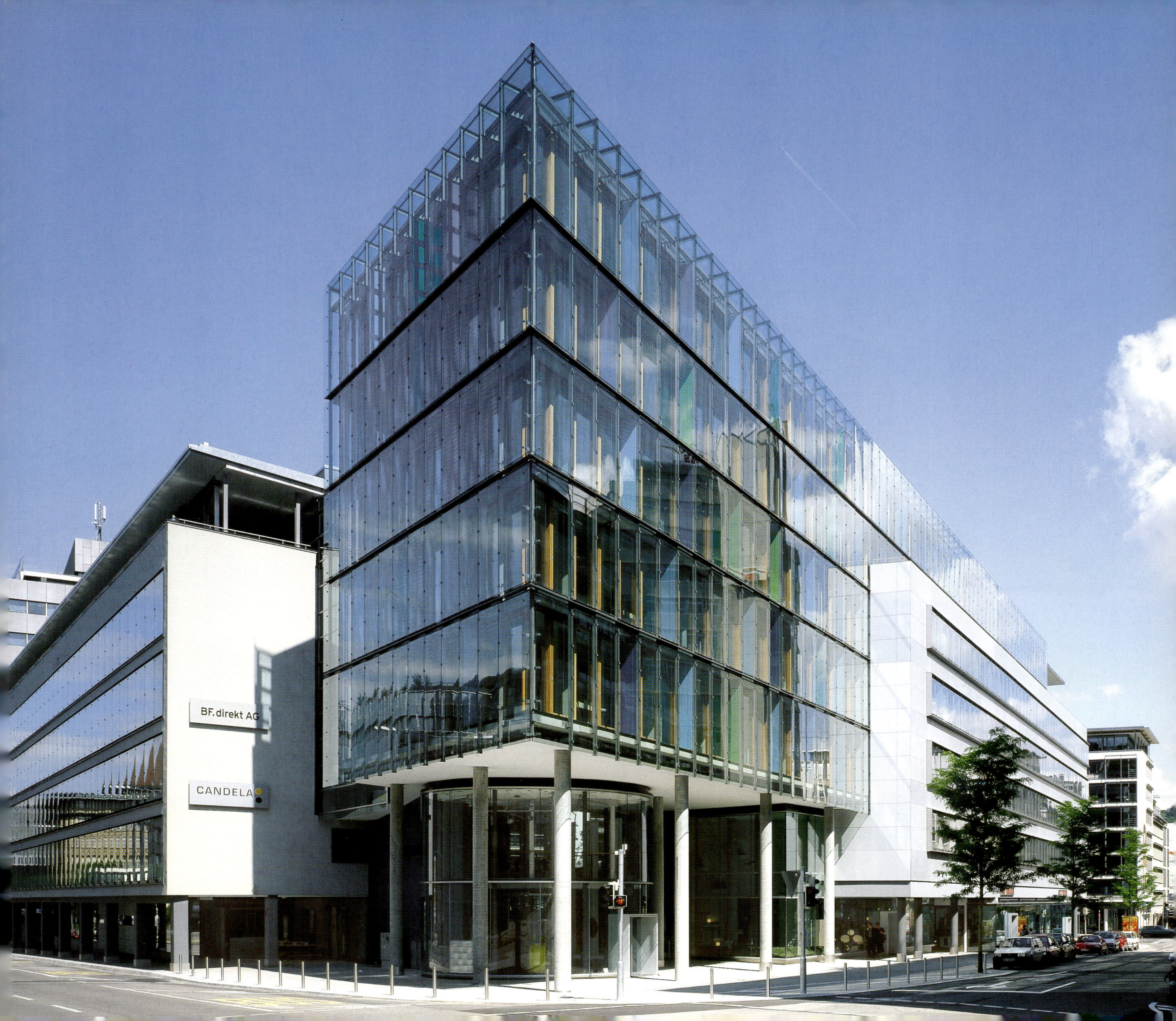
BF.direkt AG
CANDELA

Regelgeschoss / Standard floor
1:1000

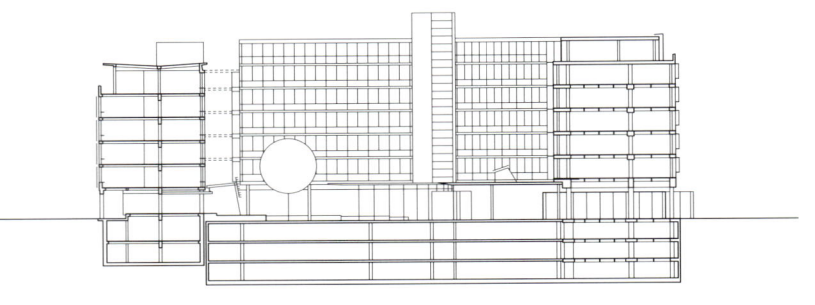

1. Begrünte Dachfläche
   Roof surface with greenery
2. Büroflächen / Office floors

Schnitt / Section
1:1000

Durchlaufende, über die Fassadenebene leicht vorspringende Fensterbänder charakterisieren den Umbau des aus dem Bestand übernommenen Gebäudeteils an der Ecke Friedrich-/Kronenstraße. Im Vergleich dazu dieselbe Situation vor dem Beginn der Sanierungs- und Umbauarbeiten (unten)

Continuous strip windows that jut out slightly from the façades characterize the conversion of the original buildings at the corner of Friedrichstrasse and Kronenstrasse. For comparison, the same location before restoration and conversion work began is shown below

Erdgeschoss / Ground floor
1:1000

1. Halle
2. Gartenhof
   Garden courtyard
3. Läden / Shops
4. Restaurant
5. Service / Service facilities

Die neue Fassade des Kronen Carré zur Friedrichstraße mit dem Hahn-Haus von Rolf Gutbrod aus den fünfziger Jahren

The new façade of the Kronen Carré, looking towards Friedrichstrasse, with Rolf Gutbrod's Hahn-House, dating from the 1950s

163　Kronen Carré Stuttgart

Obere Reihe:
Heutige Anforderungen und Möglichkeiten auf der Basis gegebener oder neuer Rohbaustrukturen führen zu unterschiedlichen Fassaden

Untere Reihe:
Der Innenausbau folgt einem flexiblen Konzept, das Vorfertigung, schnelle Montage und einen hohen Standard an technischer Gebäudeausrüstung auch in den Altbauteilen vereint sowie spätere, sich ändernde Mieterwünsche zulässt

Upper row:
The variety of façades is a reflection of today's requirements, and of the possibilities inherent in existing or new shell constructions

Lower row:
The interior design follows a flexible concept that combines prefabrication, swift assembly and a high technical level of building equipment, in the existing structures as well, and permits changing tenant requests

Blick aus den Penthouse-
Büros über Dachterrassen
auf die Stadt

The view of the city from the
penthouse offices, looking
over one of the rooftop patios

Zum geschützten Innenhof wirken die Fassaden offener und wohnlicher

Looking over the protected inner courtyard, the façades are both inviting and more accommodating

„Naturbelassene" Materialien und lichte Farben bestimmen die Atmosphäre der auf den Gartenhof orientierten Empfangshalle

Natural materials and light hues set the mood in the lobby that surrounds the courtyard

PRISMA-Haus Frankfurt am Main
2001
Wettbewerb 1996   1. Preis

PRISMA Building Frankfurt/Main
2001
Competition 1996   1st prize

Die Eingangssituation zur Bürostadt Frankfurt-Niederrad wird, von der S-Bahn aus gesehen, vom Bild des PRISMA-Hauses bestimmt.

Entsprechend den besonderen Bedingungen des Standorts fügen sich ein aufgeständerter Gebäudewinkel und eine ihn übergreifende dreieckige Klimahülle zu einer einprägsamen Großform. Der Winkel bildet eine klare Kante zur Bürostadt, das „Schaufenster" der großflächig verglasten Klimahülle öffnet sich dagegen zum Panorama der Stadt Frankfurt.

Innerhalb der Glashülle entsteht ein geschützter, vielfältig nutzbarer Hallenraum, aus dem heraus über freistehende Aufzugsanlagen und Stege alle Arbeitsebenen erschlossen sind. Gleichzeitig wirkt dieses innere Volumen im Rahmen eines intelligenten Energiekonzeptes als Klimagenerator. Von den äußeren Abmessungen bis hin zum Detail ist das Erscheinungsbild des Gebäudes geprägt von einer ganzheitlichen Konzeption unter energetischen Aspekten.

Das Konzept kommt ohne die sonst übliche mechanisch unterstützte Klimatisierung von Büroräumen aus; statt dessen nutzt es natürlich erzeugte Luftströmungen zur Versorgung des Gebäudeinneren.

Nicht nur Funktion und Konstruktion prägen die architektonische Gestalt des PRISMA-Hauses, sondern auch – als drittes Element – die Gebäudetechnik, indem Tragkonstruktion und Gebäudehülle thermodynamisch aufeinander reagieren. Wären die Luftströmungen sichtbar, so könnte man die energetische Aktivität des Gebäudes nachvollziehen und erkennen, dass es im besten Sinn des Wortes „atmet".

Viewed from the suburban railway, the initial stages of the office park in the Niederrad district of Frankfurt are dominated by the PRISMA building.

Consistent with the special conditions imposed by the location, the elevated angle of the building and triangular air-conditioning sheath meld to form a distinctive entity. The angle forms hard edges towards the office park, while at the same time the "display window" of the large-scale, glazed air-conditioning sheath opens out toward the Frankfurt panorama.

Inside the glass sheath there is a protected, multipurpose hall, providing access to all work levels via elevators and walkways. As part of an ingenious energy concept it also functions as a generator for air-conditioning. From the most extreme dimensions down to the smallest details, the building's appearance is dominated by a holistic concept that takes energy concerns into account.

This concept works without using the standard mechanically supported method of air-conditioning; instead it utilizes the natural flow of air to cool the interior of the building.

The architectural design of the PRISMA building is dominated not only by its function and construction, but by the technology behind the building where the loadbearing structure and the building sheath react to each other thermodynamically. If the currents of air were visible one would be able to see the building's energetic activity and recognize that it "breathes" in every sense of the word.

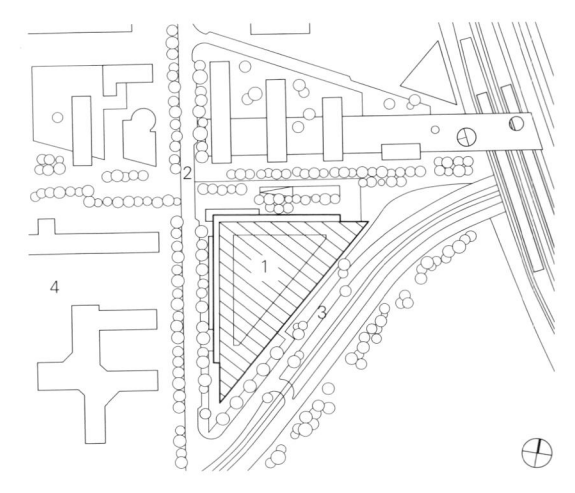

Lageplan / Site plan
1:5000

1   PRISMA-Haus
    PRISMA building
2   Hahnstraße
3   Lyoner Straße
4   Bürostadt Frankfurt-Niederrad

Ford Foundation, New York
1967
Roche, Dinkeloo & Associates

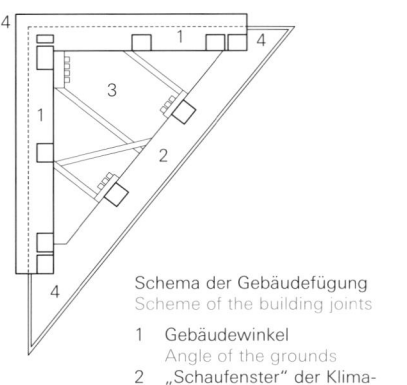

Schema der Gebäudefügung
Scheme of the building joints

1   Gebäudewinkel
    Angle of the grounds
2   „Schaufenster" der Klimahülle / "Display window"
3   Halle / Hall
4   Sonderbereich
    Special area

Regelgeschoss / Standard floor
1:1500
1. Klimahalle mit Verbindungsstegen
   Air-conditioning hall with connecting walkways
2. Büroflächen / Office space
3. Sonderbereiche
   Special areas

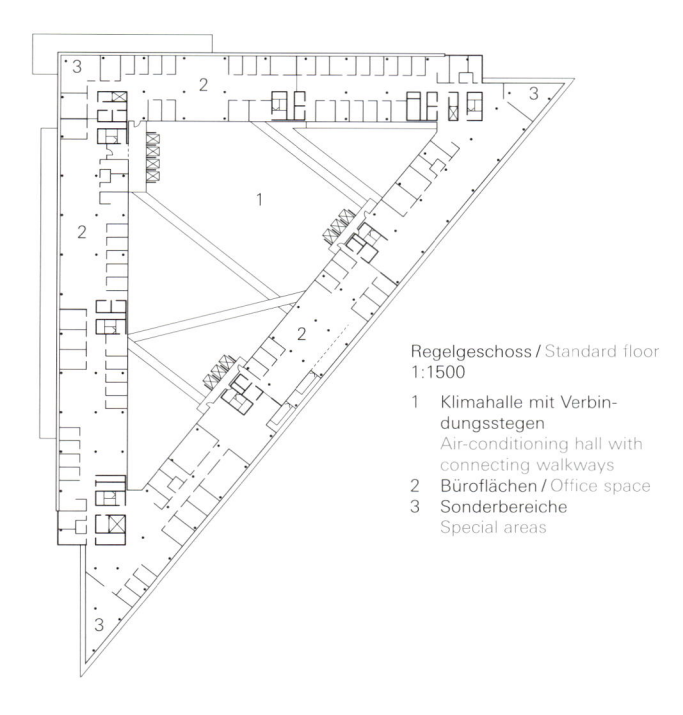

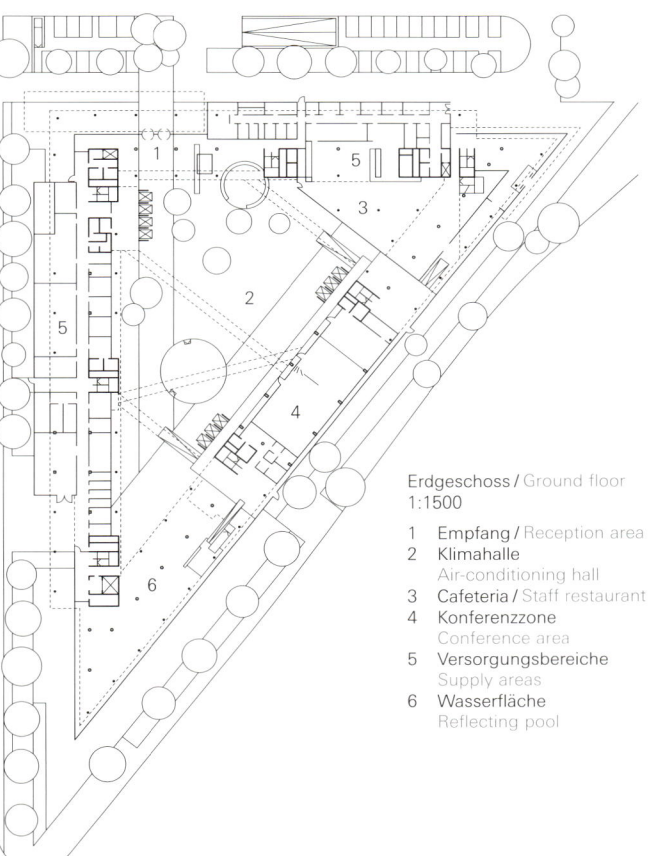

Scharfkantig und präzise stellt sich der prismatische Baukörper in den Raum. In den gläsernen Spitzen befinden sich Besprechungs- und Sonderräume. Von hier aus schweift der Blick auf den Frankfurter Stadtwald und über die Bahn auf die Silhouette der Frankfurter Innenstadt

The prism-shaped edifice stands sharp-edged and precise within its surroundings. Meeting rooms and special rooms are located in the glass corners. From here you gaze out over the Frankfurt woods and the railway towards the silhouette of downtown Frankfurt

Erdgeschoss / Ground floor
1:1500
1. Empfang / Reception area
2. Klimahalle
   Air-conditioning hall
3. Cafeteria / Staff restaurant
4. Konferenzzone
   Conference area
5. Versorgungsbereiche
   Supply areas
6. Wasserfläche
   Reflecting pool

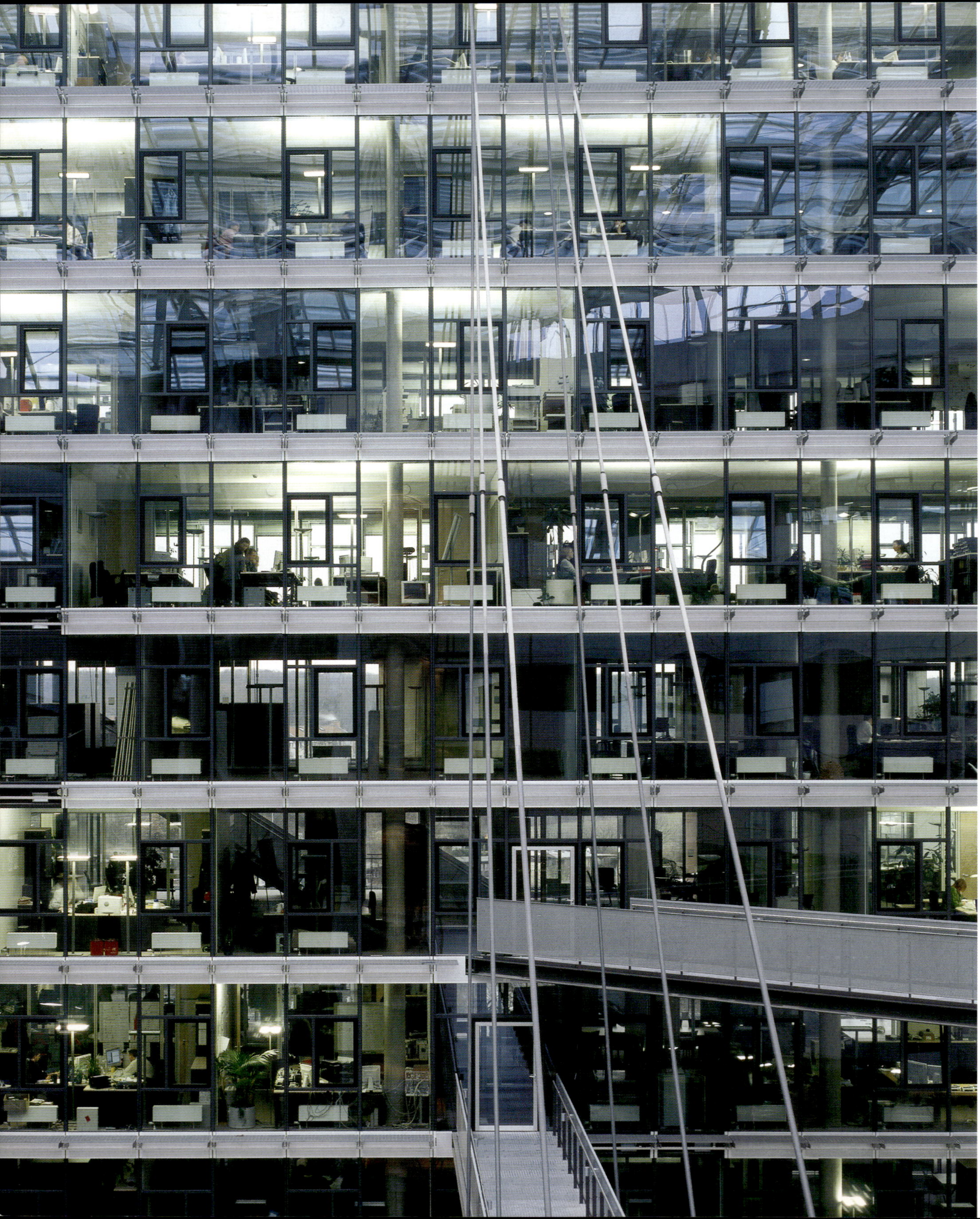

Die zur Halle orientierten Arbeitsplätze werden über ein intelligentes Lüftungssystem in den schlanken Decken mit Frischluft versorgt und stehen über transparente Innenwände auch in Bezug zur Außenwelt

Eingehängte Stege durchqueren den Hallenraum und verbinden die Arbeitsbereiche des PRISMA-Hauses über kurze, luftige Wege

Workstations facing the hall are provided with fresh air by means of an ingenious ventilation system in the thin ceilings. As a result, the transparent interior walls are not cut off from the outside world

Suspended walkways cross the hall providing short airy paths that connect the various work areas in the PRISMA building

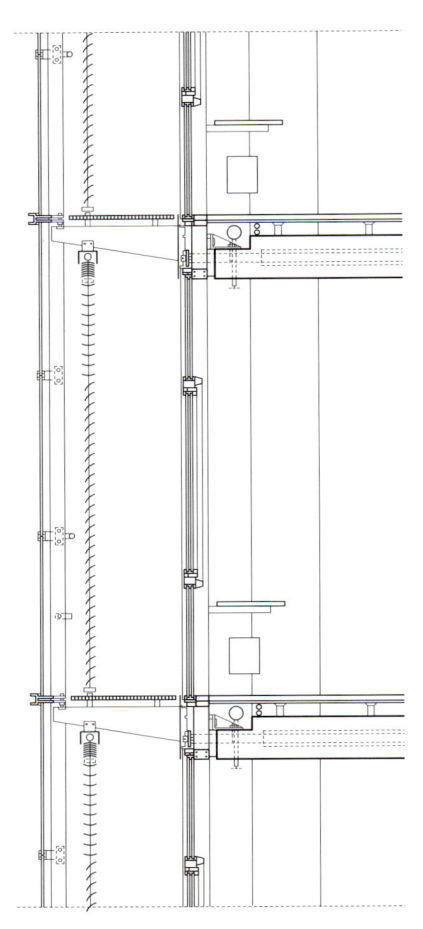

Schnitt durch die Doppelfassade / Partial section of the double façade
1:50

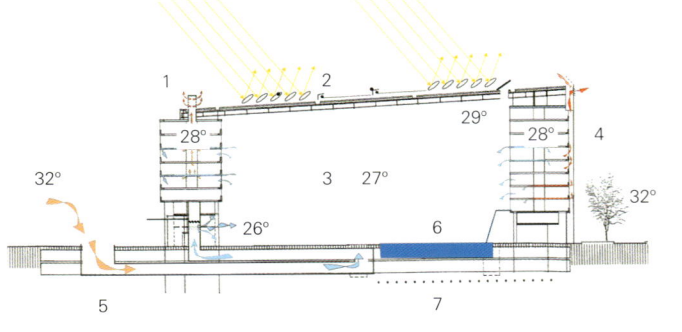

Klimakonzept
Climate control concept
Sommer / Summer

Winter / Winter

1 Solarkamin
  Solar energy collector
2 Sonnenschutz
  Sun protection
3 Hall
4 Doppelfassade
  Double façade
5 Erdkanal / Earth channel
6 Offene Wasserfläche
  Public stretch of water
7 Erdwärmetauscher
  Geothermal converter

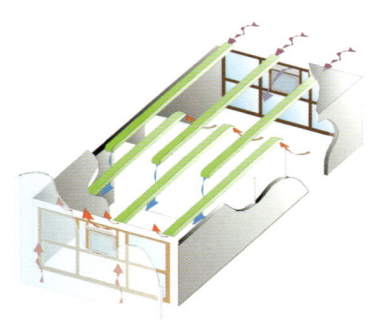

Be- und Entlüftung / Ventilation
Sommer / Summer

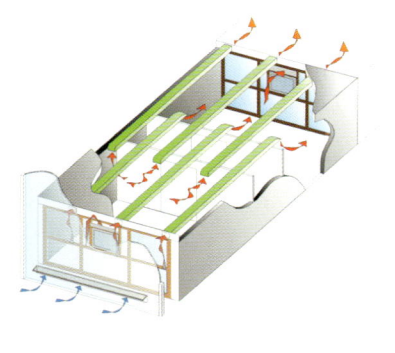

Winter / Winter

Das PRISMA-Haus orientiert sich mit seinem großen „Schaufenster" der Doppelfassade, in der die „Himmelsleiter" nach oben führt, zur Lyoner Straße und zum freien Stadtraum

With its large "display window" on the double façade – and its "Jacob's Ladder" stretching upwards – the PRISMA building faces the Lyoner Strasse and toward the open expanse of the city

Altes Rathaus Pforzheim
2001
Wettbewerb 1997 2. Preis

Pforzheim Old Town Hall
2001
Competition 1997 2nd prize

Um den gestiegenen Raumbedarf der Verwaltung an einem Ort zu konzentrieren, wurde unter Berücksichtigung denkmalschützender Belange das nach der Kriegszerstörung 1944 genutzte Gebäuderelikt des Alten Rathauses von 1911 von Grund auf saniert und erweitert. Die Erweiterung als zweigeschossiger Aufbau auf den Bestand erinnert mit einer vorgesetzten Schicht aus beweglichen Sonnenschutzlamellen an die einstige imposante Dachhaube.

Mittelpunkt und Herzstück des Alten Rathauses ist die glasüberdachte Halle mit ihren umlaufenden galerieartigen Fluren, die künftig als Bürgerzentrum auch kulturellen Belangen dient.

Der ursprüngliche Glassteinboden der Halle wurde für die Belichtung der darunter liegenden Schalterräume wiederhergestellt.

Die Oberlichthalle erhält durch eine dem ursprünglich tonnenförmigen Glasabschluss folgende Lamellenstruktur ihre historischen Proportionen zurück.

In die Glaslamellen eingelegte Hologramme zerlegen je nach Sonnenstand das Tageslicht in unterschiedliche Spektralfarben, die ein wechselndes Lichtspiel auf den Hallenwänden erzeugen.

In order to concentrate the increased demand for space under one roof, what remained of the Old Town Hall of 1911, and had been in use since it was damaged during the war in 1944, was completely gutted and then extended. In doing so, all restrictions pertaining to listed historic buildings were strictly observed. With its front of moveable lamella sunscreens, the extension, a two-story addition to the original body of the building, is reminiscent of the former domed roof.

The focal point and heart of the Old Town Hall is the glass-roofed hall surrounded by gallery-like corridors; this hall will be used in future as a civic center and a venue for cultural events.

To provide lighting for the main public hall below, the upper hall's original glass block floor was reproduced.

The historic proportions of the skylight hall were recreated by means of a lamella structure that follows the line of the original cask-shaped glass covering.

Holograms inserted in the lamellas split sunlight into various colors of the spectrum that shift with the position of the sun, thus staging an ever-changing light show on the walls of the hall.

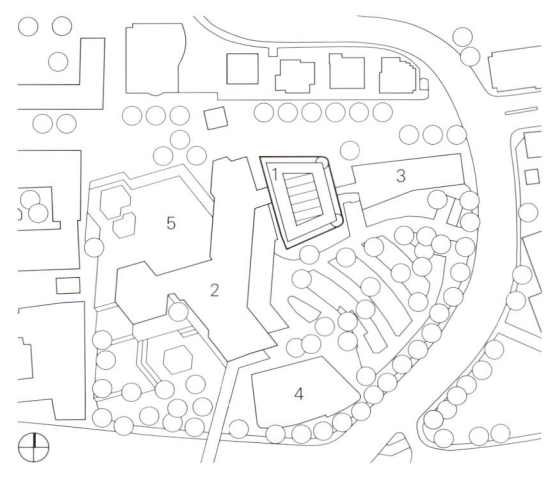

Lageplan / Site plan
1:2500

1 Altes Rathaus
  Old Town Hall
2 Neues Rathaus
  New Town Hall
3 Technisches Rathaus
  Technical city hall
4 Stadtbibliothek / Library
5 Marktplatz / Market place

Links:
Das Alte Rathaus vor der Kriegszerstörung 1944; vor dem Umbau; drei Rathäuser bilden ein Ensemble: das Neue Rathaus von 1970; das Alte Rathaus von 1911; das Technische Rathaus aus den fünfziger Jahren

Left:
The state of the building before it was destroyed in 1944 during the war; before renovation; three town halls form an ensemble: the new town hall built in 1970; the old town hall built in 1911; and the technical city hall built in the 1950s

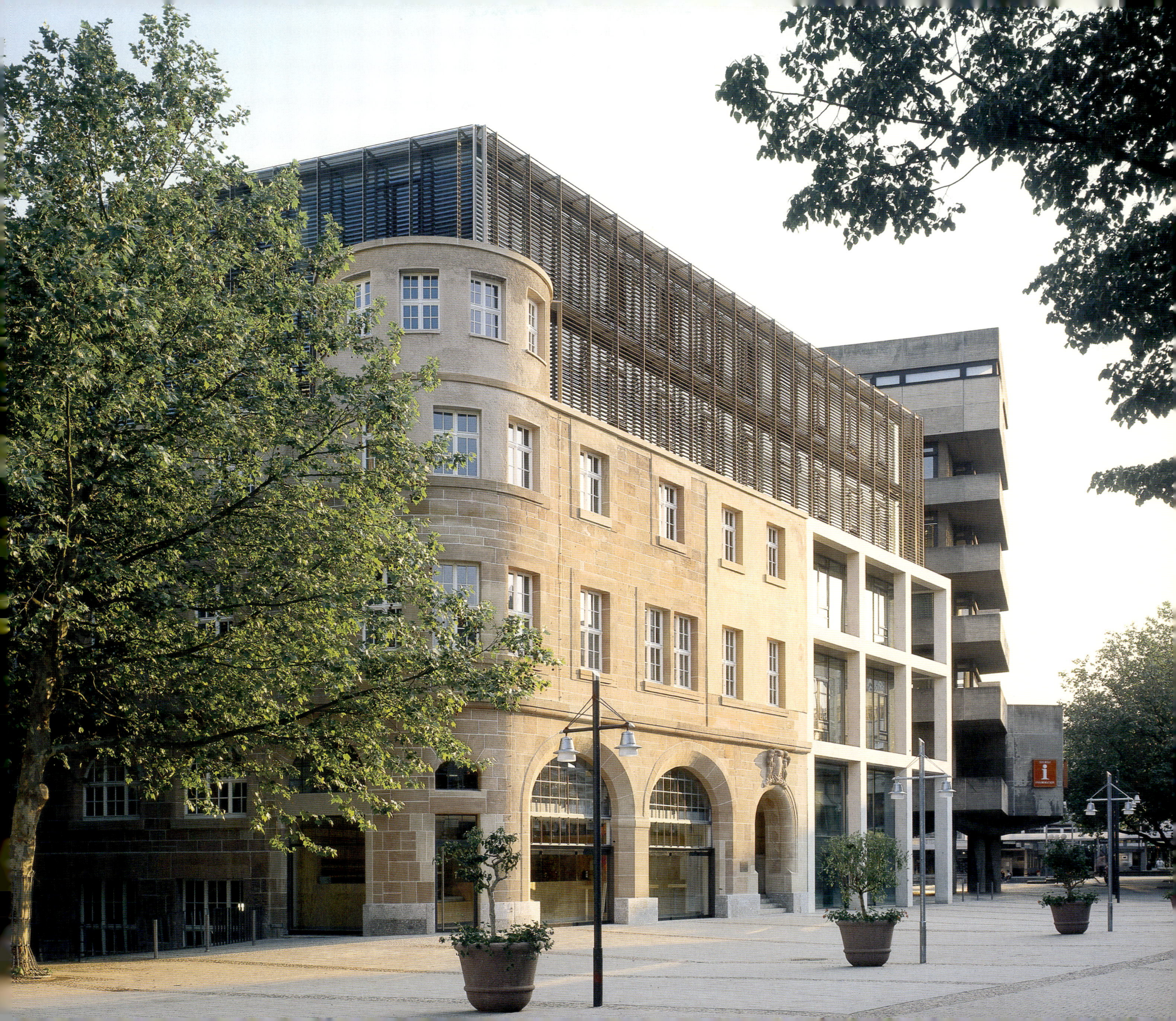

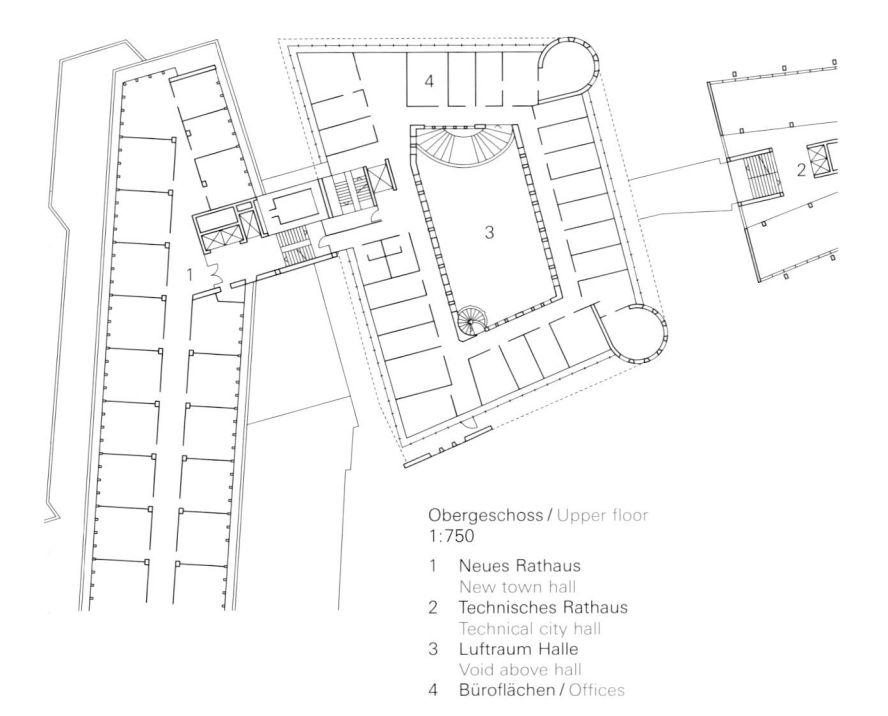

Obergeschoss / Upper floor
1:750

1. Neues Rathaus
   New town hall
2. Technisches Rathaus
   Technical city hall
3. Luftraum Halle
   Void above hall
4. Büroflächen / Offices

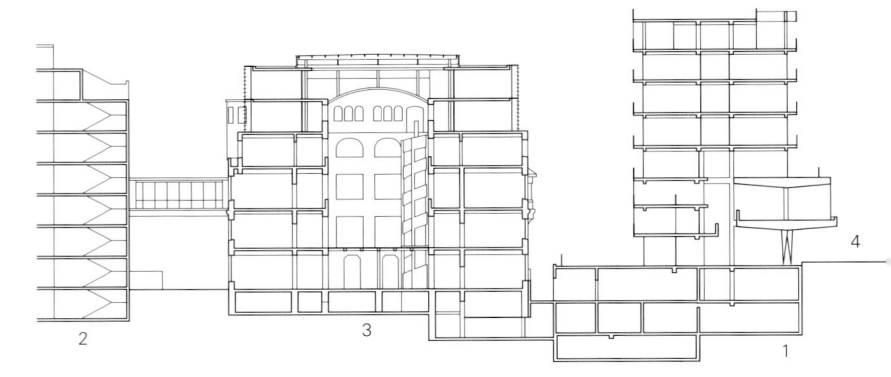

Schnitt / Section
1:750

1. Neues Rathaus
   New town hall
2. Technisches Rathaus
   Technical city hall
3. Altes Rathaus
   Old town hall
4. Marktplatz / Market square

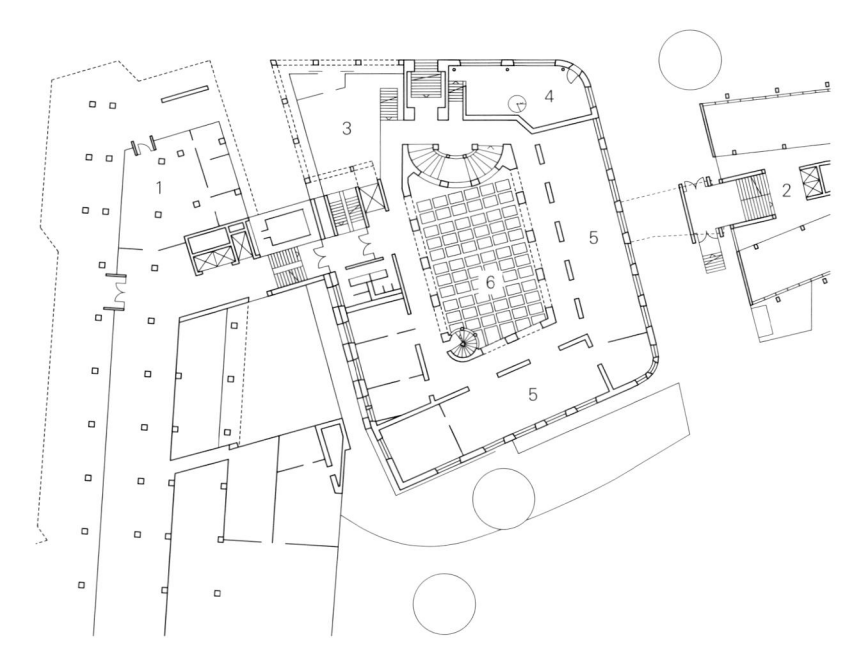

Erdgeschoss / Ground floor
1:750

1. Neues Rathaus
   New town hall
2. Technisches Rathaus
   Technical town hall
3. Eingangsfoyer
   Entrance foyer
4. Café
5. Bürgerzentrum
   Citizens' center
6. Halle / Hall

Ein Vorhang aus verstellbaren Metalllamellen bietet Sonnenschutz und fasst in Erinnerung an die frühere Dachhaube die beiden Geschosse der Aufstockung zusammen

A curtain made of adjustable metal blinds affords protection from the sun and brings the two added floors together in a manner reminiscent of the former turret

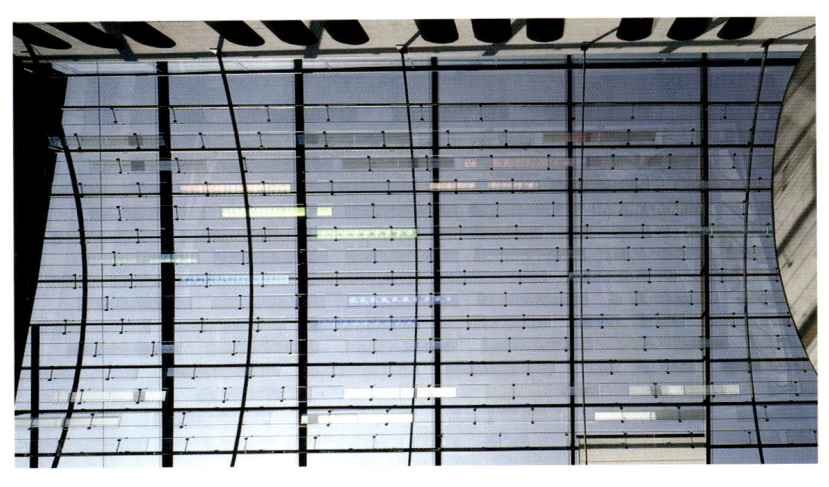

Oben und rechts:
Die Glaslamellentonne über der Halle interpretiert das historische Vorbild. Hologramme erzeugen je nach Sonnenstand unterschiedliche Spektralfarben

Mitte:
Die Schalterhalle für Meldewesen erhält Tageslicht über den Glassteinboden der Halle

Unten:
Im Fußboden des Gewölbekellers sind die Überreste eines dort vorgefundenen Brunnens aus dem Mittelalter eingelassen

Above and right:
The glass lamella drum over the hall is a modern variation on its historical predecessor. Holograms produce a variety of spectral colors depending on the position of the sun

Middle:
Daylight reaches the Aliens Registration Office through the glass block floor in the hall

Below:
In the floor of the rounded-ceiling cellar are the remains of a fountain from the Middle Ages, which was discovered there

Herzstück der Anlage und Treffpunkt für kulturelle Anlässe ist die glasüberdeckte Halle mit ihren umlaufenden, galerieartigen Fluren, den geschwungenen Treppenläufen und dem Fußboden aus Glassteinen

The focal point of the complex is the glass-roofed hall with its surrounding gallery-like corridors and glass block floor

BMW Erlebnis- und Auslieferungszentrum
München
2001
Wettbewerb   Engere Wahl

BMW Event and Delivery Center
Munich
2001
Competition   Short-listed

Dem neuen Erlebnis- und Auslieferungszentrum der BMW Group liegt die Idee zu Grunde, die Übergabe des Neuwagens an den Kunden mit einem ganztägigen Aufenthalt in einer einzigartigen Atmosphäre zu verbinden, in der die Marke BMW im Mittelpunkt steht. Den Besuchern präsentiert sich das Bauwerk entsprechend der Firmenphilosophie einer harmonischen Verbindung von Technik und Natur als vermittelndes Objekt zwischen BMW-Werk und Olympiapark. Es bereichert gleichermaßen das Erscheinungsbild des Unternehmens, bisher geprägt durch Hochhaus und Museum, wie auch das Ensemble des Olympiaparks um eine weitere Landmarke und stellt den Park, das BMW-Werksgelände und die östlich anschließenden Wohngebiete in eine übergeordnete Beziehung.

Die skulpturale Großform, die aus einer gegenüber dem Niveau der Lerchenauer Straße angehobenen Eingangsebene herauswächst und diese großzügig überlagert, umschließt ein vielschichtiges Raumgefüge. Im Inneren sind die verschiedenen Funktionsbereiche, welche die Marke BMW erlebbar machen sollen, vertikal entlang eines Weges gestaffelt, um eine übersichtliche Anordnung und dreidimensionale Verknüpfung der Programminhalte zu ermöglichen. Um den Ort des zentralen Ereignisses, die Autoübergabe, gruppieren sich verschiedene Themenbereiche, welche die Tätigkeitsfelder und die Geschichte des Unternehmens beleuchten.

Die Gebäudehülle ist ein herausforderndes Hochleistungsprodukt, welches das technologische Know-how von BMW unterstreicht und einbezieht. Sie kann auf unterschiedliche Klima- und Helligkeitsbedingungen reagieren, das energetische Versorgungskonzept aktivieren und lässt sich auch für Licht- und Ton-Inszenierungen, farbige Projektionen oder als Leinwand für Übertragungen von sportlichen Ereignissen nutzen.

The idea behind the new BMW Group Event and Delivery Center is to provide customers who wish to collect their cars in person with the chance to stay for the day and experience a unique atmosphere, focusing on the BMW brand. In keeping with the corporate philosophy, visitors experience the building as a harmonious combination of technology and nature that serves to mediate between BMW company headquarters and the Olympic Park. The building simultaneously enhances the company's appearance, already characterized by a high-rise and a museum, adds another landmark to the Olympic Park ensemble, and finally creates a cohesive whole of the Park, BMW grounds and adjoining residential areas to the east.

The overall sculptural design developing from the entrance level, raised above street level in Lerchenauer Strasse, and generously extending over the entrance, contains a complex spatial arrangement. The various functional areas, designed to allow visitors to experience the BMW brand, follow a vertical staggered line to enable a distinct arrangement of the various program components, with a three-dimensional connection between them. Various subject areas illustrating the company's fields of activity and history are grouped around the automobile collection point – the central event.

The building's shell is a sophisticated, intelligent, high-performance product, which both underscores and incorporates BMW's technological know-how. It can respond to various changes in temperature and brightness, can activate the energy supply system, and can also be harnessed for light and sound productions and color projections, or serve as a screen for viewing broadcasts of sporting events.

Das Zusammenspiel skulpturaler Großformen zwischen Werk und Olympiapark bestimmt das Erscheinungsbild von BMW am Mittleren Ring

The interplay of expansive sculptural forms defines the appearance of the BMW Headquarters

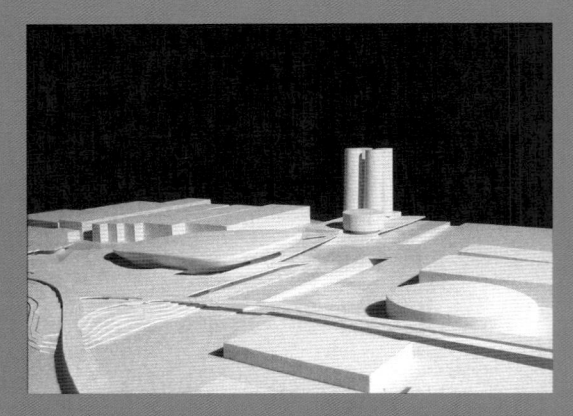

Lageplan / Site plan
1:6000

1 Erlebnis- und Auslieferungszentrum / Event and Delivery Center
2 Museum / Museum
3 BMW Hochhaus
  BMW High-rise
4 Werk / Production
5 Mittlerer Ring
6 Olympiapark / Olympia Park

Links / Left:
Schichtung der Funktionsbereiche / Layering of functional areas

1. Skybar / Skybar
2. VIP-Lounge / VIP lounge
3. Forum
4. Galerie / Gallery
5. Fahrzeugübergabe
   Vehicle delivery
6. Haupteingang / Main entrance
7. Wasserstofftankstelle
   Hydrogen filling station
8. Verwaltung / Administration
9. Gastronomie / Catering
10. Parken / Parking facilities
11. Gruppenzentrum
    Group Center
12. Übergang Museum / Werk
    Footbridge to Museum and head office

Rechts / Right:
Eingangsebene / Entrance level
1:1000

1. Haupteingang und Information / Main entrance and information
2. Fahrzeugübergabe
   Vehicle delivery
3. Vorfahrt
   Vehicle drive-up area
4. Übergang zum BMW Hochhaus und BMW Museum / Footbridge to the BMW Highrise and BMW Museum
5. Restaurant mit Außenterrasse / Restaurant with outdoor terrace

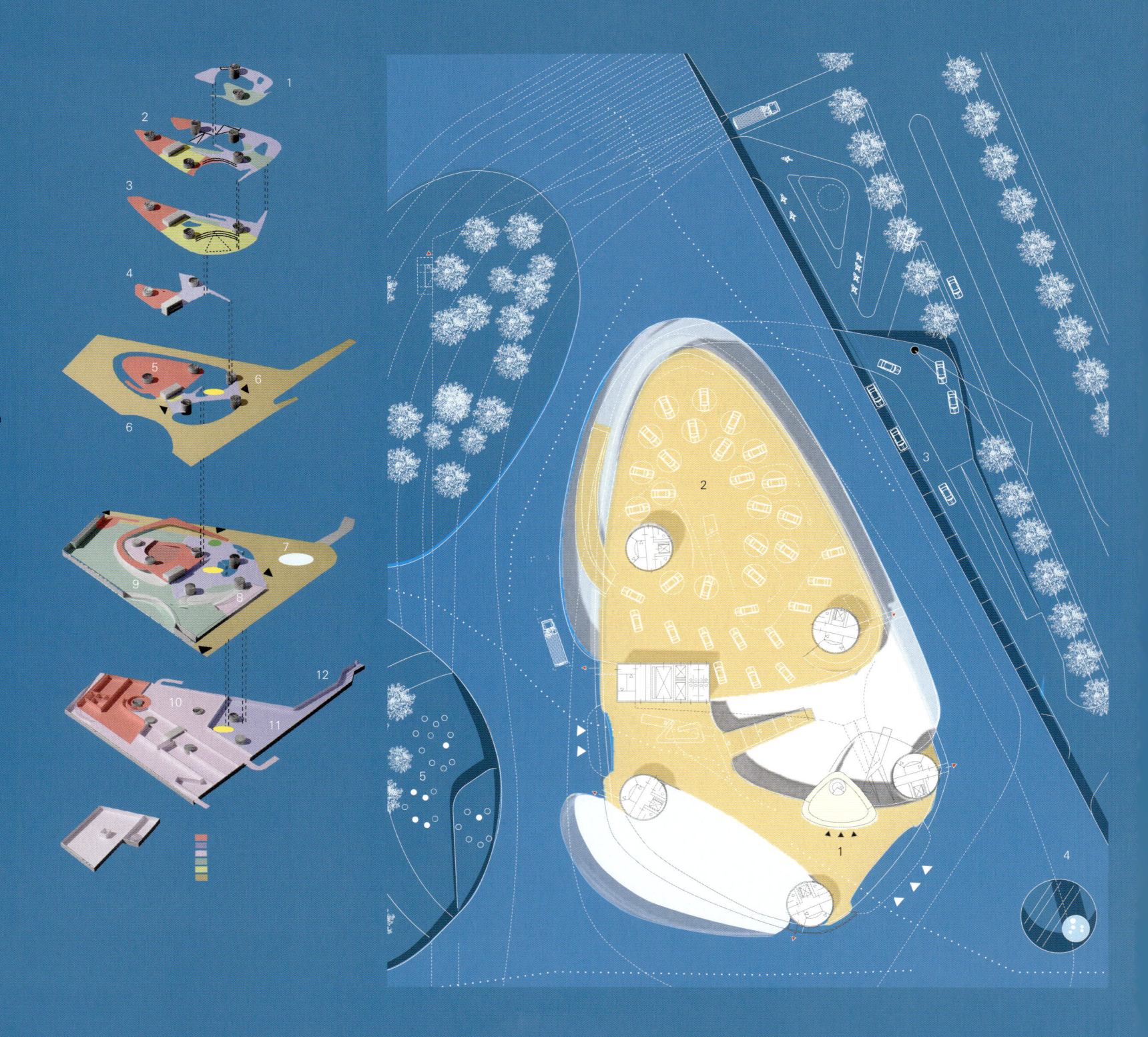

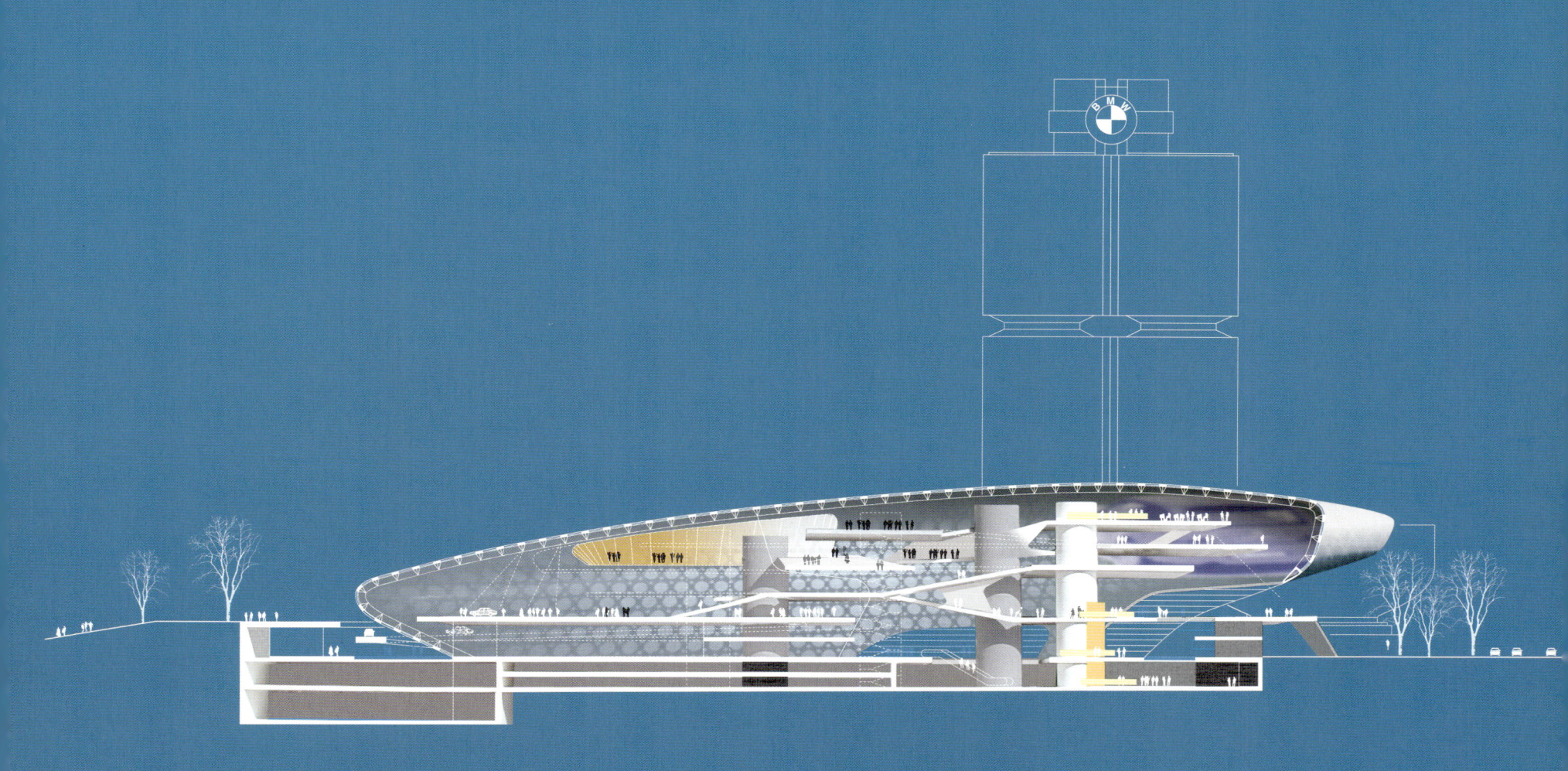

Schnitt / Section
1:1000

183 BMW Erlebnis- und Auslieferungszentrum / BMW Event and Delivery Center München

Der Organismus im Inneren wird von der frei geformten und technisch hoch entwickelten Hülle umschlossen

The interior is enclosed by a free-standing, high-performance, cutting-edge shell

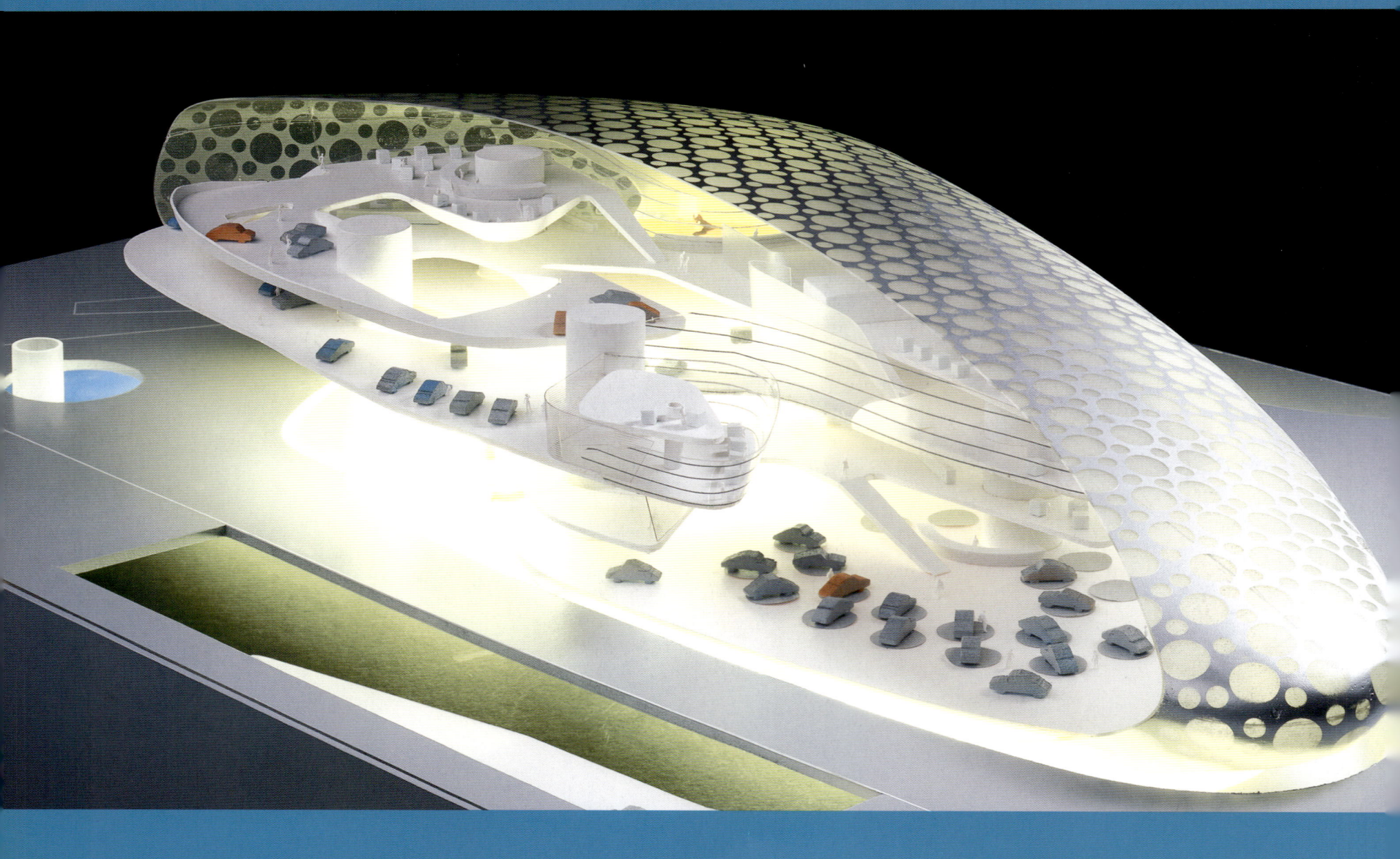

185 BMW Erlebnis- und Auslieferungszentrum / BMW Event and Delivery Center München

Büropark Fasanenhof Stuttgart
2002
Wettbewerb 2001   1. Preis
(nicht ausgeführt)

Fasanenhof Office Park Stuttgart
2002
2001 competition   1st prize
(not built)

Gesamtplan Fasanenhof Ost
Overall plan Fasanenhof East
1:8000

1. Boulevard
2. Quartiersplatz
   District square
3. Fußweg vom Wohngebiet in das Naturschutzgebiet
   Footpath from the residential area to the conservation area
4. Hochhausstandorte
   High-rise sites
5. Baublöcke am Boulevard
   Groupings on the boulevard
6. Scheibenhäuser am Wald
   Straight-line housing at the forest edge
7. Naturschutzgebiet
   Nature conservation area
8. Stadtbahn / Streetcar
9. Bundesstraße B27

Mit dem Büropark Fasanenhof wird ein am südlichen Rand der Stadt Stuttgart in Nähe des Flughafens und der neuen Messe gelegenes Gewerbegebiet neu strukturiert und aufgewertet. Die besondere Qualität des zu entwickelnden Areals besteht in der unmittelbaren Nähe zu einem unter Naturschutz stehenden Waldgebiet.

Das städtebauliche Konzept integriert das Gewerbegebiet durch Anbindung an das benachbarte Wohnquartier, das Stadtbahnnetz und die Bundesstraße 27 in das Stadtgefüge und verstärkt seine Präsenz im Stadtbild durch ausgewiesene Hochhausstandorte.

Im Schnittpunkt der Fußwegeverbindung vom Wohngebiet in das Naturschutzgebiet mit der zum Boulevard ausgebauten Hauptstraße entsteht an der neuen Stadtbahnhaltestelle ein Quartiersplatz, der das Zentrum des neuen Stadtteils bildet.

Die Bebauungsstruktur schlägt eindeutige Straßenräume entlang des Boulevards durch klar definierte Baublöcke sowie eine offene Bebauung mit zum Wald orientierten Scheibenhäusern vor. Ein Hochhaus am Quartiersplatz markiert die Mitte des Stadtteils.

Die Bebauungsstruktur wird ergänzt durch ein Freiraumkonzept, das sich vom städtischen Straßenraum über Hausgärten und die parkartige Landschaft zwischen den Scheibenhäusern bis zum Naturschutzgebiet erstreckt und Übergänge vom Kulturraum zum Naturraum ausbildet.

The objective in building the Fasanenhof office park is to upgrade and restructure an industrial area that lies on the southern periphery of the city of Stuttgart, close to the airport and the new trade fair. The special attraction of the area to be developed lies in its immediate proximity to a forested nature reserve.

The urban planning concept integrates the industrial area into the urban structure by connecting it to the neighboring residential area, to the streetcar and major road B 27, and announces its presence in the city space through striking high-rise sites.

At the point of intersection, where the path leading from the residential area to the conservation area meets the main street, which has been expanded to a boulevard, a public square that will serve as the new district's focal point and center is being constructed at the new streetcar stop.

The development structure proposes distinct blocks along the length of the boulevard through clearly defined groups of buildings, as well as an open development with straight-line housing facing the forest. A high-rise on the district's new square marks the centerpoint of the area.

An open-space concept is proposed for the development structure, extending from the urban street area via private gardens and the park-like landscape and between the straight-line housing right through to the nature reserve, and forms a graduated transition from cultivated to natural area.

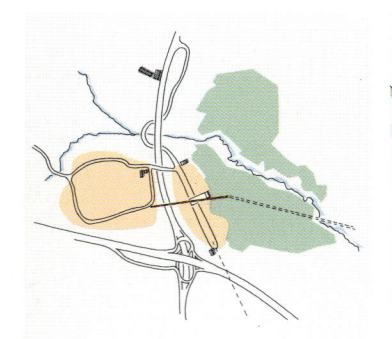

Integration

Bebauungsstruktur
Development structure

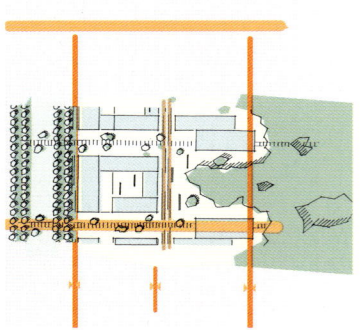

Grünkonzept / Landscape design

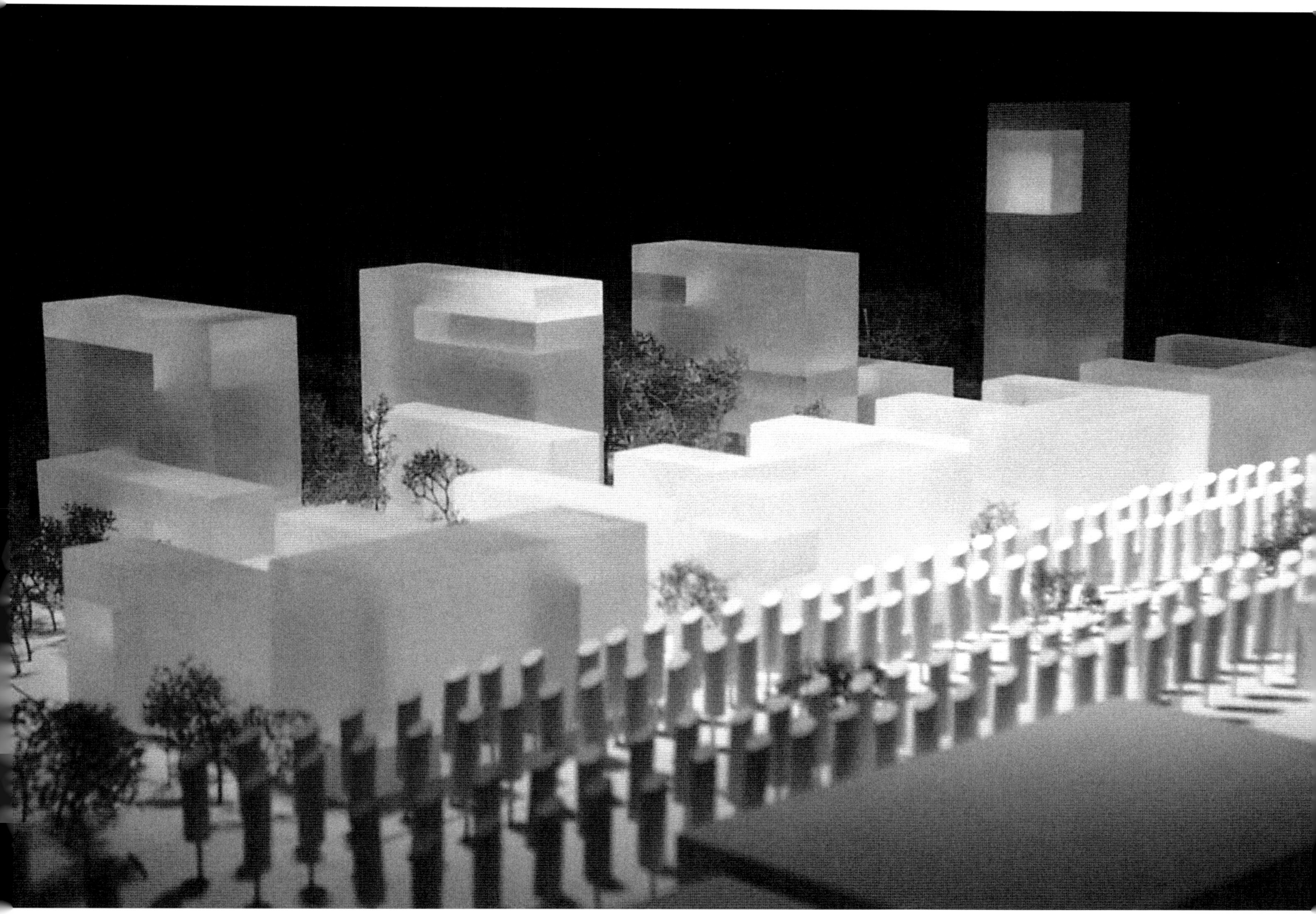

Erdgeschoss / Ground floor
1:2000

1 Boulevard
2 Quartiersplatz
  District square
3 Erschließungsstraße
  Access road
4 Blockbebauung
  Block development
5 Scheibenhaus
  Straight-line high-rise
6 Hochhaus / High-rise
7 Parkdeck unter begrüntem
  Gartenhof / Parking facilities
  underneath garden
  courtyard
8 Landschaftspark
  Landscaped park
9 Wald / Forest

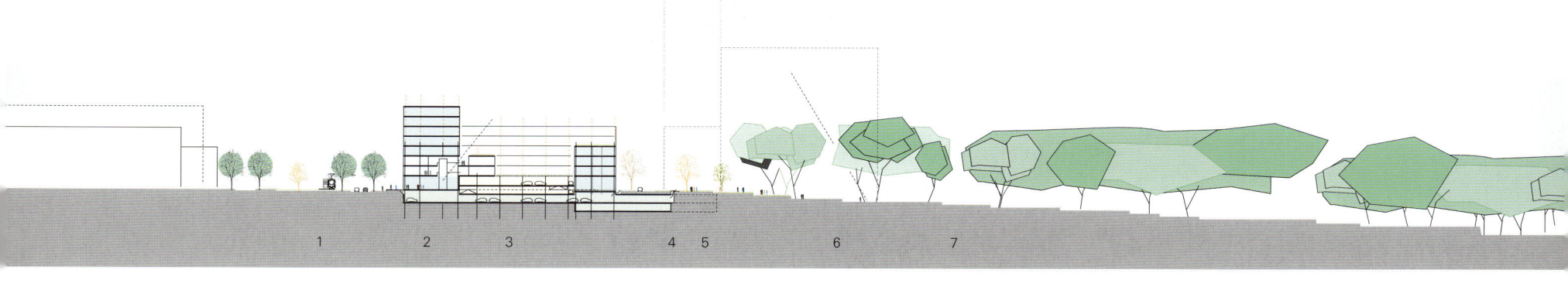

Schnitt / Section
1:2000

1 Boulevard
2 Blockbebauung
  Block development
3 Gartenhof
  Garden courtyard
4 Hochhaus / High-rise
5 Landschaftspark
  Landscaped park
6 Scheibenhaus
  Straight-line high-rise
7 Wald / Forest

Links:
Erschließungsstraße mit
Scheibenhaus am Wald

Rechts:
Quartiersplatz mit Hochhaus

Left:
Access road with straight-line
high-rise beside the forest

Right:
District square with high-rise

189 Büropark Fasanenhof / Fasanenhof Office Park Stuttgart

Neues Fußballstadion München
2001
Wettbewerb

New Soccer Stadium Munich
2001
Competition

Lageplan / Site plan
1:12 000

1 Neues Fußballstadion:
  New soccer stadium
2 Boulevard mit darunterliegenden Parkdecks
  Boulevard with parking decks below
3 U-Bahn-Station /
  Underground station
4 Windradhügel / Hill with wind-power park
5 Autobahnkreuz München-Nord / Munich's North motorway cloverleaf
6 Fröttmaninger Heide
  Fröttmaninger Heath

Nach jahrelangen Diskussionen um einen Umbau des Münchner Olympiastadions und im Hinblick auf die im Jahr 2006 in Deutschland stattfindende Fußballweltmeisterschaft entsteht im Norden der Stadt auf Initiative der beiden international renommierten Münchner Fußballvereine und unterstützt durch das Votum der Münchner Bürger ein neues Fußballstadion, das bis zum Jahr 2005 fertig gestellt sein soll.

Der vorgeschlagene Stadionbau wird von einem weit ausgreifenden horizontalen Dachschirm überspannt, der sich je nach Witterung vollständig öffnen oder schließen lässt. Die enorme Anzahl von PKW-Stellplätzen ist unter einem angehobenen Fußgängerboulevard untergebracht, welcher auch außerhalb der Stadionveranstaltungen vielerlei Freizeitangebote bereit hält. Diese sollen den Aufenthalt auf dem Stadiongelände attraktiv gestalten und so mit dazu beitragen, die Zu- und Abfahrtsströme bei Großveranstaltungen zu entzerren.

Als „Stadttor des Nordens" am Autobahnkreuz gelegen, wird das Stadion samt Dachschirm bei Tag und Nacht zu einer weithin sichtbaren Landmarke und zu einem neuen Bezugspunkt für die Stadtentwicklung in diesem Bereich.

Die Großform des Stadions entwickelt sich aus seinen inneren Bedingungen. Das Erlebnis des sich öffnenden und schließenden transparenten Daches vor, während oder nach Veranstaltungen ist ein faszinierender Vorgang, der sich scheinbar schwerelos vor den Augen des Publikums vollzieht. In spielfreien Zeiten kann der Rasen durch Öffnen des Daches natürlich belichtet und beregnet werden.

Um das enorme Volumen aufzulösen, sind Dachschirm und Arena sowohl baulich als auch architektonisch voneinander getrennt. Unter dem ausgreifenden Dach entstehen fließende Übergänge zwischen Außen- und Innenraum. Das horizontale Erscheinungsbild der Anlage wird durch eine ausgeprägte Dreigliederung der Tribünenränge erreicht; zusätzlich dazu relativiert der angehobene Boulevard die Bauhöhe.

For years there has been discussion about converting the Munich Olympic stadium. Now, in the run-up to Germany hosting the Soccer World Cup in 2006, a new football stadium is being built in the north end of the city on the initiative of two internationally renowned Munich football teams and with the backing of Munich's citizens. The scheduled completion date is 2005.

The proposed stadium will be covered by an extensive horizontal canopy that can be completely opened or closed according to the prevailing weather. Extensive parking facilities are provided under a raised pedestrian boulevard, which also offers a variety of leisure activities even when no match is in progress. These attractions are intended to encourage people to linger on the stadium grounds and will help to disperse the large crowds of people entering and leaving during big events.

As the "northern gate to the city", situated on the autobahn intersection, the stadium and canopy will create a highly visible landmark both day and night, and will provide a new focal point for urban development in the area.

The stadium's overall design derives from the intrinsic conditions entailed in such a structure. It is a fascinating experience for fans to watch the transparent roof smoothly opening or closing, during or after a game. When the field is not required for matches, the roof can be opened so the turf can benefit from natural light and rain.

In order to break up the enormous volume, the canopy and arena are separated from one another in terms of both architectural construction and design. Below the extensive roof, flowing transitions arise between the interior and exterior. The distinct division of the stands into three sections creates the stadium's horizontal appearance. The raised boulevard also serves to place the stadium's overall height in perspective.

Der über die Parkebenen angehobene Fußgängerboulevard verringert optisch die Höhe des Stadionbauwerkes und bietet auch außerhalb von Großveranstaltungen zwanglose Spiel- und Aufenthaltsmöglichkeiten

The pedestrian boulevard raised over the parking decks makes the stadium itself seem less high and also provides various opportunities for games and leisure-time pursuits when major events are not being held

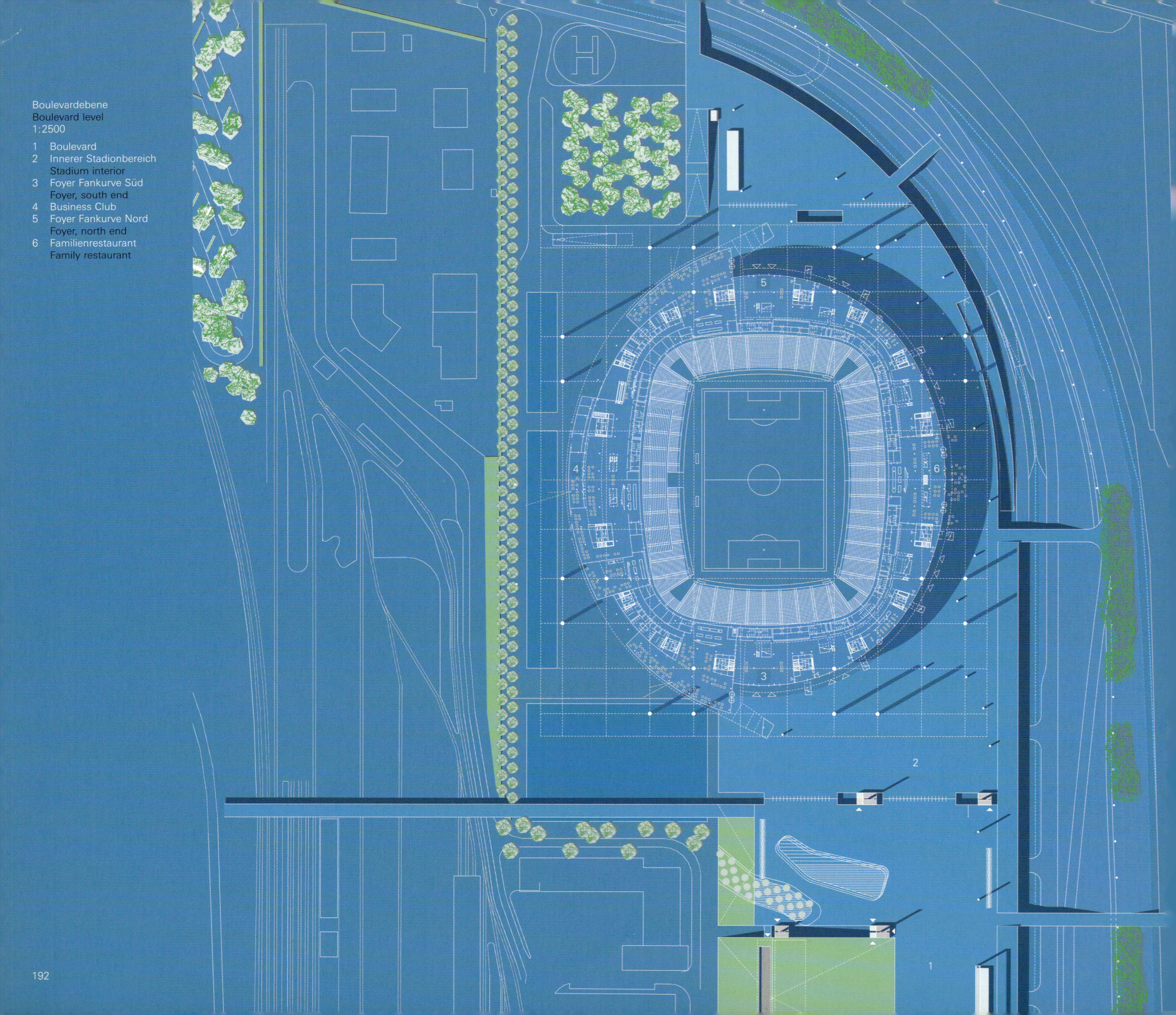

Boulevardebene
Boulevard level
1:2500

1 Boulevard
2 Innerer Stadionbereich
  Stadium interior
3 Foyer Fankurve Süd
  Foyer, south end
4 Business Club
5 Foyer Fankurve Nord
  Foyer, north end
6 Familienrestaurant
  Family restaurant

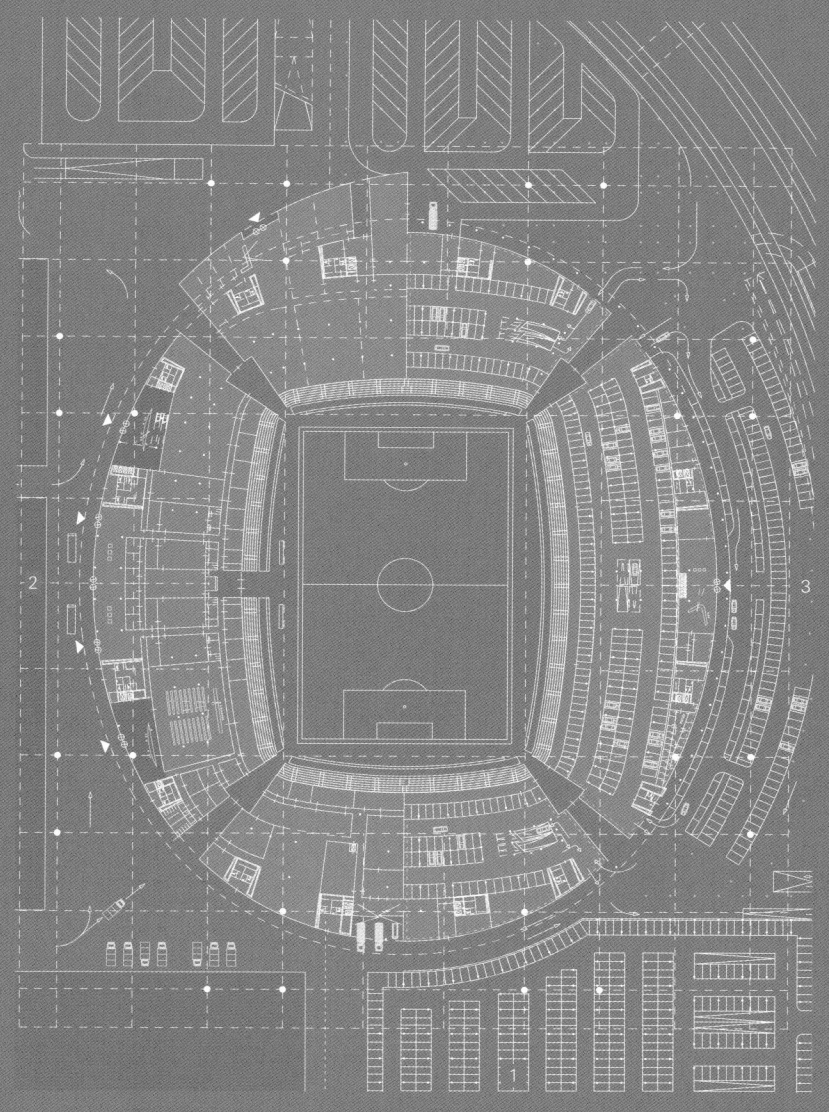

Zufahrtsebene / Access level
1:2500

1 PKW-Stellplätze
  Car parking spaces
2 VIP-Vorfahrt 1
  VIP access route 1
3 Welcome Zone,
  VIP-Vorfahrt 2 / Welcome
  Zone, VIP access route 2

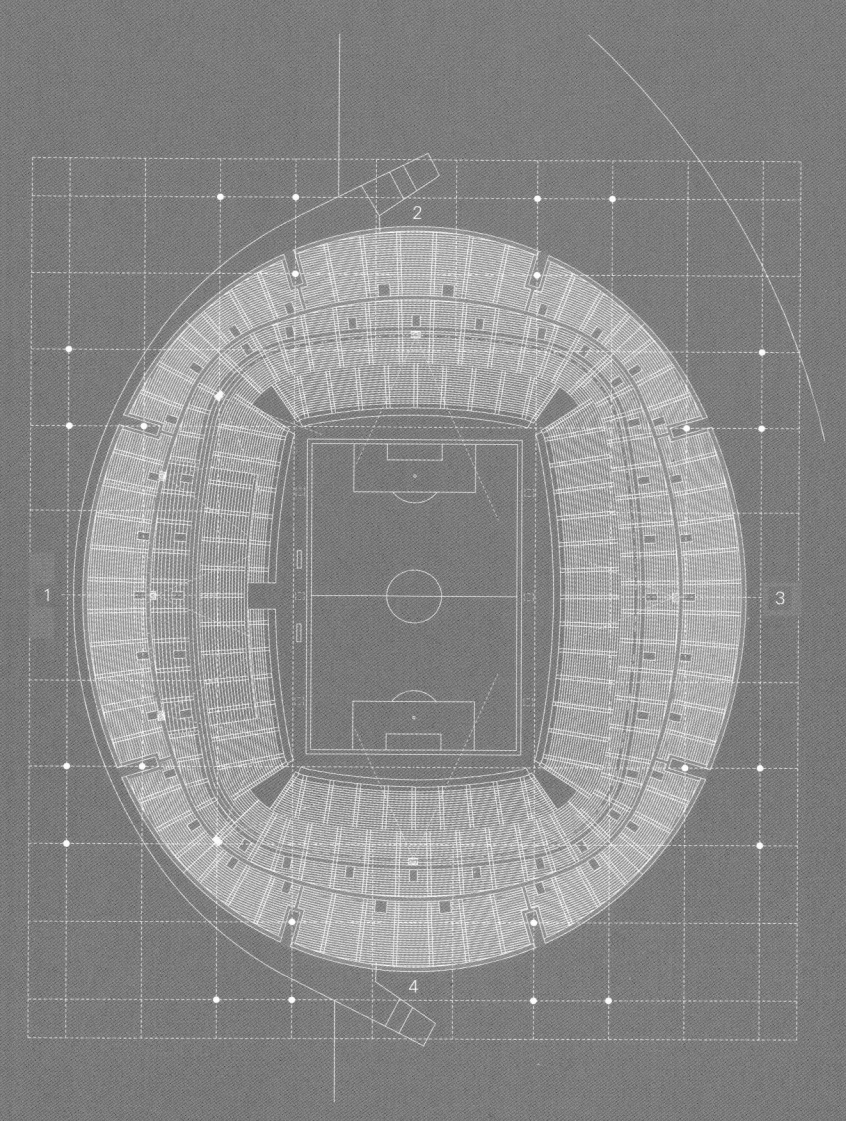

Medienebene (Rangaufsicht)
Media level (view of the stands)
1:2500

1 Haupt-Pressetribüne
  Main press boxes
2 Fantribüne Nord / North stands
3 Familientribüne / Family stands
4 Fantribüne Süd / South stands

193 Neues Fußballstadion / New Soccer Stadium München

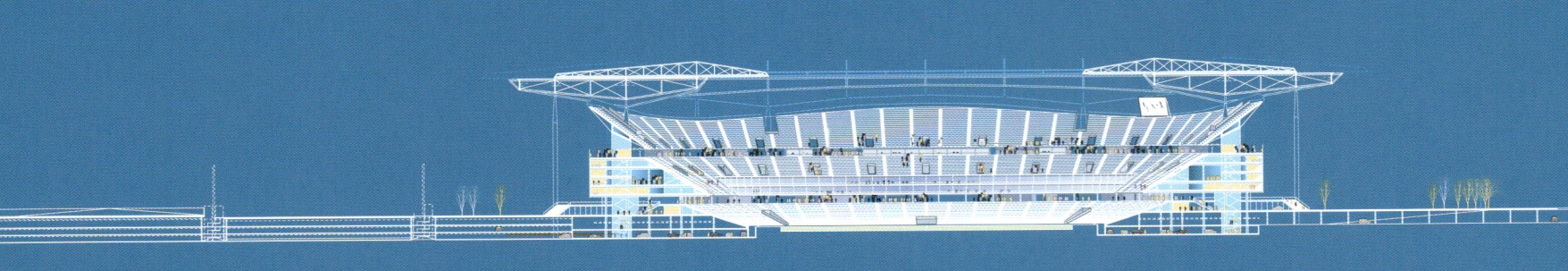

Längsschnitt
Longitudinal section
1:2500

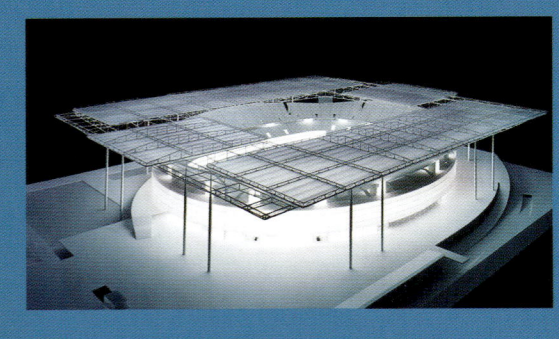

Links:
Der lichtdurchlässige Dachschirm kann vor oder während der Veranstaltungen geöffnet oder geschlossen werden

Unten:
Der Dreiklang aus aufgeständertem Tribünenring, abgelöstem oberen Rang und weit ausgreifendem Dachschirm ist bestimmend für das Stadionbild und -erlebnis bei Tag und bei Nacht

Left:
The transparent canopy can be opened or closed before or during events

Below:
The triad of raised ring of stands, a separate upper ring and a broad protruding canopy defines the face of the stadium and the experience it offers, by day or by night

Hotel der ESO am Cerro Paranal Chile
2002
Internationaler Wettbewerb 1998   1. Preis

ESO Hotel on the Cerro Paranal Chile
2002
International competition 1998   1st prize

Die Europäische Organisation für Astronomische Forschung in der Südlichen Hemisphäre (ESO) betreibt auf dem Cerro Paranal, einem Berg in der Atacamawüste im nördlichen Chile, das "Very Large Telescope" (VLT). Das VLT ist das leistungsstärkste Erdteleskop weltweit. Unterhalb des Gipfels, auf etwa 2400m Höhe, liegt das Hotel für die Wissenschaftler und Ingenieure der ESO, die hier jeweils rotierend arbeiten.

Für die relativ kurze Zeit ihres Aufenthaltes unter außergewöhnlichen äußeren Bedingungen – intensive Sonneneinstrahlung, extreme Trockenheit, hohe Windgeschwindigkeiten, starke Temperaturschwankungen und Erdbebengefahr – ist abseits der Zivilisation ein Ort entstanden, der die notwendige Erholung zwischen den anstrengenden Arbeitsphasen ermöglicht und im Sinne einer „Oase" entsprechende Annehmlichkeiten bietet: 120 Hotelzimmer, Kantine, Loungebereiche mit Swimming Pool, Fitnesscenter und Bibliothek.

Einer künstlichen Stützmauer vergleichbar, überspannt die Hotelanlage die Flanken einer Geländemulde, ohne den Horizont zu verbauen, der einen atemberaubenden Blick bis zum Pazifischen Ozean bietet. Die Erdverbundenheit des Bauwerkes steht in bewusstem Kontrast zu der von Hochtechnologie bestimmten Teleskopanlage auf dem Gipfel des Cerro Paranal.

Über den Horizont erhebt sich nur ein einziges Element, nämlich eine flach gewölbte Stahlgitterkuppel mit 35m Durchmesser. Sie befindet sich über dem zentralen Aufenthaltsbereich und stellt einen formalen Bezug zu den riesigen Hohlspiegeln der Teleskope her.

The European Southern Observatory (ESO) operates the Very Large Telescope (VLT) on Cerro Paranal, a mountain in the northern part of the Atacama desert in Chile. The VLT is the world's most powerful earth-based telescope. Beneath the summit, at a height of some 2,400 meters, lies the hotel for the ESO scientists and engineers who work here on a roster system.

For the relatively short time of their stays under extreme climatic conditions – intense sunlight, extreme dryness, high wind speeds, great fluctuations in temperature and the danger of earthquakes – a place has been created far away from civilization where they can relax and rest between the strenuous phases of their work. Reminiscent of an oasis, it provides 120 hotel rooms, a canteen and lounge areas, as well as a swimming pool, fitness center and library.

The hotel complex fits snugly into an existing depression in the ground, acting as an artificial retaining wall. It does nothing to impede the breathtaking view over the horizon out to the Pacific Ocean. This emphasis on reflecting nature sets the hotel in direct and deliberate contrast to the high-tech telescope complex atop Cerro Paranal's summit.

A single element of the hotel's structure is visible above the horizon: a slightly raised dome comprising a steel skeleton that measures 35 meters in diameter. It rises up above the central lounge area and creates a formal counterpart to the telescope's enormous concave mirrors.

Lageplan / Site plan
1:5000

Der Hotelkomplex überbrückt mit seinen vier Ebenen eine Geländemulde und schiebt sich in den Hang des Cerro Paranal. Aus den 120 Zimmern und der lang gezogenen Loggia des Restaurants reicht der spektakuläre Ausblick über die Wüste bis zum Pazifischen Ozean

The Hotel complex, comprising four levels, fits snugly into the slopes of a depression beneath Cerro Paranal. From each of the 120 rooms and the elongated loggia of the dining room there is a spectacular view out across the desert to the Pacific Ocean

Parlamentsgebäude
Parliament building
Chandigarh, Indien / India, 1958
Le Corbusier

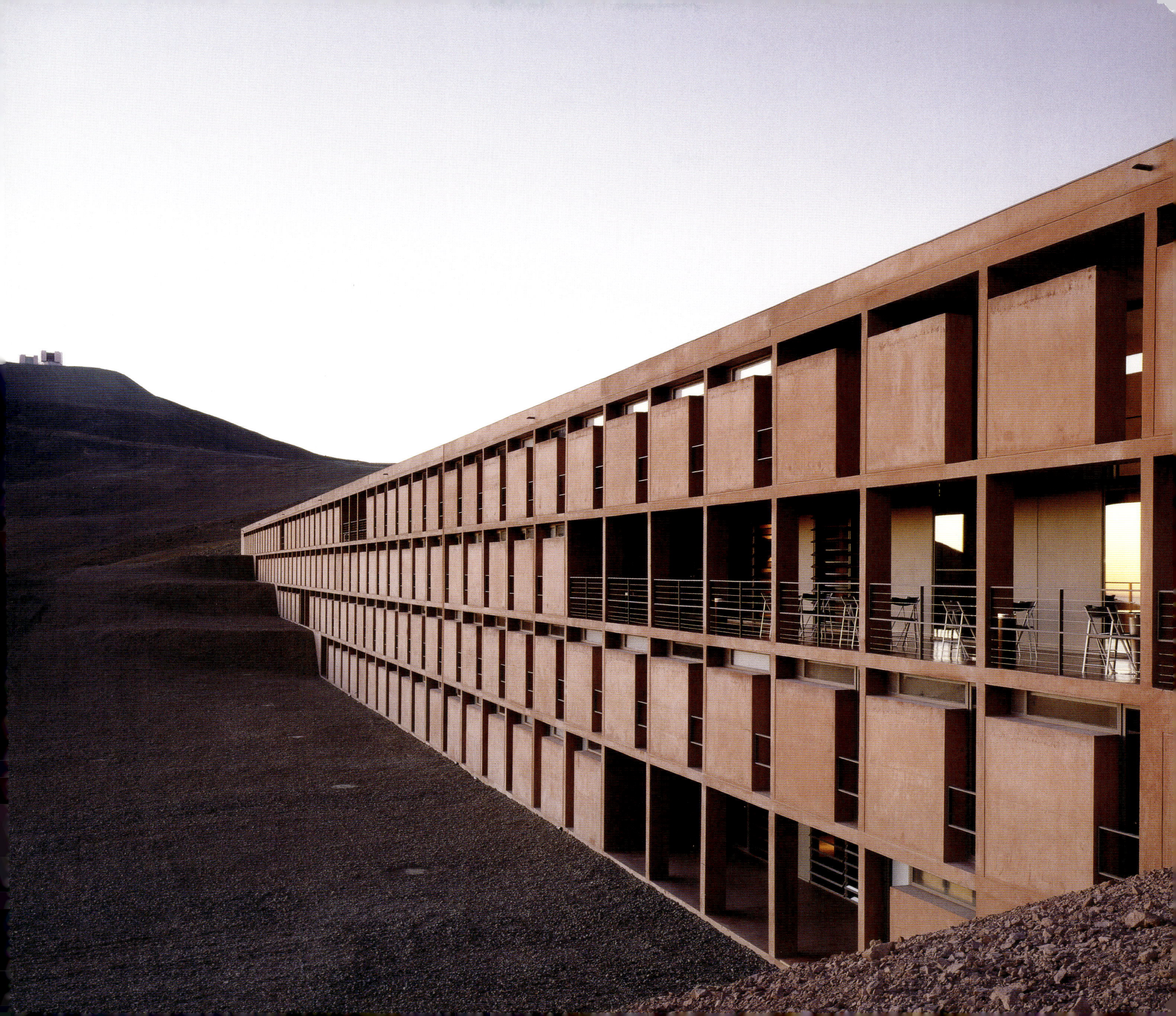

Ebene −2 / Level −2
1:1000

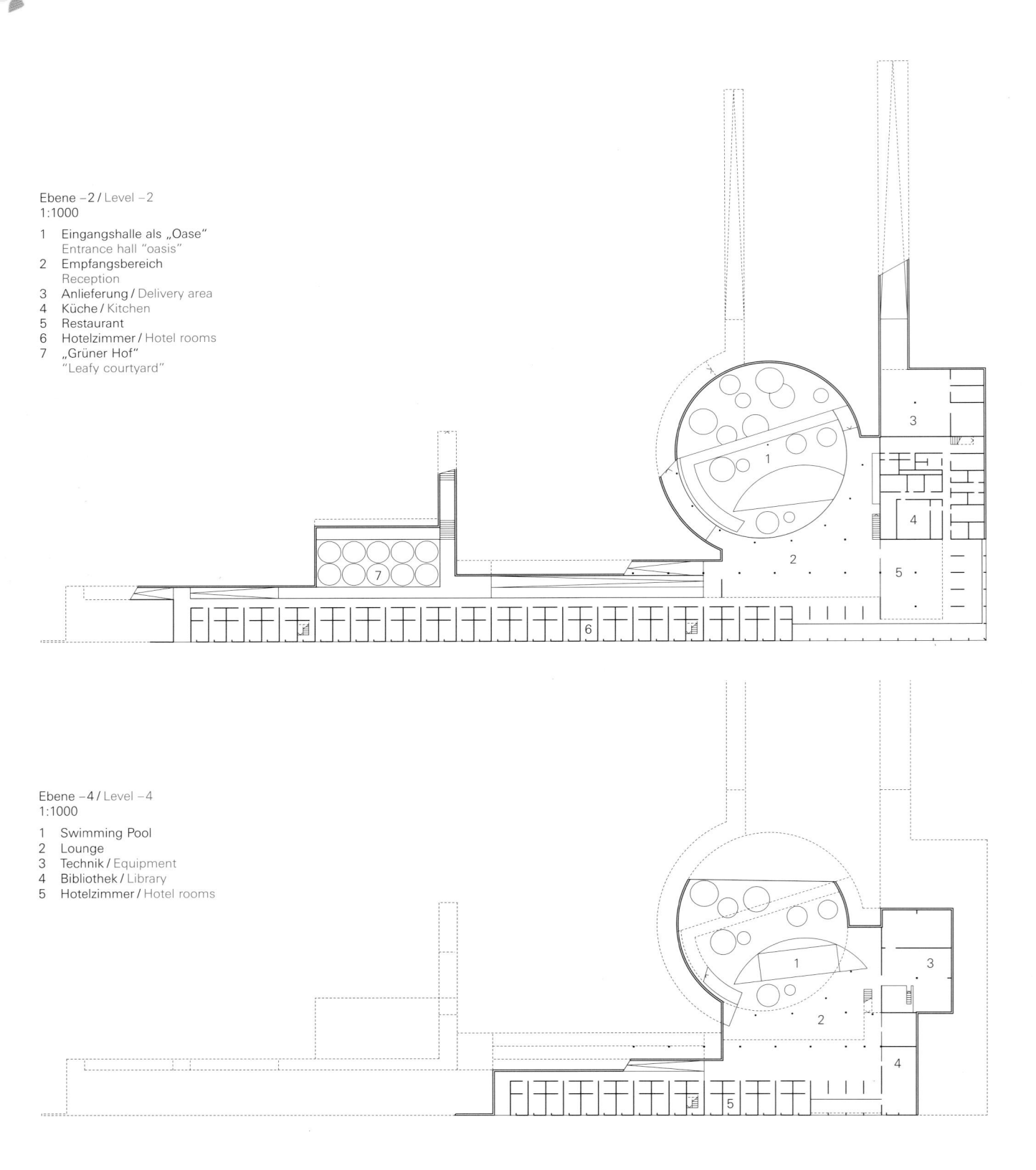

1 Eingangshalle als „Oase"
  Entrance hall "oasis"
2 Empfangsbereich
  Reception
3 Anlieferung / Delivery area
4 Küche / Kitchen
5 Restaurant
6 Hotelzimmer / Hotel rooms
7 „Grüner Hof"
  "Leafy courtyard"

Ebene −4 / Level −4
1:1000

1 Swimming Pool
2 Lounge
3 Technik / Equipment
4 Bibliothek / Library
5 Hotelzimmer / Hotel rooms

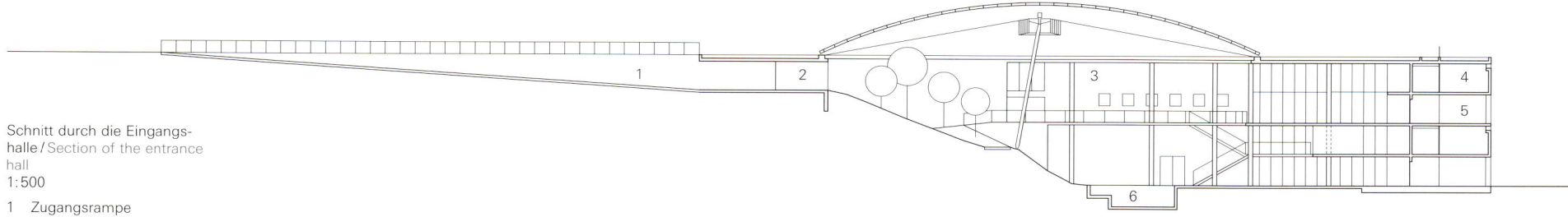

Schnitt durch die Eingangshalle / Section of the entrance hall
1:500

1. Zugangsrampe
   Access ramp
2. Haupteingang
   Main entrance
3. Eingangshalle als „Oase"
   Entrance hall
4. Hotelzimmer / Hotel rooms
5. Aussichtsterrasse
   Viewing terrace
6. Swimming Pool

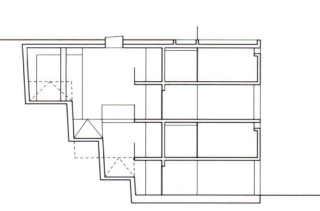

Schnitt durch den Hoteltrakt mit Erschließungsrampen
Section through hotel tract with access ramps
1:500

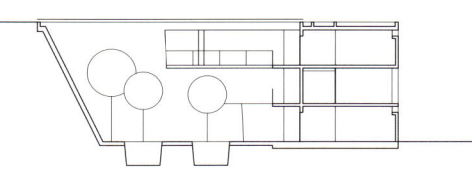

Schnitt durch den „Grünen Hof" / Section of the "leafy courtyard"
1:500

Nur die flach gewölbte Kuppel und die Zugangsrampe weisen auf die unterirdische Welt des Hotels hin

Only the shallow dome and access ramp give a hint of the subterranean hotel

Hotel der ESO / ESO Hotel Chile

Architektur- und Landschafts-
form stehen klar abgegrenzt
gegeneinander, der gefärbte
Beton verbindet sich jedoch
mit den Tönen der Wüste

Architecture and landscape
form distinct entities, and the
concrete is colored to match
the tones of the desert

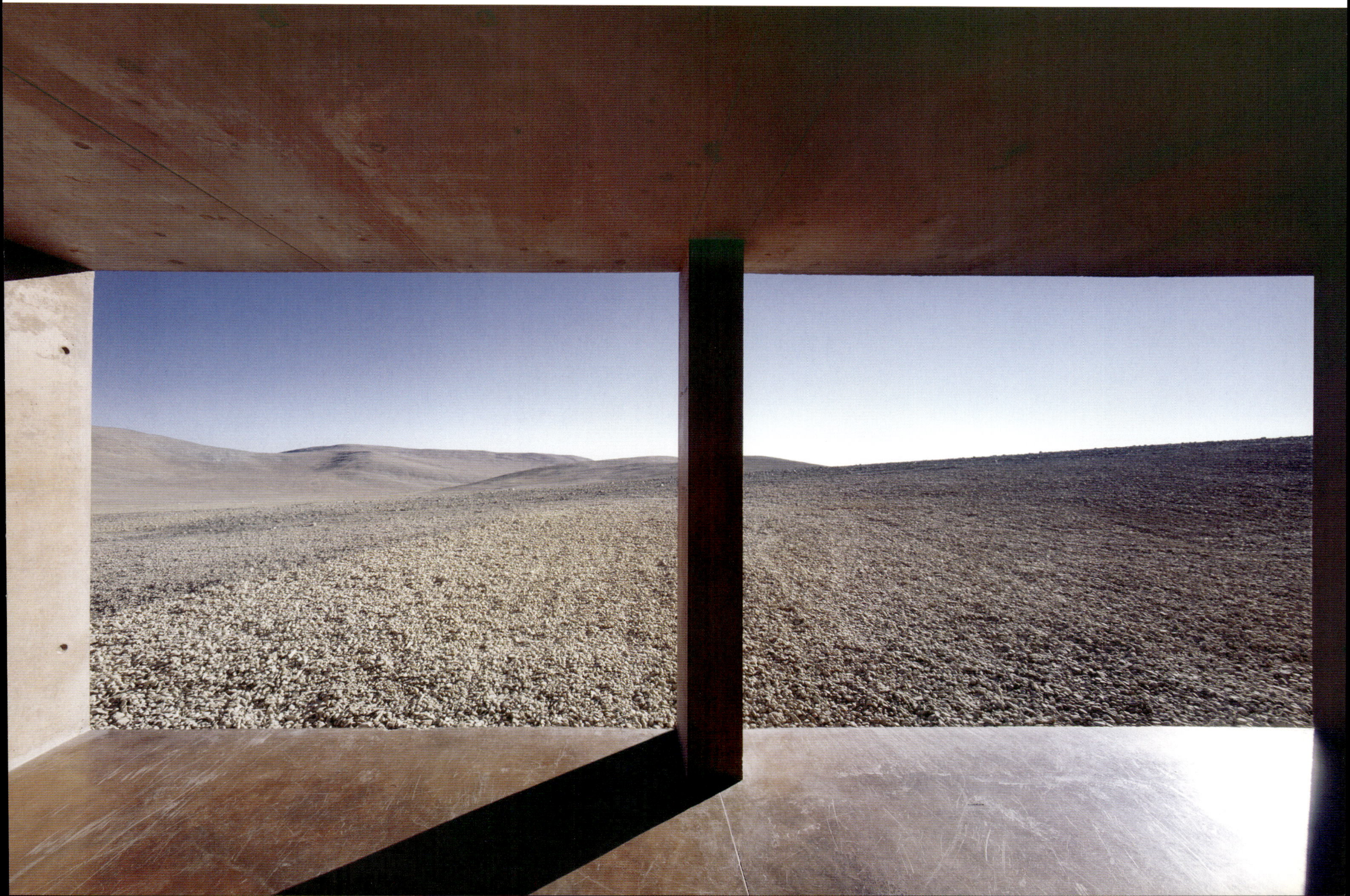

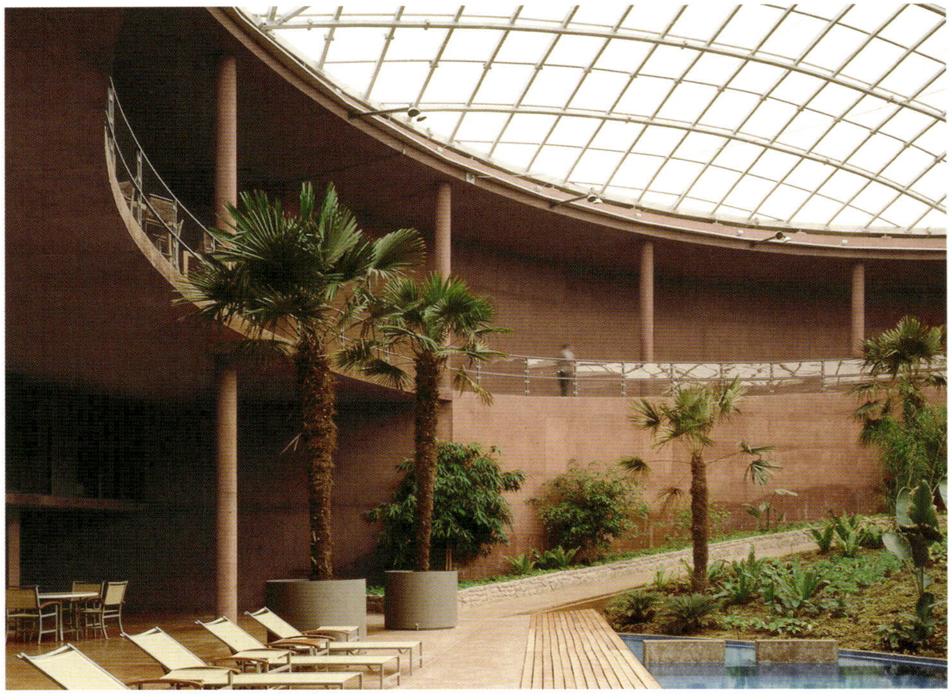
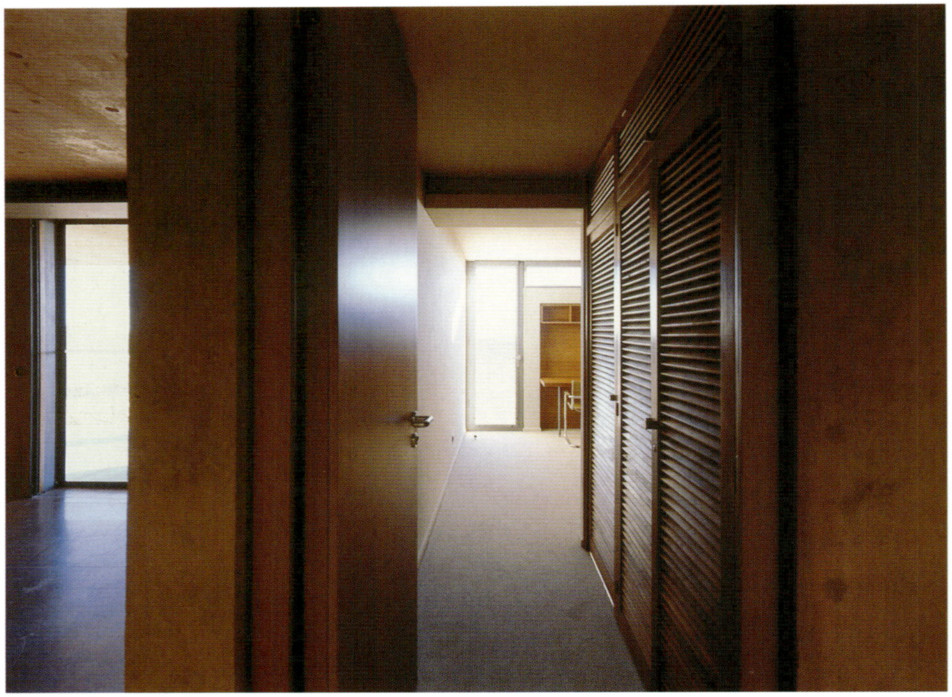
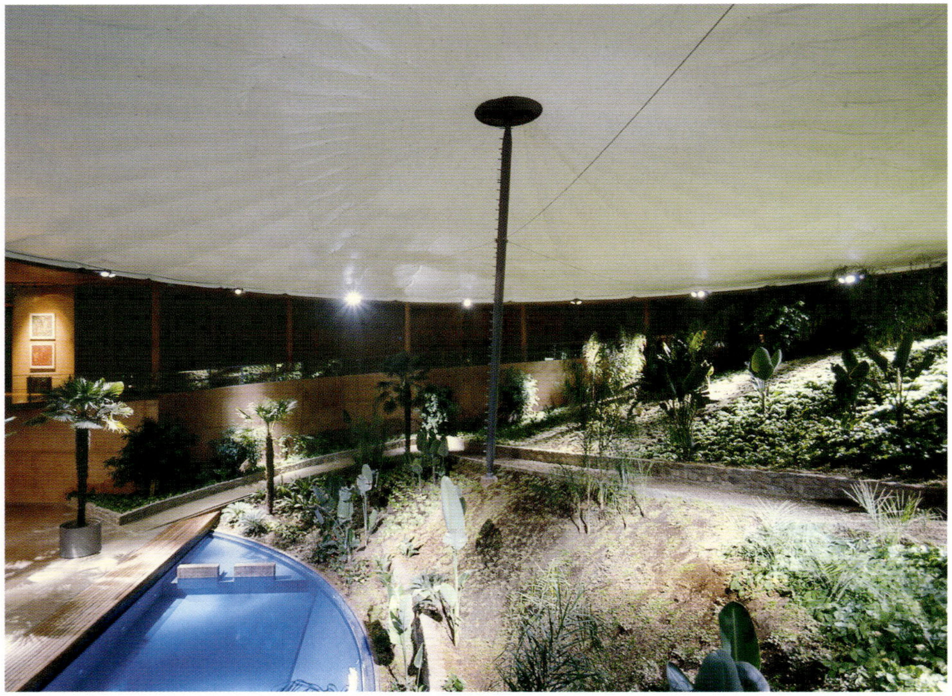
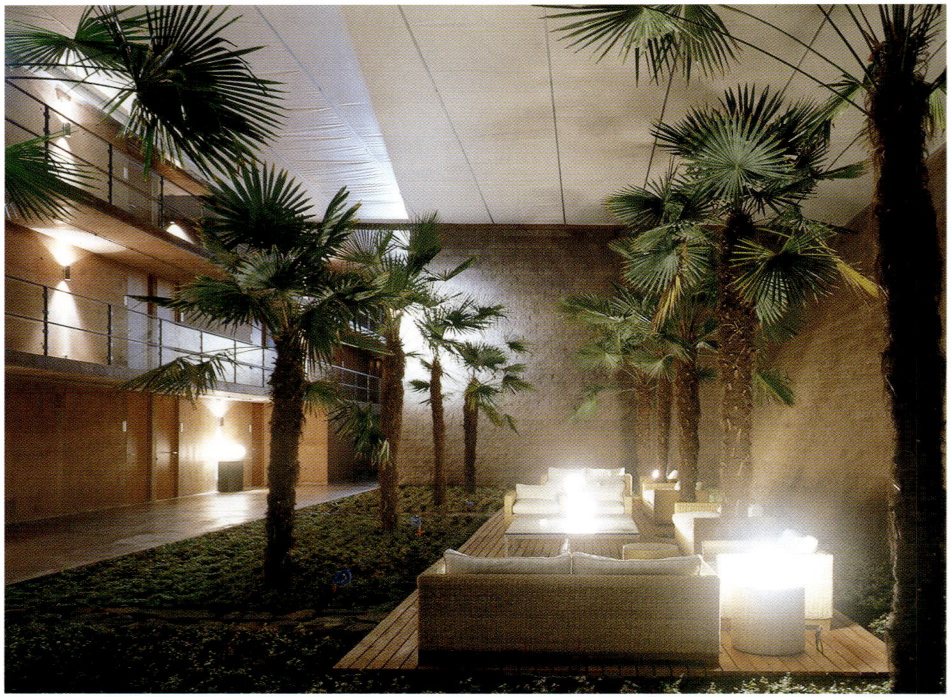

Links:
Die üppige Bepflanzung in der Eingangshalle und dem „Grünen Hof" bildet einen willkommenen Kontrast zur kargen Außenwelt. Sie bewirkt zusammen mit dem Swimmingpool die notwendige Erhöhung der auf Grund des Wüstenklimas sehr geringen Luftfeuchtigkeit

Um die Beobachtungen an den Teleskopen nicht zu beeinträchtigen, müssen sämtliche Gebäudeöffnungen nachts mittels textiler Verdunkelungsanlagen geschlossen werden

Left:
The lush vegetation in the entrance hall and "leafy" courtyard create a welcome contrast to the barren landscape. Vegetation and swimming pool help raise the low humidity of the desert climate to a comfortable level inside the hotel

Right:
So as not to impair telescope observations, special roofing closure fabric had to be used to cover all openings that might let light escape

Rechts:
Der Weg zu den offenen Fluren der Gästezimmer führt über lange Rampen

Folgende Seiten:
Die zum Pazifik ausgerichtete Fassade des Hotels bei untergehender Sonne

Das Bauwerk besteht aus Sichtbeton, der in den rötlichen Tönen der Wüste eingefärbt ist. Ins Licht der wechselnden Sonnenstände getaucht, wird es Teil der grandiosen, archaischen Landschaft

Right:
Long ramps lead to open corridors serving the hotel rooms

Next pages:
Facing the Pacific: the Hotel's façade at sunset

Exposed concrete colored to match the reddish hues of the desert is used throughout. Bathed in the light produced by the various positions of the sun, it becomes part of the breathtaking landscape

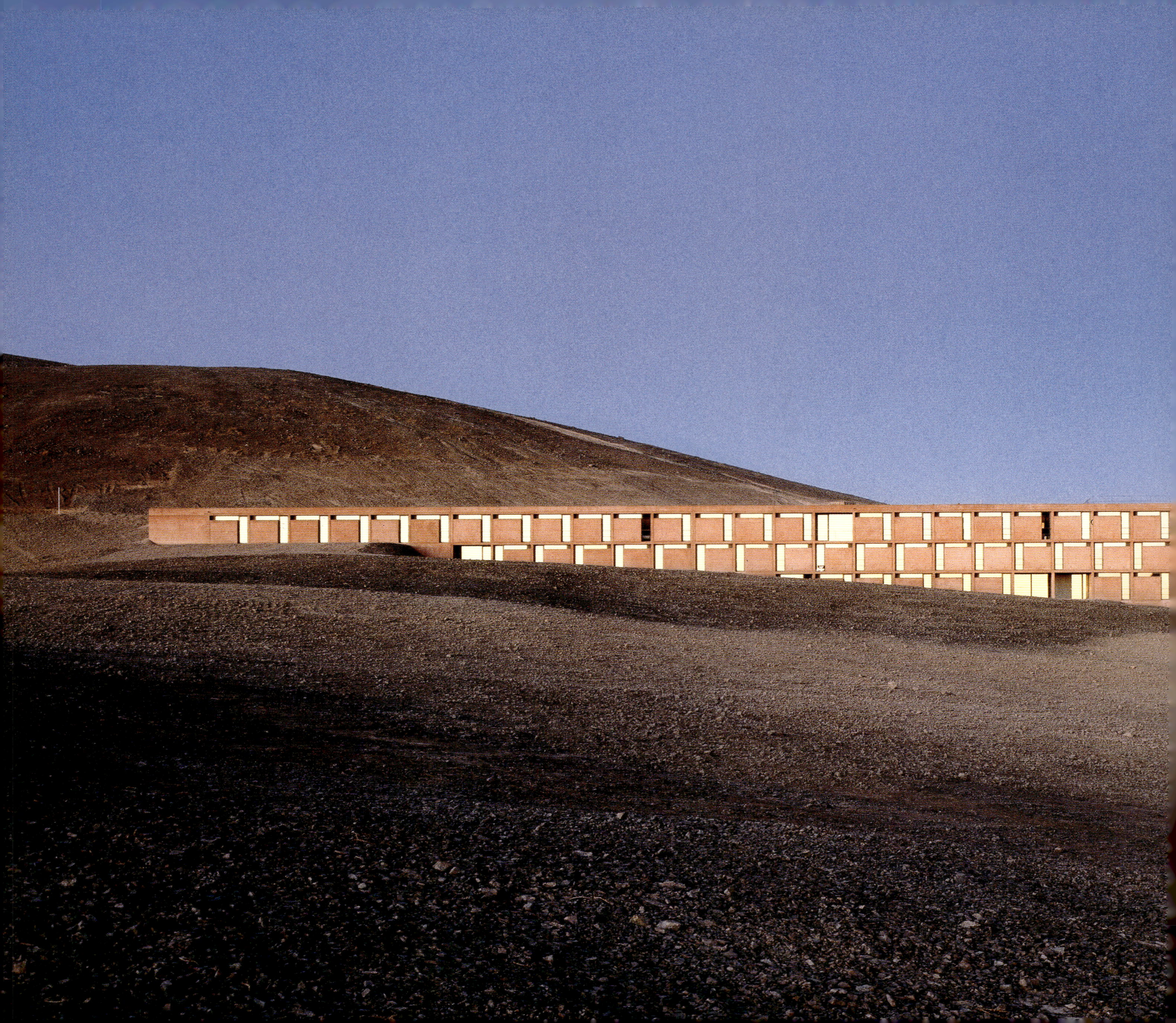

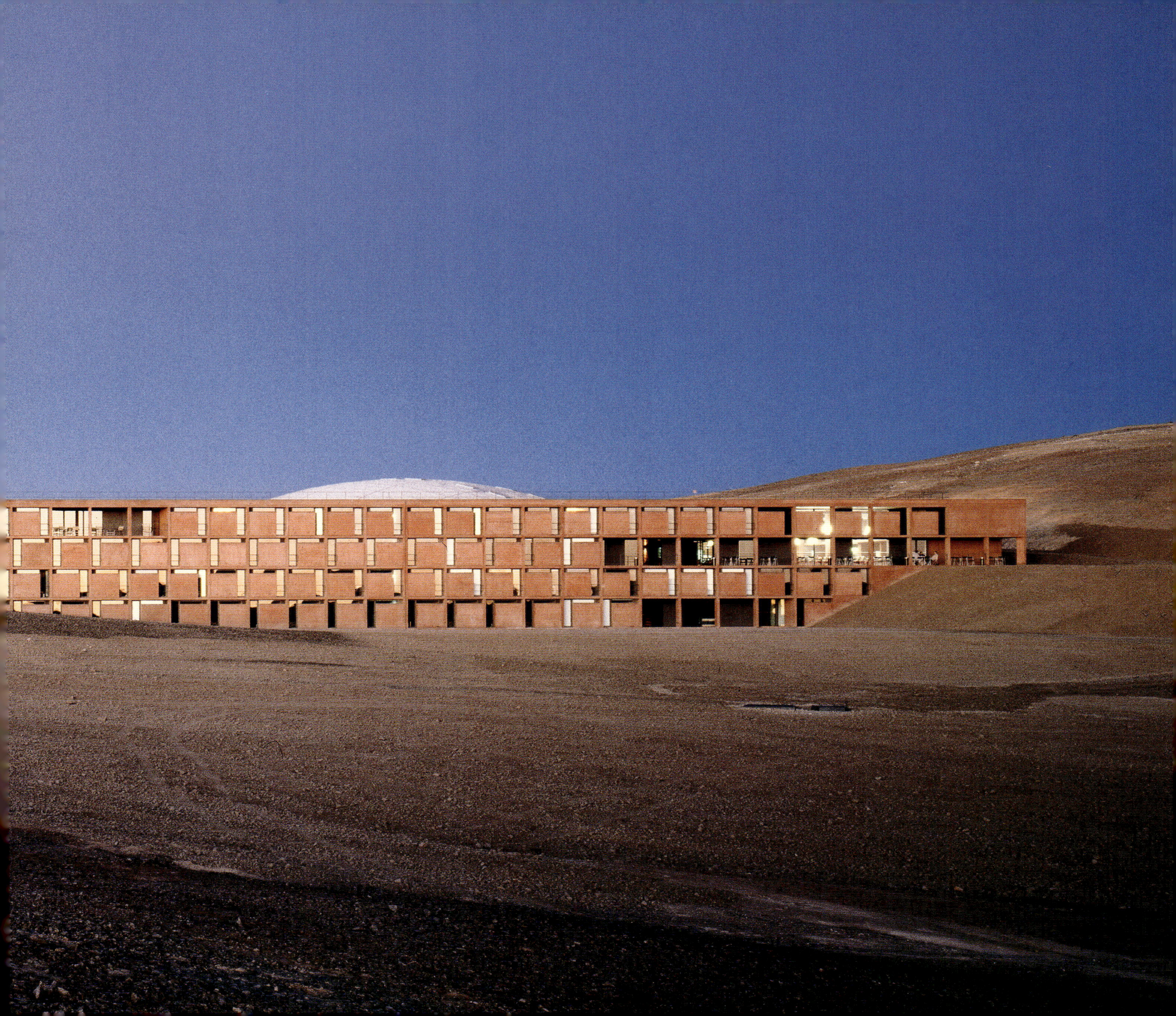

Thuringia Versicherung München
2002
Wettbewerb   Ankauf

Thuringia Insurance Building Munich
2002
Competition   Acquired

Nach der Fusion zweier großer Versicherungsgesellschaften soll deren gemeinsame Hauptverwaltung am Standort München zusammengeführt werden.

Hierfür wird die bestehende Direktion im Münchner Stadtteil Neuperlach, welche aus mehreren Einzelgebäuden besteht, durch einen Erweiterungsbau auf dem östlich angrenzenden Grundstück ergänzt.

Um dem Gebäudebestand mit seinen als Ganzes kaum erfahrbaren Konturen und differierenden Erscheinungsbildern nicht lediglich einen weiteren konkurrierenden Solitär hinzuzufügen, führen zwei bügelartige Dachschirme, die beide Längsseiten überspannen, ein übergeordnetes, zeichenhaftes Architekturelement ein, welches den Bestand und die Erweiterungsbauten zusammenfasst. Dies dokumentiert einprägsam und klar konturiert den Zusammenschluss der beiden Gesellschaften nach außen wie auch nach innen.

Innerhalb des von den beiden Dachschirmen definierten Raumes werden sowohl Kopplungselemente zwischen den Bestandsgebäuden eingefügt, als auch das weitere Neubauprogramm nach Osten entwickelt. Die südlichen und nördlichen Erweiterungsspangen nehmen die vorhandenen Baufluchten auf und lassen dadurch geschützte Hofbereiche entstehen. Fingerartige Ausleger im Wechsel zu unterschiedlich gestalteten Gartenhöfen verknüpfen die beiden parallelen Spangen.

Following the merger of two big insurance companies, the joint administrative headquarters will be located in Munich.

As a result, the existing administrative section in the Neuperlach district of Munich – which is made up of several individual buildings – is to be supplemented with an extension on the neighboring piece of land to the east.

In order to avoid adding yet another individual building that competes with the existing buildings – which have differing appearances and contours – two frame-like roofs, both of which span the longitudinal sides, will superimpose a symbolic architectural element that will unite the existing buildings with the new ones. This symbolic element will visually document the merger of the two companies both inwardly and outwardly.

Within the area defined by the two roofs, coupling elements will be introduced between the existing buildings, while the new buildings extend towards the east. The extensions to the south and the north follow the existing alignments and create protected courtyards. Finger-like sections that alternate with garden courtyards of varying designs will connect the two parallel struts.

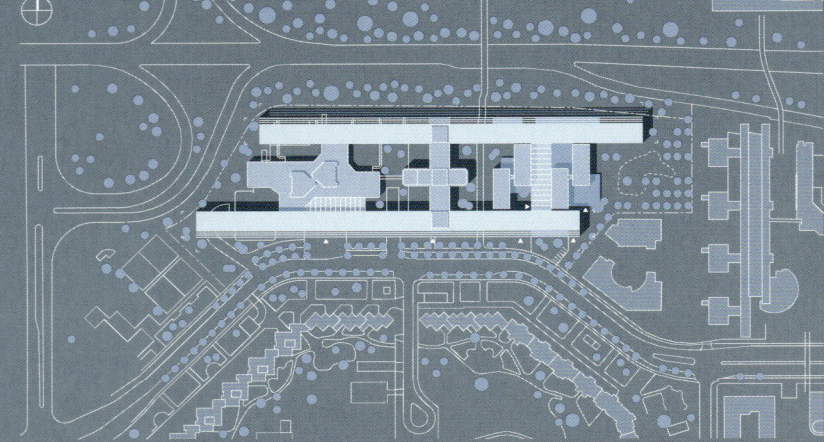

Lageplan / Site plan
1:6000

Neubau und Bestand werden durch zwei übergreifende Dachschirme zeichenhaft verbunden

New and existing buildings are all located beneath two frame-like roofs

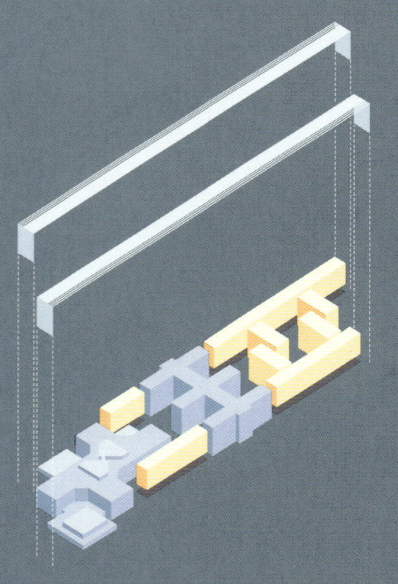

Längsschnitt
Longitudinal section
1:1500

Städtebaulicher Masterplan für die Olympiabewerbung Stuttgart 2012
2002

Master Plan for the Stuttgart Olympic submission 2012
2002

Als einer der deutschen Kandidaten bewarb sich die Stadt Stuttgart beim Nationalen Olympischen Komitee um die Austragung der Olympischen Spiele 2012.

In einem Masterplan sollte nachgewiesen werden, dass das sportliche Großereignis in Stuttgart durchführbar ist; er sollte die Einzigartigkeit der Stuttgarter Bewerbung herausarbeiten und auch Entwicklungschancen, unabhängig von der Bewerbung, für eine längerfristige Stadtentwicklung aufzeigen.

Die Lage der zentralen Sportstätten direkt am Neckar, umgeben von Parks und Weinbergen, setzt die Olympische Spiele in enge Verbindung zu Natur und Kultur, Sport und Technik, Industrie und Freizeit.

Die städtebauliche Intention einer Öffnung der Stadt zum Neckar setzt die Freiflächenplanung zur IGA 1993 und die Innenstadterweiterung im Rahmen von „Stuttgart 21" konsequent fort.

Die Nachhaltigkeit aller Maßnahmen steht im Mittelpunkt der Planung. Neubauten für das Olympische Dorf, ein Medienzentrum sowie ein Hotelstandort entstehen auf ehemaligen Gewerbeflächen.

Ein Uferpark am Neckar verknüpft die Grünräume der Innenstadt mit den Weinbergen, eine über die Geländeebene angehobene, geschwungene Fuß- und Radwegeverbindung erschließt die Sportstätten. Mit dem Olympiastadion im Zentrum formt die Anlage den „Ring der Kulturen" und bildet das Erkennungszeichen der Stuttgarter Bewerbung für die Olympischen Spiele 2012. Die Verbindung der beiden Talseiten und die Neustrukturierung der Uferbebauung gewährleisten eine Verknüpfung von Stadt und Fluss sowie eine nachhaltige Einbindung der Sportanlagen in die Landschaft.

The City of Stuttgart is one of the German candidates making a bid to the National Olympic Committee to host the 2012 Olympic Games.

The master plan aimed to demonstrate that Stuttgart is in a position to stage such a large-scale sporting event; its goal was to draw out the unique nature of the Stuttgart application as well as to present long-term development opportunities for the city that are in no way associated with the application.

The location of the central sporting venues directly on the banks of the River Neckar, surrounded by parks and vineyards, places the Olympic Games in close contact with nature and culture, sports and technology, industry and leisure time.

The urban planning concept of opening up the city to the Neckar is the logical continuation of the use of open space for the 1993 International Garden Show, and the extension of the inner city as part of the "Stuttgart 21" development.

The permanent aspect of all the measures is the focal point of the planning. New buildings for the Olympic Village, a media center and a hotel will be built on former industrial lands.

A park on the banks of the Neckar connects the green areas downtown to the vineyards, with a curved pedestrian and cycle path above ground level to connect the sporting venues. With the Olympic stadium in the middle, it forms the "Ring of Cultures" and creates the logo of the Stuttgart application for the 2012 Olympic Games. Connecting both sides of the valley and restructuring developments on the riverbanks guarantees that the city and the river will join forces and that in the long term the sports complexes will be integrated into their surroundings.

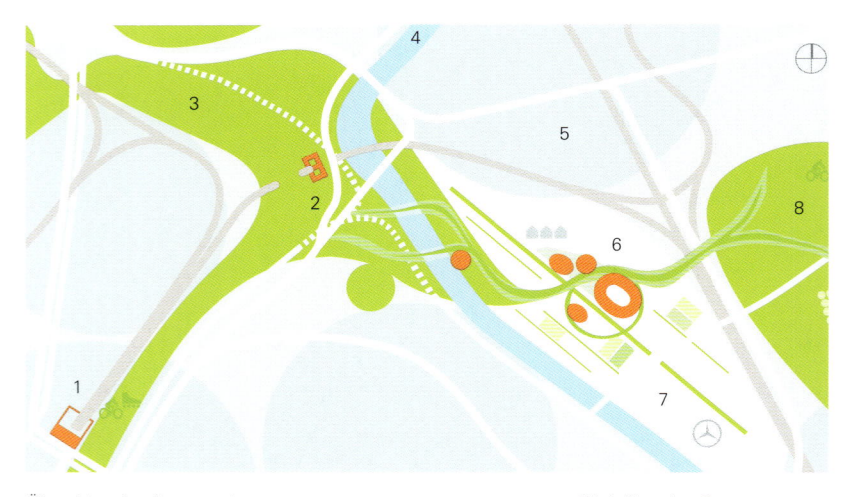

Übersichtsplan / Layout plan
1:50 000

1 Hauptbahnhof / Station
2 Schloß Rosenstein Rosenstein Castle
3 „Grünes U" / "Green U" park
4 Neckar
5 Bad Cannstatt
6 Olympisches Zentrum Olympic Center
7 DaimlerChrysler
8 Weinberge / Vineyards

Blick über den Stuttgarter Talkessel auf die Olympischen Sportstätten und das Olympische Dorf

View over the Stuttgart valley basin towards the Olympic sporting venues and the Olympic Village

Gesamtkonzept für die Bauten und Anlagen der Olympischen Spiele München 1972
Wettbewerbsmodell, 1967
Behnisch & Partner

Overall concept for buildings and facilities for the Olympic Games Munich 1972 competition model, 1967
Behnisch & Partner

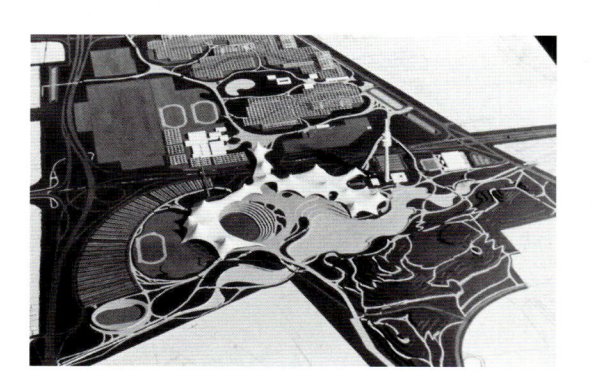

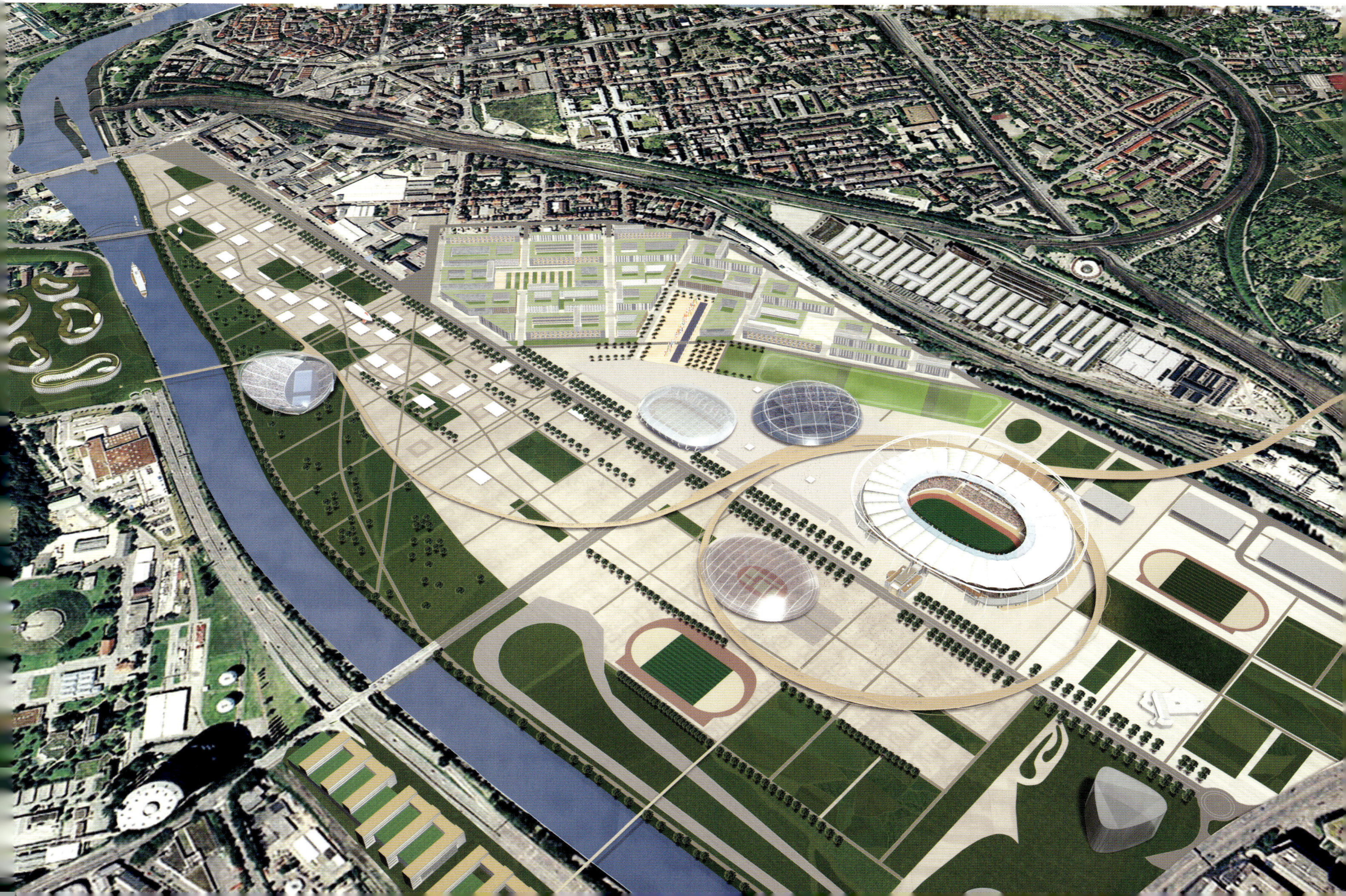

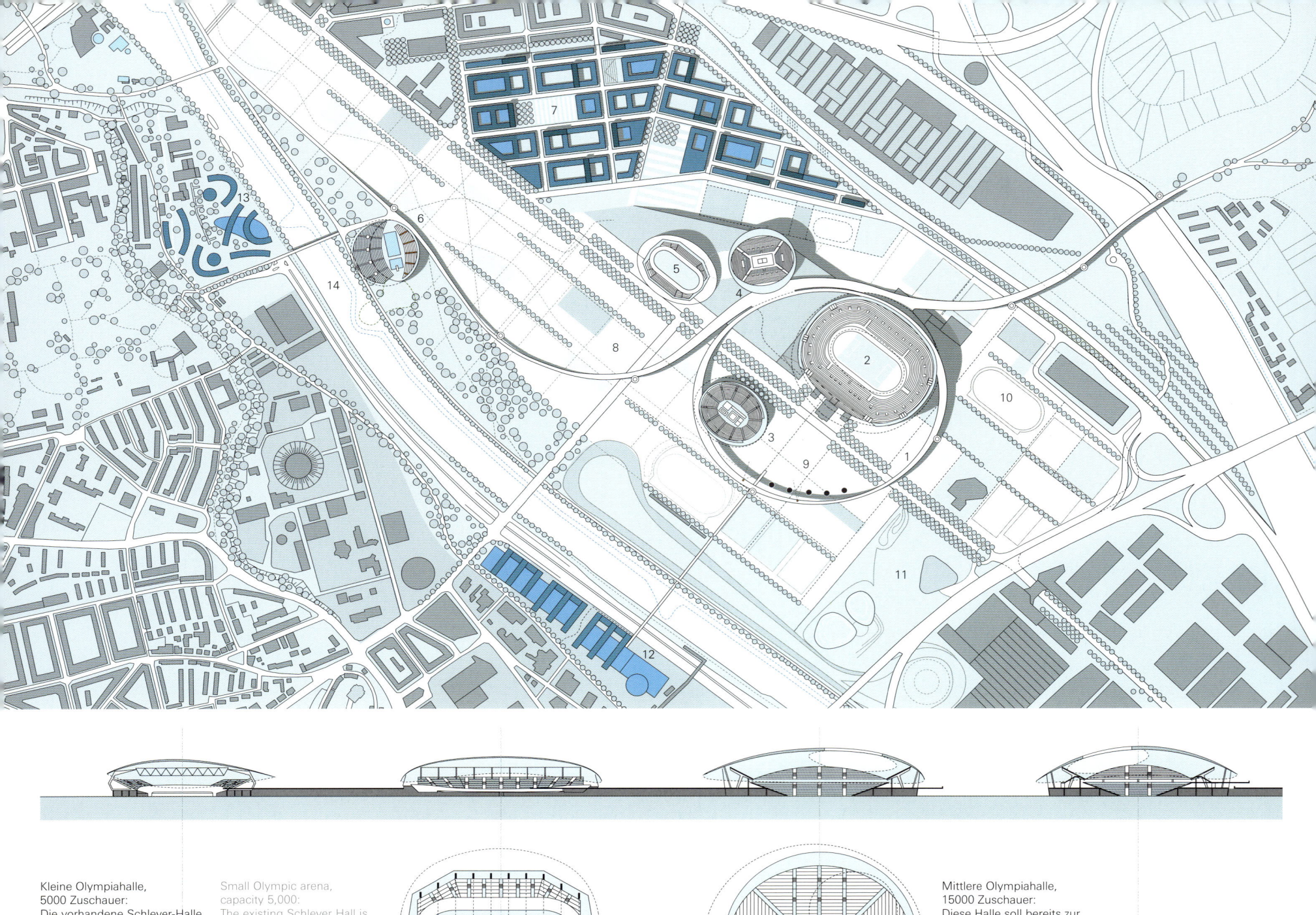

Kleine Olympiahalle, 5000 Zuschauer:
Die vorhandene Schleyer-Halle ist als Veranstaltungs- und Sporthalle bereits eingeführt und soll im Rahmen der Baumaßnahmen der benachbarten Sportstätten modernisiert werden

Small Olympic arena, capacity 5,000:
The existing Schleyer Hall is already in use as an events and sports venue, and will be modernized as part of construction measures for the neighboring sporting venues

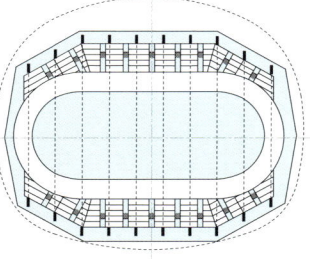

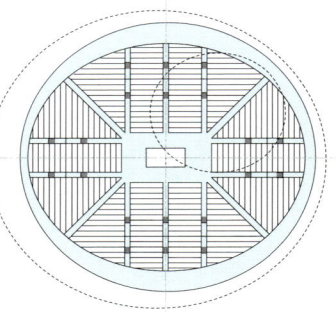

Mittlere Olympiahalle, 15000 Zuschauer:
Diese Halle soll bereits zur Fußballweltmeisterschaft 2006 verfügbar sein

Medium Olympic arena, capacity 15,000:
This arena will be completed ahead of the 2006 World Cup

Links / Left:
Lageplan / Site plan
1:10 000

1 Ring der Kulturen
  Ring of cultures
2 Olympiastadion
  Olympic stadium
3 Große Olympiahalle
  Large Olympic arena
4 Mittlere Olympiahalle
  Medium Olympic arena
5 Kleine Olympiahalle
  Small Olympic arena
6 Olympische Schwimmhalle
  Olympic swimming pool
7 Olympisches Dorf
  Olympic Village
8 Cannstatter Wasen
  Cannstatt festival grounds
9 Olympisches Forum
  Olympic forum
10 Trainingsplätze
  Training grounds
11 Mercedes-Benz-Museum
12 Pressezentrum
  Press center
13 IOC-Hotel
14 Neckar

Von links nach rechts:
Olympische Wege und Sportstätten in der Neckarlandschaft

Ring der Kulturen

Olympisches Forum

Left to right:
Olympic paths and sporting venues

Ring of cultures

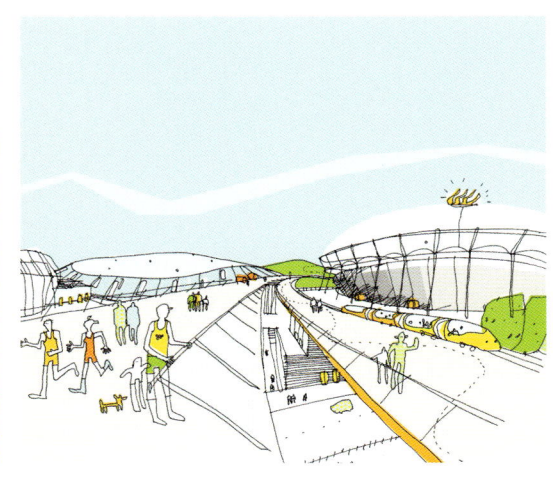

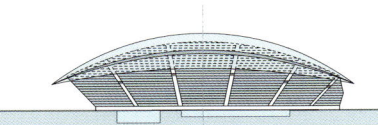

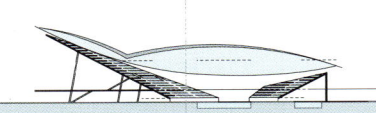

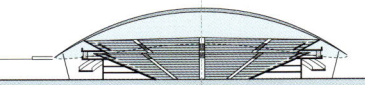

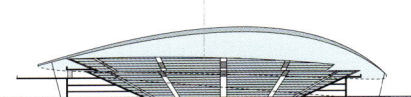

Olympic forum

Olympische Schwimmhalle, 20000 Zuschauer:
Die Olympische Schwimmhalle bildet, von der Innenstadt kommend, den Auftakt der Olympischen Sportstätten. Sie liegt im Uferpark unmittelbar am Neckar

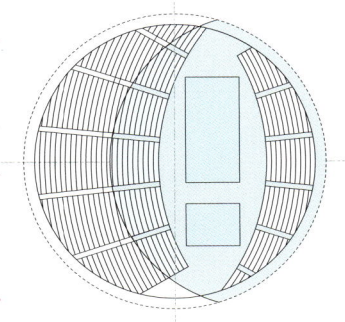

Olympic swimming pool, capacity 20,000:
Approached from downtown, the Olympic swimming pool is the first of the Olympic sports facilities. It is being constructed in the park on the banks of the Neckar and is directly adjacent to the river

Große Olympiahalle, 20000 Zuschauer:
Die große Olympiahalle ist speziell für Basketball- und Turnwettbewerbe vorgesehen

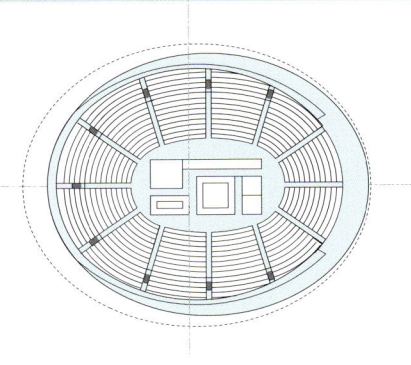

Large Olympic arena, capacity 20,000:
The large Olympic arena is intended in particular for basketball and gymnastics

211 Olympiabewerbung 2012 / Olympic Submission Stuttgart

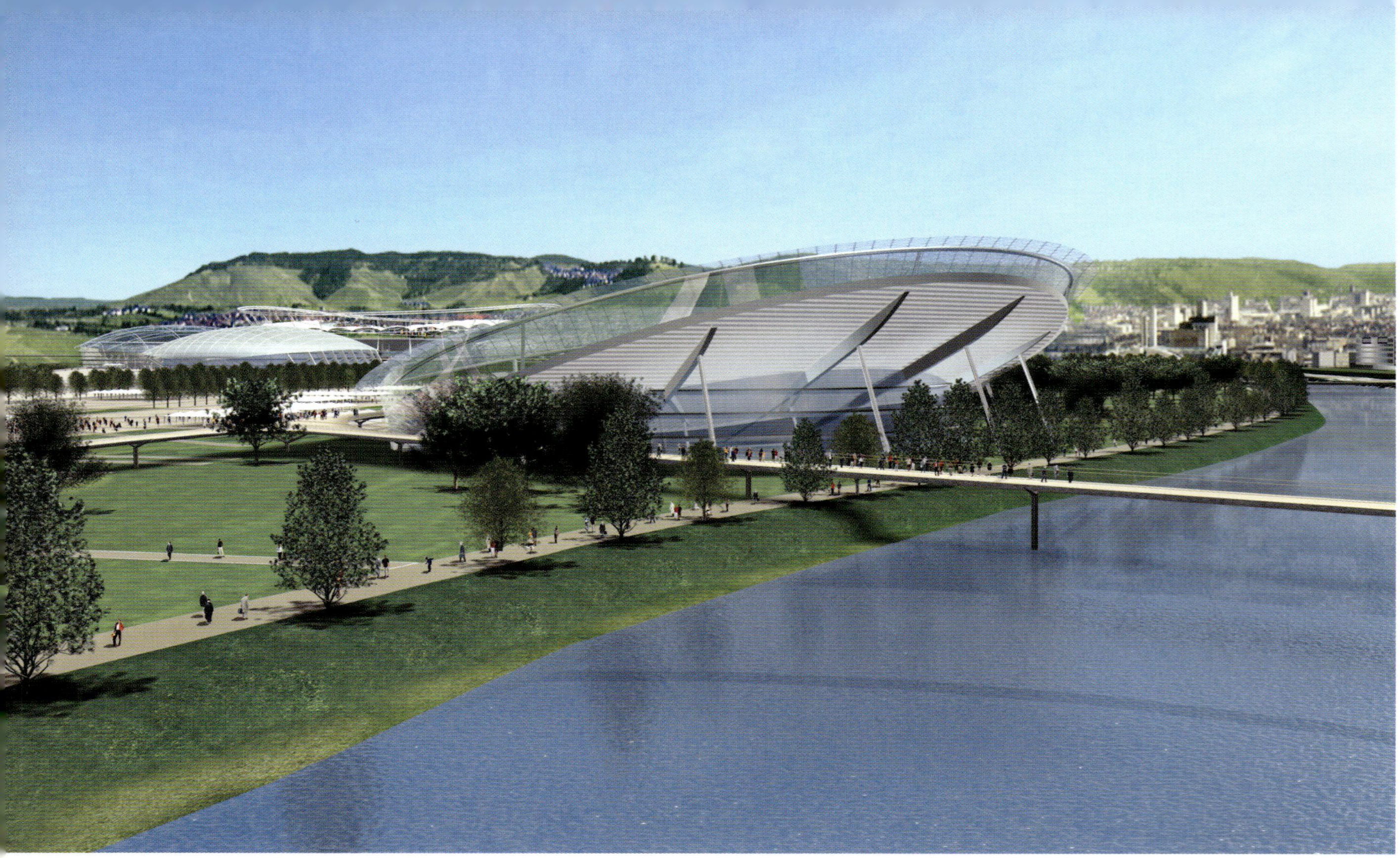

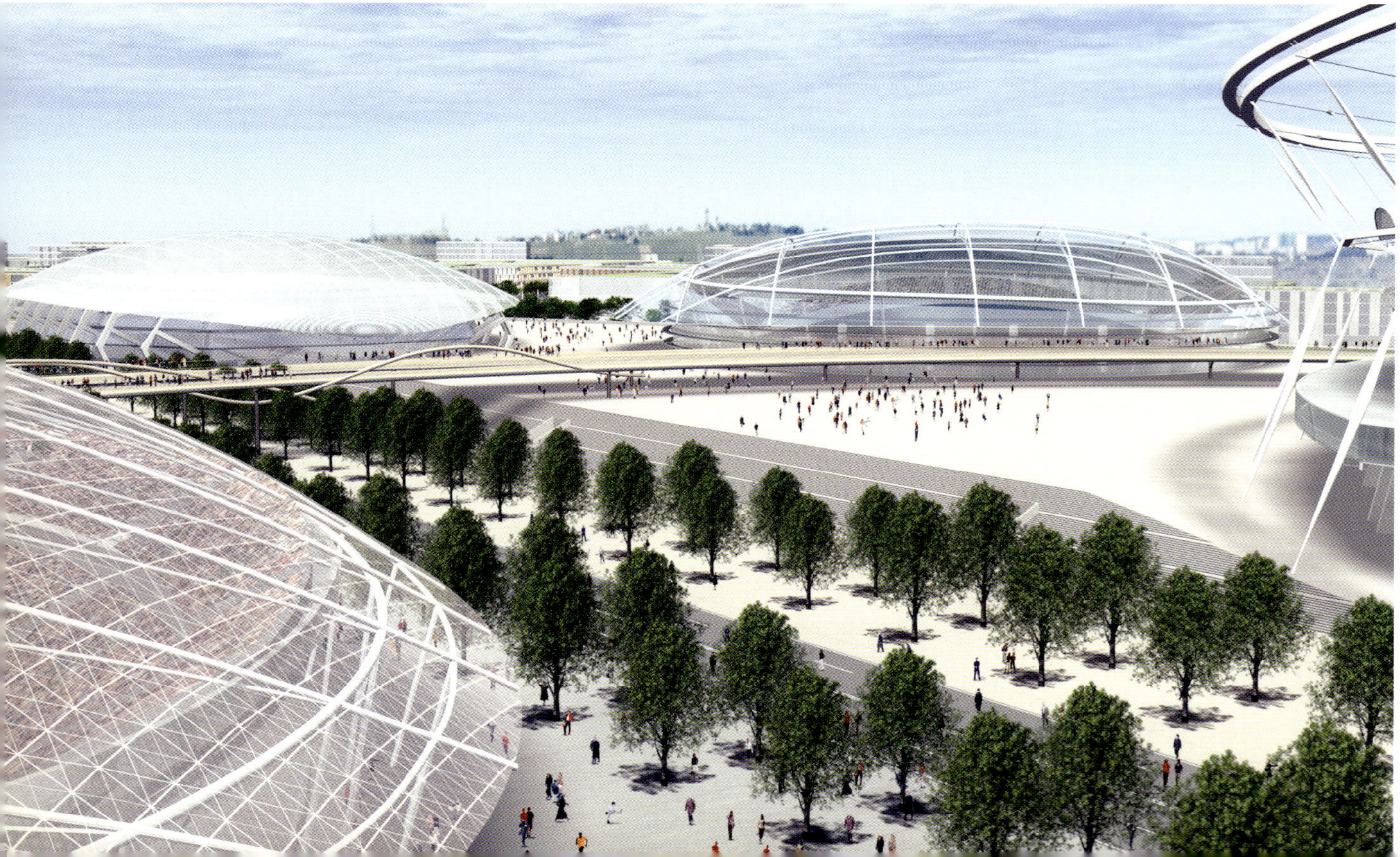

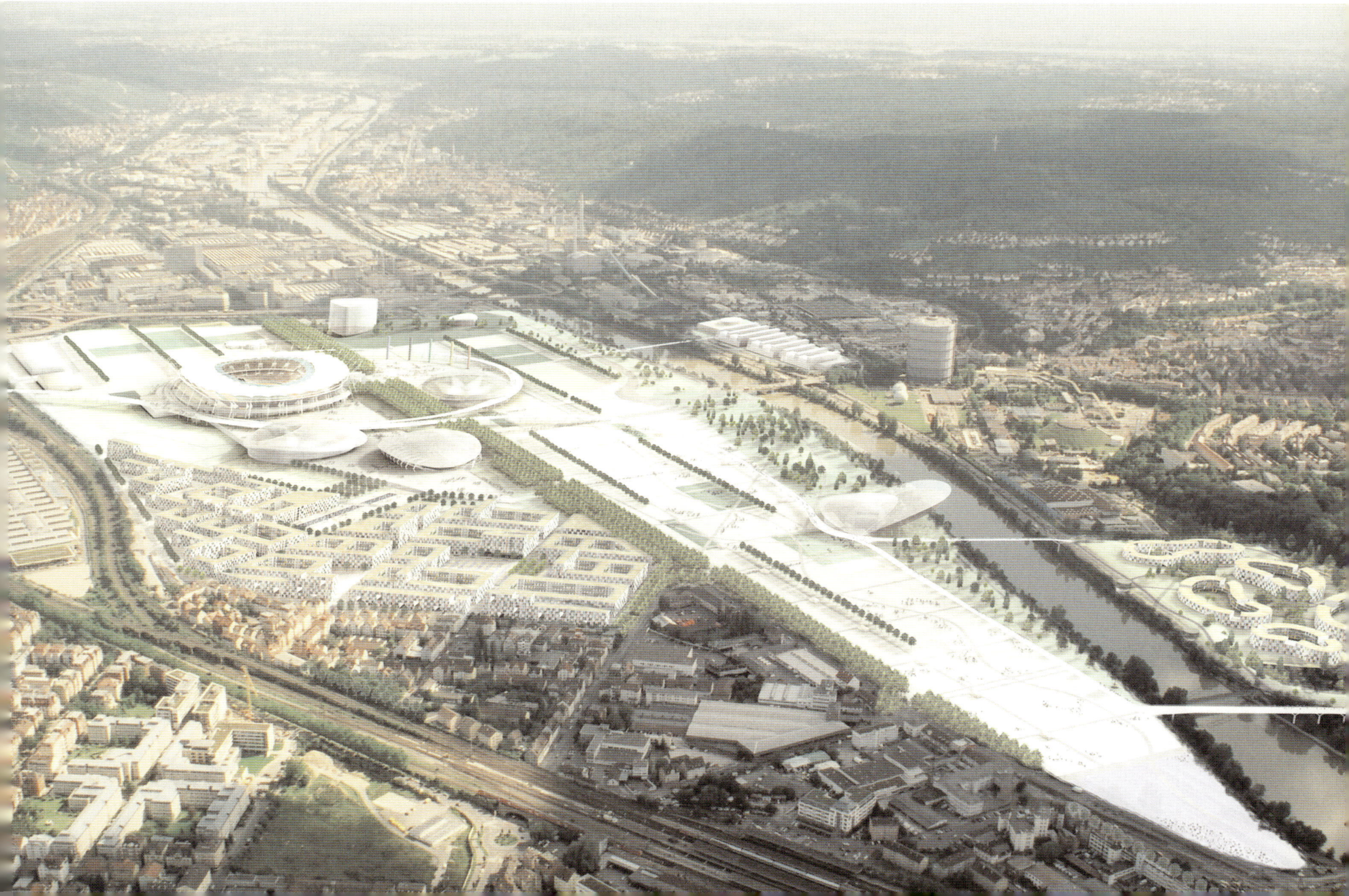

Deutsche Botschaft Mexico City
2002
Gutachten

German Embassy Mexico City
2002
Planning Expertise

Das Kanzleigebäude ist als zweigeschossiger Baukörper angelegt, der einen großzügigen Patio umschließt und sich somit auf einen überlieferten Gebäudetypus in Mexico bezieht.

Die Einfriedung der Grundstücke, welche auch Gestalt prägend für die bauliche Nachbarschaft ist, spielt als ortstypisches Thema in den Entwurf mit hinein.

Alle Räume sind auf den beschatteten Patio ausgerichtet. Das schafft eine introvertierte, gleichzeitig aber auch kommunikative Arbeitsatmosphäre und erhöht die Qualität der Arbeitsplätze durch ein verbessertes Klima. Eine Wasserwand vor der östlichen Innenhof-Fassade sorgt für zusätzliche Kühlung.

Von der Avenida Horacio aus erreicht man über einen Kontrollposten den Patio, das Foyer und die zweigeschossige Galerie. Die Büroräume werden über semitransparente Umgänge an der Außenseite des Gebäudes erschlossen, die vielfältige Ein- und Ausblicke in den Kanzleigarten und die Umgebung bieten.

The Embassy is designed as a two-story building enclosing a spacious patio, and thus evokes a traditional Mexican building type.

A local feature included in the design is the enclosure of the plot, which is typical of the neighboring buildings.

All rooms face the shady patio. This creates a feeling of seclusion, but at the same time makes for a communicative working climate; it also improves air quality, and thus enhances working conditions for employees. Additional coolness is provided through a water wall in front of the eastern courtyard façade.

Coming in from the Avenida Horacio, visitors and employees pass a checkpoint before reaching the patio, foyer and two-story gallery. Semi-transparent passages on the building's street-facing side provide access to the offices and offer views of the garden and surroundings.

Lageplan / Site plan
1:2500

1 Kanzleigebäude
  Embassy building
2 Avenida Horacio
  Avenida Horacio

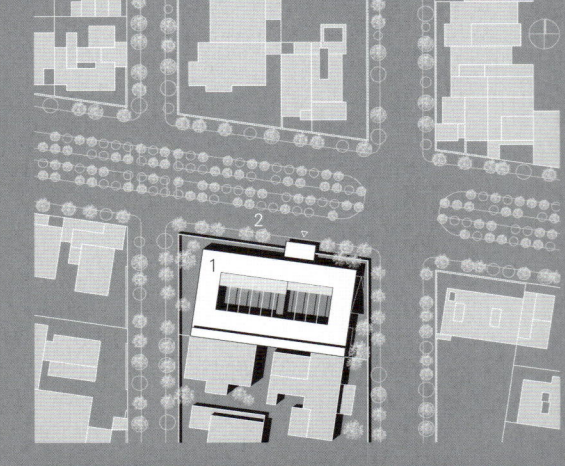

Eingang an der Avenida Horacio

Entrance on Avenida Horacio

Ansicht Plinio
Plinio elevation
1:750

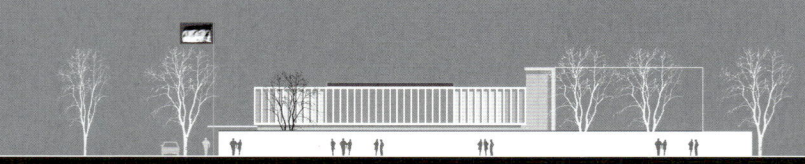

Längsschnitt
Longitudinal section
1:750

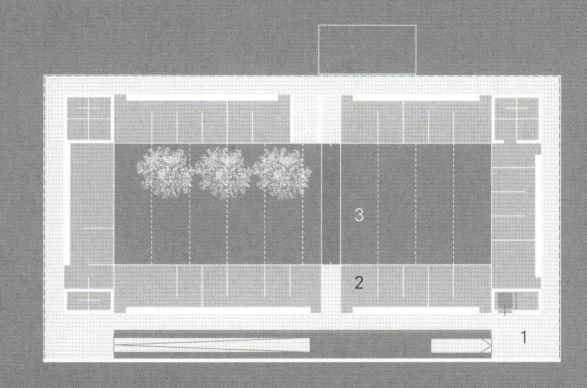

Verfahrbare Schattensegel
gewährleisten ein angenehmes
Klima im Patio

Moveable shading sails create
a pleasant climate in the patio

Links / Left:
Obergeschoss / First floor
1:750

1 Umgang / Circular walk
2 Büro / Office
3 Patio

Die Erschließungsgalerie mit
Blick in den Kanzleigarten

View from the access gallery
into the Embassy garden

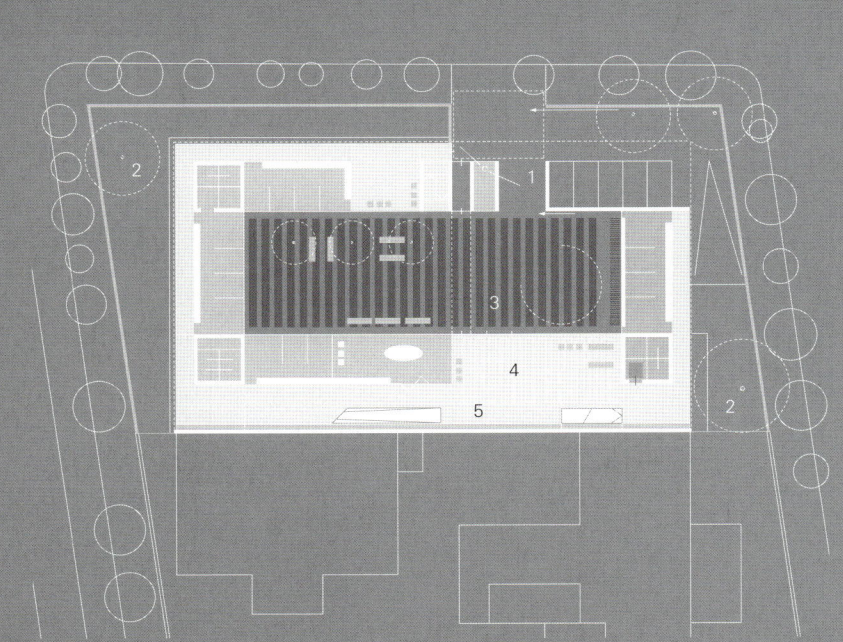

Erdgeschoss / Ground floor
1:750

1 Pforte / Gate
2 Kanzleigarten
  Embassy garden
3 Patio
4 Foyer
5 Erschließungsgalerie
  Access gallery

Hochhaus Süddeutscher Verlag
München
2002
Wettbewerb   3. Preis

Süddeutscher Verlag High-rise
Munich
2002
Competition   3rd prize

Rechts:
Blick von Osten stadteinwärts

Right:
The view from the east
towards the center

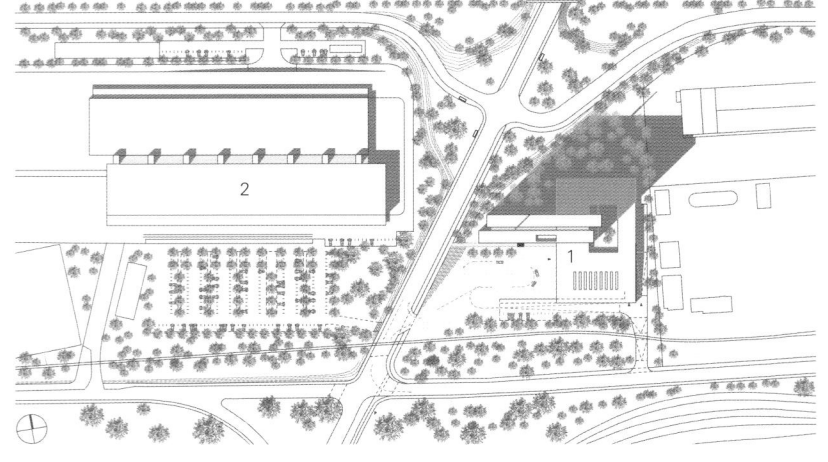

Der Süddeutsche Verlag beabsichtigt, Redaktion und Verlagsgeschäft vom Stammsitz in der Stadtmitte in die unmittelbare Nachbarschaft seines Druckhauses zu verlegen. Der Wettbewerbsentwurf schlägt ein Hochhaus mit 37 Stockwerken vor, das als extrem schlanke Ost-West orientierte Vertikalscheibe zusammen mit dem gleich orientierten, horizontal angelegten Druckhaus einprägsam den inhaltlichen Zusammenhang von Konzeption und Produktion vermittelt.

Die Nord- und Südfassaden sind transparent, glatt und großflächig verglast, die schmalen Ost- und Weststirnseiten dagegen metallisch matt. Die auch unter energetischen Gesichtspunkten exakt nach Norden bzw. Süden gerichteten „Seiten" der transparenten Fassaden eröffnen Einblicke in den Entstehungsprozess der Medienprodukte – vor allem am Abend und in der Nacht.

Ein eingeschossiger Pavillon gestaltet den Platz zwischen Zugang und Druckhaus und schirmt die Anlage gleichzeitig zur östlich angrenzenden Gewerbebebauung ab. Er „verankert" die Scheibe auf dem Gelände und erlaubt die freie Organisation des Eingangsbereichs. Haupteingang und Sonderflächen für Konferenzen und Gastronomie sind um einen Innenhof gruppiert, aus dem die östliche Stirnseite der Hochhausscheibe dramatisch in die Höhe ragt.

Äußere und innere Funktionen sind an der Schnittstelle zwischen Eingangsfoyer und Hochhaus getrennt. Eine zentrale Aufzugsgruppe erschließt das über die gesamte Gebäudehöhe nach Süden geöffnete, vertikale Hochhaus-Foyer, an das sich im Abstand von zwei bis drei Geschossen Treffpunkte mit Besucher-Warteräumen und Besprechungszimmern anschließen.

Innerhalb der Regelgeschosse lassen sich die unterschiedlichsten Büroorganisationsformen und Gruppenkonstellationen realisieren. Durch ein intelligentes Belichtungs- und Lüftungskonzept kann auf eine künstliche Klimatisierung der Büroräume, auf außen liegenden Sonnenschutz und eine aufwändige Doppelfassade verzichtet werden.

Publishing company Süddeutscher Verlag intends to move its editorial offices and publishing operations from its headquarters in the city center to the immediate vicinity of the printing plant. The competition submission proposes a highrise with 37 stories. The building is designed as an extremely narrow vertical block facing east-west. It is in tandem with the horizontal printing plant facing in the same direction and it forcefully conveys the link between conceptual work and printed output.

The north and south façades are transparent, with smooth, extensive glazing, while the narrow east and west metallic fronts are matte. Positioned perfectly north and south to save energy, the transparent façades allow views of media products in the making – especially in the evening and at night.

A single-story pavilion defines the space between the entrance area and the printing plant, and simultaneously screens off the ensemble from the industrial development adjoining to the east. It anchors the high-rise on the site, and allows for the flexible organization of the entrance area. Main entrance and special areas for conferences, restaurants, etc., are grouped around an inner courtyard from which the eastern front of the high-rise towers up dramatically.

External and internal functions are separated at the interface between entrance foyer and high-rise. A central set of elevators provides access to the vertical foyer, which extends over the entire height of the building and is accessed from the south. Every two or three stories, there are meeting points with waiting zones for visitors, while meeting and conference rooms adjoin the foyer.

The stories are designed to allow for the highly flexible organization of office and group constellations. Thanks to an intelligent lighting and ventilation system, the building can do without artificial air-conditioning in the offices, an external glare protection system, or a complicated double façade.

Lageplan / Site plan
1:5000

1   Hochhaus / High-rise
2   Druckhaus / Printing plant

Hochhaus / High-rise
Phoenix Rheinrohr
Düsseldorf, 1960
Hentrich und Petschnigg

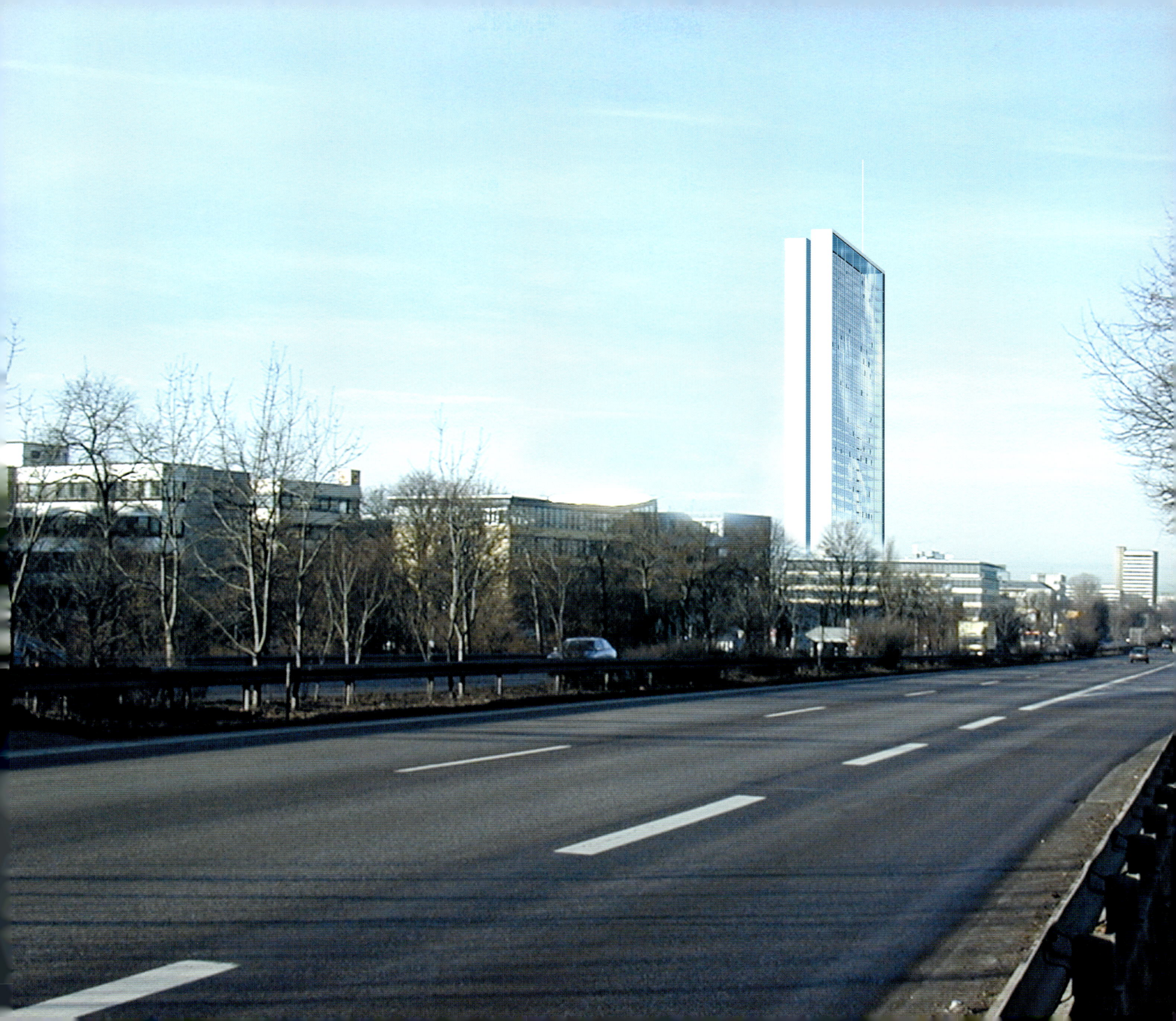

Erdgeschoss / Ground floor
1:1000

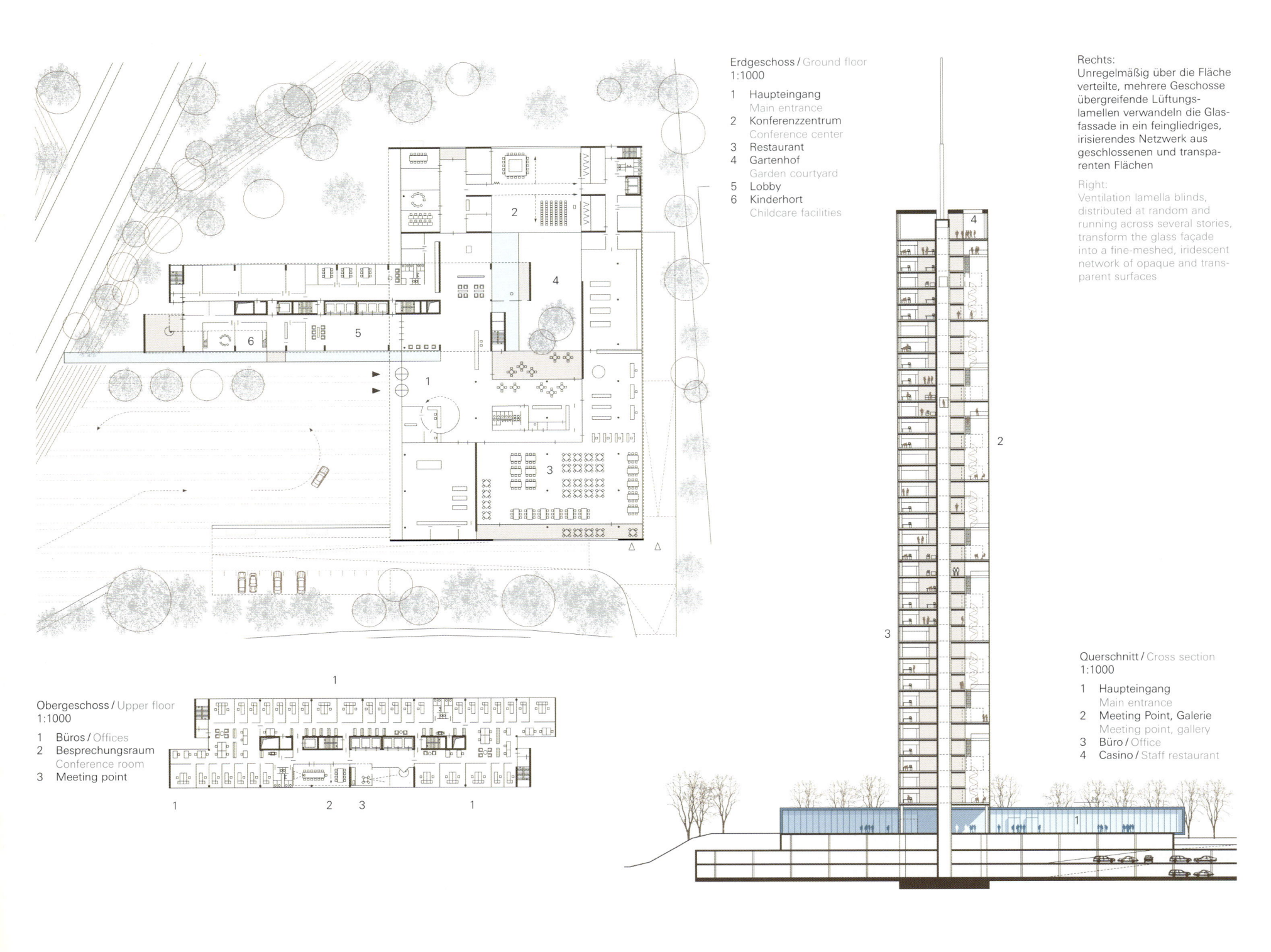

1 Haupteingang
  Main entrance
2 Konferenzzentrum
  Conference center
3 Restaurant
4 Gartenhof
  Garden courtyard
5 Lobby
6 Kinderhort
  Childcare facilities

Rechts:
Unregelmäßig über die Fläche verteilte, mehrere Geschosse übergreifende Lüftungslamellen verwandeln die Glasfassade in ein feingliedriges, irisierendes Netzwerk aus geschlossenen und transparenten Flächen

Right:
Ventilation lamella blinds, distributed at random and running across several stories, transform the glass façade into a fine-meshed, iridescent network of opaque and transparent surfaces

Querschnitt / Cross section
1:1000

1 Haupteingang
  Main entrance
2 Meeting Point, Galerie
  Meeting point, gallery
3 Büro / Office
4 Casino / Staff restaurant

Obergeschoss / Upper floor
1:1000

1 Büros / Offices
2 Besprechungsraum
  Conference room
3 Meeting point

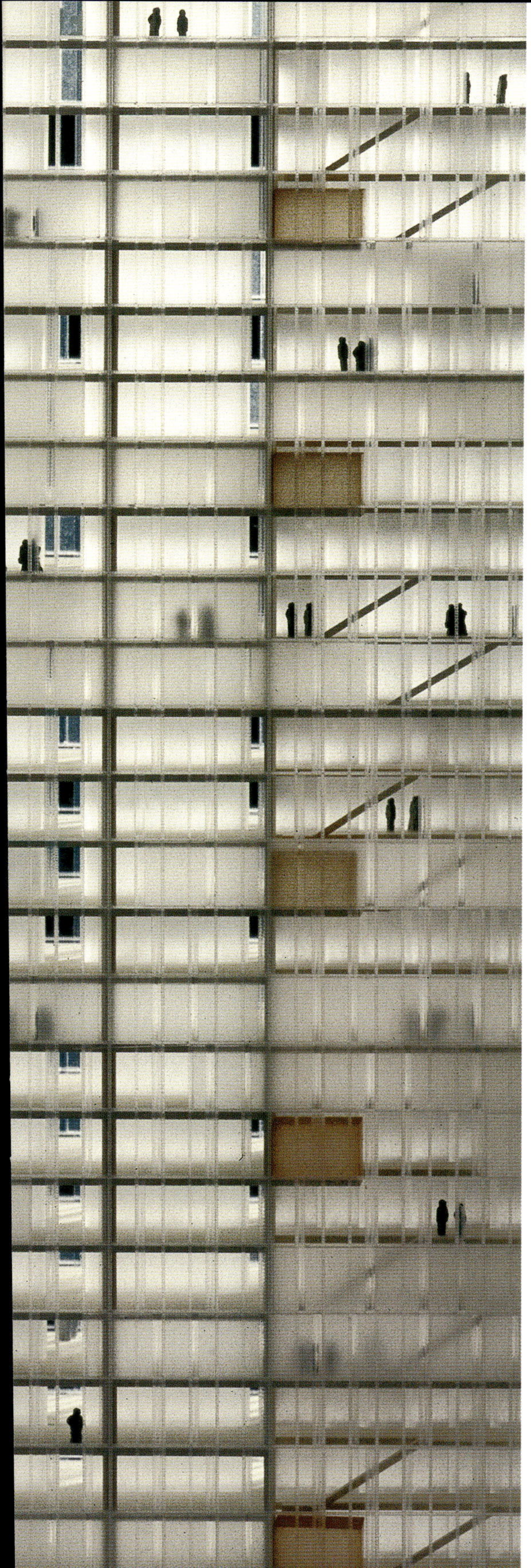

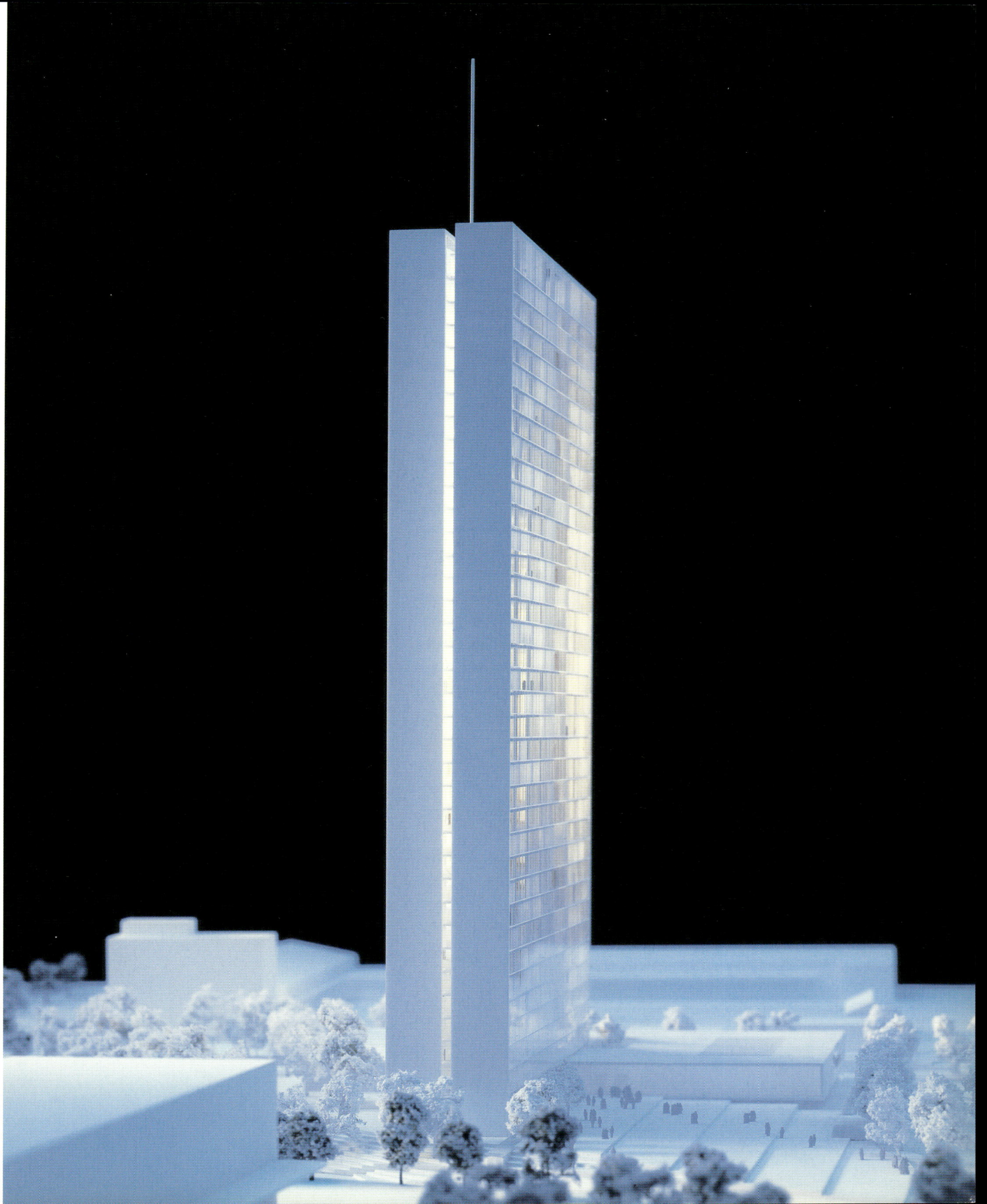

Schlossberg Böblingen
2002
Wettbewerb 3. Preis

Schlossberg Böblingen
2002
Competition 3rd prize

Bürgerzentrum und Galerie bilden das neue kulturelle und gesellschaftliche Zentrum Böblingens, das zusammen mit der Stadtkirche die Stadtsilhouette prägt. Die topografische Hangsituation überhöhend entsteht so innerhalb des Stadtbildes ein markantes Bauwerk.

Im südlichen Freiraum vor dem Bürgerzentrum, über dem ehemaligen Schlosskeller befindet sich, beschirmt von Bäumen, ein Biergarten, der die darunter liegenden Gewölbe des Jugendkulturtreffs mit einbezieht.

Eine wettergeschützte Passage, die den Serpentinenweg durch den „Schlossberggarten" fortsetzt, verbindet als gemeinsamer Eingangsraum die unterschiedlichen Funktionen von Bürgerzentrum und Galerie, welche sich in einem einheitlichen, jedoch in sich unterschiedlich ausgeformten Bauwerk präsentieren.

So genannte „Stifterhäuschen", die im näheren Umfeld an stadträumlich prägnanten Stellen platziert sind, bieten den im Raum Böblingen ansässigen Weltunternehmen Gelegenheit, einen Beitrag zum gesellschaftlichen Leben zu leisten.

The civic center and gallery form the new cultural and commercial center of Böblingen and, together with the town church, dominate the town's silhouette. Situated on top of an incline, the town is enriched by the prominent building.

In the open space to the south of the civic center, there is a beer garden above the former castle cellar which is sheltered by trees and incorporates the vaults of the youth center immediately below.

An arcade that is protected from the elements extends the meandering path through the Schlossberg garden and serves as a joint entrance to the civic center and gallery. Although the building possesses a uniform appearance, the civic center and gallery still contrast with each other.

Placed at strategic positions in the immediate surroundings, "Donors' Cottages", as they are known, present global companies in the Böblingen area with an opportunity to participate in the town's social life.

Lageplan / Site plan
1:4000

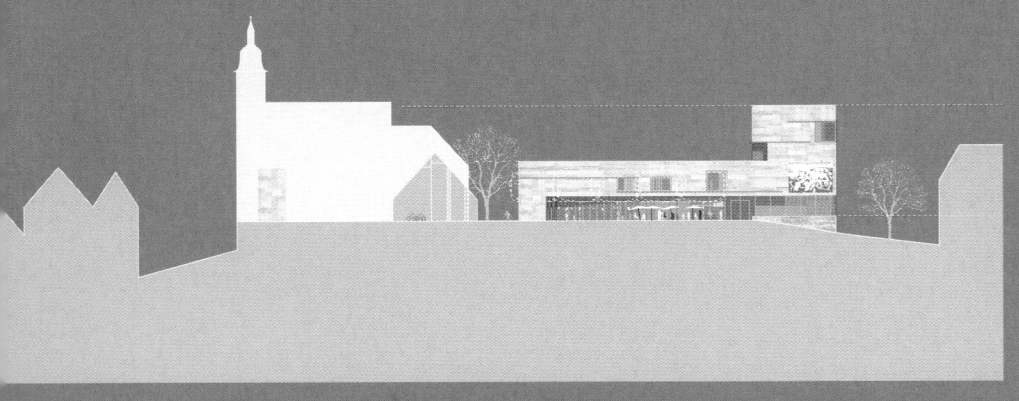

Ansicht vom Schlossbergplatz
View from Schlossbergplatz
1:1250

Querschnitt / Cross section
1:1250

Ebene Schlossbergplatz
Schlossbergplatz level
1:1250

1 Bürgerzentrum
   Civic center
2 Öffentliche Passage
   Public arcade
3 Ständige Sammlung
   der Galerie im Turm
   Permanent gallery
   in the tower
4 Schlossbergplatz
5 Schlossbergkeller
   Schlossberg cellar
6 Schlossberggarten
   Schlossberg garden

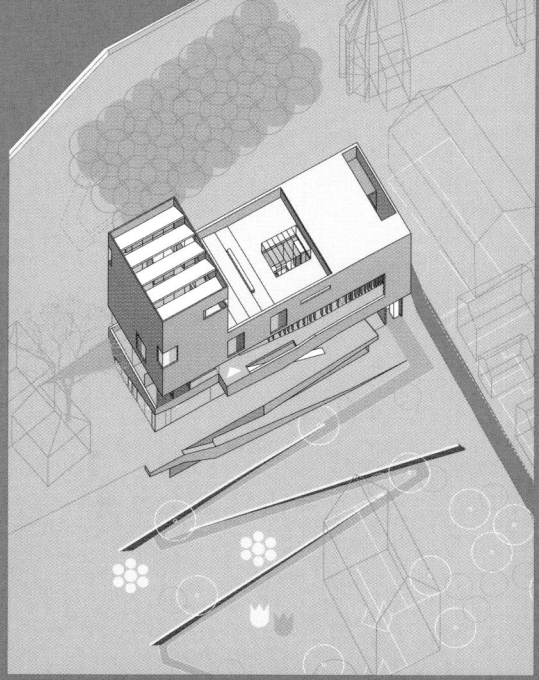

Oben:
Die neuformulierte Stadt-
silhouette des Schlossbergs
von Süden

Links:
Blick von Norden auf den
Schlossberggarten mit
Serpentinenweg

Above:
The reconstructed silhouette
of the Schlossberg, as viewed
from the south

Left:
The view of the Schlossberg
gardens and Serpentinenweg
from the north

Zentrum SolarCity Linz
2003
Wettbewerb 1999   1. Preis

SolarCity Center Linz
2003
Competition 1999   1st prize

Auf der Grundlage eines Masterplans der Architekten Norman Foster, Thomas Herzog und Richard Rogers entsteht in Linz-Pichling eine neue Stadt für rund 25000 Einwohner, die hauptsächlich durch Sonnenenergie versorgt werden soll. Das Ziel ist zudem eine maximal zulässige Dichte, eine große Vielfalt und die Möglichkeit zur Mischnutzung und Förderung sozialen Wohnungsbaus zu geringen Kosten. Mietergärten, Ruhezonen, Kinderspielplätze und Orte gemeinsamer Aktivität gliedern und individualisieren die Baufelder im kleinen Maßstab.

Das Zentrum der künftigen Solar-Stadt bildet zusammen mit einem großzügigen Erschließungsboulevard das funktionale und räumliche Bindeglied zwischen den Stadtteilen, an das sich die modularen Bausteine der verschiedenen kommerziellen, kulturellen und allgemeinen Dienstleistungen anschließen. In die entstehenden Gassen und Höfe sind lineare Gerüste als transparente Schutzdächer eingestellt. Durch die Verwendung beschichteter, farbiger und polierter Gläser können hier unterschiedliche Lichtwirkungen erzeugt werden, während die Dachflächen der Module der Erzeugung von Sonnenenergie dienen.

Der zentrale Platz, als „Sozialmagnet" von allen Punkten aus bequem zu Fuß zu erreichen, wird der künftige Mittelpunkt städtischen Lebens in der neuen Stadt.

Based on a master plan by the architects Norman Foster, Thomas Herzog and Richard Rogers a brand new town for 25,000 inhabitants, which will be powered almost entirely by solar energy, is being established in Linz-Pichling. The highest possible level of compactness, diversity and multipurpose facilities, as well as the development of low-cost municipal housing, also feature in the plans. Gardens for tenants, tranquil areas, children's playgrounds and spots for communal activities divide up the construction areas and lend them an air of small scale individuality.

Together with a wide access boulevard, the center of this future solar-powered town will form a functional and spatial link between the town's districts, including various commercial, cultural and general service providers which will be attached as modular elements. A linear supporting frame is being erected in the streets and courtyards to provide transparent roofing. A variety of lighting effects will be created by the use of coated, colored and polished glass, while the roofs of the modules will be used to create solar energy.

The plan is for the central square – a "social magnet" that can be easily reached on foot from all areas – to be the centerpiece of life in the new town.

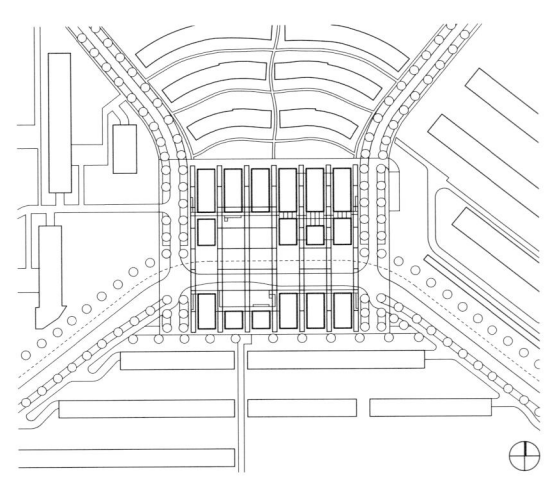

Lageplan / Site plan
1:5000

Mit seinen Raum überspannenden Gerüststrukturen verbindet das Zentrum der SolarCity die angrenzenden Stadtteile über den Verkehrsboulevard hinweg

With its supporting frames that span the area, the SolarCity center connects the adjoining neighborhoods via the boulevard

Die verschiedenen Elemente des Zentrums beziehen sich auf ein dreidimensionales, rechteckiges Grundraster. Die modularen Baukörper fügen sich hier im Wechsel mit verbindenden Gerüststrukturen ein

The various elements in the center are based on a three-dimensional, rectangular grid. The modular building elements are interchangeable with the connecting support frameworks

Schichtung der Funktionsbereiche / Layering of the functional areas
1:5000

1 Modulare Bauvolumen
  Modular building volumes
2 Gerüststruktur
  Supporting framework
3 Wetterschutz und Lichtlenkung / Weather protection and light control
4 Pneumatische Überdachungselemente
  Pneumatic roofing elements

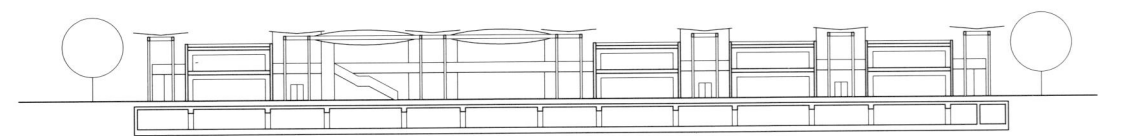

Schnitt / Section
1:1000

Erdgeschoss / Ground floor
1:1000

1 Supermarkt / Supermarket
2 Bürgersaal
  Community room
3 Seniorenclub
  Senior citizens' club
4 Café
5 Bücherei / Library
6 Läden und Dienst-
  leistungen
  Shops and services
7 Marktplatz mit Straßen-
  bahnhaltestelle / Market
  square with streetcar stop

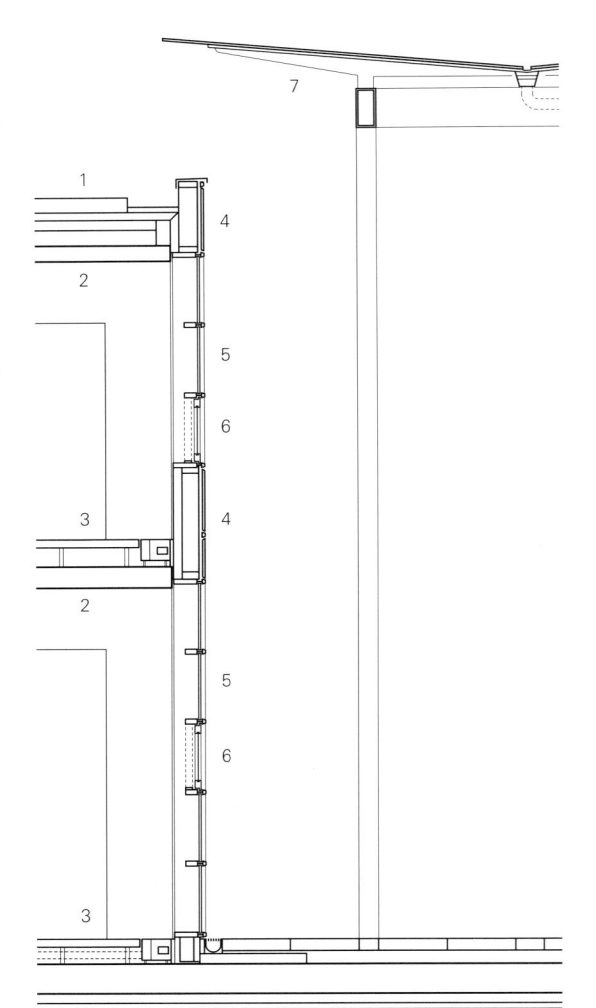

Fassadenschnitt
Façade section
1:75

1 Extensive Dachbegrünung
  Extensive roof planting
2 Sichtbetondecke
  Fair faced concrete ceiling
3 Hohlraumboden
  Hollow floor
4 Hinterlüftete Holz-Schalung
  Ventilated weather-
  boarding
5 Pfosten-Riegel-Fassade,
  Holz / Façade of stakes
  and bars, wood
6 Hebe-Schiebefenster
  Hanging sash windows
7 Glasüberdachung
  Glass roofing

Rechts:
Ein durchgehender Verbindungssteg erschließt die Dienstleistungsbereiche im Obergeschoss und die Galerie des Bürgerhauses

Unten:
Wettergeschützte Gassen führen auf den zentralen Marktplatz

Right:
A continuous connecting path provides access to the service areas in the upper story and the gallery in the municipal building

Below:
The passages are protected from the elements and lead to the central market square

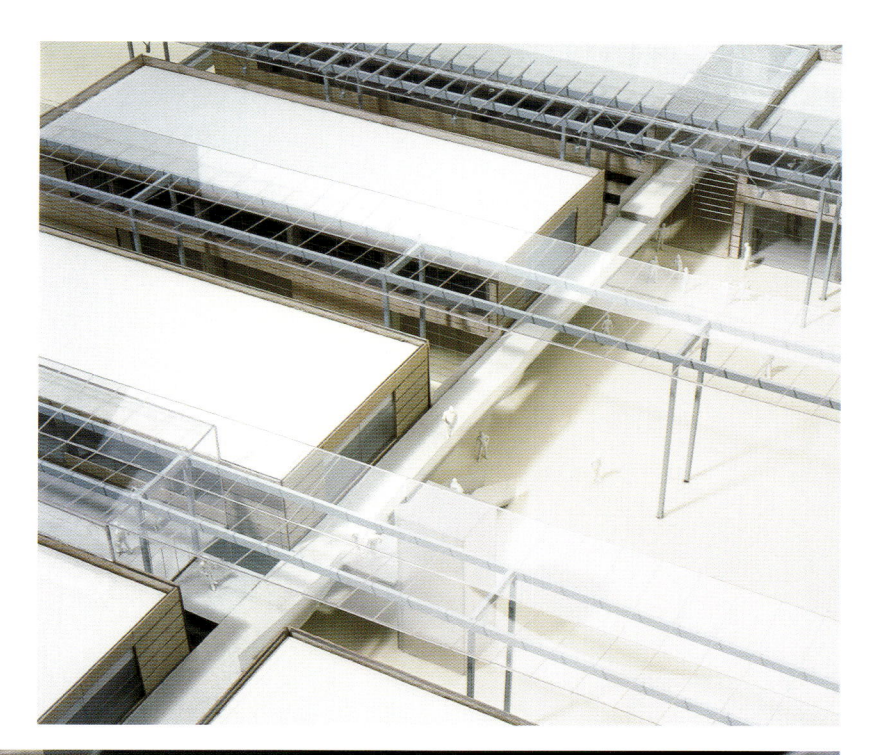

Zentraler Omnibusbahnhof München
2002
Wettbewerb   1. Preis
In Planung

Central Bus Station Munich
2002
Competition   1st prize
Planning stage

Der Baukörper des zentralen Omnibusbahnhofs fasst die Nutzungen Terminal/Büro/Hotel/Dienstleistung zusammen und bildet in seiner markanten Form stadträumlich den Auftakt der neuen „Stadtkante" nördlich des Gleisfelds zwischen Hauptbahnhof und Pasing. Er löst sich bewusst von der statisch wirkenden städtischen Bebauung. So entsteht am Ziel- und Ausgangspunkt des Fern-Busverkehrs ein Gebäude, das die Dynamik dieser Verbindungen reflektiert und auch eine attraktive Adresse für kommerzielle Nutzungen darstellt.

Alle Bereiche sind von einer karosserieähnlichen Hülle umschlossen. Über ein „Promenadendeck", welches über Stege und Fahrtreppen an die Haltestellen des zentralen Omnibusbahnhofs, den S-Bahn-Haltepunkt und die Hackerbrücke angebunden ist, besteht ein barrierefreier Zugang in alle Einrichtungen.

Die Terminal-Lounge öffnet sich auf einen großzügigen Vorplatz in Richtung Stadt und Hauptbahnhof. Von hier aus – wie auch vom Promenadendeck – hat man einen guten Blick auf die darunter liegenden Bushaltestellen, die Bahngleise und über den Hauptbahnhof hinweg auf die Silhouette der Innenstadt.

The body of the central bus station incorporates a terminal, offices, hotel and service providers. Its striking appearance marks the beginning of the "new city limit" in the area north of the tracks between the main station and Pasing. The station is a deliberate break from the static impression the city's other buildings present. The building functions as a starting point and point of return after long distances of bus travel; it reflects the dynamism of travel and is also an attractive location for commercial use.

A sheath surrounds all the station's sections like a vehicle body. A "promenade deck" is connected to the bus stops of the central bus station, the suburban railway station and Hackerbrücke by walkways and moving staircases and provides barrier-free access to all facilities.

The terminal lounge opens out onto a spacious square which faces the city and the main railway station. From here, as from the promenade deck, there is an excellent view of the bus stops below, the railway platforms and, beyond the main station, the silhouette of the downtown area.

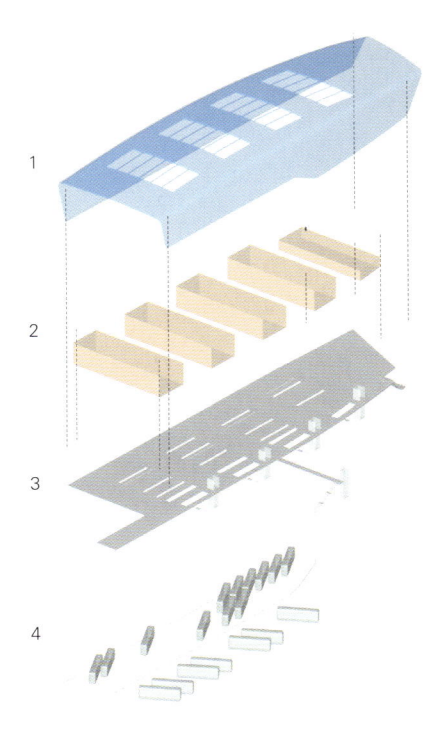

Schichtung der Funktionsbereiche / Levels of the functional areas

1 Hülle / Sheath
2 Büroflächen / Office space
3 Promenadendeck
   Promenade deck
4 Terminal / Terminal

Rechts / Right:
Lageplan / Site plan
1:5000

1 Zentraler Omnibusbahnhof
   Central bus station
2 S-Bahn-Haltestelle
   Suburban railway station
3 Hackerbrücke
4 Arnulfstraße
5 Zu- und Ausfahrt
   Entrance and exit

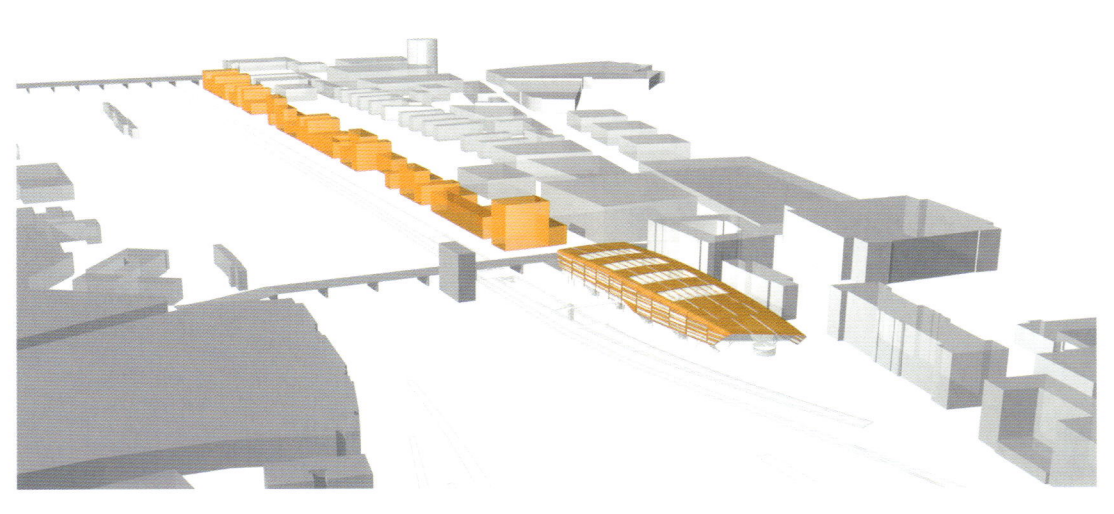

Links:
Der zentrale Omnibusbahnhof bildet den Kopfpunkt einer neuen „Stadtkante" entlang der Gleisanlagen

Rechts:
Das obere Promenadendeck öffnet sich zu ruhigen, geschützten Innenhöfen

Left:
The central bus station forms the head of the strip development along the railway lines

Right:
The upper promenade deck opens out onto quiet, protected inner courtyards

227

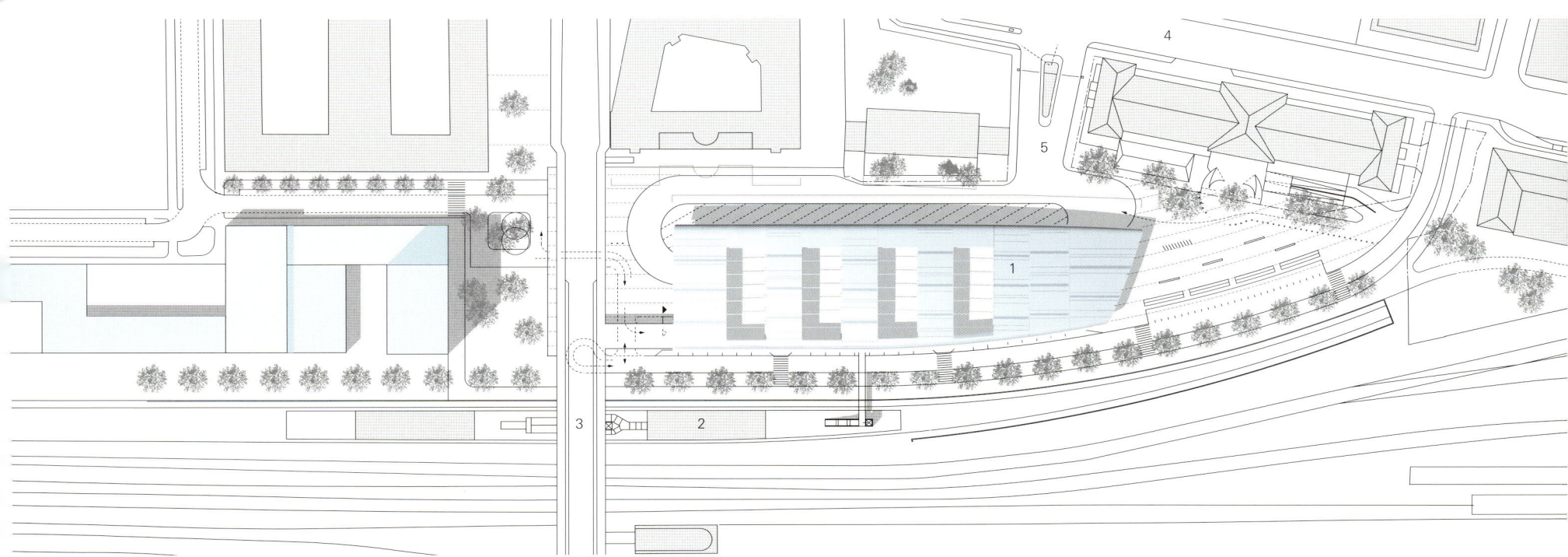

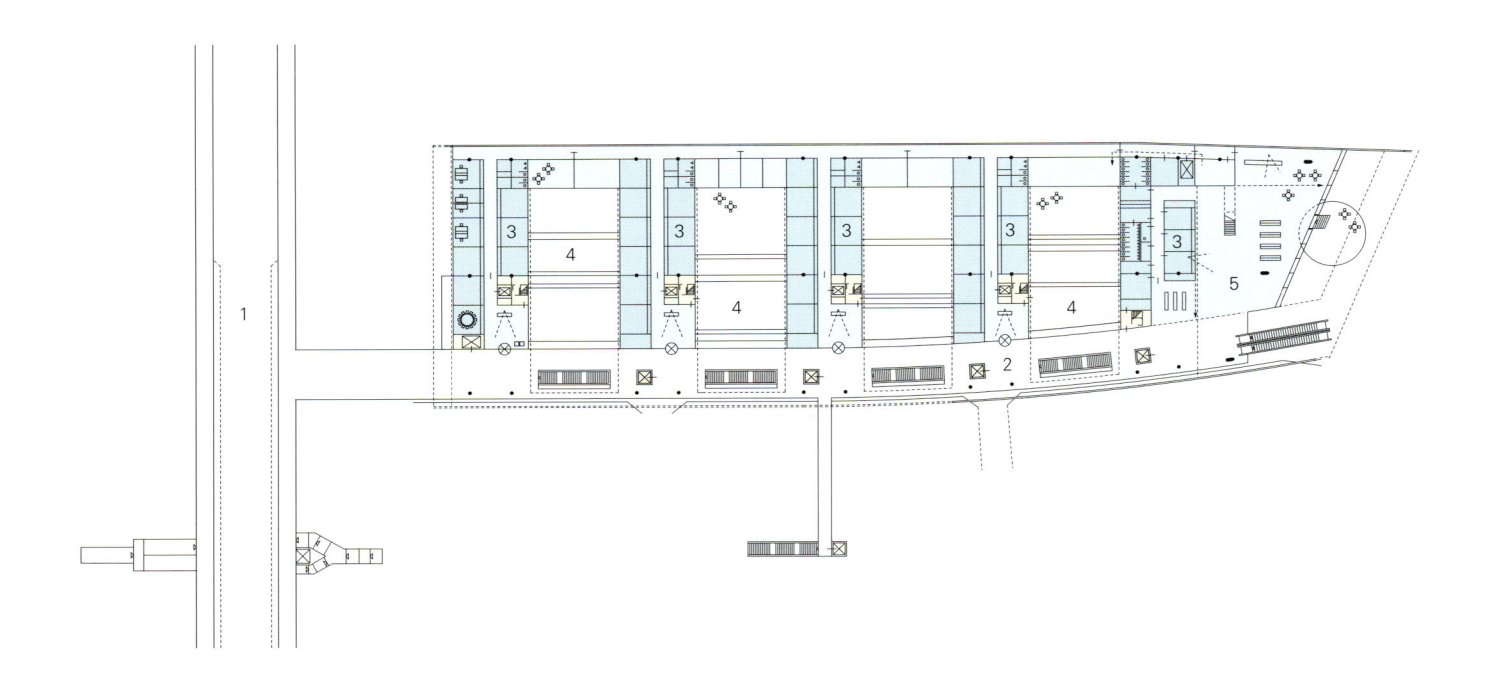

Promenadendeck
Promenade deck
1:1250

1. Hackerbrücke
2. Promenade
3. Büroflächen / Office space
4. Begrünte Innenhöfe
   Planted inner courtyards
5. Terminal-Lounge

Terminalebene / Terminal level
1:1250

1. Busabstellplätze
   Bus parking spaces
2. Ein- und Ausfahrt
   Entrance and exit
3. Information / Information
4. Kurzzeitparken
   Short-stay parking
5. Zufahrt zur Tiefgarage
   Entrance to basement garage

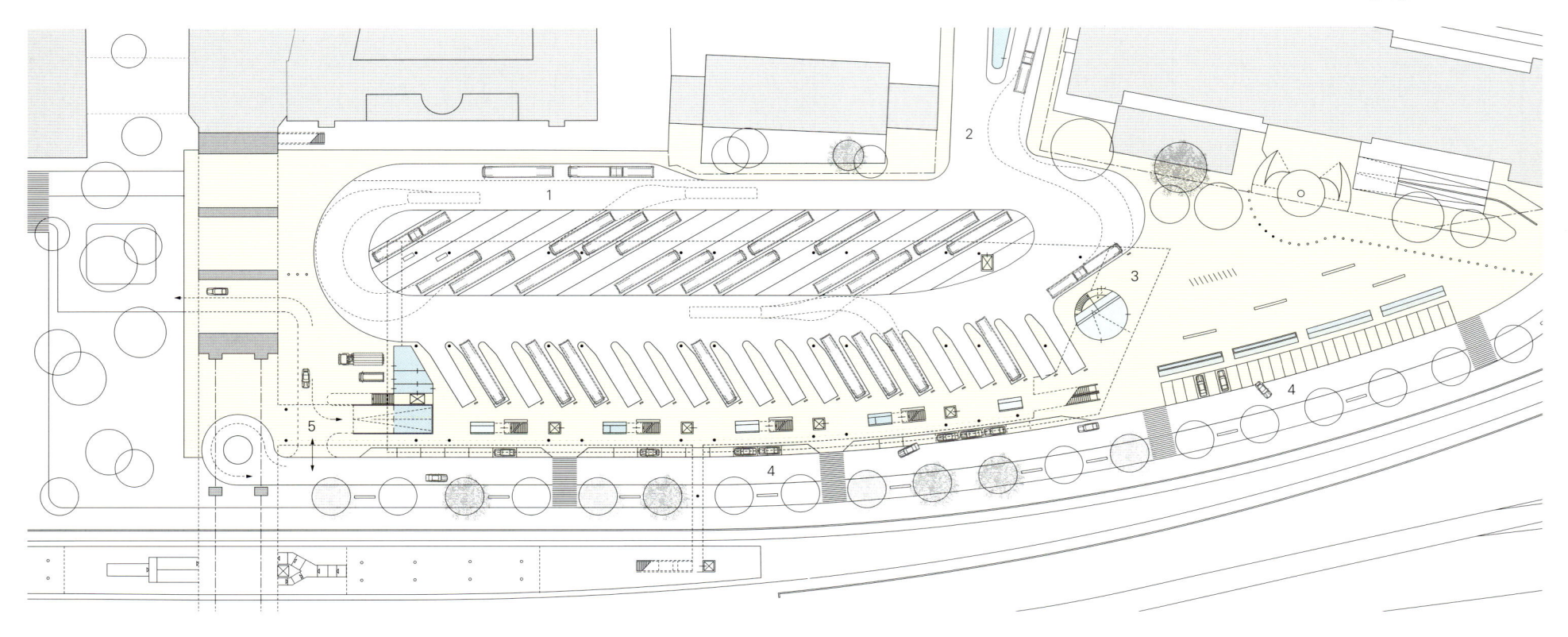

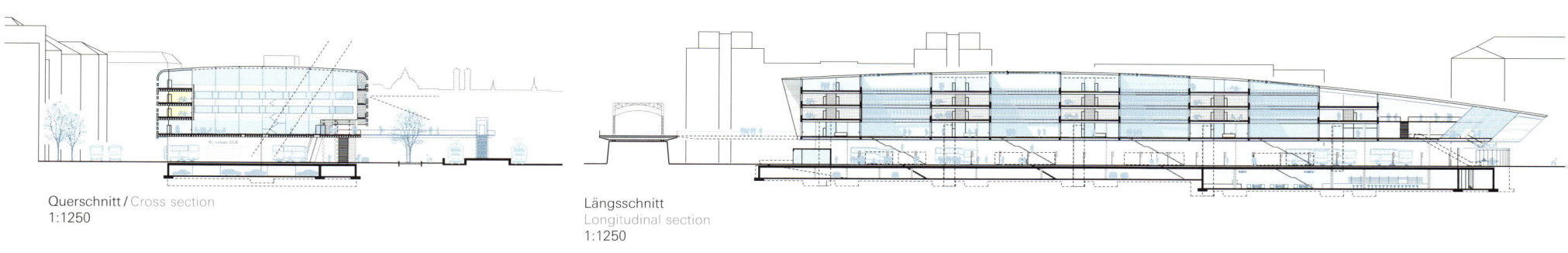

Querschnitt / Cross section
1:1250

Längsschnitt / Longitudinal section
1:1250

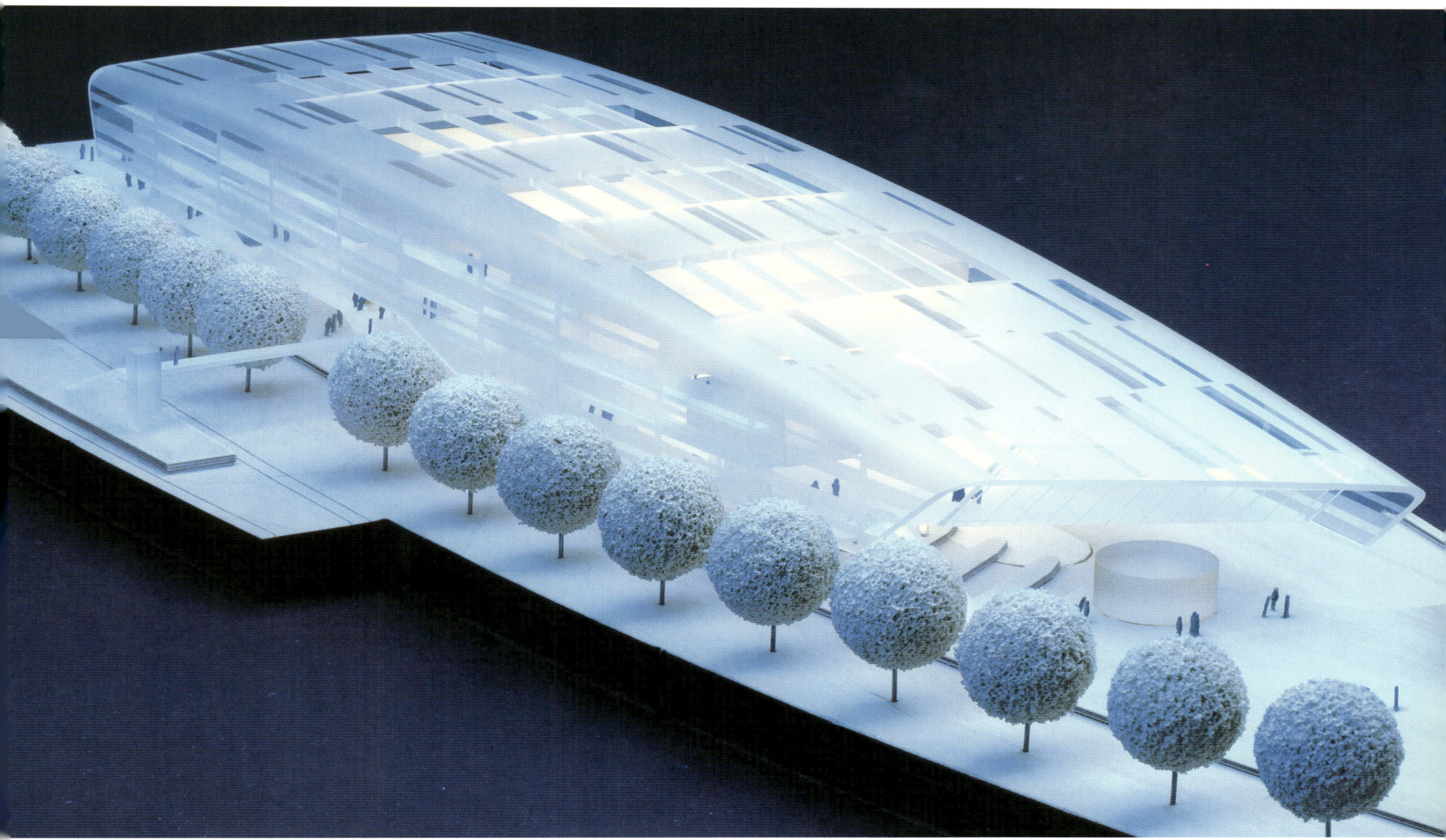

229 Zentraler Omnibusbahnhof / Central Bus Station München

Science Park III Ulm
2001
Gutachten 1. Rang

Science Park III Ulm
2001
Planning Expertise 1st place

Lageplan / Site plan
1:15 000
1. Konferenzhotel
   Conference hotel
2. Start-Up-Hain
   Start-Up Grove
3. Hangbebauung
   Buildings on the slope
4. Aussichtspromenade
   Panorama promenade
5. Parkhäuser
   Parking facilities

Ein Gewerbegebiet als Standort für Hochtechnologiefirmen, der so genannte „Science Park Ulm", soll am Ulmer Eselsberg auf einen bis dahin unangetasteten Nord-West-Hang erweitert werden.

Ohne das weithin sichtbare Hanggrundstück und den schönen Blick in die umgebende Landschaft vollständig zu verbauen, schieben sich auf insgesamt drei Ebenen Sockelbaukörper terrassenartig aus dem Hang. Auf die Sockel werden Solitärbaukörper in Form mehrgeschossiger Türme aufgesetzt als weithin sichtbare Zeichen für die ansässigen Unternehmen. Sie bilden die eigentliche Hangbebauung, hinter der die Sockelbaukörper weitgehend zurücktreten.

Ein Konferenzhotel am Entrée zum Erweiterungsgebiet dient als gemeinsames Zentrum aller Bereiche des Science Parks, der „Start-Up-Hain" in direkter Nachbarschaft ist Standort für Büros auf Zeit. Attraktives Vorfeld für den „Start-Up-Hain" ist die Aussichtspromenade entlang einer Hangstufe, die neben ergänzenden Dienstleistungsangeboten einen weiten Blick über die vorgelagerte Hangbebauung in die Landschaft bietet.

A commercial zone for high-tech companies, "Science Park Ulm", as it is called, is going to be extended to include the previously undeveloped north-west slope of Eselsberg in Ulm.

So that it does not completely obstruct the sloping site, which is visible from afar, or the attractive view out over the surrounding countryside, pedestal-like volumes protrude from the slope. Individual building elements in the form of multistory towers are set atop these pedestals, as visible symbols of the companies based there. These towers constitute the actual buildings on the slope, and the pedestal elements largely retreat behind them.

A conference hotel at the entrance to the area being extended will serve as a common center for all sections in the Science Park, while the adjacent "Start-Up Grove" will provide temporary office space. A panorama promenade, where supplementary services are located, sweeps beyond the buildings of the slope, creating an attractive approach to the "Start-Up Grove" and a view out over the surrounding countryside.

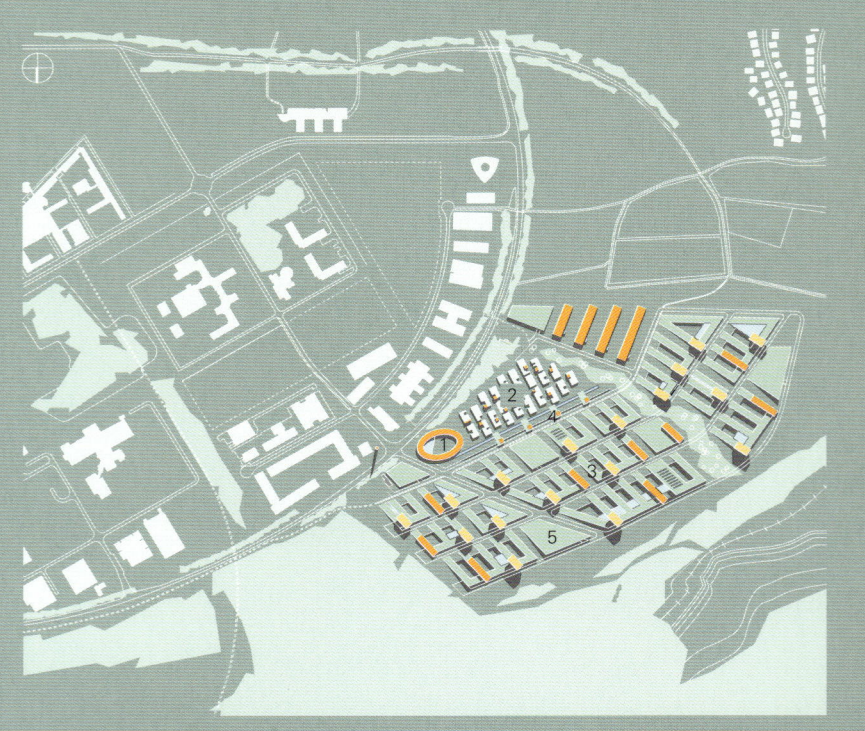

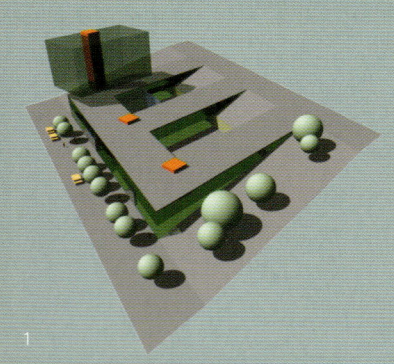

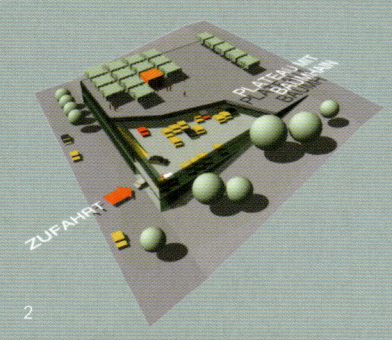

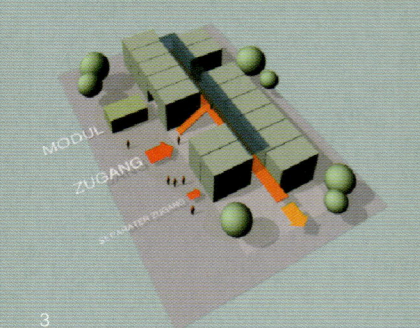

Die drei Grundelemente der Bebauung (von links):

1. die aus dem Berg heraustretenden Sockelgebäude bilden künstliche Terrassen, auf die in Hangrichtung orientierte Hochbauten aufgesetzt werden
2. terrassenförmige und mit Baumteppichen überstellte Parkdecks
3. modulare Bausteine des „Start-Up-Hains"

The three basic elements of the buildings (from left):

1. ground-floor buildings protruding from the slope form artificial terraces on which constructions facing in the direction of the slope are positioned
2. terraced tree-lined car parks
3. modular building elements of the "Start-Up Grove"

| Konferenzhotel | Start-Up-Hain | Hangbebauung |
| Conference hotel | Start-Up Grove | Buildings on the slope |

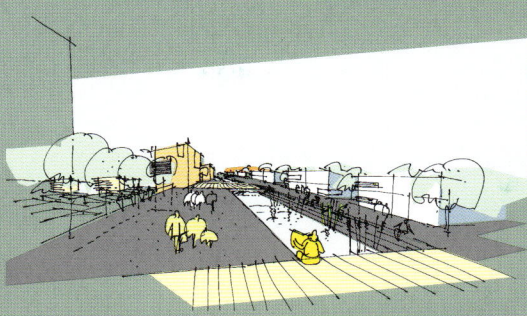

Eingangsgeschoss
Ground floor

1 Eingangshalle / Lobby
2 Bürobereiche / Office areas
3 Grünhof / Planted courtyard
4 Werk-/Lieferhof
　Work & delivery courtyard
5 Parkgarage
　Parking facilities

Obergeschoss / Upper floor

Turmgeschoss / Tower floor

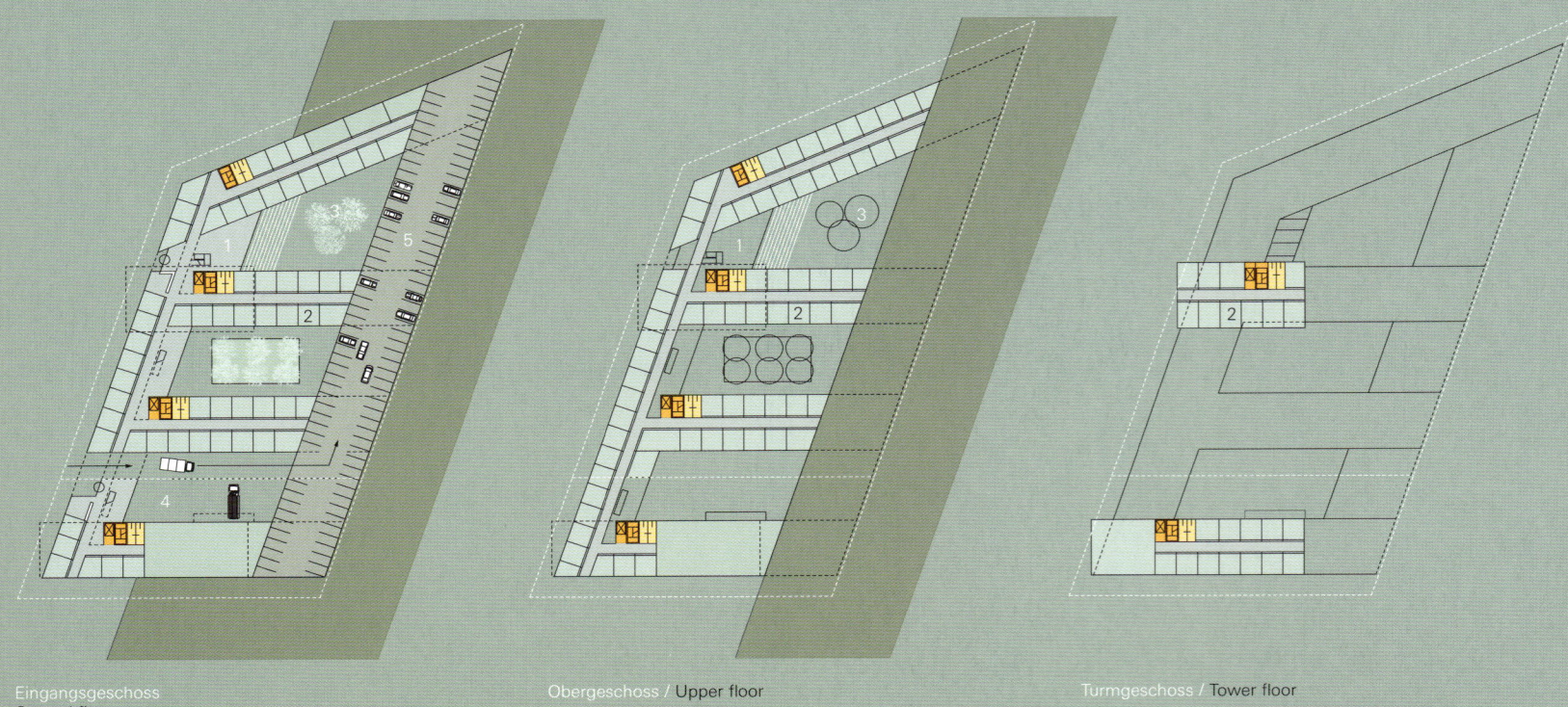

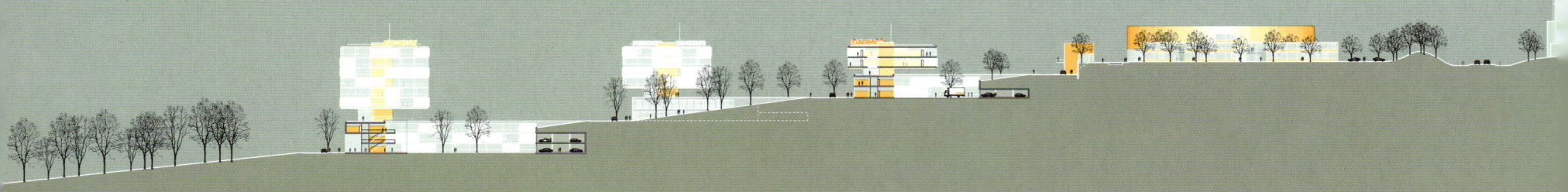

Rechts / Right:
Entwicklungsstufen,
Variationen des Hangtypus
Development phases, variations on the type of slope:

1 Parken / Parking
2 Erschließung / Access
3 Sonderfunktionen
　Special functions
4 Teilbarkeit / Divisibility
5 Erweiterung / Extension

Längsschnitt
Longitudinal section
1:1200

233 Science Park III Ulm

**Anting New Town Shanghai China
2002**

**Anting New Town Shanghai China
2002**

Übersichtsplan / Layout plan
1:40000
1 Anting New Town
2 Stadion / Stadium
3 Marina
4 Lunapark
5 Automobile City park
6 Internationale Automobilmesse / International Automobile Fair
7 Internationale Automobilcity / International Automobile City

Im Großraum Shanghai entsteht in Verbindung mit der Internationalen Automobilstadt die Anting New Town, eine Wohnstadt für 25 000 Einwohner.

Aufbauend auf einem Masterplan von Albert Speer & Partner, der auf ausdrücklichen Wunsch der chinesischen Auftraggeber das Bild einer „deutschen Stadt" vermitteln soll, erhielten fünf deutsche Architekturbüros den Auftrag, jeweils einen Sektor dieser Stadt einschließlich der gewünschten Infrastruktureinrichtungen wie Schulen, Kindergärten, Rat- und Kaufhaus, Kirche, sowie allgemeine Dienstleistungsgebäude zu entwerfen.

Der Masterplan gibt eine Mischung aus blockartig begrenzten und durchgrünten Stadt- und Straßenräumen vor, welche durch einen äußeren Ringkanal und gliedernde innere Kanäle räumlich definiert sind. Innerhalb dieses Bereichs sollen unterschiedliche Wohnformen und -typen angeboten werden.

Der hier vorgestellte Sektor 3 mit 90 000m² Bruttogeschossfläche schließt an das Stadtzentrum an und baut auf dem Prinzip Straße und Hof, also Öffentlichkeit und Privatheit auf. Diese Bauform hat sowohl in der deutschen als auch in der chinesischen Stadtkultur Tradition.

Die überwiegend geschlossenen Blockränder mit kontinuierlichen Straßenansichten und Dienstleistungsangeboten im Erdgeschoss sind durch Quer- und Kopfbauten aufgelockert. Dadurch entstehen ruhige Hofsituationen für individuelles Wohnen und Parken unter innen liegenden Gärten in unmittelbarer Zuordnung zu den Wohnungseingängen.

Unter den für eine traditionelle deutsche Stadt typischen, ziegelgedeckten Steildächern entstehen Räume, die für besondere Wohnformen genutzt werden können. Chinesische Lebensgewohnheiten und traditionelle Wohnformen waren bei der Konzeption ebenso zu berücksichtigen wie die Besonderheiten des regionalen Klimas sowie die Anwendbarkeit ortsüblicher Konstruktionsmethoden und Ausbaustandards.

In the Shanghai metropolitan area, Anting New Town, a city for 25,000 residents has been erected in connection with the International Automobile City.

Building on a master plan by Albert Speer & Partner the expressed wish of the Chinese developer was to have the area designed in the image of a "German" city. Five architectural offices were awarded contracts, each of them was to design a sector of the city including the desired infrastructural institutions such as schools, kindergartens, city hall, department stores, churches and general service buildings.

The master plan is based upon a mixture of stand alone blocks, green-city and street areas which are spatially defined by an external ring canal and a branching inner canal. Within these areas different types and forms of residence were to be offered.

Sector 3 presented here, with a total of 90,000 square meters of floor space, adjoins the city center and works on the principles of street and yard, public space and private space. This building form has its tradition in the cultures of both German and Chinese cities.

The effect of the mainly seamless block fronts, with continuous street views and service sections on the ground floor, is given a lighter touch by the quadrature and vertical buildings. This creates peaceful courtyard situations for individual living as well as parking in the direct vicinity of apartment entrances under the inner gardens.

Beneath the sloping tile roofs typical of a German town are rooms which can be used for special lifestyles. Chinese living customs were taken into account in the concept as were the peculiarities of the regional climate and the applicability of local construction methods and building standards.

Stadtplan / Town map
Villingen, 12.Jh. / 12th century

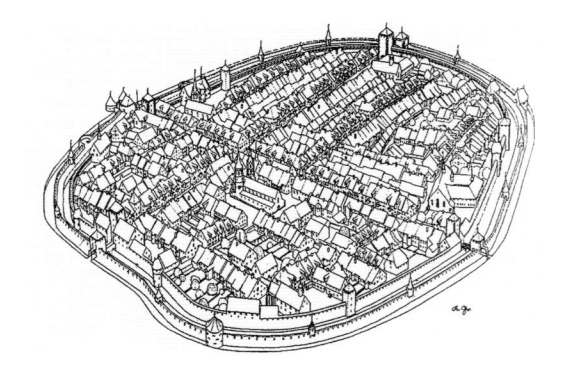

Lageplan / Site plan
1:7000

1 Zentraler Platz
  Town square
2 Zentraler Grünzug
  Central green area
3 Wohnsektor 3
  Residential area sector 3
4 Ringkanal / Circular channel
5 Öffentliche Einrichtungen
  Public facilities
6 Marina

Die Straßen begleitenden Blockränder mit öffentlichen Nutzungen auf Erdgeschossebene umschließen vielfältig gestaltete Innenhofbereiche. Es entstehen individuell nutzbare räumliche Übergänge zwischen Wohnung, privatem Garten und halböffentlichen Gemeinschaftsflächen

The block borders that line the streets house public facilities at ground level and enclose inner courtyards that display a wealth of varied designs. Spaces that can be used individually link residential areas, private gardens and semi-public communal areas

Straßenraum / Street

Hofraum / Courtyard

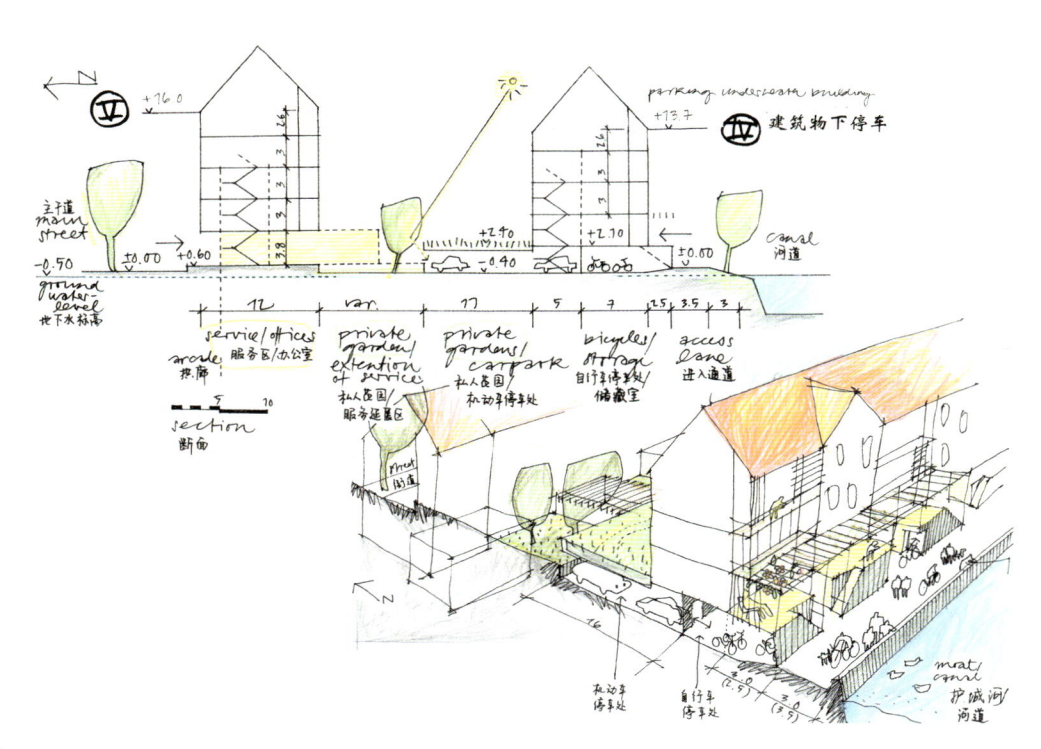

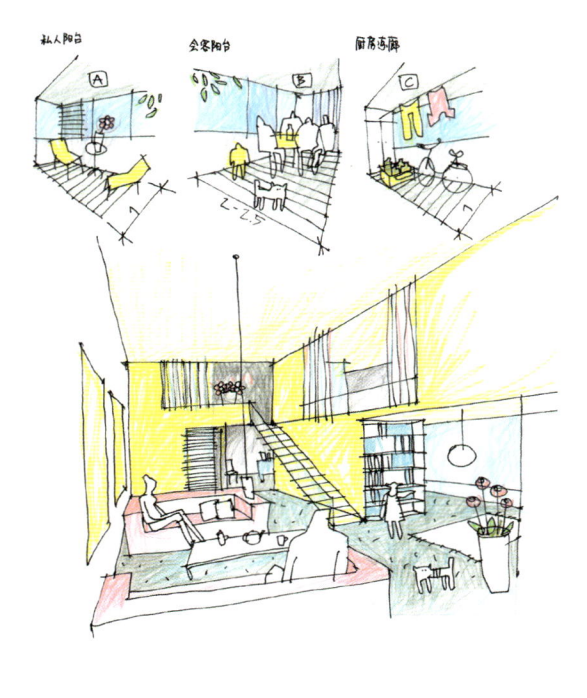

Skizzen aus der Workshop-
phase vor Ort

Sketches from the workshop
phase on location

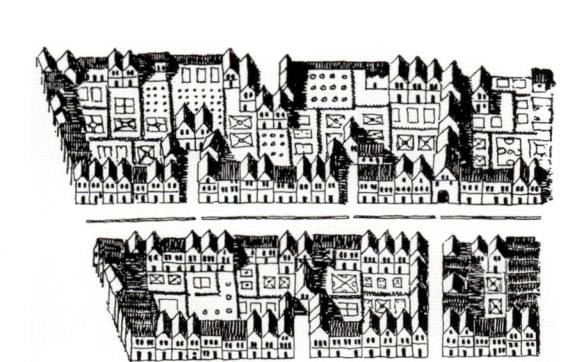

Lippstadt
Matthäus Merian, 17. Jh.

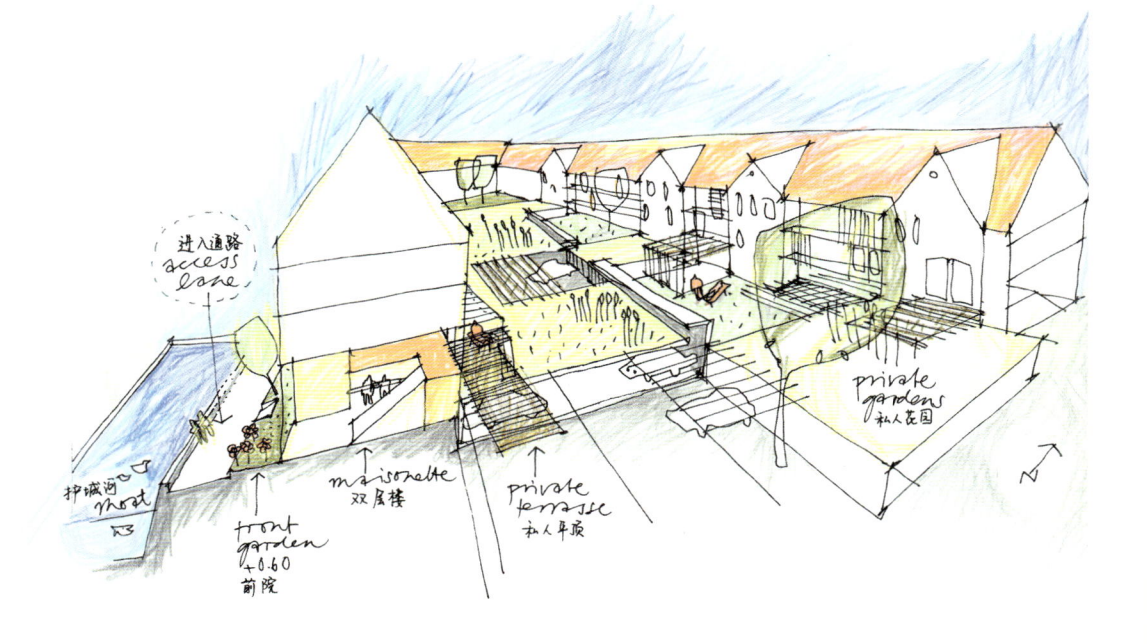

237   Anting New Town Shanghai China

Eine große Bandbreite unterschiedlicher Wohnungstypen erzeugt die abwechslungsreiche Vielfalt eines kleinstädtischen Erscheinungsbildes „deutscher" Anmutung

Combining a large variety of different apartment types creates the diverse appearance of a typical German small town

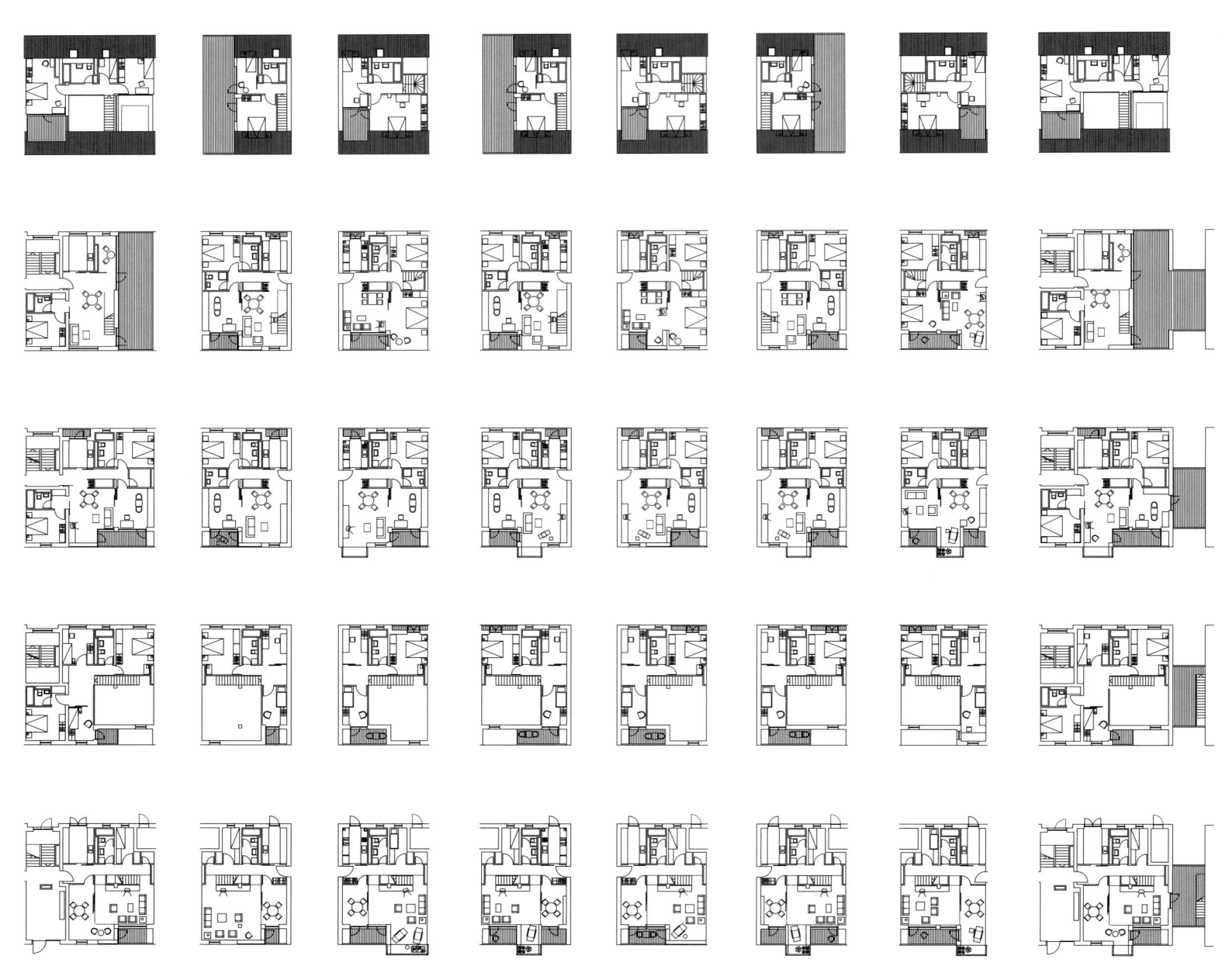

239 Anting New Town Shanghai China

Universitätsbibliothek Magdeburg
2003
Wettbewerb 1998   1. Preis

Library of the University of Magdeburg
2003
Competition 1998   1st prize

Die neue Universitätsbibliothek als Gegenüber zur bestehenden Mensa ist Bindeglied zwischen Universität und Stadt.

Die in Ost-West-Richtung verlaufende Entwicklungslinie der Universität mündet in einen Platz, der zwischen den Haupteingängen von Mensa, Bibliothek und Rechenzentrum Mittelpunkt des studentischen Lebens ist.

Nach dem Prinzip der Faltung einer bandartigen Fläche entsteht über lange, ungebrochene Diagonalen ein räumliches Kontinuum, das als „Lese-Landschaft" nach außen und innen auch zeichenhaft für die Inhalte des Gebäudes steht. An Ausleihe, Zeitschriften- und Nutzerbereich auf Zugangsebene schließen sich, nach oben ansteigend, die Buch- und Arbeitsflächen der Fachgebiete an. Ihnen sind Auskunfttheken, interne Arbeitsräume und offene sowie abgeschlossene Leseplätze jeweils direkt zugeordnet. Das vorgelagerte Atrium als räumliche Mitte ermöglicht eine klare Orientierung und Erschließung der Bibliotheksflächen sowie deren natürliche Belichtung und zentrale Entlüftung. Direkt einfallendes Sonnenlicht wird über lichtlenkende, steuerbare, vertikale Glaslamellen vor der Fassade vermieden.

The new university library, opposite the existing refectory, will connect the university with the city.

The university buildings are located at the very heart of student life: They run from east to west, and open up onto a square between the main entrances of the refectory, library and computer center.

In keeping with the principle of a folded, ribbon-like surface, a spatial continuum is created via long uninterrupted diagonals. As a "reading landscape" it represents the building's contents both on the outside and on the inside. Rising upwards, the bookshelf and working areas of the various specialized subjects merge at the access level where the borrowing, magazine and user areas are located. These areas all possess information counters, internal work rooms and both open and closed reading booths. At the center of the building, the atrium provides natural lighting and central ventilation as well as a clear sense of direction and access into all library areas. Direct sunlight is diverted by means of controllable, vertical glass shutters in front of the façade.

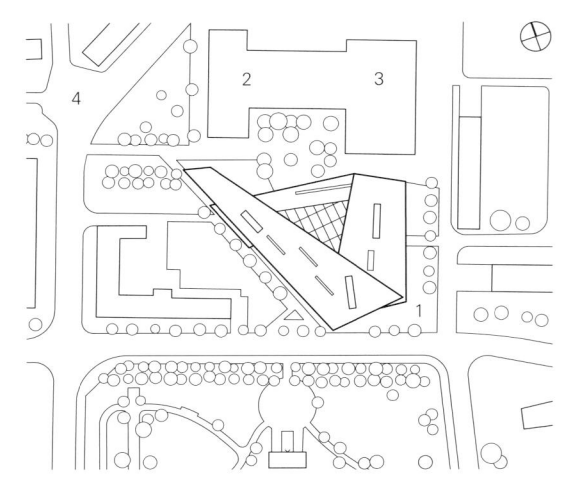

Lageplan / Site plan
1:5000

1 Bibliothek / Library
2 Mensa / Refectory
3 Rechenzentrum
   Computing center
4 Campusplatz
   Campus square

Staatsbibliothek Berlin / State Library Berlin 1978
Hans Scharoun

Landhaus Schminke / House Schminke Löbau, 1933
Hans Scharoun

Das aufgeständerte, weit ausladende „Band" der Leselandschaft definiert den Zielpunkt der Universitätsachse und markiert den Bibliothekseingang

The spandrel-braced, long "ribbon" of the "reading landscape" defines the focus of the University's axis and marks the library entrance

Obergeschoss / Upper floor
1:1000

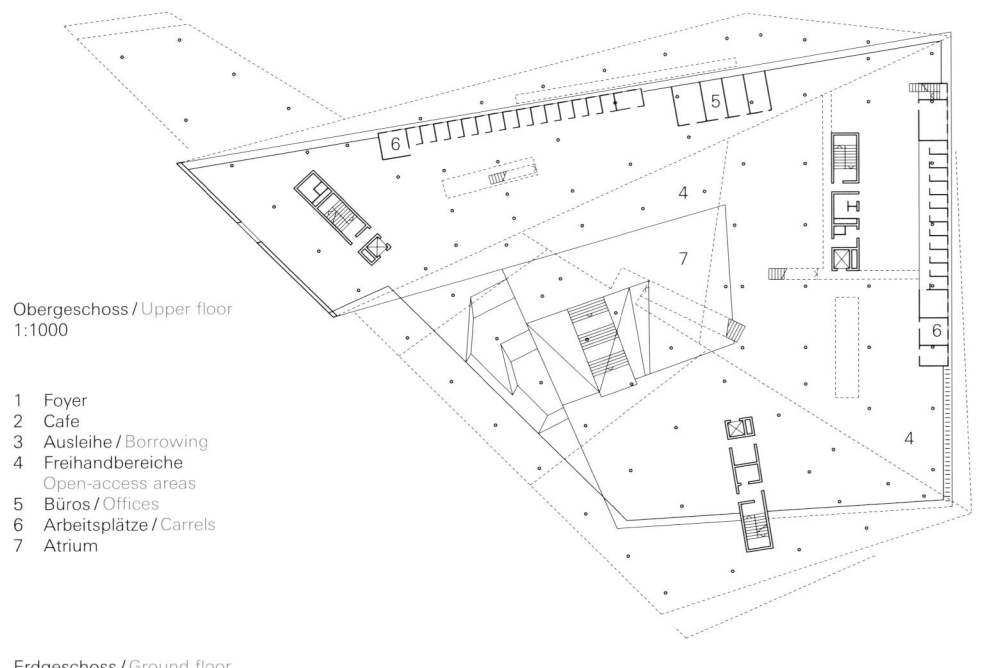

1 Foyer
2 Cafe
3 Ausleihe / Borrowing
4 Freihandbereiche
  Open-access areas
5 Büros / Offices
6 Arbeitsplätze / Carrels
7 Atrium

Erdgeschoss / Ground floor
1:1000

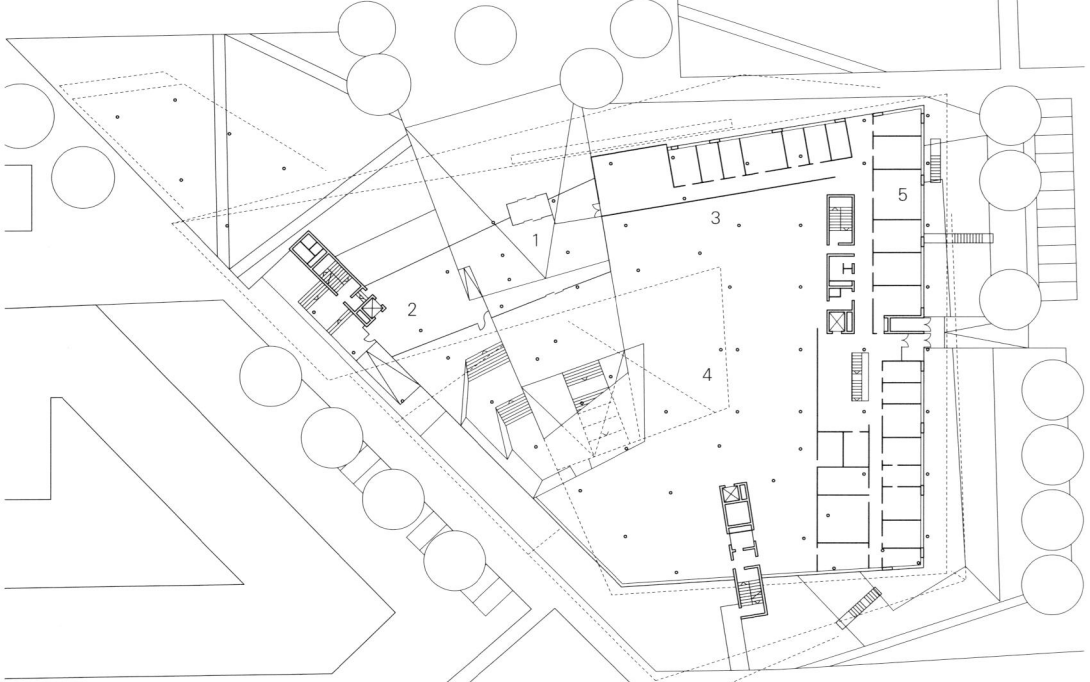

Durch Übereinanderfalten eines ebenen „Schnittmusters" entsteht eine kontinuierliche, dreidimensionale Raumfolge

A continuous three-dimensional series of rooms is achieved by folding over a level "sectional model"

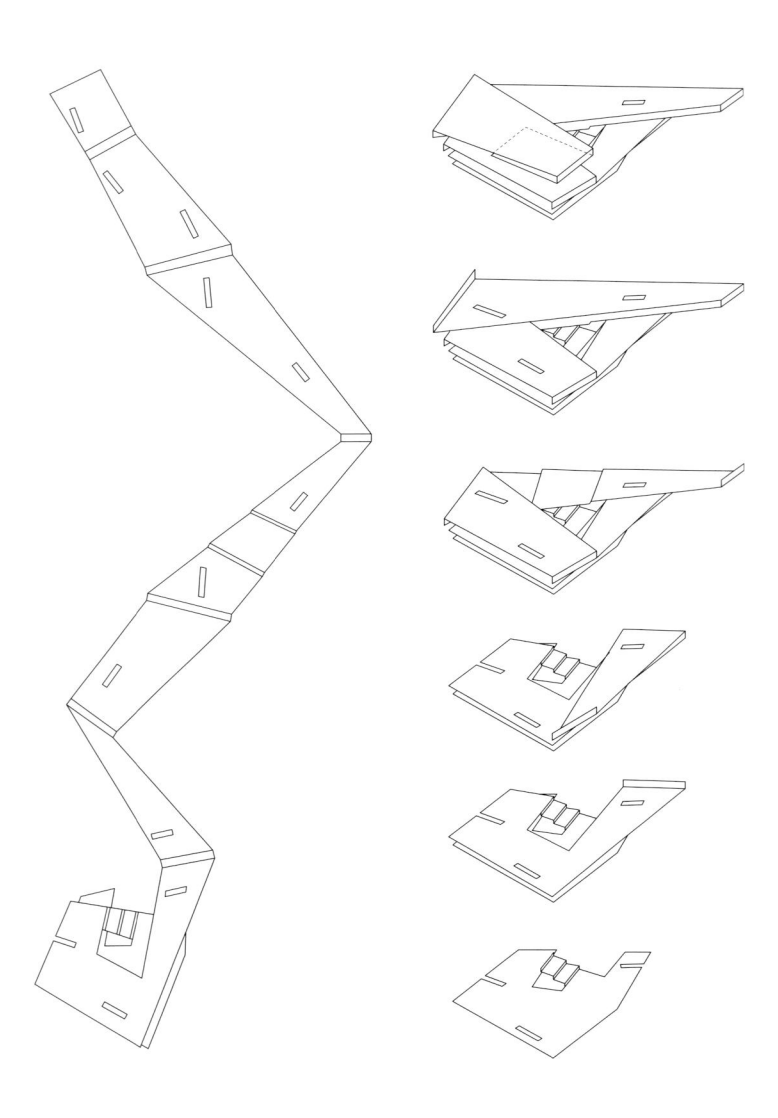

Schnitt / Section
1:750

1 Foyer
2 Atrium
3 Freihandbereiche
  Open-access areas

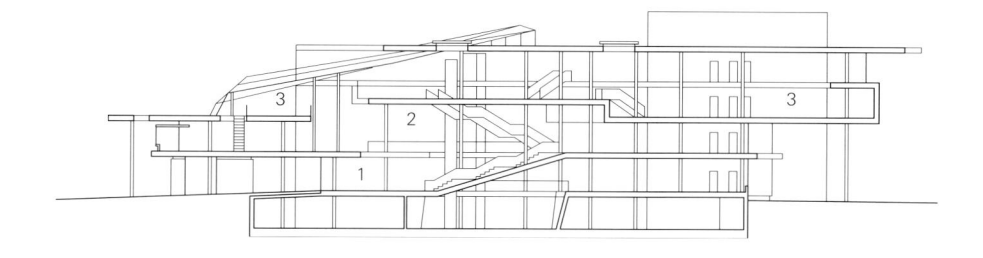

Schnitt / Ansicht von Westen
Section / elevation from the west
1:750

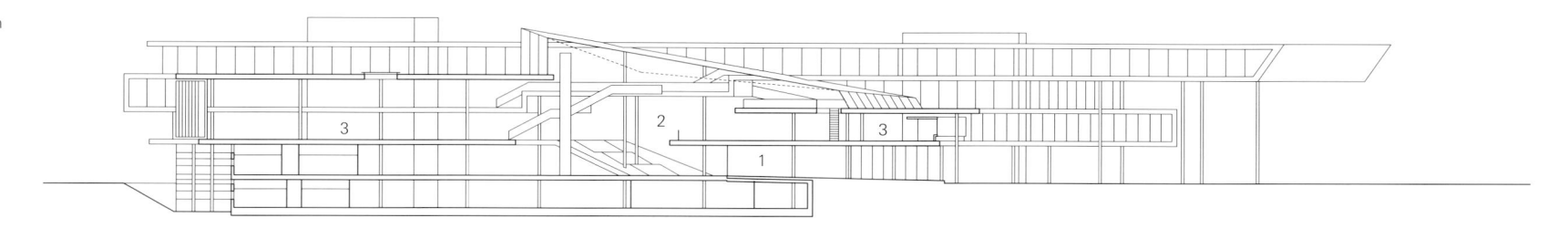

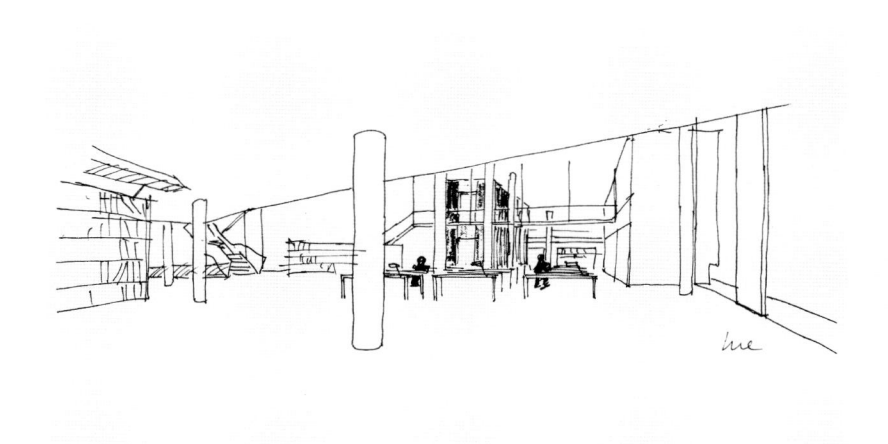

243   Universitätsbibliothek / Library of the University Magdeburg

Die Leselandschaft erschließt sich räumlich über alle Ebenen von einem luftigen Atrium aus, das von dem Kontinuum der gefalteten Geschossdecken gebildet wird

Eingehängte Treppen stellen kurze Verbindungen zwischen den Leseflächen der verschiedenen Fachbereiche her

The "reading landscape" opens out into all levels by an airy atrium, formed by the continuum of the folded ceilings

Suspended staircases provide short links between the reading floors of the different subjects

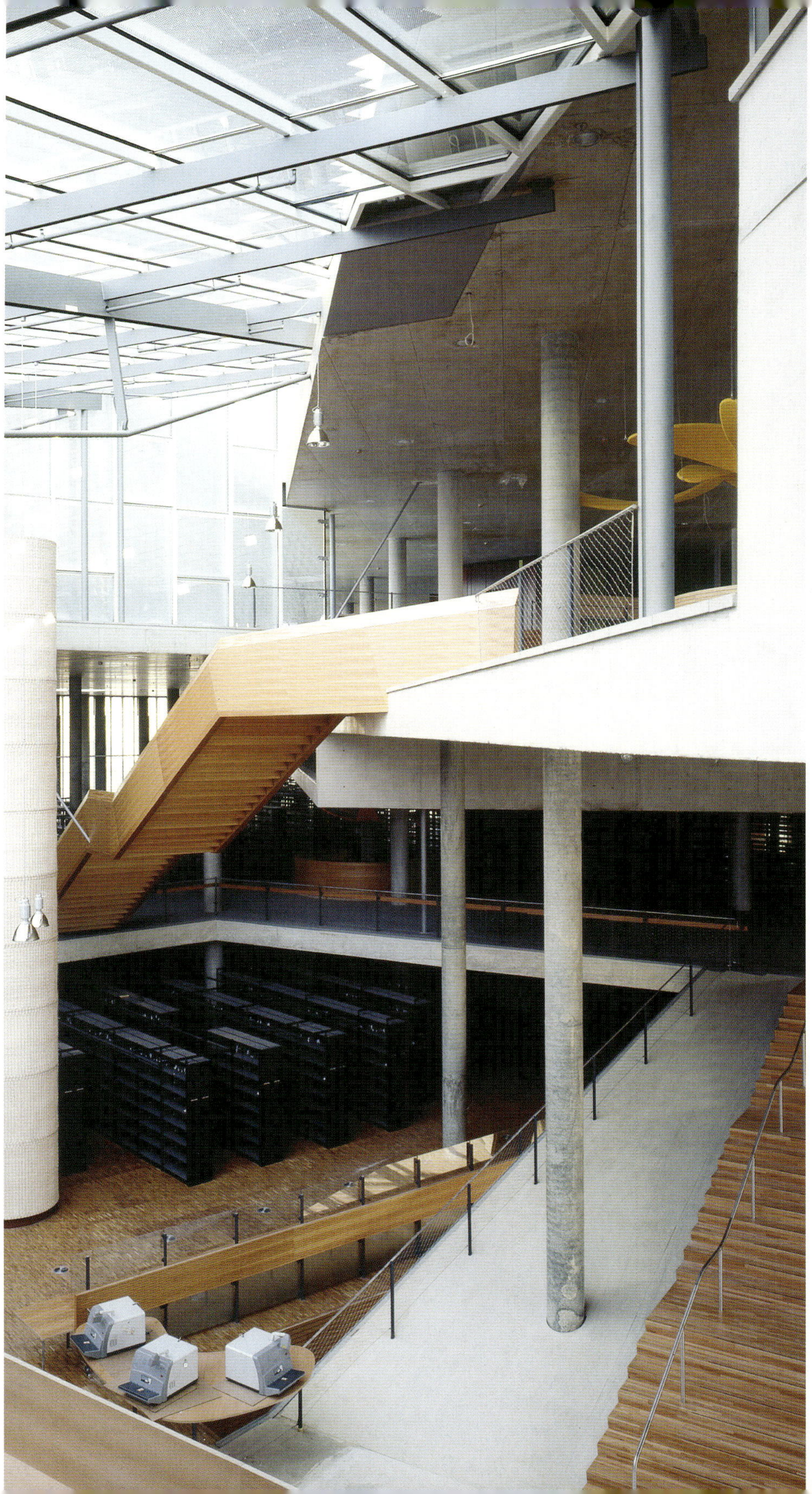

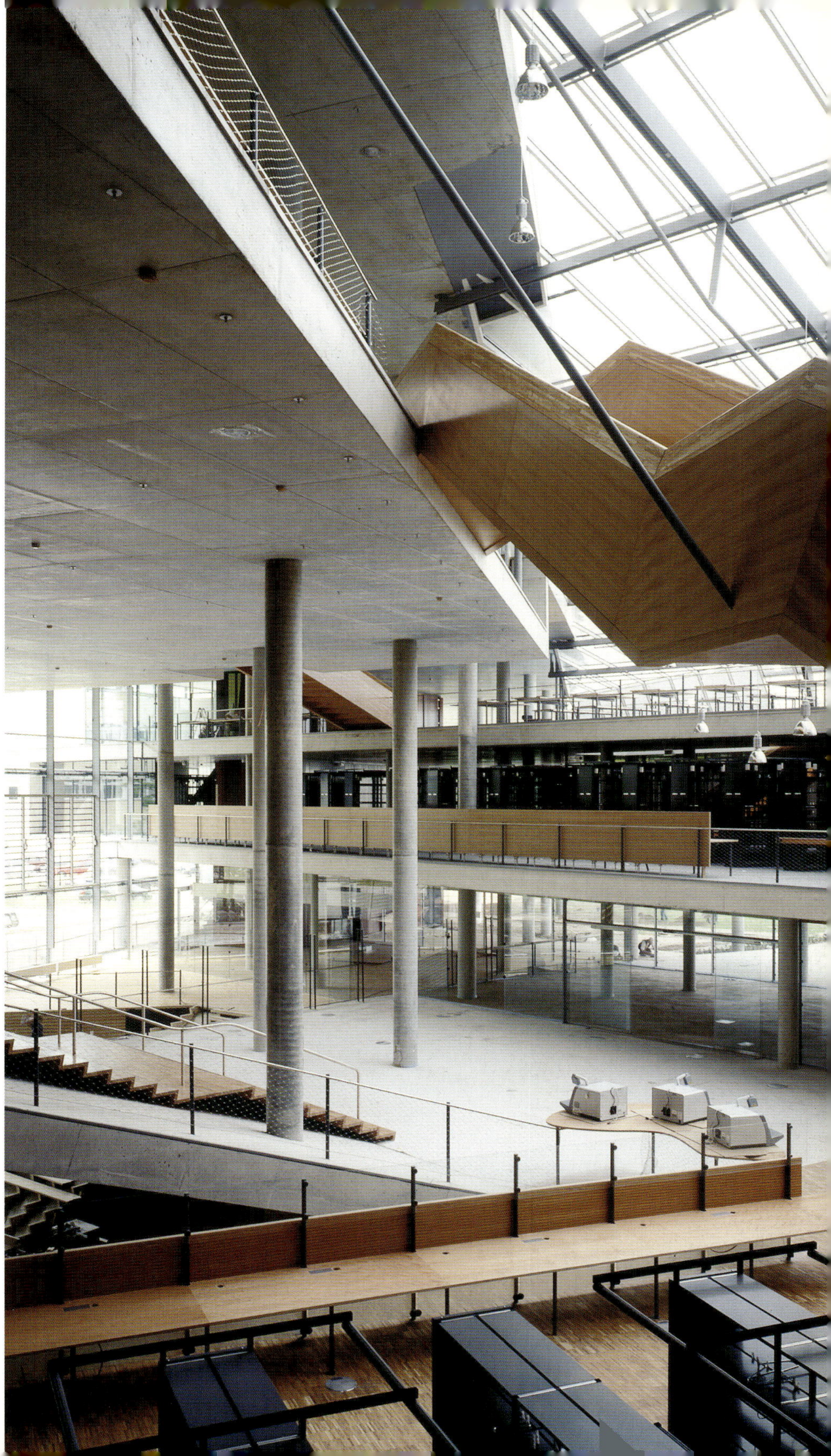

Max-Planck-Institut für Biophysik
Frankfurt am Main
2003
Wettbewerb 1997   1. Preis

Max Planck Institute of Biophysics
Frankfurt/Main
2003
Competition 1997   1st prize

Das Institutsgebäude bildet einen weiteren Baustein des neuen Campus der Johann-Wolfgang-Goethe-Universität am Niederurseler Hang und liegt zentral in unmittelbarer Nachbarschaft zu den bereits bestehenden Fachbereichen Chemie und Biologie.

Die drei Grundelemente des Gebäudes sind entsprechend ihren Inhalten unterschiedlich ausgeformt: die Laborbereiche befinden sich in den kubischen Baukörpern auf der Nordseite, die Bereiche für theoretisches Arbeiten bestehen aus aufgelockerten Raumgruppen und sind über „Decks" zum Landschaftsraum im Süden orientiert; dazwischen entsteht eine Halle, welche beide Funktionsbänder verbindet und als Orientierungs- und Kommunikationsraum den erwünschten Austausch zwischen theoretischer und Laborarbeit fördert.

Dieser „Zwischenraum" reicht als einladende Geste und großzügiger Eingangsbereich nach Westen über die beiden Funktionsbänder hinaus und nimmt damit die Nord-Süd-Verbindung zwischen den Fachbereichen Chemie und Biologie und dem zukünftigen, als Campusmitte dienenden Freiraum auf.

Der Hallenraum wird einerseits durch die monolithischen Sichtbetonwände der Laborkuben, andererseits durch die rhythmische Abfolge großflächiger Glas- und Holzwandelemente der gegenüberliegenden Bürobereiche bestimmt.

Stahltreppen, die durch Brücken zwischen den Büro- und Laborseiten ergänzt sind, verknüpfen die Gebäudeteile vertikal und horizontal. Ein filigraner Dachschirm aus Stahl und Glas überspannt die Halle und zeichnet je nach Tageszeit unterschiedliche Licht- und Schattenbilder auf Wände und Fußboden.

Die Wohnungen für Gäste und Hausmeister liegen, abgesetzt vom Institutsgebäude, als kleiner „Wohnwürfel" im Landschaftsraum.

This institute building is yet another element of the Niederursel campus of Frankfurt's Johann Wolfgang Goethe University, and enjoys a central location directly adjacent to the departments of chemistry and biology, which are already complete.

The three basic elements of the building are designed in line with their respective contents: the laboratory areas are located in the cubist bodies on the northern side: the areas for theoretical work consist of dispersed groups of rooms, and, via "decks", face south toward open countryside; in between there is a hall that unites both functional areas and, acting as a space for orientation and communication, helps promote the desired exchange of ideas between those involved in theoretical work and those involved in laboratory work.

As an inviting gesture and spacious entrance area, this "intermediate area" extends to the west beyond the two functional areas and as such accommodates the north-south axis between the departments of chemistry and biology and the open space, which in future will serve as the center of the campus.

The hall is determined on the one hand by the monolithic exposed concrete walls of the laboratory cubes and on the other by the rhythmical sequence of large-scale glass and wooden wall elements of the office areas on the other side.

Steel staircases, supplemented by bridges between the office and laboratory sides, connect the various sections of the building vertically and horizontally. A filigree roof made of steel and glass covers the hall and, depending on the time of day, casts ever-changing projections and shadows on the walls and floors.

Apartments for guests and the facility manager are located away from the institute building, in a small "living cube" in the open countryside.

Lageplan / Site plan
1:2500

1 Halle / Connecting hall
2 Laboratorien / Labs
3 Theorie / Theory class
4 Bibliothek / Library
5 Gästehaus / Guest house
6 Biologie, Chemie
   Biology and chemistry

Schnitt / Section
1:750

1 Halle / Hall
2 Labors / Labs
3 Theorie / Theory class
4 Technik / Equipment
5 Gäste, Hausmeister
   Guests and janitor

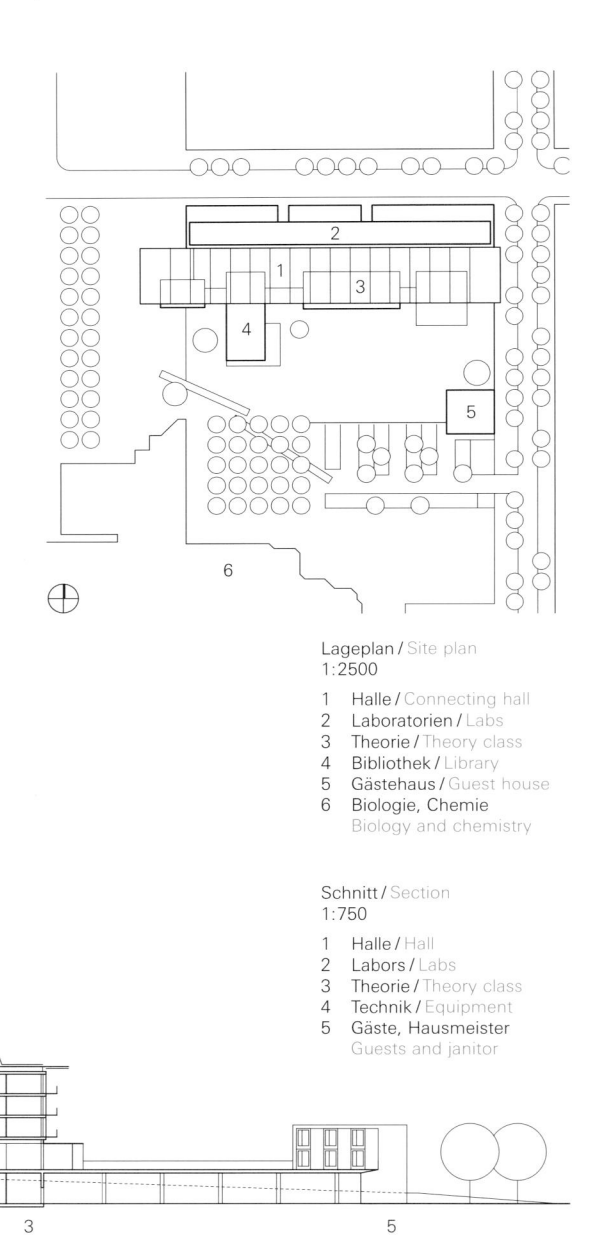

Über die lichte Eingangshalle und den weit ausgreifenden Dachschirm verbindet sich das Gebäude mit dem Freiraum zwischen den bestehenden Instituten

The bright entrance hall and the wide reach of the overhanging roof link the building with the open space between the existing institutes

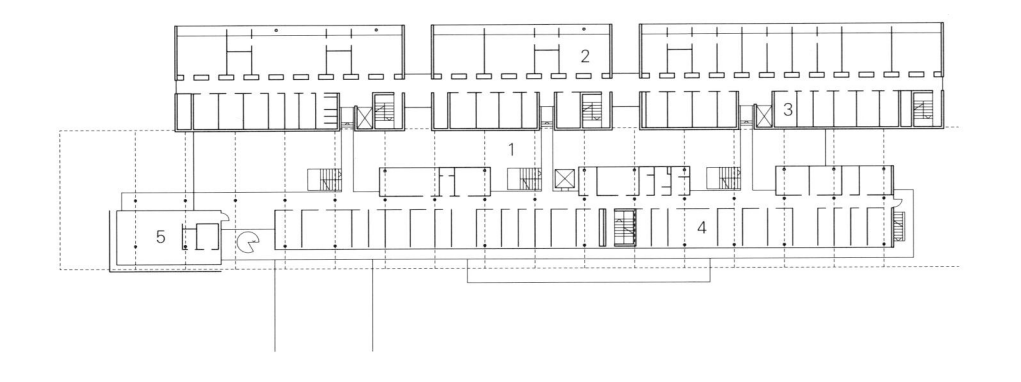

Obergeschoss / Upper floor
1:1000

1 Halle / Hall
2 Laboratorien / Labs
3 Labornebenraumzone
  Laboratory prep rooms
4 Theorie / Theory class
5 Seminarraum
  Seminar area

Die zwischen den „Häusern" der Labors und den „Decks" für theoretisches Arbeiten entstehende Halle verbindet sowohl räumlich als auch inhaltlich alle Bereiche des Institutsgebäudes

The hall between the "houses" for the labs and the "decks" for theoretical work will connect all areas of the institute building, both spatially and in terms of content

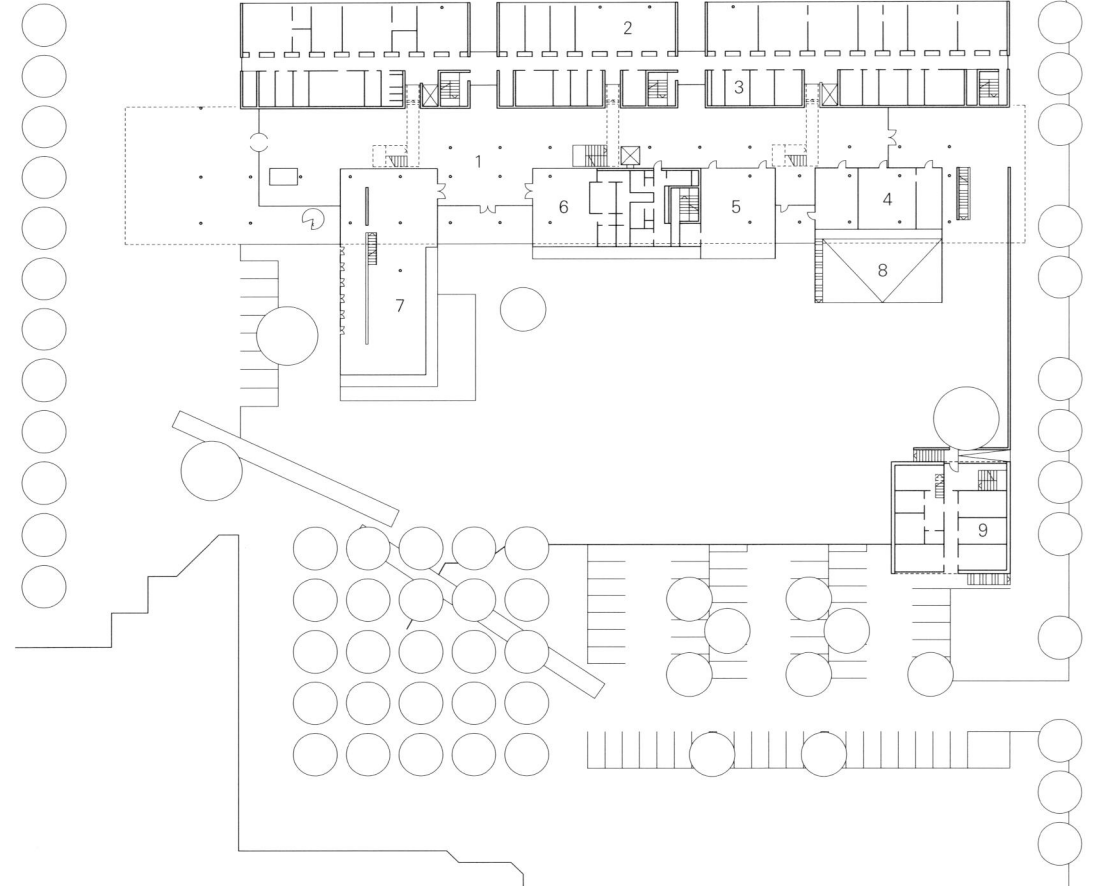

Erdgeschoss / Ground floor
1:1000

1 Halle / Hall
2 Laboratorien / Labs
3 Labornebenraumzone
  Laboratory prep rooms
4 Werkstatt / Workshop
5 Hörsaal / Lecture theater
6 Cafeteria
7 Bibliothek / Library
8 Tiefhof / Lower courtyard
9 Gästehaus / Guest house

Entwurfskizze aus der Wettbewerbsphase

Design sketch from the competition phase

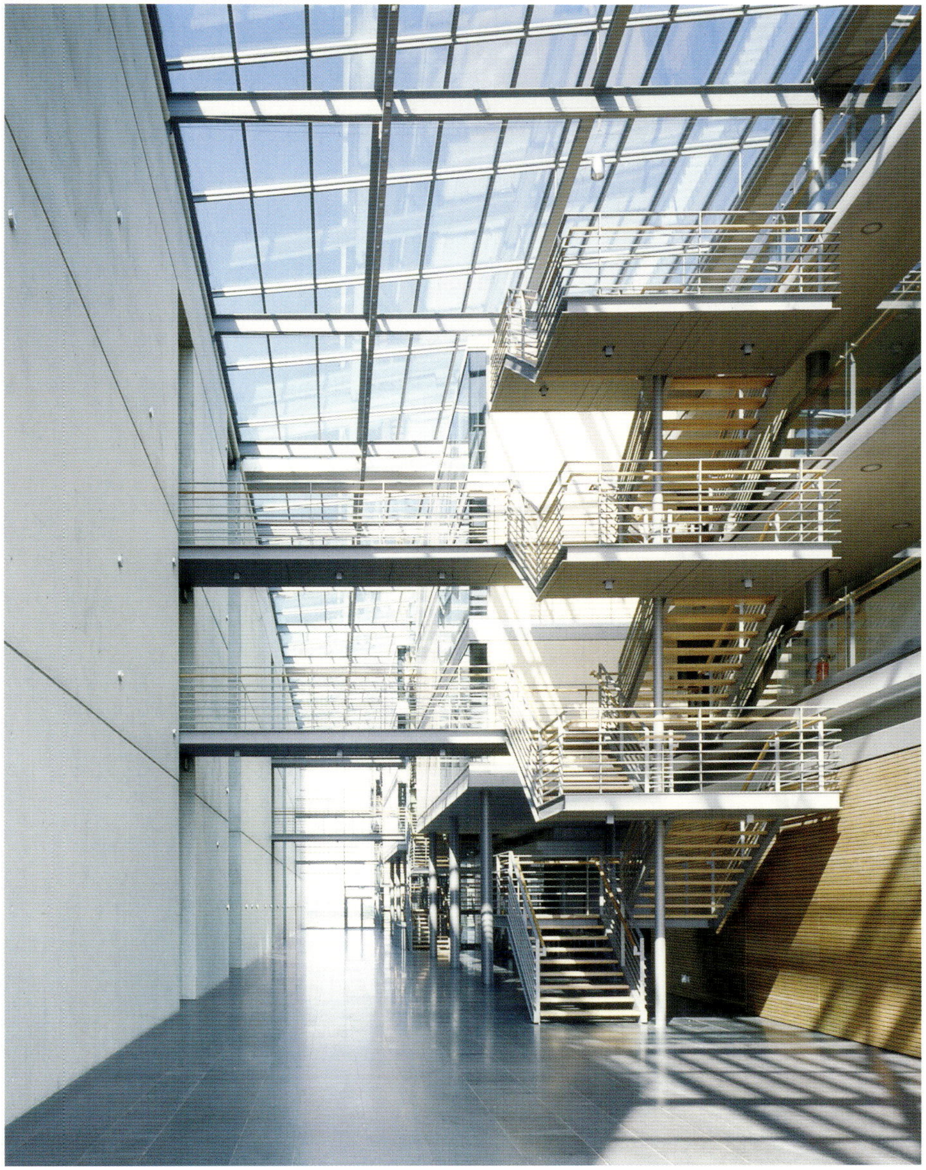

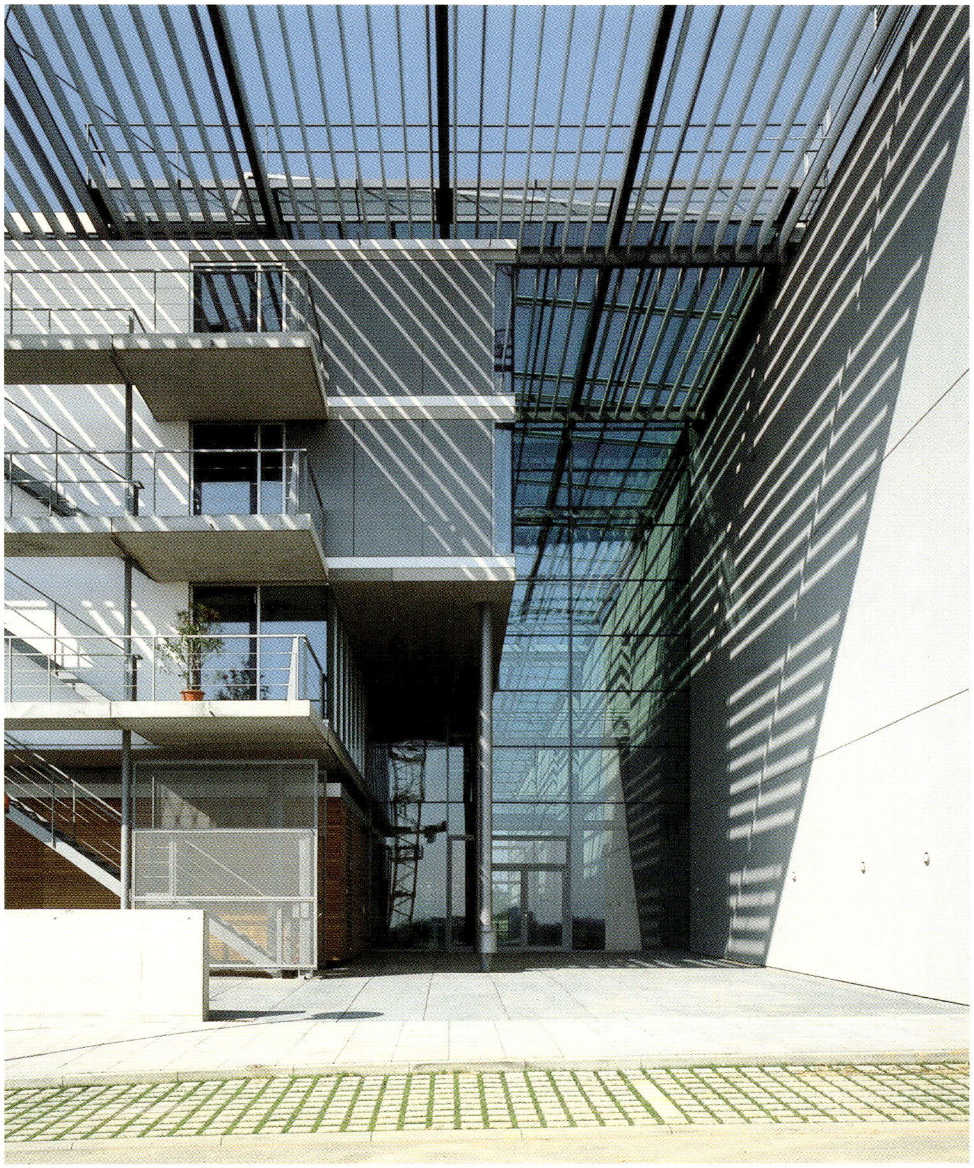

Während die nach Süden ausgerichteten Bereiche für theoretisches Arbeiten zur Landschaft hin offen und frei bespielbar erscheinen, erfüllen die technisch hochentwickelten Laborräume im Norden komplexe funktionale Anforderungen

While the areas for theory, which face south and appear open and flexible, the high-tech laboratories to the north fulfill complex functional requirements

Max-Planck-Institut / Max Planck Institute Frankfurt am Main

Fragen und Antworten / Questions and Answers

Menschenwerk / A Human Feat

Fragen und Antworten
Andrea Kiock im Gespräch mit Fritz Auer, März 2003

Questions and Answers
Andrea Kiock in conversation with Fritz Auer, March 2003

Andrea Kiock
Warum bist du Architekt geworden?

Fritz Auer
Der Beruf war mir nicht vorbestimmt. Ich hätte genauso gut Lehrer, Organist, Bäcker oder Tierpräparator werden können. Mit entscheidend für meine spätere Berufswahl war der Bau meines Elternhauses bei Tübingen 1951. Damals gab es weder Bagger noch Kran, wir mussten die Baugrube noch mit Pickel und Schaufel ausheben. Der Architekt war ein Mensch mit Künstlerhut, Bauplänen und Lichtpausen, welche den typischen Salmiakgeruch verströmten. Er gab den Bauarbeitern Anweisung, was zu tun war, – und die haben das dann tatsächlich auch gemacht. Das hat mich beeindruckt. Ein Schulfreund schenkte mir während des Hausbaus das Buch über Hans Poelzig von Theodor Heuss, mein erstes Buch über Architektur überhaupt. Außerdem hatte ich immer schon ein starkes Empfinden für haptische Situationen, für Gerüche, Temperaturen, Licht und Schatten.

All dies gab den Ausschlag, dass ich mich um einen Studienplatz an der Technischen Hochschule Stuttgart bewarb. In der Aufnahmeprüfung wurde die Frage nach einem bedeutenden zeitgenössischen Architekten gestellt. Mir fiel wieder Poelzig ein – und ich bin mir sicher, dass ich deshalb aufgenommen wurde.

AK
Wie fügten sich Studium und Berufsbeginn?

FA
Im Jahr 1954, gegen Ende des 4. Semesters, wurde ich zufällig der Korrekturgruppe von Günter Behnisch zugeteilt, der damals Assistent an der TH Stuttgart war. Er bot mir an, in seinem damals noch sehr kleinen Büro zwei Semester Zwischenpraxis zu machen. Carlo Weber, ein Studienkollege, kam dann ebenfalls dazu – wir kannten uns von den gemeinsamen Fahrten mit der Vorortbahn nach Stuttgart. Mir gefielen seine Skizzen und Freihandzeichnungen. Damals haben wir uns eng angefreundet und arbeiten, mit Unterbrechungen, seither zusammen.

AK
Welches war euer erstes gemeinsames Projekt, nachdem ihr aus der Partnerschaft mit Günter Behnisch ausgeschieden wart und ein eigenes Büro gegründet hattet?

Andrea Kiock
Why did you become an architect?

Fritz Auer
The career wasn't forced on me. I could just as easily have become a teacher, an organist, a baker or even a taxidermist. One of the deciding factors for my subsequent choice of career was the building of my parents' house near Tübingen in 1951. In those days there were no such things as excavators and cranes, we had to dig the foundation pit with picks and shovels. The architect in charge was a person with an artist's hat, building plans and blueprints, all of which gave off the typical smell of ammonium chloride. He gave the builders their instructions – and they then actually carried them out. That made an impression on me. While the house was being built, a school friend gave me a book by Theodor Heuss about Hans Poelzig; my first book ever about architecture. What's more, I had always been particularly sensitive to situations based on touch, smells, temperatures, light and darkness.

All this was what prompted me to apply for a place at the technical university in Stuttgart. In the entrance examination we were asked to name an important contemporary architect. The name Poelzig came to me – and I'm sure that's why I was accepted.

AK
How did you make the transition from student to working life?

FA
Quite by chance in 1954, towards the end of my fourth semester, I was assigned to Günter Behnisch's seminar group. At the time he was an assistant at the university. He proposed to me that I spend two semesters doing a practical internship in his company, which at the time was still very small. Carlo Weber, a fellow student, also joined in – we already knew each other from traveling into Stuttgart together by train. I was keen on his sketches and free-hand drawings. We became close friends then and, with a couple of interruptions, have been working together ever since.

AK
Having left the partnership with Günter Behnisch and set up your own company, what was your first joint project?

FA

Die Loslösung aus der Partnerschaft mit Behnisch erfolgte allmählich und übergangsweise. Ich wollte es endlich für mich selbst wissen. Carlo Weber zog mit, und so gründeten wir 1980 unser gemeinsames Büro. Wir hatten lediglich die Projekte Kurgastzentrum Bad Salzuflen und das Subzentrum für den neuen Münchner Flughafen aus der Partnerschaft übernommen. Beides waren gewonnene Wettbewerbe, aber noch keine festen Aufträge. Unser erster gewonnener Wettbewerb im eigenen Büro war das Internationale Begegnungszentrum der Universität Freiburg, ein Gästehaus für ausländische Dozenten.

AK

Hattest du von Beginn an eine Vision als Architekt im partnerschaftlichen, eigenen Büro?

FA

Mir war von Anfang an wichtig, dass ich in meine Überlegungen nicht nur den Einzelnen einbeziehe, sondern einen Schlüssel für „jedermann" finde durch die Vermittlung von Raum, Licht, Offenheit und Geborgenheit, indem ich das architektonische Konzept in Material und Konstruktion umsetze. Dabei sollte Bauherrn und Bewohnern genug Luft bleiben für Aneignung und Veränderung unter sich wechselnden Bedingungen – also kein einengender formaler Rahmen, sondern organisierter Lebensraum.

AK

Deine Bauten sind schlicht und klar, nirgends gibt es Prunk, Pomp oder Protz. Wie kommt das?

FA

Ich bin protestantisch erzogen und hatte nie das Bedürfnis, etwas, das der Raum nicht hergibt, mit Oberfläche zu kompensieren. Wichtig sind mir Raum, Freiraum und Luft zum Atmen. Meiner Meinung nach führen vordergründige Überhöhungen der Oberflächen eher zur Abwertung des Raums und stellen sich der unmittelbaren räumlichen Erfahrung in den Weg.

AK

Ich habe wiederholt eure so extrem unterschiedlichen Projekte bestaunt. Was zählt für dich zur Phänomenologie des Entwerfens?

FA

Relinquishing the Behnisch partnership was a transitional, gradual process. I really wanted to know for myself whether I was up to it. Carlo Weber came along and, in 1980, we founded our own company. The only projects we had taken over from the partnership were for the spa guest center in Bad Salzuflen and the subcenter for the new airport in Munich. Both these were competitions that we had won but for which we still hadn't been awarded a firm contract. The first competition we won in our own company was the International Meeting Center at the University of Freiburg, a guest house for visiting foreign lecturers.

AK

Did you have a vision from the very beginning of what being an architect and partner in your own company entailed?

FA

From the very start it was important to me that not just individuals feature in my ideas, but that in providing a source of space, light, openness and refuge – and by transforming an architectural concept into material and a construction – I find an opening for everyone. That said, clients and tenants were to be given enough breathing space to allow them to appropriate and alter the plans as they saw fit under changing conditions – so it wasn't a case of a restrictive formal framework, more a case of organized living space.

AK

Your buildings are straightforward and clear, there is no trace of splendor, pomp or ostentation. Why?

FA

I was raised as a Protestant and never felt the need to compensate for properties the room didn't have by dressing up the outside of the building. Space, free space, and room to breathe are important to me. To my mind excessive concentration on prominent outer surfaces degrades a room and gets in the way of experiencing it directly.

AK

On several occasions I have been astounded by the sheer variety of your projects. What do you consider to be the phenomenology of design?

FA

Wir verfolgen keinen bestimmten „Stil", sondern sind offen für das, was auf uns zukommt. Das ist unsere Philosophie. Sie kommt sicherlich aus der langen Zusammenarbeit mit Günter Behnisch und den damaligen Partnern. Für mich ist Entwerfen ein Prozess des vorsichtigen, interessierten Herangehens, verbunden mit Hören, Zuhören und Eingehen auf die jeweiligen Gegebenheiten. Auch die Eigenart der Beteiligten gehört dazu, und natürlich die eigentliche Aufgabe. Daraus entsteht die Offenheit zur Vielfalt – die allerdings manche irritiert.

AK

Kannst du dafür zwei Beispiele nennen?

FA

Der Einstieg in den Wettbewerb für das Landratsamt Starnberg ist mir in besonderer Erinnerung geblieben. Nach dem Kolloquium ging ich zum Wettbewerbsgrundstück am See. In der benachbarten Wassersportsiedlung aus den dreißiger Jahren sah ich wunderbar einfache Bauten mit weit auskragenden Dächern, mit Holzverschalungen, die nach Karbolineum rochen – alles erinnerte mich an mein eigenes Schwimmenlernen. Ich nahm ein herumliegendes Brett mit und den Entschluss: Hier möchte ich bauen.

Ein anderes Beispiel ist der Deutsche Pavillon für die Weltausstellung in Sevilla. Dort war die Herangehensweise viel schwieriger, weil aus Zeitnot keiner von uns hinreisen konnte. Obwohl es um deutsche Selbstdarstellung ging, wollten wir ja nicht ein-fach Architektur exportieren. Wir haben uns deshalb sehr früh zusammengesetzt mit Klima- und Konstruktionsberatern, um ein Konzept zu entwickeln, das für die klimatischen und technischen Anforderungen vor Ort geeignet war. Später kam dann der Bildhauer Albert Hien dazu, und mit ihm zusammen haben wir das den ganzen Pavillon prägende Thema der „Deutschlandschaft" entwickelt. Die Form und das Bild des Pavillons war also im We-sentlichen das Resultat verschiedener Einflüsse, die sich aus der engen Zusammenarbeit eines Teams ergaben.

AK

In deinen Schilderungen der Planung sprichst du mal von ICH, mal von WIR. Wie arbeitet ihr in der Partnerschaft?

FA

We don't have any particular "style", we're open to anything that comes our way. That is our philosophy. It is no doubt a remnant of the long time spent working together with Günter Behnisch and the other partners at the time. To my mind, design is a process involving a careful, enthusiastic approach, a willingness to hear, listen and adapt plans to given circumstances as they unravel. The characteristics of those involved play a part, and of course the task at hand. This results in an openness to variety – which does, however, confuse some.

AK

Can you give me two examples?

FA

I particularly remember entering the competition for the District Office in Starnberg. After the colloquium I went to the competition site by the lake. The neighboring aquatic sports center, dating from the 1930s, featured marvelous simple buildings with projecting roofs, with wooden lagging that smelled of carbolineum – it all reminded me of when I was learning to swim. I took with me a plank of wood that was lying around and had already decided: I want to build something here. Another example would be the German Pavilion for the World Expo in Seville. Our approach to this was much more difficult because, due to a lack of time, none of us was able to make the journey there. Although it was meant to represent Germany, we didn't want to just export architecture. So at a very early stage we got together with climate and construction consultants to develop a concept that was suitable for the climatic and technical challenges in Seville. Later on, sculptor Albert Hien joined forces with us and together we developed the all-pervading "Deutschlandschaft" theme. And so the form and the appearance of the pavilion were essentially the result of various influences that came about through very close teamwork.

AK

When you talk about planning, you sometimes speak in the first-person singular, sometimes the first-person plural. How does the partnership actually function?

FA

Carlo Weber und ich besprechen, wer einen Wettbewerb und das Projekt, das hoffentlich später daraus hervorgeht, betreut und wer als Mitarbeiter dazu kommt. Das sind WIR. In der eigentlichen Arbeit versuchen wir, uns große Freiheit zu lassen, uns aber trotzdem immer wieder zu beraten. Nehmen wir das Beispiel des Zeppelin Carré: Anfangs waren wir nur zu viert, die Gruppe wurde dann schnell größer. Die Gemengelage dieses Areals, mit Bauten ab 1870, unter anderem von Paul Bonatz, die vom Krieg zerstört waren, dann die veränderte Stadtplanung der fünfziger Jahre, unterschiedliche Besitzer – all das machte eine geradezu detektivische Untersuchung der baulichen Zusammenhänge notwendig. Bauherr und Architekten mussten dabei eng zusammenarbeiten. Wir hatten es also mit einer relativ großen Gruppe und einer vielfältigen, patchworkartigen Aufgabenstellungen zu tun – so viel zum WIR.

AK

Die formale Seite des Entwurfs steht also eher am Ende deiner vielen Recherchen?

FA

Es gibt auch Fälle, bei denen wir bewusst umgekehrt herangehen, – wobei das vorher Gesagte die Regel bleibt. Ein Beispiel dafür ist der Wettbewerb um das geplante Hochhaus des Süddeutschen Verlags. Das „Bild", das uns vorschwebte, war eine Zeitung. Das Gebäude sollte also nicht „dick" und kubisch sein, sondern sehr schlank, eine Art überdimensionale Informationstafel.

Ein anderes Beispiel ist der Wettbewerb für das Verlagshaus des „Spiegel". In Hamburg gab es eine zwar nicht ausgesprochene, aber durchaus bekannte Abneigung gegen Hochhäuser. Unser Vorschlag für den freien Standort an den Deichtorhallen war ein Gebäude, welches das Format des „Spiegel" maßstabsgerecht wiedergibt, mitsamt dem typischen roten Rahmen und dem Schriftzug. Wir riskierten diese Metaphern bewusst, um die „hohe" Bedeutung des „Spiegel" über Hamburg und über die Bundesrepublik hinaus zu unterstreichen.

AK

Du warst sieben Jahre lang Professor an der Fachhochschule in München, acht Jahre als Professor Leiter einer Architekturklasse an der Stuttgarter Kunstakademie. Hatte das Geben und Nehmen der Lehre Einfluss auf deine Arbeit?

FA

Carlo Weber and I discuss who is to be responsible for a competition, and hopefully the ensuing project, and which members of staff are to be involved. That's the "we" bit. As far as the actual work is concerned we try to leave ourselves a good deal of freedom, while continuing to give each other advice. Let's take as an example the Zeppelin Carré. To begin with there were just four of us, but the group quickly grew in size. The complexity of the site, with buildings dating from 1870 (some of them by Paul Bonatz) that had been destroyed in the war, then the different town planning of the 1950s, various owners – all this made some very accurate investigative work necessary into the various types of buildings, and the developer and architects had to work together closely. So we were dealing with quite a large group and a highly varied, patchwork-like set of tasks – which should answer your question about "we".

AK

So the formal part of planning comes at the end of all your research?

FA

In some cases we go about things the other way round – but as a rule what I just said is the norm. One example is the competition for the high-rise for the Süddeutscher Verlag publishing company. The image we had was of a newspaper, meaning that the building was not to be thick and cubical but very slender, a sort of over-sized information board.

Another example is the competition for a building for the publishers of Spiegel magazine. It's an open secret that in Hamburg there is an aversion to high-rises. Our proposal for the stand-alone adjacent to the Deichtorhallen was a building with an exact to-scale format of the magazine, including the well-known red edging and the lettering. It was a conscious decision to take the risk of using these metaphors, so as to highlight how important Spiegel magazine is, even beyond Hamburg and Germany.

AK

You were professor at Munich Polytechnic for seven years and professor at Stuttgart Academy of Art, where you lectured in architecture for eight years. Did the give and take involved in teaching have any influence on your work?

FA

Das Geben und Nehmen, das man sich erhofft, ist nicht ganz so einfach. Das Geben ist auf jeden Fall wichtiger, aber auch härter als das Nehmen. Die zeitliche Verpflichtung und die Anzahl der Studenten an einer Fachhochschule fordern großen Einsatz. Langwierige Diskussionen und Korrekturen können einen aussaugen, aber ich bekam auch immer wieder Anregungen für meine Arbeit im Büro. Die Zeit an der Stuttgarter Kunstakademie war ergiebiger. Die Klassen waren kleiner, ich hatte die Möglichkeit, jeden Studierenden persönlich kennenzulernen. Ob ich junge Menschen an der Universität motiviere oder Mitarbeiter im Büro, macht kaum einen Unterschied. Ich muss mir selbst Rechenschaft ablegen, reflektieren, mich darauf konzentrieren, was ich vermitteln möchte, – ich muss klare Botschaften formulieren. Dieselbe Fähigkeit benötige ich naturgemäß auch in der Argumentation gegenüber Bauherren oder Politikern.

AK

Wer fand das wunderbare Material für das erste Modell der Dachlandschaft der Münchner Olympiabauten mit der anschaulichen Netzkonstruktion? Es war jetzt im Architekturmuseum der Pinakothek der Moderne in München ausgestellt.

FA

Das Prinzip der schwebenden Dachlandschaft geht zurück auf Frei Otto und seinen Entwurf für den Deutschen Pavillon auf der Weltausstellung 1969 in Montreal. Eines Morgens, nach einer langen Arbeitsnacht am Wettbewerb, kam Cord Wehrse mit einem Zeitungsbild dieses Pavillons und sagte: „Das wäre es doch! Aber wie stellen wir das im Modell dar?" Wir hatten nämlich bislang für die Überdachung der Sportstätten mit Schalen operiert, welche die Arenen jedoch als aus dem Landschaftszusammenhang isolierte Bauwerke erscheinen ließen. Also suchten wir nach einem Material, das in jede Richtung dehnbar war und die Verformungen eines Seilnetzes nachbilden konnte. Durch den Tipp meiner Frau kamen wir auf eine Stuttgarter Strumpfwirkerei, die uns freundlicherweise Rohlinge zur Verfügung stellte. Es waren also nicht die viel zitierten Damenstrümpfe von Frau Behnisch. Cord Wehrse, vom Segeln her vertraut mit Masten und Knoten, hat dann aus Rohlingen und Zahnstochern die Form modelliert. Später veränderte sich die Konstruktion wegen der großen Spannweiten allerdings erheblich und wurde in der weiteren Zusammenarbeit mit Frei Otto und den Ingenieuren Leonhardt und Andrä zur Baubarkeit entwickelt.

FA

The give and take one might hope for is not that easy. The giving is certainly more important, but it's also more difficult than the taking. The time you have to invest, as well as the number of students at a polytechnic, mean an enormous amount of effort is required. Tedious meetings and correction work can drain your energy, but I always received great amount of inspiration for my work in the company. The time spent at the Stuttgart Academy of Art was more fruitful. The classes were smaller, and I was able to get to know all the students personally. It doesn't make much difference to me whether I'm motivating young people at university or members of staff. I have to have some form of justification for myself. I need to ponder and concentrate on the points I want to get across. I have to come up with a clear message. And this is exactly what I need when I'm dealing with clients and politicians.

AK

Who discovered the material for the first model of the roofing of the buildings at the Munich Olympics, with their vivid mesh construction? It's now an exhibit in the architecture museum at the Pinakothek der Moderne in Munich.

FA

The principle of the hovering roof landscape can be attributed to Frei Otto and his design for the German Pavilion at the 1967 World Exhibition in Montreal. One morning, after a long night spent working on the competition entry, Cord Wehrse came by with a newspaper picture of the pavilion and said: "That's it! But how do we make a model of it?" Until then we had been using shells for roofing in sports stadiums, which made the arenas seem isolated from the overall landscape. So we were looking for a material that could be extended in any direction and could reproduce the distortions of cable mesh. My wife gave me a tip, which led us to a stocking manufacturer in Stuttgart, who was kind enough to provide us with some samples. So, in fact, it wasn't Mrs. Behnisch's much-cited stockings after all! Cord Wehrse, who knew all about masts and joints from sailing, used the samples and tooth picks to make a model of the form. Later on, because of the wide spans involved, the construction was altered considerably and further development work, together with Frei Otto and engineers Leonhardt and Andrä, produced a model that was capable of being built.

AK

Welchen Wunsch für die Zukunft – für dich und für euer Büro – willst du zum Ende unseres Gesprächs formulieren?

FA

Diese Frage kann ich eigentlich nur für mich beantworten. Wir befinden uns in einer Übergangszeit, ein Generationswechsel steht an. Architektur ist mein Leben und mein Lebenselixier, das Aufregendste, was ich mir vorstellen kann. Meine Idealvorstellung wäre es, mit meinen Söhnen – beide sind seit mehreren Jahren im Büro – und einigen Anderen kongenial weiter zusammen zu arbeiten. Ich würde sie gerne im weitesten Sinn mit meiner Erfahrung unterstützen, sie anregen, neue Wege aufzuspüren. Mir liegt es, gemeinsam mit vielen unterschiedlichen Menschen Konzepte zu entwickeln, sie für meine Gedanken einzunehmen und von ihnen zu lernen. Ich wäre der Berater, dessen Wort und Stimme gehört wird, aber nicht mehr der in erster Linie Verantwortliche.

Ich würde allerdings bitten: „Haltet's Tischtuch sauber".

AK

To bring our conversation to a close, do you have any special wish for the future for yourself and the company?

FA

I can really only answer that question for myself. Right now, we're in a period of transition, a new generation is set to take over. Architecture is the elixir of my life, the most exciting thing I can imagine. For me, the ideal thing would be to continue working in the company together with my sons – both of whom have been on board for several years now – and some other colleagues. I would like to support them as much as possible with my experience and inspire them to open up new channels of discovery. I enjoy developing concepts together with all sorts of different people, captivating them with my ideas and learning from them. I would be the consultant, whose advice is valued, but who is no longer the only one in charge.

But I would ask for one thing: "Don't dirty a clean cloth."

Carlo Weber
Menschenwerk
Gedanken zum Entwerfen, Planen und Bauen

Ich werde öfters nach meiner Einstellung zu den Dingen des Bauens gefragt. Hier einige Antworten.

Dass ich Architekt wurde, hat mehrere Gründe: Als junger Mensch wollte ich Bildende Künste studieren, malen. Pragmatische und materielle Argumente aus meinem Familien- und Freundeskreis bewogen mich jedoch, ein ganz anderes Berufsziel anzusteuern: Aus einem Kohle- und Stahl-Revier stammend, entschied ich mich, einen „ordentlichen" Beruf zu wählen: Bergingenieur, Steiger.

Ich hatte mich schon in Clausthal-Zellerfeld zum Studium angemeldet. Durch eine glückliche Fügung empfahl mir mein Onkel, Landschaftsplaner, den Architektenberuf, – ein Kompromiss, der mir dann aus späterer Sicht all das bot, was ich mir erhoffte.

Meine Jugendjahre fielen mit den Aufbaujahren der Nachkriegszeit zusammen. Überall um mich herum wurde gebaut. Nicht nur als Schüler lernte und litt ich schon in den verschiedenen Bereichen des Bauhandwerks – angefangen mit Erdarbeiten per Handaushub in den Schulferien –, auch in der Studienzeit. Während meine Mitstudenten bereits in Architekturbüros zeichneten, arbeitete ich, nicht zuletzt wegen der besseren Verdienstmöglichkeiten, als Maurer und Betonbauer. Daraus hat sich wohl ein Sinn für das Machbare, das Zumutbare entwickelt.

Das Elternhaus und meine Neugierde waren wichtig für die Dinge, an die ich herangeführt wurde. Ich las Bücher über Kunst und Malerei und ging, als wir nach dem Krieg in Bad Tölz lebten, mit meinem Vater oft an die Isar zum Zeichnen. Die Erlebnisse der Jugend- und Studienjahre prägten sich tief ein; einfache Holzhäuser wie in den Bergen wollte ich bauen und entwarf schon als Studienanfänger für einen Freund ein eingeschossiges, lang gestrecktes Holzhaus, was damals an der Hochschule so gar nicht *en vogue* war.

Letztlich hatte auch die Schule großen Einfluss auf meine Berufswahl. Meine Lehrer haben es verstanden, mein Interesse für Geschichte – und damit auch Baugeschichte – und für Kunst und Ästhetik zu wecken. So wie später meine Lehrer an der Technischen Hochschule Stuttgart, von denen ich Hans Volkart, Rolf Gutbrod und Günter Behnisch nenne, dazu verhalfen, das Wirken eines Architekten in der Gesellschaft nicht nur auf dem Gebiet der Bautechnik und Ökonomie zu sehen, sondern auf breiter künstlerischer und humanistischer Basis.

Carlo Weber
A Human Feat
Thoughts about work at the drawing board, planning and building

I'm often asked about my ideas about aspects of building. Here are a few answers.

There are several reasons why I became an architect: as a young man I wanted to study fine art and become a painter. By means of an array of practical and material arguments, however, my family and friends convinced me to turn my attention to a quite different career. Since I came from an area where there was coal mining and a steel industry, I decided on a "proper" job: mining engineer, deputy.

I had already registered to study in Clausthal-Zellerfeld. Through a fortunate stroke of luck my uncle, a landscape planner, recommended architecture to me as a career option, a compromise which, in retrospect, offered me all I could ever have wished for.

My youth coincided with the years spent rebuilding the country after World War II. There was construction work going on all around me. It was not only while I was at school that I learned about and, indeed, did a fair share of suffering in various divisions of the building trade; I starting with digging ground with my bare hands during my school holidays. While my fellow students were already producing draft plans in architects' studios, I worked as a bricklayer and builder, mostly because I could earn more money. It was here that I developed a sense of what can be achieved, what can be expected.

My family and my sense of curiosity played important roles in developing my interests. I read books about art and painting and, when we were living in Bad Tölz in Bavaria after the War, I often went with my father to the River Isar to sketch. What I experienced as a child and as a student left a very deep impression on me. I wanted to construct simple wooden houses like the ones I saw in the mountains. When I was a freshman I even designed a long, single-story wooden house for a friend – something that, at the time, was not particularly "in" at university.

At the end of the day, the school I attended also had a big influence on my choice of career. My teachers managed to develop my interest in history – and by extension an interest in the history of building – as well as art and aesthetics. Later, my teachers at Stuttgart Technical University, in particular Hans Volkart, Rolf Gutbrod and Günter Behnisch, all helped me understand the architect's role in society, not only in terms of building technology and economics, but from a wider artistic and humanist perspective as well.

Was mir für meine Arbeit als Architekt wichtig ist
Die Begeisterung für diesen Beruf: Man sollte das, was man tut, konsequent und mit Freude tun. Für mich hängt Privates und Beruf, Leben und Arbeit untrennbar zusammen. Ich bin in der glücklichen Lage, sagen zu können, dass Beruf und „Hobby" ineinander übergehen.

Das Wissen um das Zusammenspiel von Ratio und Intuition beim Entwerfen: Ich bin der Meinung, gute Architektur muss beides ansprechen, das Rationale und das Emotionale.

Die Einsicht, dass Entwerfen, Planen und Bauen „Menschenwerk" ist: Beim Bauen geht es ja nicht nur um die ingenieurmäßige Erstellung eines nutzbaren Gebäudes. Die Entstehung eines Bauwerks beinhaltet sehr komplexe Abläufe. Es handelt sich um stets neue Prozesse, betrieben und beeinflusst von wechselnden Individuen auf der Bauherren-, der planenden und der ausführenden Seite. Und schließlich der Umgang mit den Menschen, mit denen man arbeitet, als eine der wichtigsten Voraussetzungen zum Gelingen eines guten Werks.

Die Achtung jedes Einzelnen, Respekt vor dem Anderen, vom Projektleiter bis zum studentischen Helfer, vom Ingenieur bis zum Bauarbeiter: Nur wenn gegenseitige Achtung und Harmonie zwischen Architekt und Bauherr herrschen, entstehen gute bauliche Ergebnisse, weil man dann „auf gleicher Wellenlänge" mit dem anderen ist, ihn ernst nimmt und ernst genommen wird – und somit auch überzeugen kann.

Ich bin sicher, dass gute Zusammenarbeit auf der menschlichen Ebene und gutes bauliches Resultat in direktem kausalem Zusammenhang stehen.

Hierfür einige positive Beispiele:
Die Planung und Verwirklichung der olympischen Anlagen München 1972 – ein Prozess, bei dem staatliche und städtische Behörden in seltener Einmütigkeit oft „über den eigenen Schatten sprangen" und unkonventionell und pragmatisch agierten; so brachten die oft heterogenen Arbeitsgruppen unseres Büros, in denen doch Eines alle gemeinsam beseelte – Ambition, hoher Qualitätsanspruch, gegenseitiger Respekt – Höchstleistungen hervor.

Die fruchtbare Zusammenarbeit – als katholisch Aufgewachsener – bei der Planung des evangelischen Studienzentrums Stuttgart-Birkach.

Das Arbeiten – als „Schwabe" – mit den Menschen im Lipper Land beim Kurgastzentrum Bad Salzuflen oder der Altenwohnanlage in Lemgo.

What is important to me in my work as an architect?
Enthusiasm for the job: One ought to be consistent in what one does, and enjoy doing it. For me, my private life and my career are inextricably intertwined. I am in the fortunate position of being able to say that my hobby is my job.

Awareness of the interaction of reason and intuition when drafting plans: I believe that good architecture must appeal on both rational and emotional levels.

The view that work at the drawing board, planning and building is a "human feat": Construction is not just about creating a usable building according to an engineer's plans. Building an edifice involves highly complex processes. These are always new processes, developed and influenced by constantly changing individuals among the clients, planners and constructors. And finally, the way you get along with the people you work with is one of the most important factors in deciding whether a project works well or not.

An appreciation for each individual and the respect of others, from the project leader to student helpers, from engineer to builder: Buildings will only succeed if architects and clients have a harmonious working relationship in which both parties are on the same wavelength, take each other seriously and can pursuade each other of a particular viewpoint.

I am convinced that there is a direct link between fruitful cooperation on a personal level and sound building results.

Here are a few positive examples to back this up:
The planning and realization of the Olympic grounds in Munich in 1972 was a rare example of state and municipal authorities going out of their way to work together in harmony and operating in an unconventional, practical manner. In this same way, the often disparate teams in our office were able to produce superb results, united as they all were in their ambition, demand for high quality and mutual respect.

Another fruitful cooperation involved me – having been brought up as a Catholic – planning the Protestant study center in Birkach, Stuttgart.

As a "Swabian" working together with the people in the Lippe region on the Bad Salzuflen spa center and the retirement and nursing home in Lemgo.

The construction of the theater in Hof: a progressive building for a rather conservative general public.

Die Entstehung des Theaters in Hof – ein progressiver Bau für ein eher konservatives Publikum.

Das Abenteuer Ruhrfestspielhaus Recklinghausen – die Baukosten mussten von 90 über 60 auf 40 Millionen DM reduziert werden – mit einer weitsichtigen staatlichen Baubehörde.

Welche Arbeitsweise halte ich für richtig?
Bei der heutigen spezialisierten Arbeitsweise in unserem Metier kann das nur die Teamarbeit sein. Während meiner Studienzeit hatte ich noch das hierarchisch gegliederte Chef-orientierte Büro kennen gelernt, in solchen Büros gearbeitet und die Nachteile erfahren.

Ich schließe nicht aus, dass es beim Bauen auch hervorragende Leistungen gibt, die „nur durch einen Kopf gehen", ich glaube aber, dass durch das Zusammenwirken Mehrerer im idealen Fall das Resultat gesteigert werden kann.

Durch meine Arbeit zunächst als Mitarbeiter von Günter Behnisch, später als einer seiner Partner und bis heute gemeinsam mit Fritz Auer lernte ich, in der Gruppe zu arbeiten, zu delegieren und durch Vertrauensvorschuss und Übertragung von Verantwortung Andere zu motivieren. Diese Arbeitsweise kann zu besseren Ergebnissen führen als die des „Einzelkämpfers", wenn man sich darauf beschränkt, das große Ziel im Auge zu haben und subjektive Teilaspekte hintanzusetzen.

Man muss dabei offen sein für Neuerungen oder sich während des Planungs- und Bauprozesses ändernde Umstände, flexibel auf Überraschungen reagieren können. Ich habe öfters den Vergleich eines Bootes in der Strömung herangezogen: Gegen die Strömung kann auf Dauer niemand anrudern, aber mit der Strömung an den entscheidenden Stellen und im rechten Augenblick einen entschlossenen Ruderschlag einzusetzen, das bringt einen zum Ziel.

Dem Austausch mit jüngeren Menschen, mit Studenten und Mitarbeitern verdanke ich viel. Nicht nur an der Hochschule, auch im Büro bearbeite ich mit Kollegen und Mitarbeitern die Probleme ungern „ex cathedra", lieber direkt an der Aufgabe, am Arbeitstisch.

Eindrücke und Vorbilder für meine Arbeit sind faszinierende Orte, Räume, Gebäude
Der überwältigende Raumeindruck der Hagia Sophia oder der Moschee in Córdoba; ein aus dem Material der Umgebung entstandenes, gleichsam aus dem Berg gewachsenes Dorf im Tessin oder in der Provence; ein aus Granit gebautes Haus in Irland

The adventure of the Ruhrfestspielhaus in Recklinghausen whose far-sighted state building authorities were forced to reduce the building's budget from 90 to 60 and then again to 40 million marks.

What work method do I consider to be the right one?
Given the specialized approach in the trade nowadays the only choice can be teamwork. As a student I came across companies where there was a hierarchical structure with the boss at the top. I worked in such companies and experienced all the disadvantages that go hand in hand with such top-down structures.

I am not ignoring the fact that, in the building trade, there are also outstanding achievements that are the brainchild of one particular individual, but I do believe that the end result will be even better if several people work together on a project.

Through my work, initially as one of Günter Behnisch's colleagues, later as one of his partners and to this day together with Fritz Auer, I learned how to work in a group, how to delegate and how to motivate others by trusting in them and giving them responsibility. When you concentrate on a collective goal and put subjective aspects lower down the agenda, you always achieve better results.

You also have to be open to innovation and changing conditions during the planning and construction stages of a project. You must also be flexible when confronted with surprises. I have often used the example of a boat in a current: you can't row against the current forever, but if you go with the flow and stroke the oar with the right amount of determination, precision and timing, you will reach your goal.

I owe a great deal to the process of exchanging ideas with young people, students and colleagues. In the office, as well as at university, I don't enjoy solving problems together with colleagues ex cathedra; I prefer to do it on-site, at the desk.

Fascinating places, ideas and buildings all provide me with impressions and models for my work
The overwhelming dimensions of the Hagia Sophia or the mosque in Córdoba; a village in Ticino or Provence that is made of local material and still stands out against the hills; a granite house in Ireland or Brittany; simply constructed wooden houses in the Walsertal that reflect the material used and contrast with the crystal-clear directness and coolness of a Dutch greenhouse; as well as unspectacular, anonymous, architecture – *architecture without architects*.

oder in der Bretagne; einfach und materialgerecht konstruierte Holzhäuser im Walsertal und im Gegensatz dazu die glasklare Direktheit und Kühle einer holländischen Gewächshausanlage; aber auch die unspektakuläre, anonyme Architektur – *architecture without architects*.

Meine Vorbilder sind Architekten, deren Werke beides spüren lassen, Ratio und Intuition: Gunnar Asplund und Frank Lloyd Wright, Jan Duiker und Le Corbusier, auch Alvar Aalto.

Zukünftige Herausforderungen
Welchen gesellschaftlichen und kulturellen Stellenwert die Architektur in Zukunft einnehmen wird, wage ich nicht zu prognostizieren. Entscheidend hierfür wird die gesellschaftliche Wertschätzung und Anerkennung genuiner schöpferischer Leistungen von Architekten und Ingenieuren sein gegenüber einer zunehmend marktorientierten Lieferung von Gebautem als verhandelbarer Ware, für die beim Architekten als „Designer" bestenfalls deren attraktive Verpackung bestellt wird. Sollte die Entwicklung in diese Richtung weitergehen und überhand nehmen, stünde damit unser Auftrag als Architekten innerhalb der Gesellschaft zur Disposition.

Ich habe jedoch die unerlässliche Zuversicht, dass Architektur, wie wir sie verstehen, als gesellschaftlicher Anstoß und kulturelles Ferment auch in Zukunft unverzichtbar bleibt.

My role models are architects, whose works display traces of both reason and intuition: Gunnar Asplund and Frank Lloyd Wright, Jan Duiker and Le Corbusier, and let's not forget Alvar Aalto.

Future challenges
I don't dare predict the social and cultural importance that will be attributed to architecture in the future. I think what will be decisive will be the value and recognition placed by society on genuine creative achievements by architects and engineers, as opposed to the increasing number of market-oriented buildings that are negotiable commodities for which architects are required only in their capacity as designers, to provide an attractive form of packaging. Should developments in this direction continue, and gain prevalence, then our function in society as architects will be called into question.

However, I am firmly convinced that in the future architecture as we know it will sow the seeds of cultural development and continue to be an indispensable stimulus for society.

Anhang / Appendix

267	Auer + Weber + Architekten 1980 – 2003
268	Bauten und Projekte / Buildings and Projects 1980 – 2003
290	Biografien / Biographies Fritz Auer und Carlo Weber
292	Biografien Partner und Assoziierte 1991 – 2003 Biographies of partners and associates
294	Mitarbeiter / Members of staff 1980 – 2003
296	Interdisziplinäre Zusammenarbeit 1980 – 2003 Interdisciplinary cooperation
298	Ausstellungen (Auswahl) / Exhibitions (Selection)
299	Veröffentlichungen (Auswahl) / Publications (Selection)
300	Abbildungsnachweis / Illustrations' credits
301	Dank / Acknowledgement
302	Impressum / Imprint

Auer + Weber + Architekten 1980 – 2003

Die Architektengemeinschaft Auer + Weber hat sich 1980 aus der Architektenpartnerschaft Behnisch & Partner herausgelöst, der beide Architekten von 1966 bis 1979 angehörten. Das Büro mit Sitz in München und Stuttgart beschäftigt im Mittel 50 bis 60 Mitarbeiter.

Von 1991 bis 2000 firmierte die Stuttgarter Niederlassung unter Auer + Weber + Partner, seit 2001 lautet die gemeinsame Firmierung Auer + Weber + Architekten.

Schwerpunkte der Tätigkeit sind Neu- und Umbauten sowie die Revitalisierung innerstädtischer Quartiere. Um zu neuen und vielschichtigen Antworten zu kommen, entwickelt sich die architektonische Gestalt aus der jeweiligen Aufgabenstellung und den Bedingungen des Ortes auf der Basis einer unhierarchischen Zusammenarbeit im Team, sowohl innerhalb des Büros als auch mit externen Fachingenieuren und Beratern.

Grundsätzliches Anliegen ist nicht ein formaler Stil, sondern – mit Qualitäten wie Offenheit, Zugänglichkeit und Lesbarkeit durch das Gebaute – Orte und Orientierungen zu definieren.

Vor dem Hintergrund einer zunehmenden Merkantilisierung des Bauens wird Architektur nicht nur als Dienstleistung, sondern als kulturelle Verpflichtung der Gesellschaft gegenüber verstanden.

Die überwiegende Zahl der realisierten Projekte resultiert aus Wettbewerbserfolgen.

Established in 1980, the architect's office Auer + Weber emerged from Behnisch & Partner, to which both architects belonged between 1966 and 1979. Operating out of Munich and Stuttgart respectively, the office employs an average of 50 to 60 staff.

From 1991 to 2001 the office in Stuttgart used Auer + Weber + Partner as company name; since 2001 the common name is Auer + Weber + Architekten.

The office's activities focus on new construction and renovation/modernization, as well as the revitalization of inner-city areas. The objective is to achieve innovative solutions that work on many levels. Architectural design evolves by factoring in specific requirements and local conditions and working in a spirit of non-hierarchical team co-operation, both within the office itself and with external specialist engineers and consultants.

A major aim is not to achieve a formal style, but rather to define places and orientations through qualities such as openness, accessibility, and readability in the finished building.

Given the increasing commercialization of construction, architecture is not only viewed as a service, but also as a cultural obligation to society.

The overwhelming majority of completed projects is the result of successful competitions.

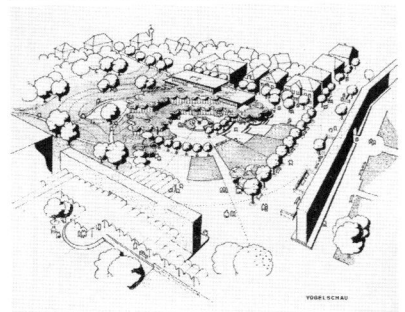

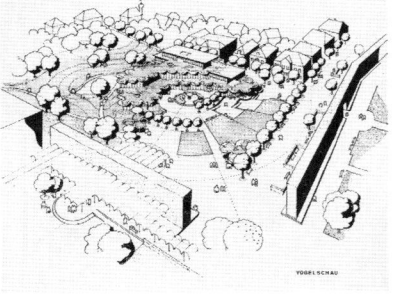

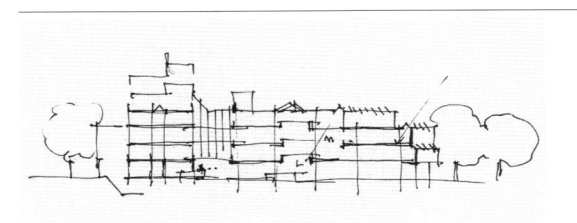

Bauten und Projekte / Buildings and Projects 1980 – 2003

Legende / Keys:
A   Auftraggeber / Client
P   Projektleitung / Project head
M   Mitarbeit / Collaboration
B   Bauleitung / Building supervision
S   Seite / Page

1983   **Kurgastzentrum** / Spa Center **Bad Salzuflen**
A   Landesverband Lippe
Wettbewerb 1976, 1. Preis (in Behnisch & Partner)
P   Reinhold Wanner
M   Fritz Eckert, Albert Fischer
B   mit Wilfried Funke, Detmold
BDA-Preis Nordrhein-Westfalen 1985, Anerkennung
Architekturpreis Beton 1985, Lobende Erwähnung
S   26

Forstwissenschaftliche Fakultät / Faculty of Forestry **der Universität München Weihenstephan**
Wettbewerb, 3. Preis
M   Stephan Wittmann, Tobias Wulf

Internationales Begegnungszentrum / International Meeting Center **der Universität Freiburg**
A   Studentenwerk der Universität Freiburg
Gutachten 1981, 1. Preis
P   Christof Hilzinger, Ilona Werz
M   Peter Freudenthal, Hans Jana
B   mit Körber, Barton, Maul, Freiburg

1985   **Staats- und Universitätsbibliothek** / State and University Library **Göttingen**
Wettbewerb, 2. Preis
M   Götz Guggenberger

Altenwohn- und Pflegeheim / Retirement and Nursing Home **Vaterstetten**
A   Johann Luft KG, Vaterstetten
Auftrag 1981
P   Boris Nedeleff
M   Hans Kremer, Eberhard von Pechmann, Michaela Schepe

1986   **Landratsamt** / District Office **Alb-Donau-Kreis Ulm**
A   Alb-Donau-Kreis
Wettbewerb 1981, 1. Preis
P   Reinhold Wanner
M   Fritz Eckert, Ilona Werz
B   mit Hans Köpple, Dietmannsried
Auszeichnung Guter Bauten 1987, BDA Baden-Württemberg

Robert-Bosch-Haus / Robert Bosch House **Stuttgart**
A   Robert-Bosch-Stiftung
Gutachten 1984
M   Götz Guggenberger, Sebastian Henrich
B   Robert Bosch GmbH, Stuttgart
S   38

1986 **Altenwohn- und Pflegeheim** / Retirement and Nursing Home
St. Marien Lemgo
A   Kreis Lippe, Detmold, Lippisches Damenstift
    St. Marien, Lemgo
Wettbewerb 1982, 1. Preis
P   Tobias Wulf
M   Ulf Decker
B   mit Wilfried Funke, Detmold
BDA-Auszeichnung Kostensparendes Bauen
bei hoher Qualität 1988, Lobende Erwähnung
S   32

1987 **Stadion** / Stadium **Nürnberg**
Wettbewerb
M   Felix Schürmann

Bundesforschungsanstalt für Ernährung / Federal Research
Institute of Nutrition **Karlsruhe**
Wettbewerb, 4. Preis
mit Wolfgang Glaser
M   Thomas Bittcher, Klaus Habisreutinger, Petra Haindl

Landratsamt / District Office **Starnberg**
A   Landkreis Starnberg
Wettbewerb 1982, 1. Preis
P   Christof Hilzinger
M   Thomas Bittcher-Zeitz, Wolfgang Glaser,
    Klaus Habisreutinger, Hans Jana, Tobias Wulf
B   Rainer Köhler, Gauting
Deutscher Architekturpreis 1989
BDA-Preis Bayern 1989
Europäischer Holzleimbaupreis 1991
Holzbaupreis Bayern 1988
Architekturpreis des Klempner-Handwerks 1988
„Stern des Jahres", Abendzeitung München 1988 ·
S   40

1988 **Büro- und Konferenzgebäude** / Office and Conference Building
des ZDF Mainz
Wettbewerb, 2. Preis
mit Wolfgang Glaser

Parlamentsvorzone / Area in front of Parliament Buildings
Bonn
Wettbewerb, 2. Preis
M   Angela Bergmann, Petra Haindl, Jörg Müller

Zentraler Omnibusbahnhof / Central Bus Station
Ludwigsburg
A   Stadt Ludwigsburg
Wettbewerb 1981, 1. Preis
P   Götz Guggenberger
M   Peter Freudenthal, Ilona Werz
B   Stadt Ludwigsburg, Tiefbauamt
Auszeichnung Beispielhaftes Bauen 1988,
Architektenkammer Baden-Württemberg
Auszeichnung Guter Bauten 1990, BDA Baden-Württemberg

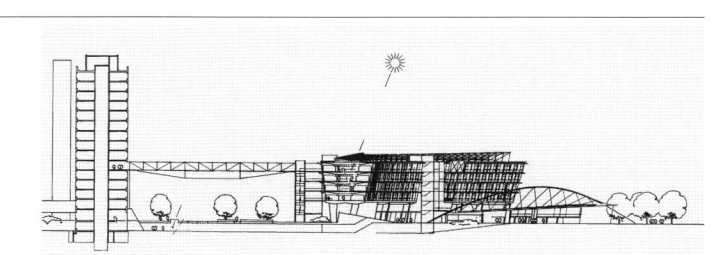

1988 **Francksteg Ludwigsburg**
A Stadt Ludwigsburg
Wettbewerb 1981
in Planungsgemeinschaft mit Ing.-Büro Hildenbrand, Ludwigsburg
P Götz Guggenberger

1989 **Kultur- und Kongresszentrum** / Cultural and Congress Center **Oberschwaben Weingarten**
A Stadt Weingarten
Wettbewerb 1986, 1. Preis
P Matthias Bruder, Reinhold Wanner
M Astrid Chwoika, Bernhard Lutz, Wolfgang Schwarz, Tobias Wulf
B mit Holletzek + Voigt, Weingarten
Auszeichnung Beispielhaftes Bauen 1989, Architektenkammer Baden-Württemberg

Hotel beim Kultur- und Kongresszentrum / Hotel at the Cultural and Congress Center **Oberschwaben Weingarten**
A Konferenzhotel Weingarten GmbH
Auftrag
in Planungsgemeinschaft mit Bernhard von Busse, München
P Manfred Michel
M Bernardo Striegel
B mit Holletzek + Voigt, Weingarten

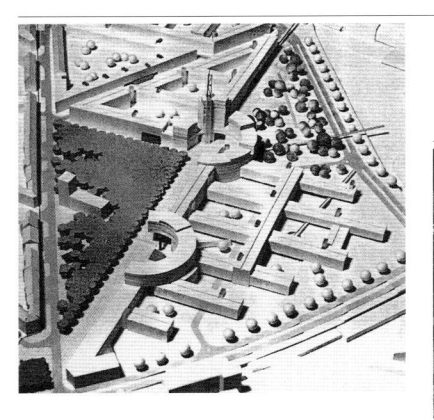

Internationales Handelszentrum / International Trade Center **Düsseldorf**
Wettbewerb, 5. Preis
M Jürgen Deger

Tank- und Rastanlage / Autobahn Service Station **Pentling**
A Autobahndirektion Südbayern
Auftrag 1987
mit Christof Hilzinger
M Klaus Habisreutinger
B mit Max Lecker, Regensburg
Deutscher Natursteinpreis 1991, Anerkennung

Bundesrat Bonn
Wettbewerb, 5.Preis
M Matthias Hotz, Jörg Müller

Mensa der Universität / Refectory of the University **Ulm**
A Land Baden-Württemberg, Oberfinanzdirektion Stuttgart
Wettbewerb 1981, 1. Preis
P Ulf Decker
M Peter Freudenthal, Sabine Füssenhäuser, Bernhard Lutz, Eugen Schweinbeck, Ilona Werz
B mit Bodo Berger, Ulm, Hans Köpple, Dietmannsried
Auszeichnung Beispielhaftes Bauen 1991, Architektenkammer Baden-Württemberg

1990 **Kollegienhaus** / College Building **der Deutschen Schillergesellschaft Marbach am Neckar**
Wettbewerb, 2. Preis
M   Petra Haindl, Achim Söding, Bernardo Striegel

Dienstleistungszentrum / Service Center **Pragsattel Stuttgart**
Wettbewerb, 5. Preis
M   Matthias Hotz, Michael Sigle, Peter Terbüchte, Matias Wenzel

Siemens-Niederlassung / Siemens Building **Stuttgart-Weilimdorf**
Gutachten
M   Volker Swiatkowski, Florian Tuczek

Pavillon der Bundesrepublik Deutschland / Pavilion of the Federal Republic of Germany **EXPO '92 Sevilla**
A   Bundesrepublik Deutschland
Wettbewerb 1990, 1. Preis
mit Bernd Meyerspeer und Alexander Mayr
P   Bernd Meyerspeer
M   Stefan Burger, Alexander Mayr, Dominik Schenkirz
Kritikerpreis 1991, Verband Deutscher Kritiker
(Projekt eingestellt)
S   50

Eiserne Brücke / Iron Bridge **über die Donau Regensburg**
A   Stadt Regensburg
Wettbewerb 1987, Sonderpreis Brücke
in Planungsgemeinschaft mit Mayr+Ludescher, München
P   Felix Schürmann
M   Ellen Dettinger, Klaus Habisreutinger, Wilfried Mayer
B   mit Stadt Regensburg, Tiefbauamt
Ingenieurbaupreis 1992, Auszeichnung
Preis des Deutschen Stahlbaues 1994, Auszeichnung
Stahl-Innovationspreis 1994, Anerkennung
Deutscher Städtebaupreis 1997, Anerkennung
S   66

Stadtportalhäuser / Portal Buildings **Frankfurt am Main**
Wettbewerb, 4. Preis
mit Bernd Meyerspeer
M   Charles Martin
S   56

Petuelpark / Park Petuel **München**
A   Landeshauptstadt München
Auftrag 1989
mit Latz+Partner, Kranzberg
P   Thomas Bittcher-Zeitz
(Projekt eingestellt)

Hotel Kapuzinerhof Biberach
A   Bauherrengemeinschaft Hotel am Kapuzinerplatz
Wettbewerb 1990, 1. Preis
M   Manfred Michel, Michael Sigle
(bis Genehmigungsplanung)

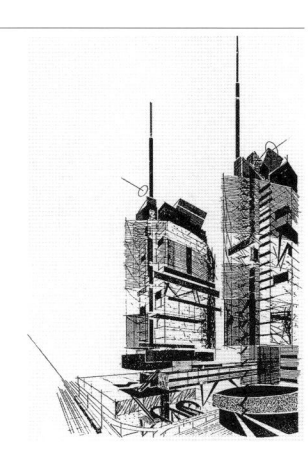

1990	**Casino** / Staff Restaurant **Bosch Bühl/Baden** A Robert Bosch GmbH, Stuttgart Auftrag 1989 M Manfred Michel, Achim Söding (Projekt eingestellt)
1991	**Ausstellungskonzept** / Exhibition Concept **Mercedes-Benz IAA '91 Frankfurt am Main** Gutachten mit Albert Hien M Konrad Deffner, Thomas Rückert

Marktplatz / Market Square **Jena**
Wettbewerb, 3. Preis
M   Achim Söding

Doppelwohnhaus / Semi-detached House **Stockdorf**
A   Bernd Rindfleisch/Jochen Hagen, München
Auftrag 1990
mit Bernd Meyerspeer
(Projekt eingestellt)

Dienstleistungszentrum / Service Center „Am Aalto" **Essen**
Wettbewerb, 3. Preis
mit Partner Götz Guggenberger
M   Dominik Schenkirz, Peter Terbüchte, Thomas Traub

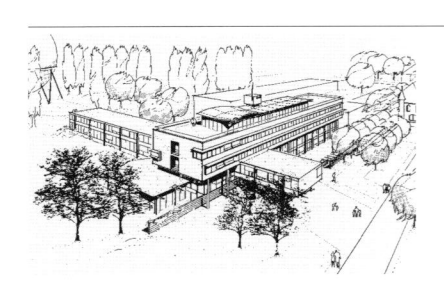

Verwaltungsgebäude / Administration Building
der Stadtwerke Reutlingen
A   Stadt Reutlingen, Grundstücksverwaltungs-
    Gesellschaft mbH
Wettbewerb 1987, 1. Preis
P   Petra Haindl
M   Bernardo Striegel
B   mit Karl-Heinz Jetter, Reutlingen
Auszeichnung Guter Bauten 1993, BDA Baden-Württemberg
Hugo-Häring-Preis 1994
S   70

Landratsamt / District Office **Schwarzwald-Baar-Kreis**
Villingen-Schwenningen
A   Schwarzwald-Baar-Kreis
Wettbewerb 1987
P   Götz Guggenberger
M   Angela Bergmann, Petra Haindl, Matthias Hotz, Leonore Kill,
    Eckhart Mauch, Jörg Müller
B   mit Ludszuweit-Rolf, Donaueschingen/Freiburg,
    Harald Nolte, Schwenningen
Auszeichnung Beispielhaftes Bauen 1992, Architektenkammer
Baden-Württemberg
Auszeichnung Guter Bauten 1993, BDA Baden-Württemberg

1991 **Subzentrum Flughafen** / Subcenter Munich Airport **München**
A   Flughafen München GmbH
Wettbewerb 1976, 1. Preis (in Behnisch & Partner)
P   Peter Fink, Bernd Meyerspeer
M Peter Freudenthal, Peter Kloncz, Wilfried Mayer,
     Tiemo Mehner, Paul Schlossbauer, Felix Schürmann,
     Manfred Stiegelmeier, Hans Wagenstaller
B   Ingenieurgemeinschaft Schlegel/Kling, München
Deutscher Verzinkerpreis 1995, Anerkennung
S   58

Fernmeldeamt 4 und Rechenzentrum / Telecommunications
Center 4 and Computer Center **München**
A   Deutsche Bundespost, Telekom
Auftrag 1990
mit Bernd Meyerspeer
M Charles Martin, Dominik Schenkirz
(Projekt eingestellt)

1992 **Landratsamt** / District Office **Tübingen**
Wettbewerb, 1. Preis
mit Partner Götz Guggenberger
M Angela Bergmann, Martin Gessert, Andreas Soppa

Neue Umweltbehörde / Environment Authority **Hamburg**
Wettbewerb, Ankauf
mit Partner Götz Guggenberger
M Bettina Gehlen, Andreas Wallner

Museen für Moderne Kunst / Museums of Modern Art
München
Wettbewerb
mit Bernd Meyerspeer
M Manfred Ehrle

Kolping-Familienerholungsstätte / Family Recreation Center
Pleinfeld am Brombachsee
Wettbewerb, 3. Preis
M Angela Bergmann, Andreas Soppa

Umbau / Conversion **des Reichstags
zum Deutschen Bundestag Berlin**
Wettbewerb
mit Partner Götz Guggenberger
M Peter Haubert, Dominik Schenkirz, Alexander Schleifenheimer

Hotel Unter den Linden Berlin
Wettbewerb, 3. Preis
M Moritz Auer, Dominik Schenkirz, Alexander Schleifenheimer

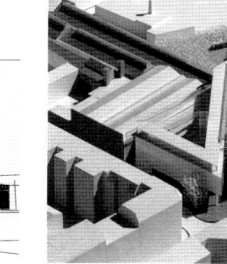

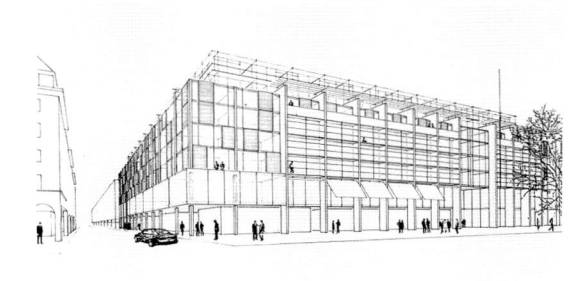

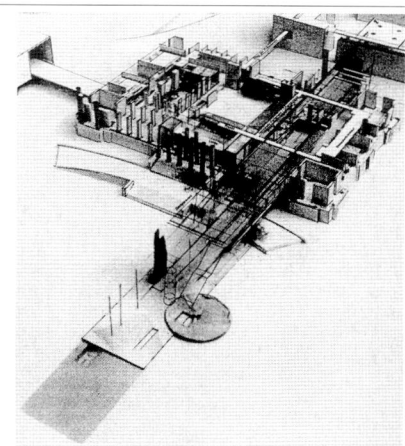

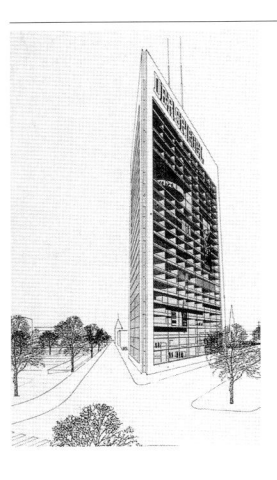

	1992	**SPIEGEL-Haus** / SPIEGEL Building **Hamburg**

1992   **SPIEGEL-Haus** / SPIEGEL Building **Hamburg**
Wettbewerb
mit Partner Götz Guggenberger
M   Angela Bergmann, Bettina Gehlen, Martin Gessert, Peter Haubert

Parkcafé im Schlossgarten Ludwigsburg
A   Land Baden-Württemberg, Staatl. Hochbauamt Ludwigsburg
Auftrag 1989
P   Angela Bergmann, Matias Wenzel
B   mit Christophers + Partner, Stuttgart
Auszeichnung Guter Bauten 1993, BDA Baden-Württemberg
Deutscher Verzinkerpreis 1993, 2. Preis

Tribüne und Überdachung / Stand and Roofing **Stadion Ellental Bietigheim-Bissingen**
A   Stadt Bietigheim-Bissingen
Gutachten 1992
P   Michael Sigle, Thomas Strittmatter
(Projekt eingestellt)

Helen-Keller-Realschule / Secondary School **München-Johanneskirchen**
A   Landeshauptstadt München
Wettbewerb 1987, 1. Preis
P   Wilfried Mayer
M   Ellen Dettinger, Matthias Jakob
S   74

1993   **Königstraße Stadt Schleswig**
Wettbewerb, 1. Preis
M   Martin Gessert, Alexander Schleifenheimer

Uppstal Stadtteilzentrum / Center of Town District **Stendal**
Wettbewerb, 1. Preis
M   Alexander Schleifenheimer

Theater der Stadt / Municipal Theater **Gütersloh**
Wettbewerb, Ankauf
M   Martin Gessert, Christof Teige

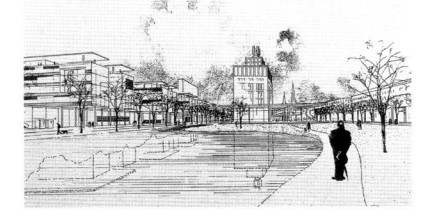

Dortmunder „U"
Wettbewerb, 3. Preis
M   Bettina Gehlen, Martin Gessert

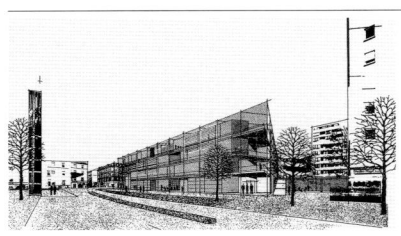

Verwaltungsgebäude / Administration Building **Badenwerk Karlsruhe**
A   Badenwerk AG, Karlsruhe
Wettbewerb 1991, 1. Preis
P   Dominik Schenkirz
M   Charles Martin
(Projekt eingestellt)

1993 **Großvoliere in der „Wilhelma" /** Large Aviary **Stuttgart**
A   Land Baden-Württemberg, Staatl. Hochbauamt
Auftrag 1987
in Planungsgemeinschaft mit Mayr+Ludescher, Stuttgart
P   Angela Bergmann, Matias Wenzel
Auszeichnung Guter Bauten 1993, BDA Baden-Württemberg
S   88

Stadthalle im Ortszentrum / Civic Hall **Germering**
A   Stadt Germering
Wettbewerb 1984, 1. Preis
mit Wolfgang Glaser
M   Edgar Burian, Ellen Dettinger, Klaus Habisreutinger,
      Michael Hüttinger, Thomas Rückert, Felix Schürmann
B   mit Zipf+Partner, München
S   80

Altenwohnanlage / Retirement and Nursing Home
St. Marien Lemgo, 2.+3. Bauabschnitt
A   Lippisches Damenstift St. Marien, Lemgo
Wettbewerb 1988, 1. Preis
P   Wilfried Funke
M   Petra Haindl, Tobias Wulf
B   Wilfried Funke, Detmold
S   32

Kurhaus / Spa Center **Bad Dürrheim, Umbau und Erweiterung**
Conversion and Extension
A   Kur- und Bäder GmbH, Bad Dürrheim
Auftrag 1990
P   Achim Söding
M   Manuela Rademaker
B   mit Fred Rolf, Freiburg, Harald Nolte, Schwenningen
Auszeichnung Guter Bauten 1996, BDA Baden-Württemberg

Kindergarten am Veitshof Freising
A   Stadt Freising
Auftrag 1990
mit Wilfried Mayer
M   Abdullah Motaleb
B   mit Streit+Partner, München

1994 **Hochschulzentrum /** University Center **mit Hörsaalkomplex und technischen Instituten der TU Dresden**
Wettbewerb, 3. Preis
M   Alexander Schleifenheimer, Christof Teige

Akademie der Künste / Academy of Arts
am Pariser Platz Berlin
Gutachten
M   Bettina Gehlen, Martin Gessert, Stefan Glück

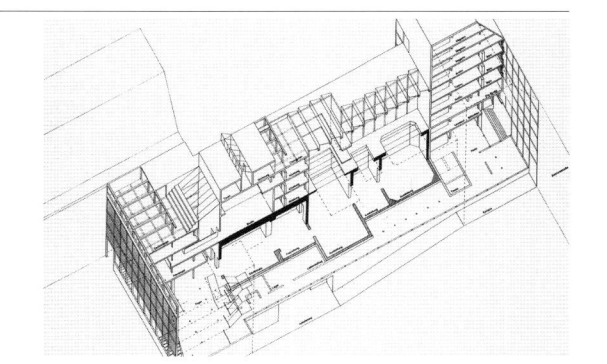

1994 **Theater Hof**
A   Stadt Hof
Wettbewerb 1987, 1. Preis
mit Thomas Bittcher-Zeitz
M   Reinhard Bauer, Stefan Burger, Konrad Deffner,
    Klaus Habisreutinger, Abdullah Motaleb, Felix Schürmann,
    Clemens Schulte-Mattler, Andreas Soppa, Herbert Stoderl
B   mit Ulrich Thies, Hof
Deutscher Architekturpreis 1995, Auszeichnung
S   94

Bibliothek im Ortszentrum / Library **Germering**
A   Stadt Germering
Wettbewerb 1984, 1. Preis
mit Wolfgang Glaser
P   Wolfgang Glaser, Klaus Habisreutinger
M   Bettina Kirchner, Christiane Müller, Felix Schürmann
B   mit Zipf + Partner, München
S   80

Kindergarten im Ortszentrum Germering
A   Stadt Germering
Auftrag 1991
mit Wolfgang Glaser
P   Wolfgang Glaser, Peter Haubert
M   Ellen Dettinger
B   mit Sieme + Partner, München
S   80

Erweiterung der Tank- und Rastanlage
Extension of Autobahn Service Station **Pentling**
A   Autobahndirektion Südbayern
Auftrag
mit Christof Hilzinger
B   mit Max Lecker, Regensburg

Sporthalle / Sports Hall **Marbacher Weg Bietigheim-Bissingen**
A   Stadt Bietigheim-Bissingen
Wettbewerb 1991, 1. Preis
P   Michael Sigle
M   Thomas Strittmatter
B   mit Bernd Raff, Bietigheim-Bissingen
Auszeichnung Beispielhaftes Bauen 1989–1999,
Architektenkammer Baden-Württemberg

Wildermuth-Wohnheim / Residential Home
Anstalt Stetten im Remstal
A   Anstalt Stetten
Gutachten 1989
P   Manfred Michel
M   Bettina Gehlen, Dietmar Lachenmann, Michael Sigle,
    Bernardo Striegel
B   mit Ulrich Gassmann
Auszeichnung Beispielhaftes Bauen 1986–96,
Architektenkammer Baden-Württemberg

1995	**Bewegungsbad** / Rehabilitation Spa **Bad Elster**

Wettbewerb, Ankauf
M   Peter Holzer, Eberhard Kastner, Christof Kimmich

Anlagen für Forschung und Entwicklung
Research & Development Facilities **SICAN Hannover**
A   SIAG-SICAN, Hannover
Wettbewerb 1995
P   Dominik Schenkirz
M   Marc Eutebach, Hans-Günter Lübben, Markus Mayer
(Projekt eingestellt)

Landratsamt / District Office **Würzburg**
Erweiterung / Extension
A   Landkreis Würzburg
Wettbewerb 1991, 2. Preis
P   Bettina Gehlen
(Projekt eingestellt)

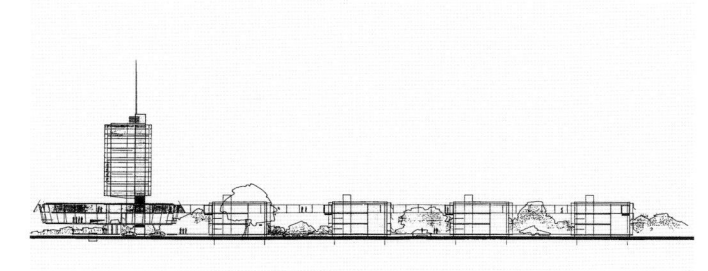

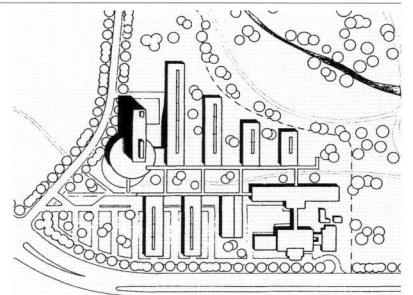

Kindergarten Sindelfingen-Darmsheim
A   Stadt Sindelfingen, Hochbauamt
Wettbewerb 1992, 1. Preis
mit Partner Götz Guggenberger
P   Angela Bergmann mit Edmund Hoke, Stuttgart
B   Stadt Sindelfingen, Hochbauamt
Auszeichnung Beispielhaftes Bauen 1986–1996,
Architektenkammer Baden-Württemberg

1996	**Landesfunkhaus** / Broadcasting Center **MDR Erfurt**

Wettbewerb, 3. Preis
M   Martin Gessert, Markus Lanz, Albrecht Randecker,
     Jörn Scholz

Landeszentralbank / State Central Bank **Halle**
Wettbewerb, 3. Preis
M   Philipp Grath, Jörn Scholz, Achim Söding

Altenwohnungen am Innenhafen / Retirement Homes
Duisburg
A   Landesentwicklungsgesellschaft Düsseldorf
Auftrag 1995
P   Bettina Gehlen, Christof Teige
(Projekt eingestellt)

1997	**Geschäftshaus und Volkshochschule**

Office Building and Adult Evening School
Degussa-Gelände, Pforzheim
A   Degussa Pensionskasse, Frankfurt am Main
Wettbewerb 1994
mit Partner Götz Guggenberger
P   Götz Guggenberger, Matias Wenzel
M   Christoph van Heyden, Eberhard Räuchle, Franz Stinner,
     Christof Teige
B   mit Wenzel+Wenzel, Karlsruhe
Deutscher Verzinkerpreis 1997, Anerkennung

1997 **Verwaltungsgebäude** / Administration Building **der DEGI Frankfurt am Main, Umbau** / Conversion
A   DEGI Deutsche Gesellschaft für Immobilienfonds mbH, Frankfurt am Main
Auftrag 1996
mit Partner Götz Guggenberger
M   Bärbel Nanz
(Projekt eingestellt)

1998 **Kongresshotel** / Congress Hotel **Karlsruhe**
Wettbewerb, 3. Preis
M   Philipp Auer, Stefan Niese, Gilbert Wilk

U-Bahn-Station / Underground Station **Westfriedhof München**
A   Landeshauptstadt München, U-Bahn-Referat
Auftrag 1995
mit Ingo Maurer, München
P   Martina Hornhardt, Heiner Reimers, Dominik Schenkirz, Stephan Suxdorf
M   Moritz Auer, Hans-Günter Lübben
B   U-Bahn-Referat München
BDA-Preis Bayern 1999, Auszeichnung
Renault Award for Traffic Design 2001
S   128

Kreissparkasse / District Savings Bank **Esslingen-Nürtingen, Hauptstelle Nürtingen**
A   Kreissparkasse Esslingen-Nürtingen
Wettbewerb 1993, 3. Preis
mit Partner Götz Guggenberger
P   Dietmar Lachenmann
M   Edgar Burian, Petra Haindl, Wallie Heinisch, Markus Huber, Matthias Weber
B   mit Martin Ott, Stuttgart
Auszeichnung Beispielhaftes Bauen 1991–2001, Architektenkammer Baden-Württemberg

Ehapa-Verlag / Ehapa-Publishers **Leinfelden-Echterdingen Umbau** / Conversion
A   Ehapa-Verlag, Leinfelden-Echterdingen
Auftrag 1996
mit Partner Götz Guggenberger und Architektenbüro 4a, Stuttgart
B   Architektenbüro 4a, Stuttgart

Wohnen am Innenhafen / Residences **Duisburg**
A   Gemeinnützige Baugesellschaft AG, Duisburg
Auftrag 1995
mit Partner Götz Guggenberger
P   Christof Teige, Bettina Gehlen,
M   Siegfried Irion
Auszeichnung Vorbildlicher Bauten in Nordrhein-Westfalen 2000, Architektenkammer Nordrhein-Westfalen
S   110

1998 **Zeppelin Carré Stuttgart**
A   DEGI Deutsche Gesellschaft für Immobilienfonds mbH,
    Frankfurt am Main
Auftrag 1995
mit Partner Götz Guggenberger und Michel+Wolf+Partner,
Stuttgart
P   Manfred Michel
M   Christian Bade, Jutta Dahlhäuser, Stefan Glück,
    Uli Hermann, Vanessa Hupertz, Bärbel Nanz, Oliver Prokop,
    Susan Schlameuß, Wolfgang Selbach, Ralph Sommer,
    Matthias Weber
B   mit Ulrich Gassmann, Stuttgart
Deutscher Städtebaupreis 2001, Besondere Anerkennung
Gestaltungspreis der Wüstenrot Stiftung 1998, Anerkennung
Auszeichnung Guter Bauten 1999, BDA Baden-Württemberg
S   114

Casino und Mensa der Offiziersschule des Heeres / Army
Officers' Mess at the Training College **Dresden**
A   Staatshochbauamt Radeberg
Auftrag 1994
P   Volker Auch-Schwelk
M   Christina Brucker, Petra Gumbrecht, Frank Schäfer,
    Martin Gessert
B   mit Jahn+Nichelmann, Dresden
Holzbaupreis Neue Bundesländer 1998
S   122

Ramada Hotel Berlin-Köpenick
A   GELIN Grundstücksverwaltungsgesellschaft mbH
    Immobilien KG, Heidelberg
Wettbewerb 1993, 1. Preis
P   Dominik Schenkirz
M   Peter Haubert, Alexander Schleifenheimer, Jochen Schwind,
    Christof Teige
(bis Genehmigungsplanung)

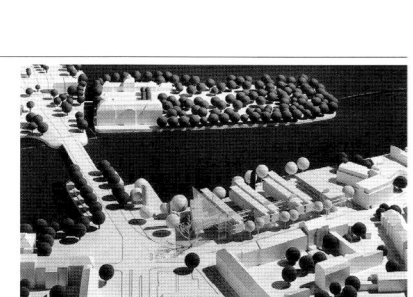

Ruhrfestspielhaus Recklinghausen
Umbau und Anbau / Conversion and Extension
A   Stadt Recklinghausen
Wettbewerb 1993, 1. Preis
P   Martin Gessert
M   Eberhard Kastner, Fleur Keller, Markus Lanz, Robert Plail,
    Albrecht Randecker, Christof Teige
B   mit Klaus Legner, Moers
Deutscher Architekturpreis 2001
Architekturpreis Nordrhein-Westfalen 2001
BDA-Auszeichnung Guter Bauten 2000
Verzinkerpreis 1999, Belobigung
S   102

1999 **adidas "World of Sports", Herzogenaurach**
Wettbewerb, 3. Preis
mit Michel+Wolf+Partner, Stuttgart
M   Moritz Auer, Sabine Heine, Fleur Keller
S   136

1999 **Stadion** / Stadium **Salzburg**
Wettbewerb
M Philipp Auer, Dieter Heigl, André Lang, Stephan Suxdorf

Bodenseetherme / Thermal Baths **Überlingen**
Wettbewerb, Ankauf
mit Partner Götz Guggenberger
M Frank Schäfer, Susan Schlameuß

MOB-Gelände / Site **Grewen**
Wettbewerb, 2. Preis
M Sabine Heine, Christof Teige

Science Center Wolfsburg
Wettbewerb, 4. Preis
mit Partner Götz Guggenberger
M Sabine Heine, Susan Schlameuß

Amazonienhaus in der „Wilhelma" / Amazonian House **Stuttgart**
A Land Baden-Württemberg, Oberfinanzdirektion Stuttgart
Auftrag 1989
P Eberhard Räuchle, Achim Söding
M Monika Metz
B mit Wenzel+Wenzel, Karlsruhe
S 132

Landeszentralbank / State Central Bank **Halberstadt**
A Landeszentralbank in Bremen, Niedersachsen und Sachsen-Anhalt, Hannover
Wettbewerb 1994, 1. Preis
P Achim Söding
M Philipp Grath, Christoph Kimmich, Bernd Liebl, Alexander Schleifenheimer, Thomas Streitberg, Christof Teige
B mit Jäger+Herbst, Halberstadt
Architekturpreis Sachsen-Anhalt 2001, Anerkennung
Magdeburger Architekturpreis 2001

Multifunktionales Sport- und Veranstaltungszentrum / Multi-purpose Sports and Event Center **Stuttgart**
Wettbewerb, 3. Preis
M Moritz Auer, Alexander Carl, Dieter Heigl, Sebastian Heine, Stefan Niese, Sonja Mutterer

Hochhauskomplex / High-rise **MAX Frankfurt am Main**
Wettbewerb, Engere Wahl
M Moritz Auer, Philipp Auer, Fleur Keller
S 140

2000 **Gewerbepark** / Industrial Estate **Neckarstatt Wendlingen**
Wettbewerb, 1. Preis
mit Partner Götz Guggenberger
M Alexander Carl, Clemens Haury, Andrea Seidel

2000   **Gymnasium** / Grammar School **Bruckmühl**
Wettbewerb, 2. Preis
M   Moritz Auer, Philipp Auer, André Lang, Sonja Mutterer

Clubhaus / Clubhouse **Bayerischer Yachtclub Starnberg**
Wettbewerb, Preisgruppe
M   Moritz Auer, Philipp Auer, Dieter Heigl, Stefan Niese

Rathaus / Town Hall **Ingolstadt**
Umbau und Erweiterung / Conversion and Extension
Rathausplatz und / and **Viktualienmarkt**
A   Stadt Ingolstadt
Wettbewerb 2000, 1. Preis
P   Martin Klemp
M   Moritz Auer, Philipp Auer, Dominik Fahr, Sonja Mutterer, Stephan Suxdorf

Kurmittelhaus / Spa Center **Bad Brambach**
A   Sächsisches Staatsministerium der Finanzen, Dresden
Wettbewerb 1996, 1. Preis
P   Peter Holzer
M   Volker Auch-Schwelk, Bernd Liebl, Monika Metz, Bärbel Nanz
B   mit Harald Schneider, Oelsnitz
Deutscher Verzinkerpreis 2001, 2. Preis
S   146

Post Carré Bonn
A   ISP Grundstücks-Vermietungsgesellschaft mbH, Bonn, ab 2000 Deutsche Post Bauen, Bonn
Wettbewerb 1996
mit Partner Götz Guggenberger
P   Ulof Rückert
M   Andreas Achilles, Christian Bade, Svetlana Curcic, Siegfried Irion, Christoph van Heyden, Frank Schäfer
B   HOCHTIEF Dortmund

Überdachung / Roofing **Niedersachsenstadion Hannover**
Wettbewerb, 2. Preis
M   Achim Söding
S   152

Neue Pforte / New Gate **Werk 1 Mann+Hummel GmbH Ludwigsburg**
A   Mann+Hummel GmbH, Ludwigsburg
Gutachten 1999
P   Fleur Keller
M   Andrea Seidel
(Projekt eingestellt)

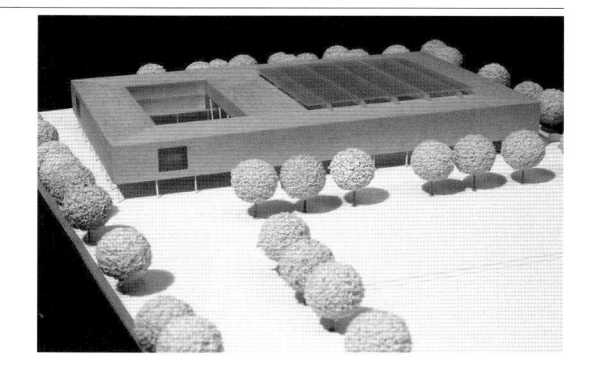

2000 **Wohnbebauung** / Residences „Altes Schlachthofgelände"
Paderborn
A   Spar- und Bauverein Paderborn eG
Wettbewerb 1998, 1. Preis
P   Christof Teige
M   Oliver Fischer, Rainer Oertelt, Karl Richter
B   mit Becker-Just + Partner, Paderborn

Realschule / Secondary School **Traunreut**
A   Landkreis Traunstein
Wettbewerb 2000, 1. Preis
P   Peter Hofmann
M   Moritz Auer, Philipp Auer, Volker Kilian, André Lang,
    Sonja Mutterer
(Projekt eingestellt)

Hochhausensemble / High-rise Ensemble „Münchner Tor"
München
Scheibenhochhaus / Straight-line high-rise
Wettbewerb, Ankauf
M   Martin Klemp, Stefan Niese

Hochhausensemble / High-rise Ensemble „Münchner Tor"
München
Twin Towers
Wettbewerb, 1. Preis
M   Moritz Auer, Philipp Auer
S   156

2001 **National Stadium of Ireland Dublin**
Wettbewerb
mit Walter Bau, Augsburg
M   Eberhard Kastner, Andrea Seidel, Achim Söding,
    Kathrin Weiß

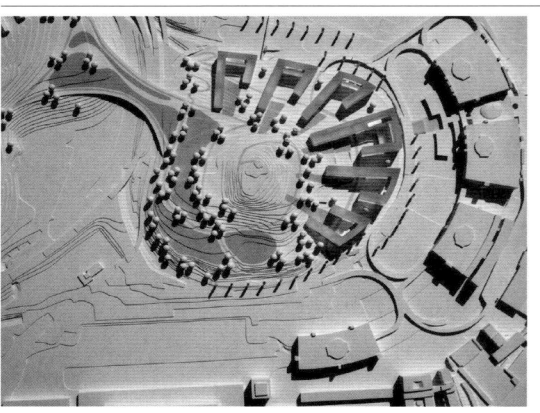

Erweiterung / Extension **Unique Airport Zürich**
Wettbewerb
M   Alexander Carl, Sabine Heine, Jörn Scholz, Kathrin Weiß,
    Felix Wiemken

Carl-Bosch-Haus / Carl Bosch House **Frankfurt am Main**
Fassade und Umbau / Façade and Conversion
A   GDCh Gesellschaft Deutscher Chemiker e.V.,
    Frankfurt am Main
Wettbewerb 2000
mit Partner Götz Guggenberger
M   Rainer Oertelt, Achim Söding
(Projekt eingestellt)

Büropark / Office Park **Fasanenhof Stuttgart**
A   STEP GmbH, Stuttgart
Gutachten 2001, 1. Preis
M   Eberhard Kastner, Andrea Seidel, Achim Söding,
    Christof Teige, Kathrin Weiß
S   186

2001 **Zentrum für Anwendungen der Informatik und Zentrum für internationale Beziehungen** / IT Applications Center and Center for International Relations **Universität Passau**
Wettbewerb, 2. Preis
M   Moritz Auer, Philipp Auer, Martin Klemp, Christian Siebert

Sportbad / Swimming Pool **Opladen Leverkusen**
Wettbewerb, 2. Preis
M   Jörn Scholz, Kathrin Weiß

Altes Rathaus / Old Town Hall **Pforzheim**
Bauliche Ergänzung, Umbau und Sanierung
Extension, Conversion and Restoration
A   Stadt Pforzheim / Grundbesitzgesellschaft Altes Rathaus
    Pforzheim mbH + Co.KG
Wettbewerb 1997, 2. Preis
mit Partner Götz Guggenberger
P   Jörn Scholz
M   Alexander Carl, Tillmann Heller, Eberhard Kastner,
    Albrecht Randecker, Matthias Weber, Felix Wiemken
B   mit Wenzel + Wenzel, Karlsruhe
Auszeichnung Guter Bauten 2002, BDA Baden-Württemberg
S   174

Kronen Carré Stuttgart
A   Sparkassen-Versicherung AG, Stuttgart
Wettbewerb 1997, 1. Preis
mit Partner Götz Guggenberger
P   Jörg Müller
M   Christian Bade, Sabine Heine, Uli Hermann,
    Thorsten Hessdörfer, Tillmann Heller, Tillmann Heuter,
    Christoph van Heyden, Siegfried Irion, Bärbel Nanz,
    Albrecht Randecker, Susan Schlameuß, Jürgen Weigl
B   Gassmann + Grossmann, Stuttgart
S   160

Stadtbahn / Suburban Railway **Heilbronn**
Überdachung Bahnhofsplatz,
Haltestellen Harmonie / Kurt-Schumacher-Platz
A   Stadt Heilbronn
Auftrag
P   Fleur Keller
B   mit Wenzel + Wenzel, Karlsruhe
DuPont Benedictus Award 2000/2001, Exceptional Merit
Auszeichnung Guter Bauten 2002, BDA Baden-Württemberg

BMW Erlebnis- und Auslieferungszentrum
BMW Event and Delivery Center **München**
Wettbewerb, Engere Wahl
M   Moritz Auer, Philipp Auer, Stefan Niese, Hartmut Windels
S   180

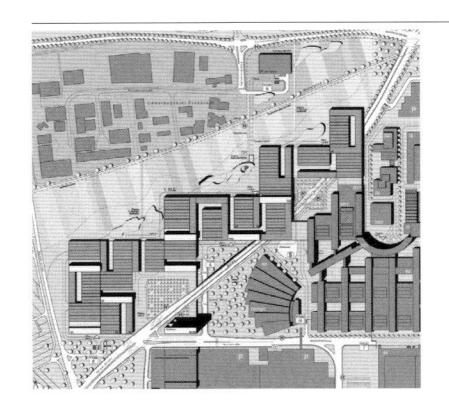

2001 **PRISMA-Haus** / PRISMA Building **Frankfurt am Main**
A   HOCHTIEF Projektentwicklung GmbH,
Niederlassung Südwest, Frankfurt am Main
Wettbewerb 1996, 1. Preis
mit Partner Götz Guggenberger
P   Frank Schäfer
M   Sonja Grimbacher, Petra Haindl, Christian Kern, Markus Lanz,
     Rainer Oertelt, Susan Schlameuß, Jörn Scholz,
     Christof Teige, Kathrin Weiß
B   HOCHTIEF AG, Frankfurt am Main
(Ausführungsplanung mit HOCHTIEF AG, Frankfurt am Main)
S   168

TH Darmstadt / Technical University **Fachbereich 13 Darmstadt**
Wettbewerb, 3. Preis
M   Rainer Oertelt, Frank Schäfer, Andrea Seidel

Hotel der ESO am Cerro Paranal / ESO Hotel **Chile**
A   ESO European Southern Observatory, Garching
Wettbewerb 1998, 1. Preis
P   Philipp Auer, Dominik Schenkirz
M   Moritz Auer, Robert Giessl, Dieter Heigl, Stefan Niese,
     Michael Krüger, Charles Martin
B   ESO
S   196

Neues Fußballstadion / New Soccer Stadium **München**
Wettbewerb
mit HOCHTIEF Construction AG, München
M   Moritz Auer, Philipp Auer, Volker Kilian, Sonja Mutterer,
     Stefan Niese, Till Richter, Stephan Suxdorf, Rolf Wenig,
     Hartmut Windels
S   190

2002 **adidas Factory Outlet Herzogenaurach**
Wettbewerb, 1. Preis
M   Moritz Auer, Philipp Auer, Till Richter, Stephan Suxdorf

Forschungszentrum / Research Center **DaimlerChrysler Sindelfingen**
Gutachten
M   Sabine Heine, Rainer Oertelt, Frank Schäfer, Achim Söding

Fachhochschule / Polytechnic **Aalen, Erweiterung** / Extension
Wettbewerb, 2. Preis
M   Christof Teige, Kathrin Weiß

Hochhaus / High-rise **Süddeutscher Verlag, München**
Wettbewerb, 3. Preis
M   Moritz Auer, Philipp Auer, Martin Klemp, Stefan Niese,
     Till Richter
S   216

2002 **Sportzentrum Alter Bahnhof** / Sports Center **Calw**
Wettbewerb, 2. Preis
M   Stefan Niese, Till Richter

Headquarter Altana Pharma Konstanz
Wettbewerb, 4. Preis
M   Jörn Scholz, Jürgen Weigl, Kathrin Weiß

Thuringia Versicherung / Insurance **München**
Wettbewerb, Ankauf
M   Moritz Auer, Philipp Auer, Till Richter, Christian Siebert,
    Hartmut Windels
S   206

LOEWE Verwaltungsgebäude / Administration Building
Kronach
Wettbewerb, 2. Preis
M   Moritz Auer, Philipp Auer, Michel Casertano, Sebastian
    Reusch, Till Richter, Stephan Suxdorf

Kreisberufsschulzentrum / District Vocational College **Aalen**
Erweiterung / Extension
Wettbewerb, 3. Preis
M   Rainer Oertelt, Achim Söding

Deutsche Botschaft / German Embassy **Mexico City**
Gutachten
M   Moritz Auer, Philipp Auer, Jörn Scholz
S   214

Klimasphäre / Climate Sphere **Bremerhaven**
Gutachten
mit Atelier Brückner, Stuttgart
M   Moritz Auer, Philipp Auer, Sophia Ben Yedder,
    Michel Casertano, Sebastian Reusch

Schmetterlingshalle in der „Wilhelma" / Butterfly Hall
Stuttgart
A   Land Baden-Württemberg, Oberfinanzdirektion Stuttgart
Auftrag 1999
mit Eberhard Räuchle, Stuttgart

Lärmschutzeinhausung / Noise Reduction Construction
Fußgänger- und Straßenbahnbrücke
Pedestrian and Streetcar Bridge **München**
A   Landeshauptstadt München, Baureferat
Auftrag 1988/1996
in Planungsgemeinschaft mit Mayr+Ludescher, München
mit Thomas Bittcher-Zeitz (bis 1989)
P   Stephan Suxdorf
M   Moritz Auer, Markus Jatsch, Gilbert Wilk, Hartmut Windels
B   mit Mayr+Ludescher, München

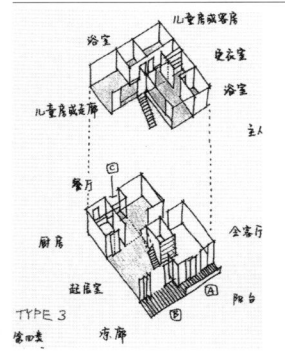

2002 **Schlossberg Böblingen**
Wettbewerb, 3. Preis
M   Sabine Heine, Jörg Müller
S   220

2003 **Max-Planck-Institut für Biophysik** / Max Planck Institute of Biophysics **Frankfurt am Main**
A   Max-Planck-Gesellschaft zur Förderung der Wissenschaften e.V., München
Wettbewerb 1997, 1. Preis
P   Matthias Goetz, Dominik Schenkirz
M   Peter Hofmann, Volker Kilian, Nicola Krämer, Hans-Günter Lübben, Stefan Niese, Gilbert Wilk
B   Doranth Post Architekten, München
S   246

Bachhaus / Bach House **Eisenach**
Wettbewerb, 3. Preis
M   Sophia Ben Yedder, Christof Teige

Anting New Town Shanghai China
A   Shanghai International Automobile City Real Estate Co. Ltd, Anting
Auftrag 2002
P   Christoph Lueder
M   Svetlana Curcic, Sabine Heine, Christof Hemminger, Britta Knobel
(bis Genehmigungsplanung)
S   234

Kaufhaus / Department Store **Welle Bielefeld**
A   Ulrich Möllmann GmbH & Co.KG
Wettbewerb 2000, 1. Preis
P   Achim Söding
M   Rainer Oertelt, Andrea Seidl
(bis Genehmigungsplanung)

Fußgängerbrücke / Pedestrian Bridge **Neckartailfingen**
A   Gemeinde Neckartailfingen
Auftrag 2001
in Planungsgemeinschaft mit Mayr+Ludescher, Stuttgart
P   Thorsten Hessdörfer, Jörg Müller
B   mit Mayr+Ludescher, Stuttgart

2003 **Zentrum** / Center **SolarCity, Linz**
    A   Magistrat der Landeshauptstadt Linz, Hochbauamt
Wettbewerb 1999, 1. Preis
    P   Stephan Suxdorf
    M Philipp Auer, Volker Kilian, Sonja Mutterer, Till Richter,
         Gilbert Wilk
    B   STRABAG AG, Linz
    S   222

Städtebaulicher Masterplan für die Olympiabewerbung Stuttgart 2012 / Master Plan for the Stuttgart Olympic Submission 2012
    A   Stadt Stuttgart
Auftrag 2020
    P   Achim Söding
    M Sabine Heine, Rainer Oertelt, Andrea Seidel
    S   208

Universitätsbibliothek / Library of the University **Magdeburg**
    A   Land Sachsen-Anhalt, Staatshochbauamt Magdeburg
Wettbewerb 1998, 1. Preis
mit Partner Götz Guggenberger
    P   Christoph Lueder
    M Svetlana Curcic, Christoph van Heyden, Armin Kammer,
         Holger Schurk
    B   mit Martin Ott, Magdeburg
    S   240

Sporthalle / Sports Hall **im Aurain Bietigheim-Bissingen**
    A   Stadt Bietigheim-Bissingen
Gutachten 2000
    P   Felix Wiemken
    M Christof Teige, Jürgen Weigl
    B   mit KMB, Ludwigsburg

Landratsamt / District Office **Alb-Donau-Kreis Ulm**
Erweiterung / Extension
    A   Kreisbaugesellschaft mbH Alb-Donau
Auftrag
    P   Stefan Dinkel, Stephan Suxdorf
    M André Lang, Christian Siebert
    B   mit Bodo Berger, Ulm

Sporthallen / Sports Hall **im Sportpark, Ulm-Nord**
    A   Stadt Ulm, Abteilung Hochbau
Gutachten 1999, 1. Preis
    P   Stephan Suxdorf, Rolf Wenig
    M Volker Kilian, Sonja Mutterer, Christian Siebert
    B   Seidel Architekten, Ulm

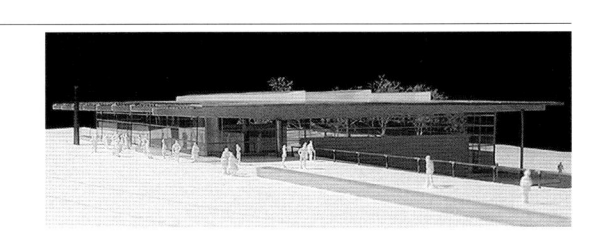

2003 **Ammersee-Gymnasium** / Grammar School **Dießen**
Wettbewerb, 2. Preis
M Moritz Auer, Philipp Auer, Michel Casertano, Stefan Niese, Till Richter

Science Park III Ulm
A Stadt Ulm
Gutachten 2001, 1. Preis
P Till Richter
S 230

2004 (voraussichtlich / expected)
Pavillon / Pavilion **Merckle–ratiopharm Ulm**
A VEM Vermögensverwaltung GmbH, Dresden
Gutachten, 1. Preis
P Rainer Oertelt, Achim Söding
M Britta Knobel

2004 (voraussichtlich / expected)
Wohnen am Altenhof / Residences **Essen**
A Thyssen-Krupp Immobilien Development GmbH
Wettbewerb 1993, 1. Preis
P Martin Gessert
M Bettina Gehlen

2005 (voraussichtlich / expected)
Fachoberschule / Senior Technical College **Aichach-Friedberg**
A Landratsamt Aichach-Friedberg
P Peter Hofmann, Stefan Niese
M Till Richter

2005 (voraussichtlich / expected)
Landratsamt / District Office **Tübingen**
A Landkreis Tübingen
Wettbewerb 2002, 3. Preis
P Jörn Scholz
M Thomas Köhler, Markus Seifermann, Kathrin Weiß
B mit Wenzel+Wenzel, Karlsruhe

2005 (voraussichtlich / expected)
Zentraler Omnibusbahnhof / Central Bus Station **München**
A Landeshauptstadt München, Kommunalreferat
Wettbewerb 2002, 1. Preis
mit Latz+Partner, Kranzberg
P Martin Klemp
M Moritz Auer, Philipp Auer, Dominik Fahr, Till Richter, Hartmut Windels
S 226

2005 (voraussichtlich / expected)
Wohnen und Arbeiten / Living and Working **im Alten Hof München**
Wettbewerb, Preisgruppe
M   Moritz Auer, Philipp Auer, Michel Casertano, Stefan Niese, Sebastian Reusch, Till Richter

2005 (voraussichtlich / expected)
Ausstellungsgebäude / Exhibition Building **Brühl'sche Terrasse, Dresden**
A   Freistaat Sachsen, Sächsisches Staatsministerium der Finanzen
Wettbewerb 1999, 1. Preis
mit Rolf Zimmermann, Dresden
P   Christof Teige

2006 (voraussichtlich / expected)
Sparkassenzentrale / District Savings Bank's Head Office **der Kreissparkasse Tübingen**
A   Kreissparkasse Tübingen
Wettbewerb 2002, 1. Preis
P   Christof Teige
M   Sophia Ben Yedder, Andrea Tontsch
B   mit Martin Ott, Stuttgart

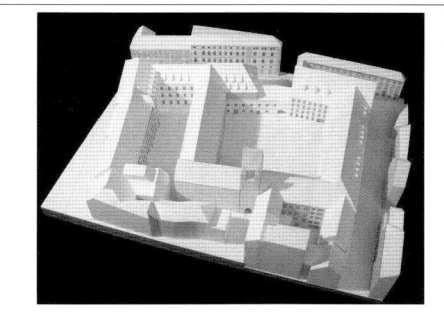

Auer+Weber+Architekten 1980 – 2003

Fritz Auer

1933	geboren in Tübingen
1953 – 1962	Studium TH Stuttgart
1958 – 1959	Stipendium Cranbrook Academy of Arts Bloomfield Hills, Michigan, USA, Master of Architecture
1962	Diplom TH Stuttgart
1960 – 1965	Behnisch und Lambart, Stuttgart
1965	Yamasaki + Associates, Birmingham, Michigan, USA
Jäger und Müller, Stuttgart
1966 – 1979	Partner in Behnisch & Partner
seit 1980	Architektengemeinschaft Auer+Weber
1985 – 1992	Professur für Baukonstruktion und Entwerfen FH München
1993 – 2001	Professur für Entwerfen Staatliche Akademie der Bildenden Künste Stuttgart
seit 1993	Mitglied der Akademie der Künste Berlin

Fritz Auer

1933	born in Tübingen
1953 – 1962	studied at TH Stuttgart
1958 – 1959	Scholarship to Cranbrook Academy of Arts, Bloomfield Hills, Michigan, USA, Master of Architecture
1962	graduated from TH Stuttgart
1960 – 1965	Behnisch und Lambart, Stuttgart
1965	Yamasaki + Associates, Birmingham, Michigan, USA
Jäger und Müller, Stuttgart
1966 – 1979	Partner in Behnisch & Partner
since 1980	Office Auer+Weber with Carlo Weber
1985 – 1992	Professor of Building Construction and Design at FH Munich
1993 – 2001	Professor of Design at Staatliche Akademie der Bildenden Künste Stuttgart
since 1993	Member of Akademie der Künste Berlin

Carlo Weber

1934	geboren in Saarbrücken
1953–1961	Studium TH Stuttgart
1959–1960	Stipendium Ecole Nationale Supérieure des Beaux Arts in Paris
1961	Diplom TH Stuttgart
1960–1965	Behnisch und Lambart, Stuttgart und Düsseldorf; Les Frères Arsène-Henry und Prof. Louis Arretche, Paris
1966–1979	Partner in Behnisch & Partner
seit 1980	Architektengemeinschaft Auer + Weber
1980–1990	Dozent Universität Stuttgart
1992–1999	Professur für Gebäudelehre und Entwerfen TU Dresden
seit 1996	Mitglied der Sächsischen Akademie der Künste

Carlo Weber

1934	born in Saarbrücken
1953–1961	studied at TH Stuttgart
1959–1960	Scholarship to the Ecole Nationale Supérieure des Beaux Arts in Paris
1961	graduated from TH Stuttgart
1960–1965	Behnisch and Lambart, Stuttgart and Düsseldorf Les Frères Arsène-Henry and Prof. Louis Arretche, Paris
1966–1979	Partner in Behnisch & Partner
since 1980	Office Auer + Weber with Fritz Auer
1980–1990	Lecturer at Universität Stuttgart
1992–1999	Professor of Building Theory and Design at TU Dresden
since 1996	Member of the Sächsische Akademie der Künste

Wichtige Auszeichnungen Auer + Weber

1972	Großer Architekturpreis des BDA*
1972	I.C.P. Award of Honour* Hugo-Häring-Preis*
1977	Architekturpreis der Stadt München*
1981	Internationaler Architekturpreis der UIA* Auguste-Perret-Preis* Anlagen und Bauten für die Olympischen Spiele München 1972
1989	Deutscher Architekturpreis, Landratsamt Starnberg
1991	Kritikerpreis für Architektur, Deutscher Pavillon EXPO '92 Sevilla
1991	Fritz-Schumacher-Preis
1995	Anerkennung Deutscher Architekturpreis Theater Hof
2001	Deutscher Architekturpreis Ruhrfestspielhaus Recklinghausen

*als Partner in Behnisch & Partner

Major awards Auer + Weber

1972	Architecture Award from the German Association of Architects (BDA)*
1972	I.C.P. Award of Honour* Hugo Häring Award*
1977	Architecture Award from the City of Munich*
1981	International Architecture Award from the UIA,* Auguste Perret Award* Sports grounds and buildings for the Olympic Games, Munich 1972
1989	German Architecture Award, Landratsamt Starnberg
1991	German critics' Architecture Award for the German Pavilion, EXPO '92 in Seville
1991	Fritz Schumacher Award
1995	German Architecture Award, official recognition, Theater in Hof
2001	German Architecture Award, Ruhrfestspielhaus in Recklinghausen

* as partners in Behnisch & Partner:

Partner und Assoziierte / Partners and Associates 1980–2003

Götz Guggenberger

1955	geboren in Stuttgart
1976–1977	Studium der Kunstgeschichte und Germanistik, Universität Tübingen
1977–1984	Studium der Architektur, TH Darmstadt und Universität Stuttgart Hilfsassistent am Lehrstuhl für Baukonstruktion und Entwerfen
1984	Diplom TH Darmstadt
seit 1984	Auer + Weber, Stuttgart
1992	Wissenschaftlicher Mitarbeiter, Institut für öffentliche Bauten, Universität Stuttgart
1991–2000	Partner in Auer + Weber + Partner, Stuttgart

1955	born in Stuttgart
1976–1977	studied History of Art, German language and literature, Tübingen University
1977–1984	studied Architecture TH Darmstadt and Stuttgart University Graduate lecturer for Building Construction and Design
1984	graduated from TH Darmstadt
since 1984	Auer + Weber, Stuttgart
1992	Technical assistant, Institute of Public Buildings, Stuttgart University
1991–2000	Partner at Auer + Weber + Partner, Stuttgart

Fritz Auer, Götz Guggenberger, Carlo Weber, 2000

Moritz Auer

1964	geboren in Stuttgart
1987–1988	Studium Kommunikationsdesign Folkwangschule / Gesamthochschule Essen
1988–1996	Architekturstudium TH Berlin J.P. Kleihues, Berlin, Büttner Neumann Braun, Berlin, Auer + Weber, Stuttgart / München
1996	Diplom TH Berlin
1996–2000	Mitarbeit Auer + Weber, München / Stuttgart
seit 2001	Assoziiert in Auer + Weber + Architekten, München

1964	born in Stuttgart
1987–1988	studied Communication Design Folkwangschule / Gesamthochschule Essen
1988–1996	studied Architecture TH Berlin J. P. Kleihues, Berlin, Büttner Neumann Braun, Berlin, Auer + Weber, Stuttgart / Munich
1996	graduated from TH Berlin
1996–2000	Auer + Weber, Munich / Stuttgart
since 2001	Associate at Auer + Weber + Architekten, Munich

Philipp Auer

1967	geboren in Stuttgart
1988–1991	Architekturstudium TU Stuttgart
1991–1995	Architekturstudium TH Darmstadt StadtBauPlan, Darmstadt Auer + Weber, München / Stuttgart
1995	Diplom TH Darmstadt
1995–1997	David Chipperfield Architects, London
1997–2000	Auer + Weber, München / Stuttgart
seit 2001	Assoziiert in Auer + Weber + Architekten, München

1967	born in Stuttgart
1988–1991	studied Architecture TU Stuttgart
1991–1995	studied Architecture TH Darmstadt StadtBauPlan, Darmstadt, Auer + Weber, Munich / Stuttgart
1995	graduated from TH Darmstadt
1995–1997	David Chipperfield Architects, London
1997-2000	Auer + Weber, Munich / Stuttgart
since 2001	Associate at Auer + Weber + Architekten, Munich

Jörg Müller

1954	geboren in Köln
1974–1982	Architekturstudium TH Darmstadt
1980–1981	DAAD Stipendium ETH Zürich
1982	Diplom TH Darmstadt
1982–1984	Selbständige Tätigkeit in Darmstadt
1985–1997	Behnisch & Partner, Stuttgart Auer + Weber, Stuttgart Klein + Breucha, Stuttgart
1997–2000	Auer + Weber, Stuttgart
seit 2001	Assoziiert in Auer + Weber + Architekten, Stuttgart

1954	born in Cologne
1974–1982	studied Architecture TH Darmstadt
1980–1981	DAAD grant (German Academic Exchange Service) ETH Zurich
1982	graduated from TH Darmstadt
1982–1984	freelance in Darmstadt
1985–1997	Behnisch & Partner, Stuttgart Auer + Weber, Stuttgart Klein + Breucha, Stuttgart
1997–2000	Auer + Weber, Stuttgart
since 2001	Associate at Auer + Weber + Architekten, Stuttgart

Stefan Niese

1969	geboren in Nürnberg
1990–1997	Architekturstudium Universität Kaiserslautern, Tutor an mehreren Lehrstühlen, AS-Plan, Kaiserslautern
1994	Sommerakademie Salzburg bei Coop Himmelb(l)au
1994–1995	Meisterklasse Wolf D. Prix, Hochschule für angewandte Kunst in Wien, Coop Himmelb(l)au, Wien, Eisele + Fritz, Darmstadt
1997	Diplom Universität Kaiserslautern
1997	BdB Preis
1997–2001	Auer + Weber, München
seit 2002	Assoziiert in Auer + Weber + Architekten, München

1969	born in Nuremberg
1990–1997	studied Architecture Kaiserslautern University, several tutoring appointments, AS-Plan, Kaiserslautern
1994	Salzburg summer academy with Coop Himmelb(l)au
1994–1995	attended Wolf D. Prix's Master's course, Hochschule für angewandte Kunst, Vienna, Coop Himmelb(l)au, Vienna, Eisele+Fritz, Darmstadt
1997	graduated from Kaiserslautern University
1997	BdB Award
1997–2001	Auer + Weber + Architekten, Munich
since 2002	Associate at Auer + Weber + Architekten Munich

Jörn Scholz

1967	geboren in Hameln
1988–1995	Architekturstudium Universität Stuttgart
1992–1996	Prof. Rainer Scholl, Stuttgart Klein und Breucha, Stuttgart
1995	Diplom Universität Stuttgart
1996–2001	Auer+Weber, Stuttgart
seit 1998	Lehrauftrag für Gebäudelehre und Entwerfen Universität Stuttgart
seit 2002	Assoziiert in Auer+Weber+Architekten, Stuttgart

1967	born in Hamelin
1988–1995	studied Architecture, Stuttgart University
1992–1996	Prof. Rainer Scholl, Stuttgart Klein und Breucha, Stuttgart
1995	graduated from Stuttgart University
1996–2001	Auer+Weber, Stuttgart
since 1998	Lecturer in building theory and design at Stuttgart University
since 2002	Associate at Auer+Weber+Architekten, Stuttgart

Achim Söding

1961	geboren in Hannover
1982–1988	Architekturstudium Universität Hannover
1985–1987	Architekturstudium TU Wien
1986–1987	Atelier Prof. Anton Schweighofer, Wien
1987	Rudolf Lodders Preis
1988	Diplom Universität Hannover
1989	Büro Wilke, Hannover
1989–2002	Auer+Weber, Stuttgart
seit 2001	Assoziiert in Auer+Weber+Architekten, Stuttgart
2001–2002	Lehrauftrag Baukonstruktion und Entwerfen, Hochschule Magdeburg/Stendal FH

1961	born in Hanover
1982–1988	studied Architecture Hanover University
1985–1987	studied Architecture TU Wien
1986–1987	Studio Prof. Anton Schweighofer, Vienna
1987	Rudolf Lodders Award
1988	graduated from Hanover University
1989	Büro Wilke, Hanover
1989–2000	Auer+Weber, Stuttgart
since 2001	Associate at Auer+Weber+Architekten, Stuttgart
2001–2002	Part-time lecturer at the Institute of Building Construction and Design Hochschule Magdeburg/Stendal FH

Stephan Suxdorf

1966	geboren in Hamburg
1987–1992	Architekturstudium FH Konstanz
1992	Diplom FH Konstanz Förderpreis des Dt. Zementverbandes
1990–1997	Steidle+Partner, München/Berlin Bauer Kurz Stockburger, München
1997–2000	Auer+Weber, München
seit 2001	Assoziiert in Auer+Weber+Architekten, München

1966	born in Hamburg
1987–1992	studied Architecture FH Konstanz
1992	graduated from FH Konstanz Awarded grant, German Cement Association
1990–1997	Steidle+Partner, Munich/Berlin Bauer Kurz Stockburger, Munich
1997–2000	Auer+Weber, Munich
since 2001	Associate at Auer+Weber+Architekten, Munich

Christof Teige

1963	geboren in Würzburg
1983–1985	Architekturstudium Universität Kaiserslautern
1985–1992	Architekturstudium TH Darmstadt
1987–1992	Shore Tilbe Irwin & Partners, Toronto, Canada Behnisch & Partner, Stuttgart
1992	Diplom TH Darmstadt
1992	Joachim Schürmann, Köln
1992–2000	Auer+Weber, Stuttgart
seit 2001	Assoziiert in Auer+Weber+Architekten, Stuttgart

1963	born in Würzburg
1983–1985	studied Architecture Kaiserslautern University
1985–1992	studied Architecture TH Darmstadt
1987–1992	Shore Tilbe Irwin & Partners, Toronto, Canada Behnisch & Partner, Stuttgart
1992	graduated from TH Darmstadt
1992	Joachim Schürmann, Cologne
1992–2000	Auer+Weber, Stuttgart
since 2001	Associate at Auer+Weber+Architekten, Stuttgart

Mitarbeiter / Members of Staff 1980–2003

Dass das bisher geschaffene Werk nicht allein unser persönlicher Verdienst ist, versteht sich von selbst. Insofern stehen unsere Namen für eine große Zahl von qualifizierten und engagierten Mitarbeiterinnen und Mitarbeitern, die im Laufe der Jahre durch unser Büro gegangen oder bis heute mit uns zusammen sind und deren individuelle Beiträge das vielschichtige und vielgestaltige Werk mit geprägt haben. Ihnen allen gilt unser Dank.
Fritz Auer und Carlo Weber

It goes without saying that our achievements to date cannot be attributed entirely to us in person. Our names stand for a large number of qualified and dedicated members of staff who over the years have at some stage worked with us or indeed remain with us today. Their individual contributions have helped shape our complex and diverse work. Our thanks go to all of them.
Fritz Auer and Carlo Weber

Andreas Achilles
Volker Auch-Schwelk
Ingrid Auer
Moritz Auer
Philipp Auer
Christian Bade
Sophia Ben Yedder
Angela Bergmann
Dagmar Bieselt
Thomas Bittcher-Zeitz
Christina Brucker
Matthias Bruder
Stefan Burger
Edgar Burian
Alexander Carl
Michel Casertano
Astrid Chwolka
Svetlana Curcic
Jutta Dalhäuser
Ulf Decker
Konrad Deffner
Jürgen Deger
Ellen Dettinger
Stefan Dinkel
Fritz Eckert

Sylvia Elges
Marc Eutebach
Dominik Fahr
Peter Fink
Albert Fischer
Oliver Fischer
Peter Freudenthal
Gabriele Fröhlich
Wilfried Funke
Sabine Füssenhäuser
Bettina Gehlen
Martin Gessert
Robert Giessl
Wolfgang Glaser
Stefan Glück
Matthias Goetz
Philipp Grath
Sonja Grimbacher
Götz Guggenberger
Petra Gumbrecht
Klaus Habisreutinger
Ursula Hafner
Petra Haindl
Peter Haubert
Clemens Haury
Dieter Heigl
Sebastian Heine
Sabine Heine
Wallie Heinisch
Tillmann Heller
Christof Hemminger
Renate Henkel
Sebastian Henrich
Thorsten Hessdörfer
Tillmann Heuter

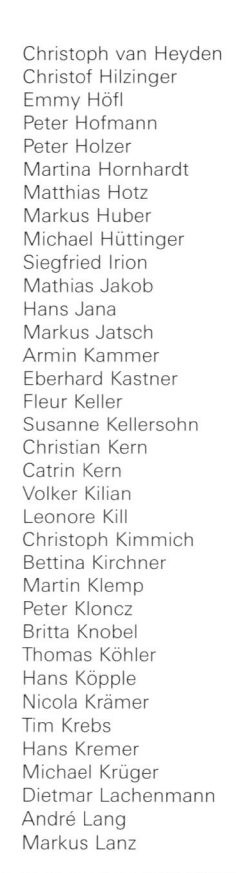

Christoph van Heyden
Christof Hilzinger
Emmy Höfl
Peter Hofmann
Peter Holzer
Martina Hornhardt
Matthias Hotz
Markus Huber
Michael Hüttinger
Siegfried Irion
Mathias Jakob
Hans Jana
Markus Jatsch
Armin Kammer
Eberhard Kastner
Fleur Keller
Susanne Kellersohn
Christian Kern
Catrin Kern
Volker Kilian
Leonore Kill
Christoph Kimmich
Bettina Kirchner
Martin Klemp
Peter Kloncz
Britta Knobel
Thomas Köhler
Hans Köpple
Nicola Krämer
Tim Krebs
Hans Kremer
Michael Krüger
Dietmar Lachenmann
André Lang
Markus Lanz

Derek Lawton
Klaus Legner
Bernd Liebl
Hans-Günter Lübben
Christoph Lueder
Bernhard Lutz
Charles Martin
Wilfried Mayer
Markus Mayer
Alexander Mayr

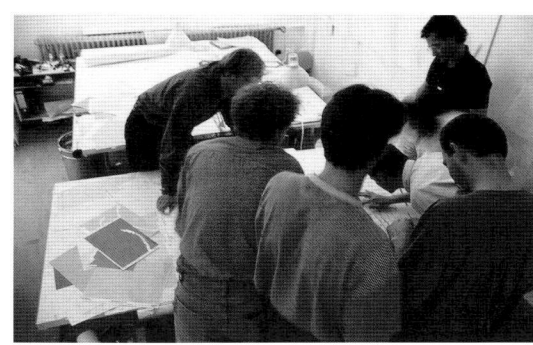

Johanna Meckes	Eberhard Räuchle	Michael Sigle
Tiemo Mehner	Heiner Reimers	Achim Söding
Martina Meinert	Sebastian Reusch	Andreas Soppa
Carmen Melero	Karl Richter	Gerda Stammer
Monika Metz	Till Richter	Ursula Staudenmaier
Bernd Meyerspeer	Thomas Rückert	Manfred Stiegelmeier
Manfred Michel	Ulof Rückert	Franz Stinner
Abdullah Motaleb	Frank Schäfer	Herbert Stoderl
Christiane Müller	Dominik Schenkirz	Thomas Streitberg
Jörg Müller	Michaela Schepe	Bernardo Striegel
Sonja Mutterer	Susan Schlameuß	Thomas Strittmatter
Bärbel Nanz	Alexander Schleifenheimer	Stephan Suxdorf
Boris Nedeleff	Paul Schlossbauer	Volker Swiatkowski
Anne Niemann	Jörn Scholz	Christof Teige
Stefan Niese	Clemens Schulte-Mattler	Peter Terbüchte
Rainer Oertelt	Holger Schurk	Andrea Tontsch
Eberhard von Pechmann	Felix Schürmann	Thomas Traub
Robert Plail	Wolfgang Schwarz	Florian Tuczek
Uta Podufal	Eugen Schweinbeck	Hans Wagenstaller
Heiner Probst	Jochen Schwind	Reinhold Wanner
Nina Pulm	Andrea Seidel	Matthias Weber
Manuala Rademaker	Markus Seifermann	Jürgen Weigl
Albrecht Randecker	Christian Siebert	Kathrin Weiß
		Rolf Wenig
		Matias Wenzel
		Bianka Werth
		Ilona Werz-Rein
		Ursula Wetzel
		Felix Wiemken
		Gilbert Wilk
		Hartmut Windels
		Stephan Wittmann
		Tobias Wulf

Interdisziplinäre Zusammenarbeit / Interdisciplinary Cooperation 1980 – 2003

Unsere Arbeit über die Jahre hat uns mit vielen verwandten Disziplinen zusammengeführt, deren Beiträge auf dem Wege einer interdisziplinären Zusammenarbeit, aus der wir immer wieder neue Erkenntnisse gewinnen konnten, in die Entwürfe und Projekte eingeflossen sind und diese wesentlich mit geprägt haben. Hierfür sei an dieser Stelle allen Leitern und Mitarbeitern unsere Anerkennung und unser Dank ausgesprochen.
Fritz Auer und Carlo Weber

Over the years, our work has brought us together with many related disciplines, whose contributions to interdisciplinary collaboration have repeatedly given us new insights, which were incorporated into designs and projects and influenced them significantly. We should like to express our recognition and thanks to all managers and staff.
Fritz Auer and Carlo Weber

Tragwerk / Structure

ARUP, Düsseldorf
Beer + Partner, Ulm
Ing.-Büro Bienert, Starnberg
Bollinger + Grohmann, Frankfurt am Main
Bornscheuer Drexl Eisele, Stuttgart
Prof. Eisenbiegler, Stuttgart
Fischer + Friedrich, Stuttgart
Ing.-Büro Frenzel, Offenburg
Furche + Zimmermann, Wendlingen
Ing.-Büro Geiger, Bietigheim-Bissingen
Ing.-Büro Gleich, Ravensburg
Ing.-Büro Grad, Ingolstadt
Gruoner + Partner, Ulm
Guyer, Schmid + Steinich, Villingen-Schwenningen
Ing.-Büro Haringer, München
Ing.-Büro Held, Germering
Herrmann + Partner, Stuttgart
Ing.-Büro Hildenbrand, Ludwigsburg
Ing.-Büro Lachenmann, Vaihingen/Enz
Ing.-Büro Lange, Detmold
Leonhardt, Andrä + Partner, Stuttgart
Lintl + Siebensohn, München
Mayr + Ludescher, München/Stuttgart
Müller Merkle, Bietigheim-Bissingen
Ing.-Büro Natterer, Lausanne
Ing.-Büro Otto, Stuttgart
Pfefferkorn + Partner, Stuttgart
Ing.-Büro Rathenow, Dresden
Rauch + Geyer, Hof
RFR, Paris/Stuttgart
Sailer Stepan und Partner GmbH, München
Schlaich, Bergermann + Partner, Stuttgart
Ing.-Büro Schneider, Ravensburg
Ing.-Büro Schönbeck, Freising
Seidl & Partner, Regensburg
Ing.-Büro Simon, Bietigheim-Bissingen
Werner Sobek Ingenieure GmbH, Stuttgart
Ing.-Büro Tischner, Dachau
Tomaschewsky-Gathmann-Reyer, Bochum
Ing.-Büro für Tragwerksplanung, Duisburg
Wegner + Klamt, Hof
Ing.-Büro Wehlmann, Recklinghausen
Weiske + Partner, Stuttgart
Ing.-Büro Zimmerle, Stuttgart

Gebäudetechnik / Technical equipment

Ing.-Büro Bamberger, Pfünz
Bauer Bauplanung, München
Bauer Planungsgesellschaft, Aichtal
Budde IFG, Villingen-Schwenningen
Burk GmbH, Ravensburg
Ing.-Büro Christoffel, Bonn
Ebert Ingenieure, Berlin
Ing.-Büro Fischer, Kalletal
Ing.-Büro Fleischmann, München
Gackstatter + Partner, Stuttgart
Gewes GmbH, München
Ing.-Büro Gladen, Paderborn
Haerter AG, Zürich
Ing.-Büro Hausladen, Kirchheim
Ing.-Büro Heckel, Steinenbronn
Heusel + Mezger + Partner, Reutlingen
Hildebrand + Hau Ingenieurgesellschaft mbH, München
HL-Technik AG, München
Ing.-Büro Hoffmann, Detmold
IBF, München
Ing.-Büro Illmayr, Hof
Jäger, Mornhinweg + Partner, Stuttgart
Ing.-Büro Jobst, Beimerstetten
Ing.-Büro Keppler, Ulm
Koch Frey Donabauer, Ingolstadt
Korner Ingenieurgesellschaft mbH, Ulm
Kraner + Partner, Stuttgart
Lang + Jochum, Ravensburg
Laux, Kaiser + Partner, Stuttgart
Oskar von Miller GmbH, München
Ing.-Büro Minati, Detmold
Möllers + Westermeier, Konstanz
Ing.-Büro Oberle, Villingen-Schwenningen
Obermeyer Planungsgesellschaft mbH, München
Ott + Spiess, Langenau
Paul + Gampe + Partner GmbH, Esslingen
PESAG, Paderborn
PFI GmbH, Wuppertal
Planungsbüro für Haustechnik, Duisburg
Pro Elektroplan, Ottobrunn
Rawe + Partner, Wuppertal
Rentschler + Riedesser, Stuttgart
Rohling Planungsbüro, Osnabrück
Ing.-Büro Schippert, Waiblingen
Schlaefle Neher Butz, Konstanz
Ing.-Büro Schnell, Stuttgart
Scholze Ing.-Gesellschaft, Leinfelden
Schreiber Ingenieure Gebäudetechnik GmbH, Ulm

Schwarz + Partner, Stuttgart
Ing.-Büro Schwarz, Grünkraut
Ing.-Büro Schwarzmann, Kornwestheim
Ing.-Büro Simon, Bietigheim-Bissingen
Ing.-Büro Stankewitz, Dorsten
Stotz GmbH, Ravensburg
Technoprojekt, Germering
Ing.-Büro Truckenmüller, Stuttgart
Ing.-Büro Wach, Baldham

Bauphysik / Building physics

Baumgartner, Stuttgart
Bayer Bauphysik, Fellbach
Bobran Ingenieure, Nürtingen
Ing.-Büro Borchard, Dossenheim
Gertis + Fuchs, Stuttgart
Graner & Partner, Bergisch-Gladbach
Gutbrod Bauphysik, Markgröningen
Horstmann + Berger, Altensteig
Kurz + Fischer, Winnenden
Müller BBM, Planegg
Schäcke + Bayer, Waiblingen
Ing.-Büro Sorge, Nürnberg

Freianlagen / Landscape design

Holm Becher, Germering
Bezzenberger + Schmelzer, Stuttgart
Bödecker Fenner Steinhauer, Düsseldorf
Brunken + Partner, Stuttgart
Burger & Tischer, München
Burger Landschaftsarchitekten, München
Irene Burkhardt, München
Copiyn, Utrecht
Dettling + Wirthensohn, Dießen
Volker von Gagern, Dresden
Gesswein, Henkel + Partner, Ostfildern
Grünplan GmbH, Freising
Haase + Sömisch, Freising
Michael Hink, München
Jedamzik + Reinboth, Stuttgart
Jühling + Bertram, München
Kerker Müller Braunbeck, Ludwigsburg
Peter Kluska, München
Latz + Partner, Kranzberg
Rita Lex-Kerfers, Bockhorn
Luska Karrer Partner, Dachau
Luz + Partner, Stuttgart
Mahl + Wartner, Landshut
Ulrich Pötzl, Vogt bei Ravensburg
Schmidt + Eppinger, Leonberg
Schube + Westhus, Magdeburg
Stötzer + Neher, Sindelfingen
Gert Wegner, Reutlingen
Welsner + Welsner, Nürtingen
Anna Zeitz, München

Gastronomie / Catering

Albrecht + Partner, München
Brunnenkant, Wiesloch
K & P Consulting GmbH, Düsseldorf
Mövenpick Projects AG, Adliswil, CH
Rainer Schneidewendt, Ostfildern
Ing.-Büro Welskopp, München

Lichtplanung / Lighting design

Bamberger, Pfünz
Bartenbach Lichtlabor, Innsbruck
Werner Lampl, Dießen
Ingo Maurer GmbH, München
Gerd Pfarré, München
Werning Tropp Schmidt, München

Bühnentechnik / Stage technology

Beneke, Daberto + Partner, München
Biste + Gerling, Berlin
Ing.-Büro Isandoro, München
Ing.-Büro Wiczkowiak, Recklinghausen

Verkehrsplanung / Traffic planning

Dorsch Consult, München
Gericke, München
Lang + Burkhardt, München
Planungsgruppe Jendreyko, München
Ing.-Büro Schönfuß, Stuttgart

Energie und Fassadentechnik
Energy and façade technology

R+R Fuchs, München
Transsolar GmbH, Stuttgart

Brandschutz / Fire protection

Kersken + Kirchner GmbH, München

Baukosten / Construction costs

IB Schmid, München

Modellbau / Modeling

Frieder Grüne, Wolfratshausen
Tilmann Heller, Stuttgart
Homolka, Stuttgart
Peter Hönigschmid, München
Emanuel Schima, München
Stephan Schwab, Stuttgart

Visuelle Kommunikation / Visual communication

avcommunication GmbH, Ludwigsburg
Baumann & Baumann, Schwäbisch Gmünd
Valerie Kiock, München
Rolf Müller, München
Jutta Sailer-Paysan, Stuttgart
Barbara Wojirsch, Stuttgart/Piani

Ausstellungsgestaltung / Exhibition design

Atelier Brückner, Stuttgart
Goetz + Schulz, Stuttgart
Atelier Lohrer, Stuttgart
Hans A. Muth, Design Consultant, Kiensau

Künstler / Artists

Thomas Barnstein, München
Tony Cragg, Wuppertal
Günter Dohr, Duisburg
Franz Mayer'sche Hofkunstanstalt GmbH, München
Sebastian Heinsdorff, Obergolding
Albert Hien, München
Stephan Huber, München
Magdalena Jetelová, Düsseldorf
Joseph Kosuth, New York
Michael Kramer, Bergisch-Gladbach
Rainer Kummer, Berlin
Armin Martinmüller, Stuttgart
Hubertus Menke, Feldafing
Maurizio Nannucci, Florenz
Panamarenko, Antwerpen
Gary Rieveschl, New York
Josef Schwaiger, Salzburg
Margund Smolka, Berlin
Dietmar Tanterl, München
Peter Vogel, Freiburg

Ausstellungen (Auswahl) / Exhibitions (Selection) **1980 – 2003**

1990	**Pavillon der Bundesrepublik Deutschland EXPO '92 Sevilla** Galerie Aedes, Berlin Architekturgalerie, München Architekturgalerie am Weißenhof, Stuttgart
1991	**Albert Hien** **Projekte – Zeichnungen – Bozzetti** Städt. Galerie im Lenbachhaus, München
1993	**Werk + Schnitte** Architekturgalerie, München
1997	**3 kulturelle Orte** Galerie Aedes East, Berlin
1998/1999	**Maßstabssprung** Deutsches Architektur-Museum, Frankfurt am Main
2001	**8 Architekten - 8 Stadien** Stadtmuseum, München
2001	**Architektur, die bewegt** Designers' Saturday, Stuttgart
2002	**BMW Erlebnis- und Auslieferungszentrum** BMW Group Pavillon, München
2002	Aedes East Forum, Berlin
2002	exporeal, München
2002	**Nacht der Architekten**, München
2003	**climadesign**, BAU 2003, München
2003	**Metamorphose München** Stadtmuseum, München
2003	**Werkstatt Stadt** **Münchner Planungen und Projekte** Rathaus, München

Veröffentlichungen (Auswahl) / Publications (Selection) 1980 – 2003

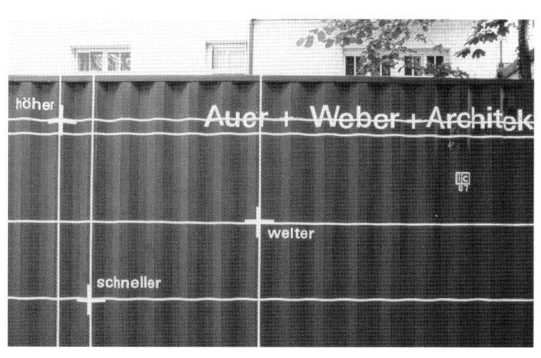

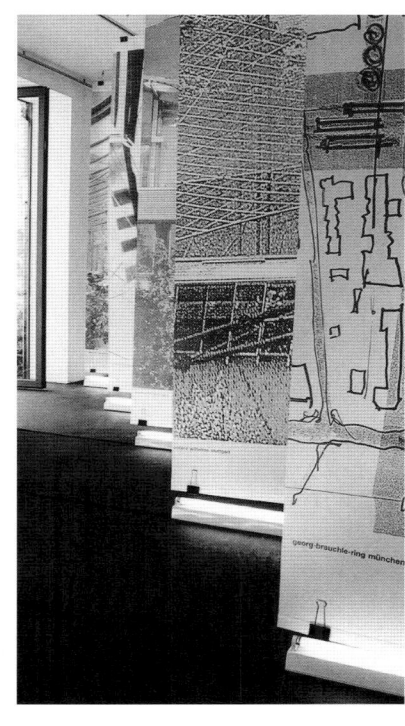

Bücher

Galerie Aedes, Pavillon der Bundesrepublik Deutschland für die Weltausstellung EXPO ´92 in Sevilla. Ausstellungskatalog. Berlin 1990

Weiß, Klaus-Dieter, Auer+Weber – Positionen und Projekte. München 1993

Galerie Aedes East, 3 kulturelle Orte. Ausstellungskatalog. Berlin 1997

Bächer, Max, Zeppelin Carré Stuttgart – Die Verwandlung eines innerstädtischen Quartiers. Tübingen/Berlin 1999

In Büchern

Jödicke, Jürgen, Architektur in Deutschland '89. Stuttgart/Zürich 1990

Flughafen München GmbH (Hrsg.) Flughafen München, Landschaft, Erscheinungsbild, Architektur. München 1992

Akademie der Künste Berlin (Hrsg.), 18 Entwürfe. Berlin 1995

de Bruyn, Gerd, Zeitgenössische Architektur in Deutschland 1970–1995. Inter Nationes 1996

Aicher, Florian, Im Gespräch – Bauen in Bayern. München 1996

Diemer, Peter, Architekten in Bayern – Bauten und Projekte. Wiesbaden 1996

Jödicke, Jürgen, Architektur in Deutschland '95. Stuttgart/Zürich 1996

Jödicke, Jürgen / Heinz Windfeder, 25 Jahre Deutscher Architekturpreis. Stuttgart/Zürich, 1997

Diemer, Peter, Architekten in Baden-Württemberg – Bauten und Projekte. Niedernhausen 1998

Stemshorn, Max, ulm neu – Stadtraum und Architektur. Ulm 1998

Jaeger, Falk, Eine Stilfrage. In: Architektur Jahrbuch Bayern 2001. München 2001

Matzig, Gerhard, Licht am Ende des Tunnels. In: Architektur Jahrbuch Bayern 2001. München 2001

Durth, Werner, Architektur in Deutschland '01. Stuttgart/Zürich 2002

Diemer, Peter, Architekten in Bayern – Bauten und Projekte. Niedernhausen 2002

Wahr, Andrea, ESO-Hotel, Cerro Paranal, Chile. In: DAM Jahrbuch 2002 – Architektur in Deutschland. München 2002

Wahr, Andrea, Wüstenplanet. In: Architektur Jahrbuch Bayern 2002. München 2002

In Fachzeitschriften

Ullmann, Gerhard, Nach Behnisch. In: Deutsche Bauzeitung 02/1992

Weiß, Klaus-Dieter, Skulptural und Strukturell. In: Deutsche Bauzeitschrift 05/1992

Kähler, Gert, A robust light architecture. In: archis 41, 03/1999

Abbildungsnachweis / Illustrations' credits

Abbildungen, zu denen kein Verfasser genannt ist, stammen von Auftraggebern, von Mitarbeitern oder aus dem Archiv der Autoren.

Der Abbildungsnachweis ist nach bestem Wissen und Gewissen zusammengestellt. Die Autorenschaft einiger Abbildungen war zu Redaktionsschluß noch ungeklärt. Verwendungs- und Veröffentlichungsrechte bleiben gewahrt.

Pictures for which no credit is given came from the clients, our staff or the authors' own archive.

The list of picture credits has been assembled to the best of our knowledge. The ownership of some pictures was still unknown at the time going to press. Rights of use and publication are reserved.

AS&P - Albert Speer & Partner GmbH, Frankfurt am Main   234, 235
Dimitri Baikov, Stuttgart   189
Zooey Braun, Stuttgart   292
CPS, Stuttgart   209, 212, 213
Wilfried Dechau, Stuttgart   73
Martin J. Duckek, Ulm   231
Engelhardt / Sellin, Aschau   276
Gottschall Photo Design, München   51, 55, 57, 59, 60, 62–65, 67–69, 75, 77–79, 95, 97–99, 269, 271, 272, 273
Siegfried Gragnato, Stuttgart   164
Roland Halbe, Stuttgart   105–109, 124, 126, 133–135, 147–151, 161, 162–167, 169–171, 173, 175, 177–179, 197, 199–205, 277–281, 283, 284
Werner Hennies / FMG, München   62
Marc Hillesheim, Köln   288
Oliver Jung, München   194, 195
Jungled Nerves, Stuttgart   153
Beate Harrer, München   274
Christian Kandzia, Stuttgart   27–31, 33, 36, 37, 44–48, 70–73, 266, 268, 275
Angelo Kaunat, Graz   81, 83–87, 129, 130, 223, 273
Klaus Kinold, München   100
Reiner J. Klein, München   297
Friedhelm Krischer, Duisburg   111–113, 276
Karl Kusidlo, Gilching   41
Christoph Lison, Frankfurt am Main   120
Archiv Ingo Maurer, München   131
Mayr + Ludescher, Stuttgart   90, 91
Stefan Müller-Naumann, München   283
Uli Oehme, Stuttgart   38
Rakete, München   191
Simone Rosenberg, München/Berlin   219
Wolfgang Rübartsch, Leimen   39
Richard Schenkirz, Leonberg   268
Jan Schmiedel, München   184, 219, 225, 229, 233
Oliver Schuster, Stuttgart   274
Petra Steiner, Dresden   123, 127
Manfred Storck, Stuttgart   93, 115, 160
SV Versicherung, Stuttgart   162
Transsolar, Stuttgart   172
Dr. Ferdinand Ullrich, Recklinghausen   103
Klaus-Dieter Weiß, Minden   272
wettbewerbe aktuell, Freiburg im Breisgau   174
Bernhard Widmann, Stuttgart   273
Valentin Wormbs, Stuttgart   89, 90, 92, 117–121, 142, 272, 275

Dank / Acknowledgement

Schon lange hatten wir uns vorgenommen und wurden von vielen Seiten dazu angeregt, ein „richtiges" Buch über unsere bisherige Arbeit herauszubringen. Nach einigen Anläufen, die immer wieder von den täglichen Herausforderungen des eigentlichen Berufes aufgehalten wurden, hat uns Johannes Determann 2001 mit dem Birkhäuser Verlag, namentlich Dr. Ulrich Schmidt und Annette Gref, in Verbindung gebracht und dort das Interesse und die Bereitschaft für eine umfangreiche Veröffentlichung unseres bisherigen Werkes geweckt.

Und da sich dazu Andrea Kiock als engagierte Herausgeberin, die unsere Arbeit über die Jahre schon immer aufmerksam verfolgte, mit Nachdruck für die Verwirklichung des Buchprojekts einsetzte, gab es für uns kein Zurück mehr. Valerie Kiock und Philipp Auer haben sich der Aufbereitung des umfangreichen Materials angenommen und es, unterstützt durch die Erfahrung von Johannes Determann, faktisch und grafisch in eine veröffentlichungsreife Form gebracht.

Allen mit dem Buchprojekt Befassten gebührt unser Dank nicht zuletzt auch für die Ausdauer und Geduld, die sie für eine angemessene Darstellung unseres bisherigen Werkes aufbrachten. Wenn mit dem nun vorliegenden Buch der neueren deutschen Architekturentwicklung eine weitere Seite hinzugefügt wird, so wäre dies für alle Beteiligten die schönste Bestätigung ihres Engagements.
Fritz Auer und Carlo Weber

We have wanted to publish a "proper" book of our work today, and many people encouraged us to do so. After a few starts, which were repeatedly delayed by the daily challenges of our actual profession, in 2001 Johannes Determann put us in contact with Dr. Ulrich Schmidt and Annette Gref at Birkhäuser Verlag, and awakened their interest and willingness to publish a wide-ranging book of our work.

And since Andrea Kiock, as a committed publisher, who had followed our work carefully for years, urged the book project, there was no going back for us. Valerie Kiock and Philipp Auer took on the preparation of the extensive material and, supported by Johannes Determann's experience gave it a publishable form in terms of both facts and graphic design.

All those involved with the book project deserve our thanks, not least for their stamina and patience they required for an appropriate presentation of our work. If this book adds a further chapter to recent developments in German architecture, this would be the best recognition of the committment of all those involved.
Fritz Auer and Carlo Weber

Impressum / Imprint

Auer+Weber+Architekten

Haußmannstraße 103 A
D-70188 Stuttgart
T 0711 268 40 40
stuttgart@auer-weber.de

Georgenstraße 22
D-80799 München
T 089 381 61 70
muenchen@auer-weber.de

www.auer-weber.de

Konzeption Concept	Philipp Auer, Auer + Weber + Architekten
Beratung / Consultant	Johannes Determann, München
Englische Übersetzung English translation	Jeremy Gaines, Frankfurt
Englisches Copy editing English copy editing	Susan James, Janice Zawerbny, Toronto
Gestaltung und Satz Layout / graphic design	Valerie Kiock, München
Reinzeichnungen / Drawings	Auer + Weber + Architekten, Katrin Ledl Friederike Michalek, München

A CIP catalogue record for this book is available from the Library of Congress, Washington, DC, USA.

Bibliografische Information der Deutschen Bibliothek.
Die Deutsche Bibliothek verzeichnet diese Publikation in der Deutschen Nationalbibliografie; detaillierte bibliografische Daten sind im Internet über http://dnb.ddb.de abrufbar.

Bibliographic information published by Die Deutsche Bibliothek.
Die Deutsche Bibliothek lists this publication in the Deutsche Nationalbibliografie; detailed bibliographic data is available in the Internet at http://dnb.ddb.de.

Dieses Werk ist urheberrechtlich geschützt. Die dadurch begründeten Rechte, insbesondere die der Übersetzung, des Nachdrucks, des Vortrags, der Entnahme von Abbildungen und Tabellen, der Funksendung, der Mikroverfilmung oder der Vervielfältigung auf anderen Wegen und der Speicherung in Datenverarbeitungsanlagen, bleiben, auch bei nur auszugsweiser Verwertung, vorbehalten. Eine Vervielfältigung dieses Werkes oder von Teilen dieses Werkes ist auch im Einzelfall nur in den Grenzen der gesetzlichen Bestimmungen des Urheberrechtsgesetzes in der jeweils geltenden Fassung zulässig. Sie ist grundsätzlich vergütungspflichtig. Zuwiderhandlungen unterliegen den Strafbestimmungen des Urheberrechts.

This work is subject to copyright. All rights are reserved, whether the whole or part of the material is concerned, specifically the rights of translation, reprinting, reuse of illustrations, recitation, broadcasting, reproduction on microfilms or in other ways, and storage in databases. For any kind of use permission of the copyright owner must be obtained.

© 2003 Birkhäuser – Publishers for Architecture,
P. O. Box 133, CH-4010 Basel, Switzerland.
Member of the BertelsmannSpringer Publishing Group.

www.birkhauser.ch

Printed on acid-free paper produced of chlorine-free pulp. TCF ∞
Printed in Germany

ISBN 3-7643-7017-3